JESUS AND OTHER LOVERS:
AN INTIMATE MEMOIR OF A CATHOLIC NUN

JUDY THEO LEHNER

outskirts press

You will read this novel and smile and weep for sadness and joy. This amazing novel gives the reader deep soul poetic language and grace filled prose.

Marianne Lyon, Napa County Poet Laureate

Judy Lehner attended Catholic high school. She had dreams of becoming a nun. She also dreamed of boys. A lively and painfully honest portrait of a woman's coming of age in San Francisco of the 1950s, forced to choose between her God and her needs.

Andy Weinberger, Author & owner of Readers Bookstore

Throughout this masterfully crafted memoir, Lehner vividly describes her physical and emotional states, her hard choices with honesty, humor and understanding.

Ana Manwaring, Author of numerous novels including the recent: Set Up: Secrets and Lies in Zihuatanejo

This nun's memoir will entertain and shock as it explores the mix of the holy and the hedonistic within the convent walls. This insightful version, told with rare honesty, will captivate the reader by its details and intimacy.

Evelyn Connolly, Ed.D, author, "Art Matters"

TABLE OF CONTENTS

PART ONE

Jesus and Other Lovers: An Intimate Memoir of a Catholic Nun

The Motherhouse – San Francisco 1966   3

Chapter One: The High School Years – San Francisco 1951   5

Chapter Two: Sophomore Year – September 1952   25

Chapter Three: Junior Year – September 1953   46

Chapter Four: Senior Year – 1954   61

Chapter Five: Last Part of Senior Year   80

PART TWO

Chapter Six: The Novitiate – Berkeley, July 1955   101

Chapter Seven: Life in the Novitiate   116

Chapter Eight: The Unbearable   124

Chapter Nine: The Veil   134

Chapter Ten: Life as a Novice – 1956   148

Chapter Eleven: The Move to the Mountains   160

Chapter Twelve: Motherhouse – Spring/Summer 1958   175

PART THREE

Chapter Thirteen: First Mission – Saint Anne's of the Sunset

San Francisco 1958   183

Chapter Fourteen: East Los Angeles – August 1959   188
Chapter Fifteen: The Wild Red Pointsetia   211
Chapter Sixteen: Motherhouse – Summer After East L.A.   221
Chapter Seventeen: Teaching – Motherhouse, San Francisco
    August 1962   236
Chapter Eighteen: After Final Vows 1963   260

PART FOUR
Chapter Nineteen: Summer 1964 San Francisco   283
Chapter Twenty: The Changes   300
Chapter Twenty-One: Vacation, Santa Cruz Mountains
    August 1964   310

PART FIVE
Chapter Twenty-Two: Motherhouse – September 1964   317
Chapter Twenty-Three: December 1964   336
Chapter Twenty-Four: Summer 1965   358

PART SIX
Chapter Twenty-Five: Motherhouse 1965   369
Chapter Twenty-Six: Vacation in the Santa Cruz Mountains   382
Chapter Twenty-Seven: Motherhouse – San Francisco Fall 1966   391

PART ONE

Jesus and Other Lovers: An Intimate Memoir of a Catholic Nun
The Motherhouse
San Francisco 1966

I COULD HEAR her coming after me with slow deliberate steps. I was hiding in my third floor bedroom cell but she would find me. Sister Aquinas always found me. How could I escape? I looked at the window of the bedroom cell, hesitated, then, I threw it wide open, tucked up my habit and pulled myself to the sill. I swung my black stockinged legs outside and eased my headgear out, hoping my veil wouldn't catch on the window frame and hold me back. Inhaling nervously, I slowly stood up on the ledge three stories above the manicured lawn of the front of the motherhouse. I pressed my back against the outside of the convent and, though my palms were sweaty against the wood, it was warm against my back. I squinted, as the sun was startlingly bright after the dim bedroom.

Suddenly, my body sagged. To stay calm, I focused on my breathing and recalled that I had never been afraid of heights. Three stories below cars whizzed through the intersection. Across the street the gas station bell sounded as cars came and went. Two old women waited at the bus stop. I was like an omniscient observer. I edged even further away from the window in case Sister Aquinas happened to look out. She wanted me to love her and was angry that I couldn't love her anymore.

After ten years I was weary of the struggle to be a good nun. And lonely. I felt overcome again by that feeling I had weeks ago when I was driving and coming off the Golden Gate Bridge and tempted to accelerate on a curve and simply speed into space. Now I could just fall forward and I'd be free. The long struggle to be a good nun would be over. Peace, yes, peace. Oh, it was tempting. Cautiously, I shifted and looked down. I was weary of the struggle of working with the *Old Guard* nuns, trying to be a good biology teacher, though I wanted so much to teach art. Would my biology students miss me? Would my Mom, always so proud of my decision to become a nun, now be ashamed? Would the Superior try to hush the fact that a young nun, only 27, killed herself.

I stood breathing deeply for a long time, away from everything, the rules, the teaching, the loneliness. Then I recalled suicide was punishable by everlasting hell fire. No, no, I didn't want hell fire.

Slowly, I edged back to the open window. When I slid inside, it was dim and quiet and cool. I collapsed on my bed in my small cell. I had a sense of having been away a very long time.

CHAPTER ONE

THE HIGH SCHOOL YEARS
SAN FRANCISCO 1951

IN THE FALL of 1951, Harry Truman's last year in office, I was a freshman at the largest Catholic all-girls school in San Francisco and I was hot to meet a boy. After school, Muni buses carried us in every direction. Eagle-eyed Sister Agnes Ann patrolled the gate to see that we climbed onto buses, not into one of the cruising cars full of boys that magically pulled up around 3 p.m. With flailing arms, she would screech and wave them past. We would have to meet them somewhere else.

In our quest to meet boys, after school Tessie, my best friend, and I rode a crowded bus to the Colonial Creamery on Irving St. or to Mel's Drive-In on Geary St. When we passed the boys' high school, Saint Ignatius, the bus seemed as if it might tip over from the weight of girls peering out the left windows to catch sight of any boys, but few ever boarded our bus as they had an earlier dismissal time than we did; an arrangement surely contrived by the nuns and the Jesuits.

At the creamery we poured nickels into the table jukebox and laughed loudly to attract the attention of the boys from Saint Ignatius

5

and Sacred Heart who sat in other booths. The boys, lean, some pimply faced, didn't wear uniforms as we did but we knew who they were. Perhaps because their haircuts were less greasy than the boys at the local high school or because their pants were pressed. Unerringly, we knew them.

Wherever we went boys always noticed Tessie. She wore a C cup and Revlon's latest lipstick, Fire 'n Ice and had high cheekbones and a single mole on her cheek. With my thick glasses, too-curly hair and braces, what chance did I have? If a boy offered Tessie a ride home, which was often, I would have to take the bus alone as the fog rolled into the Sunset and Richmond districts.

At school we discovered our parish had a majority among the class of two hundred-ten freshmen. That meant power. Tessie ran for class president and I took a stab at class secretary. Smart and wearing horn-rimmed glasses, I looked the part. We pulled it off. For our first meeting, we class officers sat in a semi-circle on stage under the hot lights of the school's Little Theater. We gazed at the large freshman class sitting alphabetically and wearing identical white blouses, navy jackets and skirts. I tried to keep my skirt well over my knees as Sister Clara, the freshman Moderator, instructed but I was tempted to hoist it up because my legs were my best feature. Microphone in hand, Tessie called the meeting to order, led us in a prayer, the Pledge of Allegiance, and then the school song. The first order of business was a motto for our class.

"Girls," said Tessie, "Sister Clara gave me a great suggestion for our motto: *Noblesse Oblige*." The girls all turned to gaze at tall Sister Clara, who stood at the rear of the Little Theater, blushing at this attention. "Sister explained the meaning of this to me," Tessie went on. "Since you are not all taking French, I'll tell you what it means: by our Baptism we are nobility. You're all baptized, right?" The whole class nodded. "Baptism made us God's children and that is our nobility but with that comes obligations. We've got an obligation to be role models-- doing things like making the Sign of the Cross before you shoot a basket or not smoking in uniform." Fake coughs arose from the class as everyone knew Tessie smoked after school. "Or giving your seat to an old lady on the bus—that is, if you ever get a seat. And being generous—like donating to the Missions and helping with the Christmas baskets. Okay, all those in favor of Noblesse Oblige as our motto, raise your hand and say 'aye'." Everyone raised a hand and said, "aye."

"Those opposed, say nay." I heard Janice, who frequently made fun of the nuns, mutter, "Nay." With gusto, Tessie banged the gavel and said, "The ayes have it!" Everyone clapped. I took furious notes as I would have to read them aloud at the next meeting.

I felt it was going to be a great year. I was meeting interesting girls from other parishes in San Francisco. I was hopeful I'd meet a nice Catholic boy. My friend, Vicky, who lived across the street, was elected sophomore class president and sold me her old Freshman books at a great price. I was grateful Mom was able to pay my five dollar a month tuition and the dollar a month for both Steve, now in seventh grade, and Ellen, in sixth grade at Saint Monica's. I loved my classes, except for Latin, taught by a colorless nun, who barely spoke above a whisper and though she looked old, she probably wasn't. However for the college bound, Latin was a requirement

My favorite class, the last of the day, was Christian Family Living or CFL for short, a course designed by the brilliant nun, who was our main counselor. It was a series of practical six-week classes that included cooking, home decorating, how to use the library, home nursing and more. In addition to our scholastic courses, it was intended as training for married life, our supposed destinies. The cooking class, though it had a fancy name like 'Nutrition and Cleanliness in the Kitchen,' was held in the cafeteria. I took a seat at one of the long tables and saved a place for my new friend, Eva, who sat next to me alphabetically in many classes. I was a Lyons and she was a Mazarov. When I saw the tall blond with the worried expression, I called, "Over here, Eva." Tessie sat further down, applying another coat of lipstick. Eva plopped her load of books on the table, complaining, "I have so much homework and now Sister Patrice is giving a Latin test tomorrow. I don't know how I'm going to do it." The harsh electric bell inturrupted her.

Sister Maureen's prompted us, "Girls, let's stand for our prayer." Thirty of us stood to face the crucifix on the wall. "In the Name of the Father and of the Son and of the Holy Ghost. Amen. Hail Mary, full of grace . ...." Mechanically we recited prayers for the seventh time that day. In grammar school we said prayers twice a day, but here, we prayed at the beginning of every class and soon it was a rote exercise, rather than a meaningful prayer.

"Good afternoon, girls. Welcome to Nutrition and Cleanliness in the Kitchen. I'm Sister Maureen and I see some familiar faces from my algebra class." Her eyes sparkled as she surveyed us. I was in her algebra class and I leaned to one side, hoping for recognition, thankful when our eyes connected for a split second. She was the most beautiful nun I'd ever seen. She had a friendly face with blue eyes under perfectly arched brows and, though her nose was large, she had dimples and a wide smile, too wide for a nun, revealing perfectly white teeth. Petite, at five feet three, she tightly cinched in her leather waistband with the huge black rosary hanging from it, and the graceful way she moved, I knew she could've been a dancer.

"You'll have to take notes as we have no text. I want. . ." The muni bus roared past on Turk St., drowning out her words.

"What did she say?" asked Eva looked over at my scribbling, worried she'd missed something.

"See, she's holding up that marble composition book. I think she wants us to have a notebook tomorrow. Relax, we won't have homework in this class." Sister began giving notes on how to defrost a refrigerator, a subject not remotely of interest to any us. Yet Eva, already aiming to go to Cal Berkeley, took careful notes. Her parents had escaped from Russia when the Czar was overthrow and were determined their only child would do well here.

A few days later the afternoon arrived for our first cooking project:

baking powder biscuits. Sister handed out white bib aprons, bowls, spoons, sifters and more. Soon everyone was jabbering, mixing the ingredients, running back and forth from the cafeteria tables to the kitchen where we baked the biscuits in the two huge ovens in the black iron stove. Neither Eva, who was mixing the ingredients, nor I, had ever made biscuits from scratch. Tessie, big spoon in hand, was chatting with the girls in the next group, but Eva was concerned about over-mixing.

"Judy, go get Sister. I want her to check out at our dough."

Sister, wedged in among the girls already at the big ovens, was checking mixtures, answering questions. She'd pinned the hem of her habit around her waist and tied on a long, starched white apron which left the back of her legs exposed. I'd never seen a nun's legs and, even in black stockings, hers were very shapely. When she caught me staring, she turned crimson. Quickly, I looked away. At our table, Sister reassured Eva our mixture was perfect.

Eva, who had to go to her Russian lesson, asked Tessie and me take care of the clean-up in the kitchen. At the deep stainless steel sink Tessie was washing the bowls and trays, barely getting things clean. I was drying the pans and bowls.

"Dry faster," Tessie, commanded. She wanted to be at the boys' football practice where we would sit in the front row of the rickety stadium seats watching for guys we knew from grammar school. About now they'd be dashing out of the Saint Ignatius gym wearing dirty jerseys with over-sized pads and helmets, trotting past the bleachers, intent on the coach's indecipherable commands. When we saw familiar faces, we'd yell out their names, but they'd ignore us and head onto the field, trying to look tough.

Sister came out of the pantry singing softly and carrying a sack of flour. There was a smudge of flour on her nose. Tessie turned from the sink and boldly asked, "Are you Irish, Sister?" Anything personal about a nun was a life or death secret! What was Tessie thinking? I bolted to take the sack of flour from Sister.

Handing me the sack, Sister broke into an Irish brogue, "And why would ya' be thinkin' that?" For a moment I thought that she'd do a jig.

"Because of that Irish song, *"Danny Boy"* that you're humming. I thought nuns only sang hymns," said Tessie. Sister flushed and laughed, a braying, un-nun-like laugh.

"Come on, Tessie," I interrupted. "We're finished. We'll see you tomorrow, Sister." As we gathered our books, Sister was putting samples of our biscuits on a tray to be graded while singing softly to herself. Surely now, it would be a hymn. I sidled up behind her and was amazed to hear the soft syllables: "That old Black Magic has me in its spell."

Riding the bus home, I wondered about this young nun, so vibrant under the austere habit. Most of our teachers were solemn and serious but the way she handled herself after class reminded me more of a fun-loving young woman than a nun. At that moment, I had no idea of how strongly she would influence my life.

Some nights on the phone, I bragged about our nuns to Sandy, who'd risked the wrath of our grammar school sisters who'd told her she'd *lose her soul* if she went to a public school—and was attending near-by Lowell, a public high school.

"The nuns I have for my classes now aren't like the ones we had in grammar school. Many are young and pretty; some are really intelligent, not like Sister Rafaela who whacked us with yardsticks. These nuns know their stuff and I'm learning a lot."

"Sounds good, Judy, but I can't talk now. I'm expecting a guy I met at school to call. I'm hoping he'll ask me to our school dance. Let's talk later."

That was the hard part: no boys.

Soon after that conversation, Tessie gushed, "Judy, today you've got to come with me! I've got a ride to The Colonial."

"What? In whose car?" I asked.

"Margie's."

Margie was her Big Sister, a senior who'd been assigned to help with the transition to high school. Each freshman had an assigned senior and Lois, who was mine, was helpful, but she didn't have a car. We ditched our blue uniform jackets in our shared locker. I pulled on my car coat, while Tessie stood at the mirror applying another layer of 'Fire 'n Ice.' She rolled up her skirt to expose her shapely calves and I did the same. At least, I had good legs, but I hated my thick glasses.

As we exited through the gate, Sister Agnes Ann asked us freshmen, "Going to catch the bus, dearies?"

"No, Sister, we've got a ride."

"Not with boys I hope?" she replied, motioning a car full of boys that was slowing at the curb, to keep moving.

"No, with my Big Sister," replied Tessie, pointing to the seniors who were a few steps ahead. Soon we were stuffed four in the back, cruising in Margie's Chevy across the Golden Gate Park toward the Sundset district. On the radio Tony Bennett was crooning *Because of You*. Mary Ann, a blond senior sitting next to Tessie, was pulling out a pack of Viceroys.

"Are we out of sight of Sister Evil-eye?" she laughed, offering each of us a cigarette. I took one and tapped it lightly on the armrest as I'd seen my Mom do, then stuck it between my lips. I inhaled gently so I wouldn't cough, though I did anyway. When we turned onto Irving Street, the seniors began to name the boys they saw standing in front of the fake columns of the Colonial Creamery, remarking who was cute, who was fickle, who was 'all hands' on a date. As we walked in, I pushed up the collar of my car coat, held my cigarette, which had gone out, at my side and tried to look sophisticated. The booths were filled with teenagers, boys with boys and girls with girls. At one booth a white-haired lady was hunched over a bowl of soup, crumbling in her saltines, ignoring the noisy teenagers. Tessie and I crammed into the booth with the four seniors. A seasoned waitress in a pastel uniform with pad in hand, arrived at our table.

How did this work with the seniors? Separate checks? I peered into my wallet and found three quarters. I ordered a chocolate soda and Tessie, a cherry phosphate. They each cost fifteen cents.

One of the seniors said in a stage whisper, "Look, Ernie is staring at us." It was true that a group of boys was looking our way and laughing.

"Hey, Mary Ann, come on over," one boy invited.

"Oh, that Ernie," said Mary Ann, shaking her head. After a few more raucous invitations, Mary Ann gave in. "He'll just keep at it if I don't go over." As she walked, she swung her generous hips. I heard Ernie say, "Hubba, hubba, shake it but don't break it." Once in the booth, he threw his arm around her, then tried to kiss her.

"Just shut up and gimme a cigarette," she retorted, pushing him away.

Our booth was quieter now and Tessie, sitting next to the table jukebox, asked, "What do ya wanna hear *Come-on-a My House* or *Mona Lisa?*"

I said, "I like "Come-on-a My House," but she dropped in a dime and hit the button for "Mona Lisa." After we finished our sodas and shakes, Margie said, "Okay, girls, ante-up for your drinks." My soda cost fifteen cents, but I handed her a quarter. She didn't even look at what we each put in her hand, just tossed the change in her purse, paid, and left a fifty-cent tip. Would I ever be as self-assured as these seniors?

As much as I wanted to meet a boy, the only place I actually talked to boys was at St. Monica's choir practice where Tessie and I still sang in the parish choir on Sundays. Then it was the same old boys from grammar school. It was 'Hi' or 'How's it going?' Nothing exciting. One Saturday on our way to choir practice, we sauntered past the flats and stucco houses of our parish that were pressed shoulder-to-shoulder with not a blade of grass between them. Tessie offered me a piece of Juicy Fruit. I refused because the nuns said that chewing gum made us look like cows chewing their cuds. Undeterred, Tessie began chomping on a stick and chattering, "So I'm walking home, minding my own beeswax when this black Buick starts tailing me. Then John sticks out his head and right , 'Hubba, hubba.' Tessie.' I yelled back, 'You guys, get lost.'"

I was so glad it wasn't me they were tailing, but Tessie could handle it. She could out-shout any of them. "Who do you think will be at the choir practice today? The Goodwin twins?" I mused.

"Who knows? Anyway, those boys said something about you, too." Tessie cracked her gum.

"They did not! I wasn't even there. Why would they say anything about me? Who was in the car?"

"John and Paul Riley and the Murphy brothers."

"Okay, what did they say?"

"You wouldn't want to know."

"Just tell me!" I demanded.

"Okay, but just remember you're making me tell you. One guy yelled, 'Hey where's your pal, Judy?' Then another one screamed out the back window, 'Who cares about that four-eyed pile of shit?" Snap went her gum.

"You are making this up!"

"Am not! Cross my heart, hope to die," she said as she traced a cross on her ample left breast.

Tessie was being as crude as those boys. I wanted to push her into the gutter. Tears began to slosh behind my eyes. Yet her mom had recently been diagnosed with cancer and I knew this weighed on Tessie. She was becoming callous.

I tried to pretend it didn't bother me, yet her words confirmed what I suspected: boys thought I was ugly because of my thick glasses and too-curly hair. For weeks, I couldn't stop the wound from oozing.

Meanwhile at school we completed our cooking class and our section moved to the next six-week series called, Art in the Home. I deliberately didn't sit near Tessie. She was so annoying and vain, always putting on more lipstick, but I loved anything to do with art and the class project of making a mock-up living room was great fun for me.

Though I saw Sister Maureen as my algebra teacher, I missed seeing her at the end of the day. One day I decided to ask her help with some difficult algebra problems.

"Come down to the cafeteria after school and bring your book," she said smiling.

As it was a baking day, girls were cleaning up and joking with Sister. I stood around with my algebra book feeling far too studious. After most of the girls left, Sister motioned me to one of the cafeteria tables. When she sat next to me, I felt awkward and wished I had something interesting to say. A lavender odor clung to her. How could she smell so fresh at 3:30 in the afternoon? I pointed out the troublesome math problems. While she was writing out equations, reminding me of axioms I'd forgotten, I noticed she had broad, rough working hands with the nails filed short across blunt fingers.

With her explanations, the problems seemed simple. When we finished the math I wanted to keep her attention, so I told her bits of school gossip, who smoked in the bathrooms, who skipped study hall. She laughed easily and seemed interested in my chatter. I told her how I loved the Art in the Home section and that I'd be glad to help with her bulletin board in her algebra classroom.

"Yes," she said, "I'd love you to put something my bulletin board. Maybe a picture of the Sacred Heart or the Blessed Virgin with some flowers."

"Yes, Sister, I can do that. I did bulletin boards at St. Monica's. In fact, this funny thing happened. One time my friend Sandy—she goes to Lowell—and I made this big mural of parts of American history that was on a big paper roll. Sister Patricia sent us to the other sixth grade to repeat the presentation, but then we just kept going to other classrooms where they weren't expecting us and made the presentaion again to the surprise of the nun and the students. Finally, Sister Patrice sent someone to call us back! We really had fun."

Now only one freshman I hardly knew was still puttering around in the kitchen. Della was tall and awkward with stringy hair, a crooked nose and a Tennesee accent. When Sister stood to leave, she bolted to grab Sister's books; then we three left the cafeteria together and went through the atrium, the fancy name for our locker room, that was empty now. I was glad as I didn't want other girls to think I was a 'kiss-up kid' to a nun. At the edge of the garden, Sister took her books and disappeared down a path that led to the back of the convent. I was beginning to feel that Sister was more fun to be with than trying to meet boys at the Colonial Creamery where Tessie always captured the boys' attention.

One Monday at last bell, we students flowed down into the atrium like a tidal wave of navy blue. Tessie called, "Hey, Jude, you've got to come on with me to Mel's. Heard some guys from St. Monica's might be there." As we headed for the bus, Tessie jabbered about her date for the upcoming Trophy Ball at Saint Ignatius, boasting she'd wear a strapless dress no matter what the nuns or Jesuits said. Listening to her, I felt the thickness of my glasses, the curliness of my hair, the pimple on my chin. Then I thought of Della in the cafeteria, making jokes with Sister Maureen; soon she'd be Sister's favorite.

As the bus rumbled up, I stepped out of line and said, "Oh, Tessie, you go on. I forgot my history book. Got homework. I'll catch up later." I darted back to the cafeteria where Sister Maureen smiled at me when I came in.

"Need some help?" I asked, noticing that a couple of girls were putting away the butter and cheese that was delivered for school lunches.

"Absolutely," replied Sister.

Della, far from awkward, was delivering a stream of witty remarks and though I knew boys wouldn't notice her, still with her Tennessee accent and constant wisecracks, she kept Sister laughing. At four-thirty, only Della and I remained. We carried Sister Maureen's books and the cooking samples through the atrium to the garden path that led to the rear of the convent.

"God bless you both," Sister said, taking her books and the tray. At the bus stop, Della and I jabbered about the things Sister said and did that day and though each of us wanted to be Sister's favorite, we were becoming friends.

The Sodality, of which every student was a member, was the school organization that dealt with our spiritual activities: Mass, Mission collections, Christmas baskets for the poor and such activites. The organization was divided in two groups: upper classmen: juniors and seniors; lower classmen: freshmen and sophomores. Sister Maureen who was in charge of the lower division group, met one Friday a month after school with the sophomore Sodality officers. As freshman, Della and I had to go home. One Friday, just as we reached our lockers, Sister called after us, "Oh dear, Della, Judy," I almost forgot the medals! Do you think you both could come tomorrow afternoon to help me, even though it's a Saturday? The medals have to be ready by Monday."

"Yes," we both replied eagerly, "we'd love to come."

The next afternoon I caught the #31 bus to school. As I left the bright sunlight and walked into the dim atrium, a strong disinfectant odor stung my nostrils. With its rows of lockers, low ceiling and cement floor, it was an unpleasant place without the girls' mayhem. I hoped the janitor, the creepy man we nicknamed, Quasimodo, wouldn't appear. At the end of the atrium, I pushed open the swinging doors. The cafeteria was empty. She had forgotten! I've given up a Saturday for nothing. Then, I heard humming in the kitchen.

"Sister Maureen," I called, "it's Judy, here."

"Hello, there," she appeared with pad in hand, her face lit with a smile. "I was just making an order. Let's sit at one of the tables and get started. Della called and said her mother has to work so she has to stay home and watch her little brother. I'm so glad you are here."

When Della was here we three joked and laughed. How could

I make conversation alone? Sister got right to work. She set up her equipment on the table, plugged in a soldering iron and set out a roll of metal, spools of thin blue ribbon and a pile of medals of Our Lady. As I sat opposite her, I was again aware of that lavender scent.

"Judy, look here." She held up a medal of the Virgin on a tiny silver ring. "We have to seal the opening so the medals don't come off the ring. Then you Sodality girls can wear them on a silver chain or put the medal on a key ring. You'll always have the Blessed Virgin with you." As I watched, she deftly heated the silver wire, held it over the opening and sealed the opening with a liquid silver drop. After she'd done three or four, she asked if I wanted to try. Awkwardly, I held the soldering iron and tried to get a tiny silver droplet to seal the opening, but I dropped a big blob of silver which made a mess. I tried again with a similar result.

"Until you get the hang of it, I think you'd better just tie on the blue ribbons," she said laughing. In answer to my query she said, "My father gave me this equipment. He's such a darling. He's a real saint and he can fix anything." I hadn't heard anyone talk of their father in such endearing terms. I felt envious of their bond.

"My father died of cancer was I was three and a half," I ventured. My only vision of him was the handsome face and wavy brown hair in the hand-colored photograph in the gold frame on my dresser. "My uncle Hube, my mom's oldest brother, a pharmacist, lives in the flat above us. He's been like our dad and helped my Mom raise us three kids. I've got a younger brother, Steve, and a sister, Ellen." I continued in a softer tone, "But now, uncle Hube's got M.S., you know, multiple sclerosis." It was painful to speak about the fate of uncle Hube, the one who told me bedtime stories, taught me to love opera and took me to the horse races at Bay Meadows in his Plymouth coupe while playing *Red River Valley* on the radio. Now I wanted to hear more about her father.

"Judy, it sounds like you've had some difficult things in your life. But, you know," she said, pausing and looking directly at me, "I'm sure your father is watching out for you in heaven. He's proud of you."

I hadn't ever thought of him in that way. These were comforting thoughts. I was surprised she was sharing so much about her own father. Most nuns would never do that and I understood she expected me to keep her confidence.

One afternoon when Sister said she had to leave right after school, she noticed Della and I were glum-faced as we headed to our lockers. Sister paused at the door and said, "Would you two like to come to Benediction in the convent?"

Would we ever! We were dying to see the inside of the convent. We raced around the corner and sprinted up the front steps of the imposing columned entrance. I rang the bell that was so piercing Della said it would raise the dead. Sister ushered us in though the vestibule by the formal parlors with Oriental carpets, past the statue of the Blessed Virgin extending her arms in welcome from a golden niche. Our shoes clumped loudly on the bare boards as we followed Sister up the wooden stairs. Older girls at school had said the nuns' cloister began on the second floor at the chapel door. I tried to sneak a look down the dim corridor with rows of doors and archaic light fixtures. I wondered which one was Sister's but she hurried us into the chapel. To my astonishment there were no pews, only rows of wood monastic stalls bathed in soft light from the stained-glass windows. I'd never seen a chapel like this. Sister led us to stalls right inside the door and pointed where we were to kneel. Then she disappeared. Della and I tried to angle our knees on the little ledge of the stall, but our legs with our scuffed saddle shoes, stuck out for miles.

Sister re-entered wearing a flowing white serge cloak over her habit. I gasped; she looked like St. Theresa, the Little Flower. In unison with another nun, she slowly genuflected in the center of the chapel and moved to her stall. When I dared glance around, I was stunned to see my ordinary teachers wrapped in white cloaks and wearing beatific expressions. The Blessed Sacrament was high on the altar in the golden monstrance, the ornate container that displayed the sacred consecrated host. Tall brass-tipped tapers were lit and red gladioli sent fingers of flames heavenward. A priest came out of the sacristy wearing a long brocade cape. The organ swelled and the nuns, sounding like a choir of angels, sang the "Tantum Ergo" written long ago by St. Thomas Aquinas. "Down in adoration falling, Lo! the sacred Host we hail." The sweet odor of burning incense swirled as the priest swung the brass censor toward the altar and then over us. As a nun tinkled a bell, I bowed my head low while the priest raised the gold monstrance that displayed the Blessed Sacrament and gave us a slow blessing. I felt as if I was in the antechamber of heaven. Deep inside something stirred. I wondered if I could ever join this holy Community.

Yet as much as I loved being around Sister Maureen, I was still intent on meeting a boy. When one of my new friends at school invited me to her New Year's Eve party, I was at first reluctant to accept because she wasn't from my parish and I wouldn't know the kids invited to the party. She sensed my hesitation and assured me that only nice Catholic boys were invited.

I spent hours putting together trial outfits, finally choosing a salmon-colored cashmere sweater and plaid skirt. Though I was worried about a couple of pimples, mom told me how nice I looked when she dropped me off at Barbara's house. Nervously, I rang the bell. Opening the door wide, Barbara greeted me loudly. She laughed and had even more pimples that I did. I felt better. Her basement was hung with bright colored steamers where I joined other girls, giggling around the big punch bowl, some of whom I knew but I didn't know any of the boys who hovered around the record player. Barbara introduced each of them and I immediately noticed a cute guy with curly blond hair. As good as the music was for dancing, not one boy, with the exception of the guy 'going steady' with a slim girl with a hard mouth, asked any of us to dance, not even to Nat King Cole's *Too Young* or Tony Bennett's *Because of You*. Only the steady couple danced, draped all over each other. The party was disappointing.

Just before midnight, the steady couple got into a noisy argument and she stomped upstairs in tears and left. At least something interesting was happening, but at the stroke of midnight, every boy bolted for a girl. Five or six different guys kissed each of us. After planting a kiss on every girl, the boy whose girlfriend had left in tears, pulled me to his lap and started kissing me. Then he began running his hands up above my nylons, fiddling with my garters, edging his fingers into my underpants. I was shocked and crossed my legs tightly, but he was persistent in trying to find that special spot inside me. I knew that spot, but I didn't want this guy touching me there. I wished I was sitting with the cute blond-haired guy that at midnight had given me a sweet kiss.

I was uncomfortable, but I didn't want to make a big commotion. Still I couldn't be with this guy any longer. Abruptly, mumbling something about the bathroom, I bolted off his lap, leapt up the stairs to the kitchen and grabbed the phone and calling Mom. "Please will you please come and get me right now?" When I got in our car, I was quiet.

"Was it a nice party? Did you have a good time?" Mom asked, tapping her Lucky Strike in the ashtray.

"It was okay," I shrugged. I couldn't tell her what happened. The only conversation we had had about sex was the time in sixth grade when I got my period. I still thought a girl could get pregnant from French kissing. It wasn't until next year in biology, a class taught by the wonderful Sister Joseph, that I got the facts straight.

Mom and I never discussed important things. We were quite different. She was tall and attractive, the youngest in her family with two older brothers who adored her. She told me she had worn a forbidden red, strapless dress to her senior prom. Now she was busy with her elementary teaching job and in the evening she worked with my eleven-year-old brother, Steve, to help him complete his homework. I wasn't like her and she just didn't understand me.

After the party, I felt depressed. So as winter set in, I started to join Della in helping Sister Maureen nearly every afternoon, both of us competing for her attention. I could tell that Sister liked me as she gave me important jobs to do and often let me carry her books at the end of the day. However, when the warm spring weather arrived, I was restless. I yearned to join Tessie again in the trek to the Colonial Creamery or Mel's Drive-in or to the Saint Ignatius games. Maybe I would meet a boy who would take me out or even invite to a prom at the boys' schools.

One warm day when we were to get out of school early, I promised Tessie I would go with her to The Creamery, but that afternoon Sister Maureen had a big project and she needed help to set up the cafeteria tables for an adult Sodality dinner in the evening. I attempted get her attention to let her know I was leaving, hoping to see disappointment in her eyes. Over the press of girls around her, she mouthed, "I've a special job for you. You're so artistic that I want you to arrange the centerpieces."

I sucked in my breath at the words *so artistic*. It was tempting to help her, but I replied, "I can't stay today. I've got things to do."

Puzzlement, then disappointment flitted across her face, but I hurried out to meet Tessie at the bus stop. As we waited, I began to feel uncomfortable with Tessie because wherever we went she would get all the attention. As the bus rumbled up, I yelled to her as she was already getting her yellow bus pass punched, "Tessie, I forgot my Latin book. Test tomorrow. I'll catch the next bus."

I sauntered back into the school, but I didn't go into the cafeteria with all those girls competing for Sister Maureen's attention. It was a glorious spring afternoon and the garden was empty. Boldly, I walked into the area reserved for seniors and plunked myself on a bench, turning my back on the Sacred Heart statute reigning from its pedestal. Overhead the beautiful Japanese plum was in blossom so I stretched out my legs on the bench and pulled up my uniform skirt to expose my thighs. Though I opened my Latin book, I closed my eyes and soaked in the sun. I pondered: *why didn't I go with Tessie? Meeting a boy was very important to me.* In fact yesterday, I had a conversation with a pretty, blond freshmen who confided to me that she was transferring to nearby Lowell high school. She said her parents thought it was a better school. Public better than Catholic? That was heresy! She had protested when I expressed shock, that she would still go to Mass and everything but then she added, 'Don't forget there are boys at Lowell.' I suddenly imagined myself sitting in a class with boys, not one taught by a nun who made the boys sit on one side of the class and the girls on the other. Possibly it might even be an interesting man teacher. Just then I heard a crunch of gravel and feared someone was coming who would remind me that this section was for *seniors only,* but out of the corner of my eye, I was surprised to see Sister Maureen walking in my direction. Quickly, I pulled my skirt down and stared at my Latin book and pretended not to notice her.

"Judy, I thought you already left. Are you studying for a test?" she asked.

I feigned surprise at her presence. "Have you finished in there?" I asked, trying to sound indifferent.

"Almost, but I missed you."

"I've got things on my mind."

"Tell me," she said, sitting and focusing her intense blue eyes on me.

"Well, Sister," I sighed, looking down at my book, "I'm thinking about transferring to Lowell for my sophomore year. I really would like to meet boys." I now had her attention, but I braced myself for her lecture: *transferring to Lowell was like selling my soul to the devil.* Yet Sister was strangely silent, her dark brows knit together, her face as pale as the blossoms that swayed overhead. Wafting from the third floor music room was the lovely *Panis Angelicus.*

She quietly studied her broad hands and after a long pause she said, "If you don't come back next year, I won't care where I'm sent. They could send me anywhere, even Siberia. If you're not here, it won't be the same." Her face flushed and she reached out, covered my hand and squeezed it. Was I hearing right? I mattered to her? Me, a lowly freshman was important to this beautiful woman vowed to God? She held my hand a long time. I knew I would never transfer to Lowell. Yet for a moment, like a prey catching a foreign scent, I sensed danger ahead.

As the school year drew to a close, I learned Sister was going to study at college in Saint Paul, Minnesota for summer. I would miss her ,but I looked forward to going to the Camp Fire Girls camp with Sandy in the high Sierras, far from the City's fog. On the last day of school, Sister pressed a small envelope into my hand. I waited until I got home to open it. In the privacy of my bedroom, I opened the envelope and a holy card fell out, a picture of Saint Therese, the Little Flower. The note, penned in her usual turquoise ink, read:

> *Dear Judy, I want to thank you for all your help and generosity this year. I hope you have a good time at camp. Don't forget to get to Mass and Communion often. I'll be thinking of you. You know how special you are to me.*
> *Love and prayers,*
> *Sister Maureen*

With her praying for me I felt I had an intermediary, someone who God really listened to. I reread her words. *You know how special you are to me.* I etched them in my memory.

Summer camp in the high Sierras held an entire month of freedom. Since sixth grade, Sandy and and I went to Caniya, the Camp Fire Girls camp near Sierra City. It was an adventure for us city girls to sleep on cots under the stars, to swim in alpine lakes, to hike the mountain peaks and all in 'mixed' company, meaning with girls from public schools. Sometimes we would sneak down to the creek and smoke forbidden cigarettes and tell dirty jokes. This freedom was wonderful! There were horses to ride. I loved the fine big animals because Uncle Hube loved them and told me stories of Man'O War and Seabiscuit. I made friends with a white horse named Bucky by bringing him apples or carrot sticks saved from my lunch. He whinnied when he sensed me approaching. I adored riding him along the steep trails, following behind the leader, Tommy, who took care of the horses and stables. We even went on overnight pack trips and I learned to saddle and bridle my horses. It was glorious to be away from the city and live in nature. At mail call, I hung around in my rayon Hawaiian shirt with the big yellow pineapples, my jeans rolled to mid-calf and tried to look casual, but I was dying for an envelope addressed to me in turquoise ink. If I received a letter, Sandy, with prying eyes, would peak over my shoulder, unless she was distracted with a box of cookies or letter from home for herself, and say, "Can't you ever take a break from the nuns, Judy?"

I'd find a tall pine, settle under it and savor every word she wrote. She said she welcomed my letters and though she spoke of her classes, I detected that she was lonely far from the sisters of her own convent. She always wrote that she was remembering me daily in her prayers and that made me feel special.

In August, tanned and sassy, we boarded the big yellow school bus, loaded with our duffel bags and suitcases and sang "One hundred Bottles of Beer on the Wall" on the long trek home. Sad as it was to leave camp, I was looking forward to seeing Sister Maureen.

CHAPTER TWO

SOPHOMORE YEAR
SEPTEMBER 1952

"ELLEN, HAVE YOU seen my brush?" I asked my younger sister with whom I shared a bedroom. She was always borrowing my things.

"No," she replied.

"I left it on my side of the dresser. I bet you used it."

"I did not. You're always accusing me. Look in your top drawer?" With her excessive modesty, she ducked into the walk–in closet to put on her St. Monica's uniform, a white middy blouse and navy uniform skirt

"I'm looking now." I rummaged through my underwear drawer, a tangle of silky pants, bras, slips and stockings then my fingers struck the pack of envelopes bound with a rubber band, each addressed to me in turquoise ink, each capital letter written with a flourish—Sister Maureen's summer letters. I couldn't wait to see her.

"Mom, is my brush in the bathroom?"

"I don't see it, Judy."

"I'm going to miss the bus if I don't find it," I screamed, "and you'll have to drive me to school."

"Can't, Judy. First day of school. I have to get there before my students come in. Come in here and use my brush."

Just then my fingers struck the bristles in my own drawer. I plucked the bobby pins from my pin curls and whisked the brush through my short brown hair. Then I stepped into the bathroom. "You look sharp. New suit?"

"No, just a new blouse. I have to look good at school."

"Bye, Mom." I gave her a peck on the cheek.

Bye, Steve," I said as I passed the solitary room, a place where my twelve-year old brother spent much time. I heard a grunt from the toilet.

Pulling my car coat on over my navy uniform, I bolted down the front stairs of our flat and ran to the corner to look for the #31 bus. It was a clear autumn day. The sun made everything brighter after the summer fog.

Hurry up, Tessie, I thought, as I saw her coming up the block. The bus was lumbering toward the stop. I got on slowly and carefully pulled out my bus ticket and handed it to the driver to punch. Tessie puffed up behind me.

"Whew, glad you made it," I said. As we slid into seats, Tessie started jabbering about her new boyfriend, digging in her purse to pull out his photo. Even though I wasn't interested, I gazed at the thin, handsome guy, a year older than us who went to Sacred Heart High. Now she 'd have a date for all the boys' school dances. I was jealous of Tessie's boyfriend. I knew I'd have to go to parish teen club meetings and Camp Fire Girls' socials to try to meet a boy—hopefully one that I liked.

I pushed through the crowd, waving to friends in the high school locker room electric with first day fever. I scanned the bulletin board to find my Homeroom. I was sporting a Stevenson button on my navy school jacket in anticipation of the presidential election. Other girls were wearing 'I like Ike' buttons. My Irish family were Democrats. Mom, uncle Hube, and cousin Alice, who was principal in another

San Francisco school, all liked Stevenson. In truth, we kids didn't really understand the issues of the election at all and thought the endless speeches were boring. Still, we liked taking competing sides in history class and were happy the nuns let us violate our uniforms with these big campaign buttons. I just wanted to get through the atrium crowd to the cafeteria. I pushed through the swinging cafeteria doors and heard Sister Maureen's voice in the kitchen.

"And that, Mrs. Petrini, is the lunch menu for the week. I'll be down at fourth period to see how it's going." When Sister turned and saw me, she smiled so broadly that the plump cook in her crisp, white uniform turned to see who'd just come in.

"Hi there, Judy," she said, her blue eyes crinkling at the corners, dimples creasing her cheeks. I sucked in my breath, feeling as if I was seeing a movie star in person. Ignoring the cook, we gazed at each other for a full minute. Her blue eyes were even more expressive than I remembered.

"Are you glad to be back? " I asked with a mischievous grin.

"As a matter of fact, very glad . . . " The electric bell cut off her sentence.

Together we walked to the stairs with our shoulders barely touching. Then I heard, "Hi, S'ter, can I carry your books to class?" It was Della with her straight hair hanging at the sides of her long face, coming 'round like a cocker spaniel, slurring Sister's name in that familiar way. Luckily I was going to have Sister Maureen for my geometry class and Della didn't. That would let me use the 'I need extra help' routine to spend more time alone with Sister. Now Della was reaching for Sister's books.

"Thank you," Sister said, but winking at me, as she handed her books to Della, who started jabbering to her as they went up the stairs. I saw Sister put her finger to her lips to remind Della talking wasn't permitted on the stairs. I followed, knowing she still cared. Late that afternoon, Della and I, in an unspoken truce, agreed to share a locker together, while still competing for Sister Maureen's affection.

As freshmen we were required to take Physical Education as our elective class, but now as a sophomore, I was free to take any elective. I was dying to take Art I. On the first day, entering the art room on the third floor, I found the smell of linseed oil and turpentine more intoxicating than any perfume. Sister Antoine, the art teacher, was an attractive nun with startling blue eyes and a teasing, playful manner. She assigned us each our own easel and small art locker. After a couple of weeks of pencil sketching of the plaster models of hands, feet, sunflowers and the like, we would begin using real oil paints and canvas. When I told Mom how much the oil paints cost, she frowned, but handed me a twenty and told me to get what I needed.

In class, the smiling Sister Antoine came round, putting her hand on our shoulders, giving us directions or praise. I had set up my easel next to my friend, Marilyn, who stayed after school daily to help Sister Joseph with her tasks. Sister Antoine directed us to choose something for our first oil painting. On my easel I pinned a picture of Man O' War that Uncle Hube gave me. For her image Marilyn chose St. Therese, the Little Flower and as we sketched or painted, we chatted about our beloved idols. Then I told Marilyn stories about my uncle Hube, who had taken me to horseraces at Bay Meadows when I was young. She confided that her father was a manager for prizefighters and that in his business, he used another name, Joey Foxx. This sounded seamy, even dangerous and I was fascinated, but she was embarrassed by his work and switched the conversation back to the nuns.

Soon Sister Antoine encouraged me to enter the competition to become the artist for our school paper, *The Reflector.* I had been one of the best artists in my grammar school class, but this was a much larger challenge and open to all the art classes. I was surprised when my entry of a pen and ink drawing of the Holy Family won. This led to a standing order to do pen and ink drawings or linoleum block images for the monthly issue of *The Reflector*. Now the whole school would see my work and I'd have to buy more tools and more linoleum blocks. Luckily, Mom gave me the money. I was happy that I could do some of my artwork after school at a cafeteria table and still be near Sister Maureen, who told me she was pround of my accomplishment.

As a sophomore, I decided to run for a Sodality office instead of a class office as I would get to spend time planning meetings with Sister. As good fortune would have it, I was elected Sodality Secretary and Della, who was not afraid of planning skits, was voted the Sodality Social Director. We'd have great fun with Sister planning the meetings and the entertaining skits that were performed at the end the meetings.

In addition to the cafeteria, Sister Maureen had another responsibility: the coat checkroom, right off the atrium. When it rained or was very cold, it was impossible for two girls to get their coats into one locker. As in a fancy restaurant, a system was set up to check one's coat and receive a tag to redeem it at the end of the day. After school, Della and I set about making new tags and setting up the system. Sister Maureen could do almost anything, but what she hated doing, was nothing. After the cafeteria was in order, she'd come into the coatroom off the atrium where Della and I were laughing and joking as we made the new coat tags. She'd bring out her leather tools and deftly stitch leather covers for prayer books and pouches for rosaries.

In time, she showed us how to use a leather punch to make slits, then how to stitch up the book covers with a special needle made to drag the thin leather lacing through the slits. If we broke a needle or pulled the lacing too tight, Sister got quite cross. Once, when she broke a needle, I heard her whisper, "Damn it."

Occasionally, a couple of seniors hung around Sister in the coatroom as well. One afternoon, Della began teasing Sister. "Sister, you've been stitching up quite a few covers. How many prayer books do you have?"

"These are not for me. I give them to the Superior," Sister replied serioiusly, looking up from her work.

"How many can she use?" asked Della, throwing up her hands.

"She doesn't use them," said Sister.

"Now this really makes a lot of sense. She just keeps a big stash that she doesn't use!" said Della squealing.

"Della, she gives them away as gifts to Sisters on their Feast days or gives them to the novices," Sister replied with a hint of annoyance.

Della settled down next to Sister, trying to be calm, but she was having too much fun with this subject. The two seniors seemed interested in hearing about the novices and gathered closer. I, too, liked hearing about the novices, those figures in starched white veils we'd occasionally see floating around the garden near the convent.

Della continued, "The novices? Those sisters that wear white veils and never leave the convent? What do they do all day?"

"They're learning to live the religious life and they pray a lot," explained Sister.

"What? Like five rosaries, a dozen Stations of the Cross, three Masses?" Della doubled over at her own joke and even the seniors were laughing.

Sister pursed her lips and replied sternly, "Don't make fun of the novices. We love them. They take classes and pray. They do the laundry, sew and have recreation."

"Sounds like a real good time," laughed Della. " I really envy them."

It soon became apparent Sister's mood was turning dark because she didn't like the way Della was talking about the novices. Abruptly she put away her things. This was rare, and in an effort to redeem ourselves, we jumped up, fawning over her and vying to carry her things to the convent. At the garden's edge, she rewarded us with a smile and a thank you as she hurried off to Vespers.

Occasionally, Sandy and I got together for social activities sponsored by the Camp Fire Girls. Both of us had been part of this group since fifth grade. One of the attractions of belonging to this troop, was that most of the girls were Jewish, as was our leader, Alice Jewel. Her daughter was shy and not nearly as attractive as her mother and I think Alice Jewel became a troup leader to support her daughter with social skills. We adored Alice Jewel who piled her dyed, jet-black hair high on her head and wore big gold earrings and taught us wonderful crafts. For Mother's Day, we sewed sequins on felt slip-on slippers we made for our mothers. We made flower baskets for older folks and did lots interesting activities, such as ushering at performance of the Tamalpais Moumtain Theater in Marin. As Catholics, our lives were sheltered. All our friends were Catholic and we were forbidden to enter any church that was not Catholic. So to mingle with others from a different faith, felt worldly.

Sandy and I planned to go to the Camp Fire Girls fall dance at our clubhouse on Arguello St. Attending these dances felt kind of daring, especially since the nuns tried to discourage us from going to these events when they learned that most of the boys at these dances were from public schools and many of the girls were Jewish. That, of course, made it all the more fascinating for us.

As we entered the old wooden clubhouse, the band, already on the stage, was playing Nat King Cole's *Unforgetable*. Sandy and I tried to look sophisticated. I was wearing a peach cashmere and low heels. Sandy had on a white blouse with a Peter Pan collar, a navy skirt and a matching cashmere cardigan draped over her thin shoulders. Standing at the edge of the dance floor next to the pretty Jewish girls, I decided on a drastic move: I tore off my glasses and stuck them in my purse. In minutes a bulky guy in a maroon sweater said, "Wanna dance?" I nodded and grabbed his arm. If he moved a foot away, I'd be lost.

Soon I was moving 'round the dance floor with George while the band played "Auf Wiederseh'n Sweetheart." His face was a blur above his fuzzy sweater, but I noticed he wore glasses. As we danced, he pressed me tightly into his soft, bulging middle. He told me he was a freshman at S.F. City College. Nice, I thought; he might invite me to a dance at his school. After our first dance, Sandy sidled up to me. She was wearing. She grasped a glass of punch with both hands.

"Jude, I saw you dancing. Was he nice? I mean, was he at least half-way decent? Did you get his name?"

"Sandy, he seems nice enough, though I could barely see him. We only had one dance."

"Did you notice he's wearing glasses? I mean if anything came of this and you put on your glasses, it wouldn't be too awful. Right? Oh golly, Judy, here he comes again!"

George and I danced several times and later in the evening, he asked if he could drive me home. I agreed. At the end of the evening we climbed onto the bench seats of his battered black Chevy and we were off. Without my glasses, I didn't notice he'd passed my block. Now we were driving on the Great Highway at the ocean beach and he parked along the stretch in front of the great sea wall. The hazy hunk pulled me close and gave me slobbery kisses with his thick lips while on the radio, Eddie Fisher crooned *Oh! My Pa-pa.*

I could hear the waves crashing on the long stretch beach and thought it would be more fun to run barefoot along the water's edge. Of course, two or three kisses were a girls' obligation, but when his stubby fingers started groping under my cashmere sweater toward my breasts. I tried to push his hands away. *Oh my Papa* droned on. Now he began fiddling with the back of my bra. I panicked. What could I do? I didn't really know this guy. I couldn't stand it another minute. What to do? Should I jump out of the car? Suddenly, with one hand, I reached into my purse, pulled out my thick glasses, shoved them, cock-eyed, on my nose and blurted to his startled face, "You know George, I'm a Catholic and petting like this is a mortal sin. Take me home right now!" As he pulled back, his hands now on the wheel, I added, "If I were killed in an accident before I could go to Confession, I'd go straight to hell."

"Jeez, straight to hell, my ass," he muttered as we sped past the other parked cars.

I wondered if all boys were like this with girls. I couldn't help feeling I was failing in an important ritual that other girls were mastering, but my friends at our very Catholic school never talked about these kinds of activities.

One October night at 2 a.m., Mom was awakened by a phone call from cousin Alice telling her Uncle Hube died of a heart attack. When I heard noise, I got up and went to the kitchen. Mom was sobbing and I put my arm around her, trying to hold back my own tears. One of us had to be strong. When uncle Hube was afflicted with MS some years ago, the laughter and music disappeared from our family. Watching this tall, kind man fall easily was agony for me. He flew to the Mayo Clinic for help, but nothing could stop the progress of the disease. Much of my childhood was spent in his flat above upstairs with him, where the yellowing shades were half-drawn and housework left undone. Mom never went to the flat upstairs. She had enough to do without worrying about Hube's housekeeping.

Hube's living room was better than any room full of toys. Strewn about were musical instruments: a violin, mandolin, harmonica and even a bass fiddle. A Western saddle straddled the back of the couch where I could ride imaginary steeds. A fine 4 x 5 view camera sat next to his big easy chair. On the floor I'd find piles of books, mostly history and mysteries, and always, next to his big chair, a huge bag of jellybeans. When he came home from the pharmacy where he worked, he cooked his own dinner, unless it was Friday when we went to Fisherman's Wharf or North Beach for seafood. On weekdays he ate rare steak and french fries that he made in his deep fryer. After my dinner, I'd come upstairs and he'd wind up the Victrola and put on his favorite records--Enrico Caruso, John McCormack, Grace Moore or Lilly Pons. At our favorite parts, Hube and I would sing along. I was his favorite and it was wonderful to be special.

Watching the disease disable uncle Hube, was a terrible event, especially for my Mom. Finally, when he could no longer climb the stairs to the flat above us, he reluctantly moved to a basement room at cousin Alice's place. She brought in a fine wingback chair and his phonograph, but it was never the same after he moved. I'd not known either of my grandfathers, and my dad died of cancer when I was three. Now with uncle Hube so ill, I I began to feel that men could not be a reliable source of comfort. The saddest part of the service was the final blessing of uncle Hube's casket with Holy Water as the pallbearers rolled the coffin to the hearse for the final ride. I told Mom I didn't want to go to the cemetery because Hube was being buried in our plot in Santa Clara with other relatives, rather than our closer plot in Holy Cross cemetery, where my father was buried. I wanted to return to school to share my sadness with Sister Maureen. Though I knew I was letting Mom down, I needed to be with someone who was alive and fun.

When I returned to school, it was time for English class and Sister Fidelity was having us read aloud portions of the *Merchant of Venice*. Long ago uncle Hube had told me that story, though he'd inserted a couple of characters that were his own invention. When she asked me to read aloud, after a couple of sentences, I began to cry. I told her about uncle Hube's funeral and she kindly, but quickly, sent me to the school chapel to pray for him so I would no longer disturb her English lesson.

I wanted to talk to Sister Maureen about uncle Hube's death, but after school was a time for joking and doing chores. Still, when I saw her between classes, I asked her if I might talk to her privately after school. She smiled and promised me a few minutes.

When I went out behind the school to the ball court to wait for Sister Maureen, I thought not only about Hube, but also about my dad's death. He was only thirty-two when he died of stomach cancer. Though I had few memories of him, one remained vivid. It occurred when my brother, Steve, was born. My dad took me to St. Mary's hospital and held me up in front of the window where a dozen or so wrinkled newborns lay sleeping or crying. He told me I could pick out a baby brother to take home. I pointed to a dark-haired sleeper, "That one. He won't make a lot of noise."

"Good choice. We'll take him." Then he took me outside to the lawn and we stood underneath my Mom's window. She waved and threw chocolates to me. At that time children weren't allowed to visit with new mothers who then stayed in the hospital for ten days after childbearing. I loved being with my dad. In the middle of these thoughts, I saw Sister striding toward me. In spite of a biting wind that made us shiver, we walked up and down in the empty ball court. As I was relating the painful story of uncle Hube, she slipped her arm through mine and listened intently. When I stopped talking, she put her arms around my shoulders and gazed into my tearful face, saying, "Judy, my dearest, you can be sure that I'll make a remembrance of this dear and wonderful man in my prayers at Mass tomorrow and I'll always remember you." I felt better.

As we headed back into the school, Della marched toward us. Looking straight at Sister, she complained, "I've been looking all over for you. All the other kids have gone home and everything's done in the kitchen. Where have you been?" Sister handed her books to Della, said something cheerful and we headed toward the convent. I sensed a difficult competition ahead, as each of us wanted so much to be Sister's favorite.

In time I began to come to help Sister Maureen on Saturday afternoons. Often Della came too, but sometimes she had to watch her younger siblings because her mom worked at the Emporium in the lingerie department. There were four kids in her family. She had an older brother and Della was the second child with a large space before the next two. The very mention of her mom's job humiliated Della.

Occasionally when I was at Della's house, her mother would say laugh-ingly, "I've got to sell enough girdles to pay the tuition for all you kids." Della would cringe.

Sister and I would sit in the ball court out of the line of vision of the school windows. With our knees touching, we'd correct mounds of algebra and geometry papers and then, enter the grades in her class books. Occasionally, I'd try to pry information from her. She'd confide interesting tidbits. She told me the nuns slept in rooms that were called 'cells' and then she pointed to a window in the convent that she said was her cell. She also told me nuns made a vow of poverty so nothing was called 'mine,' but 'ours.' I found out she hadn't been able to keep the box of stationery I'd given her at Christmas. Everything had to be turned in to the Superior. It was weird that the nuns, who seemed so powerful in school, had to submit to such rigid, trivial rules.

I asked about her life before she entered the convent. Did she have any boyfriends? She blushed and stopped correcting papers. Her eyes got a faraway look. She said softly, "At first, the only social gather-ings we went to were the Knights of Columbus' gatherings where my four older sisters and I were part of the entertainment; we danced Irish jigs, but then, during the war, they had real dances to entertain the troops. One night I was standing against the wall, watching my sisters dance with service men. When a soldier asked me to dance. I was very shy, but he insisted," she giggled and continued, "His name was Brian and had red hair and freckles that reminded me of my favorite cousin, Johnny. We went out on the dance floor." She smiled at the memory, continuing." He said I was a good dancer. I saw him a couple more times and we danced and . . . " Then Sister was quiet. I was sure she was thinking of Brian.

"And . . ." I encouraged her, feeling jealous of him.

"And he asked me to wait for him, but of course, I didn't because here I am," she blushed. "But I do remember him in my prayers, along with you. Now you know all about me," she said, playfully slapping my knee. After we had corrected a ton of papers, I paused and she looked at me with a smile and put her hand over mine. Slyly, I asked how long her hair was. She blushed, but leaned toward me and whispered it was close-cropped for comfort under her complex headgear. I longed to put my hand under the layers of serge and feel her hair, to know its exact color.

Often when I was helping her on a Saturday, her call bell would often ring--that loud insistent set of sounds, like a piercing Morse code. Each nun had a bell code. In the midst of our correcting papers, she'd head off to the convent to answer her call bell. I hated sitting alone and soon I'd think of the others things I could be doing----swimming at the Town and Country Club in Fairfax or going to a ballgame with friends. She was always gone too long. Impatiently, I'd pull on my jacket, sling my purse on my shoulder and start to write a terse note. Then I'd think of how sad she be to find me gone, but soon I'd put away the pen because I knew I'd be the one that would be miserable. When she finally returned, I often smelled coffee on her breath. However, spending so much time with Sister affected my social life. Now at lunchtime in the cafeteria when the girls were talking about what they'd done on the weekend, I had less and less to contribute. Gradually, I felt left out of their conversations.

It was spring when Mom met Sister Maureen. I'd spent the afternoon stuffing envelopes for a Mission project. It was late, so I called Mom to pick me up at the convent rather than the school. In the high-ceil-inged vestibule, I performed the introduction as the nuns had taught us, presenting my mother to Sister who was younger, but was accorded deference as a nun. Mom looked sophisticated in her red fitted coat and freshly painted nails. In her heels, she seemed to tower over Sister who stood with her hands hidden in her detachable large sleeves, which she never wore at school. Her veil was pulled out like blinders, instead of pinned back. She looked formal, not like the spirited nun I knew.

Mom extended her hand and Sister shook it but she was acting shy and deferential, not presenting the charm or humor she showed at school. She complimented Mom on the fine job she was doing of raising three kids alone. Then she patted my shoulder and said, "Really Mrs. Lyons, you must be proud of Judy with her good grades and artistic talent."

"It's true, Sister, I never have to worry about her studies, but where her art work is concerned, I think she copies too much. I'd like to see her do more original things."

"Mo-om!" I made a disgusted, clicking sound. The remark infuriated me. True, at home I had notebooks full of ballerinas and horses that I'd drawn from photos for years, but Mom was overlooking the competition I'd recently won as top artist for our school paper with my original design. She was treating me like her little girl and omitting my recent artistic accomplishments. This meeting wasn't going well as I'd hoped Mom would see how special Sister was, but the Sister I loved wasn't making an appearance. They weren't connecting as I'd hoped. On the way home, I was irritated with Mom and annoyed at Sister for appearing so reserved, hiding the appealing side of her that I knew so well.

Yet, I got over my irritation the next day when Sister Maureen asked Della and me to come help with a Sodality project on the next Saturday afternoon. Of course, we agreed. We were going to have a new task, sewing up little flannel shirts for the Missions.

Saturday morning Della called me and said with annoyance that she wouldn't be able to help. Through the phone, I could hear Della's dad shouting in his Tennessee accent, "Money doesn't grow on trees and you should be thankful your mother 's got a job!"

"Isn't this awful?" Della whispered. Then he yelled, "Get off the damn phone. Get in here and do the dishes."

"Gotta go."

What good fortune--an afternoon alone with Sister. I picked out a fuzzy, light blue, angora sweater and a pleated skirt and ran for the bus. Instead of working in the cafeteria or in the ball court correcting her students papers, we worked in the second floor sewing room. Shirts for the Missions had to be stitched up. Fortunately, Sister Esther, the sewing teacher, an, older nun, was never in the room on weekends. I was taking a sewing class so I knew how to use the machines. Sister gave me a stack of tiny shirts with a baby pattern to stitch together. At one of the Singer sewing machines, I began sewing them as Sister showed me. Soon my stack of stitched shirts rose high. As often as I dared, I knelt next to Sister with my work, asking her approval. Among the rows of cold sewing machines and slick Formica tables, she seemed warm and vital, softly singing snatches of her favorites, "Danny Boy" and "Zing, Zing, Zing went the Trolley."

By late afternoon, the fog was rolling over Twin Peaks, snaking into the school garden. My pile of flannel shirts now rose in soft towers and Sister, who'd finished hers, stood behind me, her hands resting on my shoulders as I sewed my last shirt. Slowly I left the shirt under the needle and put my hands over hers. I leaned back and felt the warmth of her body against mine. She leaned forward. I sat very still, barely breathing as we leaned against each other. She bent over with her lips close to my ear. "You're a good seamstress, Judy. Much better than I imagined."

She drew a deep breath, picked up a stack of shirts and whirled away into the small pressing room. I followed her with another stack. Sister was standing at the ironing board with her back to the door, the sputtering steam iron in one hand. A tower of shirts lay on the end of ironing board. I came up behind her and paused; then daringly, holding my breath, I slid my arms around her waist. In the mirrors, which were on three sides of the room, our images were reflected over and over--my fuzzy, angora arms violating her body encased in black serge. She was biting her lip. I lay my cheek against the back of her head. My hands felt the hard leather cincture binding her waist. Slowly Sister turned in the circle of blue angora and drew me against her. I felt the stiffness of the bib that covered her breasts. Nervous bubbles gurgled in my throat. With the steam iron hissing a sensuous song, we held each other tightly, her cheek soft against mine, her English lavender scent intoxicating.

Over her shoulder, I peered through the crack in the drawn yellow shade to the empty ball court below. On weekdays it was crowded with girls in cobalt gym suits playing softball. What would they think if they looked up and saw me, an ordinary sophomore, embracing their teacher, Sister Maureen? Would they condemn me, stone me? At that moment, I didn't care.

"My dearest Judy," Sister murmured. In slow motion we stepped back and looked at each other. Sister's eyes were clouded with emotion. Neither of us spoke, but we both understood something had now changed. Quickly we gathered up the shirts and put them in boxes. She took out her pocket watch. "Time for Vespers," she announced in a husky voice. I took her hand, put it to my cheek, and kissed the rough fingers. I was no longer an ordinary sophomore, who helped a favorite nun but Sister and I were in love.

When I got home, Mom was in the kitchen fixing dinner. I could hear the ice tinkling in her highball. I put on Chopin's *Polonaise* and stretched out on the couch, pondering what had happened this afternoon.

"Judy, set the table," Mom called from the kitchen. Still in a trance, I didn't move.

That Sister deeply cared for me was the wonder of my existence. I savored it constantly: *she loves me.* In the midst of activities at school—Sodality functions, Father's club or Mother's club meetings—we'd squeeze hands, have a quick hug in the pantry, an embrace in the furnace room where we hung wet dishtowels to dry on a collapsible rack. Between classes, Sister passed me a notes written in turquoise ink and folded like origami pieces. I'd dart into a bathroom stall and open the note that always began: *My dearest, or my darling Judy.* She'd often write: *I hope you'll help unpack the cans after school?* Or: *Could you come this evening and serve the ladies of the Good Council meeting? They'll have coffee and cake around 7:30? You're a sweetheart.*

Under my bed, I kept a wooden box that was filling up with her notes. I could never throw away anything from her.

At home things were shifting. Mom had a boyfriend, the first one in years. When we three were young, Mom had several serious suitors, and in hindsight, it would've been easier for her if she'd married again. Yet she always counted on uncle Hube to help; they got on very well and he loved us kids. Now with Hube gone, it shouldn't have surprised us that Mom was ready for a new man in her life.

Ray was younger than Mom, a tanned former lifeguard, who looked like Howard Keele, straight out of *Showboat*, mustache and all. He had a slight limp from an old injury, but that didn't keep him from bouncing when he walked. Steve, Ellen and I couldn't stand his eagerness, his super-politeness and he wasn't even Catholic! He punctuated ordinary conversation with so many *pleases, thank yous*, and *would you mind's* that it made us want to puke. Soon he was a regular, bringing Mom flowers, and when she entered the room in a cloud of her favorite cologne, White Shoulders, he'd almost burst out singing "Make Believe" from *Showboat*. He'd try to buddy up to Steve and me, saying things like: "Hey kids, excuse me, but I've got a great idea. If you don't mind me making a suggestion, why don't we all go out for dinner and then I'd be pleased to take you and your beautiful mother to a movie." He drove a green M.G. two-seater with a running board. How was he going to get all of us to dinner and a movie in his M.G.? Impossible. He was really talking about driving our family car.

Mom would fix highballs and we would sit we around the living room with us kids sulking in silence and watching TV, while they'd cozy-up on the sofa, exchanging lovey glances. Often Steve would pretend to gag and

I'd snicker at his antics. But then a familiar pattern set in: too much drinking, followed by arguments that we sometimes heard, but didn't witness. Ray would disappear for a time; Mom would mope. We hoped he wouldn't return. But he always did. Once I overheard Mom talking on the phone to cousin Alice. "Frances, you've got to stop running around with that young man," Alice scolded. "It's foolishness. Think of your career. This could seriously interfere with potential school promotions."

Mom replied, "He doesn't interfere in my work. You don't know him, Alice. He's a fine person and the kids like him. You're making too much of this." Cousin Alice was an influential school principal and was active in getting Mom a promotion to assistant principal after only four years of teaching in the classroom. Mom owed her. She had to listen.

I yearned to tell Sister about Ray, but it felt disloyal to talk about my Mom drinking, driving around in Ray's M.G., wearing a bright scarf to keep her hair in place. One day after school Sister and I were wrestling the huge No. 10 cans of peaches and tomato sauce that had been delivered for school lunches up to the pantry shelves. It was late and the other helpers had already left. I was up on the stepladder; Sister was below, handing me the big cans out of the carton. I began to blurt out a recent unpleasant Ray episode. One winter weekend. Mom and Ray decided to take us for a play-day in the snow in the Sierras. We all piled in our roomy Hudson and had a great time sledding, building snowmen and throwing snowballs. When it got dark, Ray said, "Why don't we hunker down in the car and drive home at daylight?"

"Do you think that's a good idea?" Mom asked.

"Oh, the kids can snuggle in the back and get warm. They'll be asleep before you know it." He was too cheap to pay for a motel. Mom, as usual, gave in to Ray. All three of us scrunched in the back seat under a couple of blankets, cold and cranky, while Mom and Ray were reclining in the front seat. I couldn't see them clearly, but I think they were kissing and hugging. I wanted to get out and walk home. Luckily, I had the rosary Sister gave me and I fingered the beads several times for the sins that I was certain Ray and Mom were committing.

While telling the story, I started down the stepladder and began crying. To my surprise, Sister didn't censure my mother, but put a comforting arm around me, shaking out her large linen hankie, since I had no tissue.

"There now don't cry, Judy. Your mother has been a widow a long time and I'm sure she's lonely. She deserves a chance for happiness."

"Why is she trying to find it with this creep?"

"Sounds like he loves her."

"He's icky. I hate him! You can't understand. You have perfect parents." I retorted, leaning my head on her shoulder. I could hear Sister's breath quickening. Then very slowly our lips grazed, her full lips, slightly chapped, met mine. A current ripped through me. Then, our mouths meshed again, hungrily.

"My darling Judy," Sister whispered as she pulled back, "What am I to do with you?" She crooked her finger and hit my nose affectionately.

As I rode the bus home, still feeling awed. I pondered what had just happened. Sister and I were in love and we had been hugging and touching for a long time. I knew I was special to her. Yet, I wondered if this happened with any other nuns and students? Many students adored a favorite nun and spent time with the nun after school. Surely, there were hugs, but I didn't know if it became as physical as it now was with Sister and me. I knew we had to keep it secret, but it seemed natural because our feelings for each other were so genuine.

I recalled that summer at camp when Sandy and I had a huge crush on one of the counselors, and when we returned to the city, we called her frequently. One afternoon we even took her to a movie, each of us sitting on either side of her. We were very disappointed when she didn't return to camp as counselor the next summer. It didn't seem strange at all to love other women, usually a bit older, someone we looked up to and would like to be close to them.

Sister was different from the other nuns, younger, only ten years my senior, and open with her feelings. In fact, she seemed to need loving herself. I recalled Tessie remarking when we were freshmen that Sister was not like the other nuns. "In fact, Judy," she'd said, "she seems too much like one of us kids." But now considering our feelings for each other, it seemed completely natural for us to kiss. We had been embracing for a long time. I'd never had a satisfactory kiss with a boy. We had no fear of being discovered as Sister's domain, the cafeteria and kitchen and the little pantry where we embraced was very private. We both were of a passionate nature and at this moment, we were in love and nothing else really mattered to me.

In June, once again, Sister was going to Minnesota for summer college classes. I dreaded our parting. On the dreaded last day of school, we waited 'til everyone else had gone home. I hid in the pantry waiting for her. When she came in, she came straight into my arms. We hugged and kissed tenderly but too soon our time was up. She said she'd think of me every day and keep me in her prayers. Then from deep in her pocket, she pulled out an envelope and gave it to me me. She told me not to open it 'til she'd gone.

Later that afternoon, I walked to St. Monica's and sat in a pew at the back of the empty church. Every nook and cranny was familiar. I'd sung in the choir, cleaned the sanctuary, arranged the flowers and the candles on the altar and confessed my sins in the confessionals. In the comfort of my church, I opened Sister's letter. She wrote that she'd miss me and would remember me in her prayers, but the surprise was at the top. She had pasted a tiny photo of her beautiful face in the center of a gold foil heart. I knew then that I'd never have a love like hers ever again.

When I came home from Camp in the Sierras that August, Mom said she was ready to trade in our old grey Hudson with the running boards that we had since 1938 for something new. Steve, Ellen and I went with Mom to the car dealer on Geary St. and collectively, we finally agreed on a four-door Studebaker in a new color, Ojai green. Then Ray, still Mom's boyfriend, did one good thing. He gave me driving lessons because he thought it would make Mom's life easier if I could run errands for her.

I sat behind the wheel of the new Studebaker, that looked as if it should have a propeller attached, anxious to begin, but Ray, reeking of after-shave, sat too close for my comfort. He'd review the gears about a hundred times. Finally, he'd let me turn on the engine and pull away from the curb, followed by many jerks and false starts. As we approached every intersection, he tapped my shoulder, repeating, "Heads up, heads up, all alert." I was sure I'd have a permanent dent in my shoulder. He was such a jerk, but I had to learn to drive to gain my freedom. Traffic was minimal in San Francisco's Richmond district and we'd head out to the Great Highway where I could get up to thirty-five miles an hour without having to stop at intersections. Though occasionally I mixed up second gear and reverse, at the end of August, I passed both the written and driving tests.

CHAPTER THREE

———~~~———

JUNIOR YEAR
SEPTEMBER 1953

WHEN I RETURNED to school in September, I couldn't wait to see Sister and to surprise her with the news I had my driver's license. I raced to the cafeteria to tell her I could legally drive! I could run errands for her and I could pick up the boxes of doughnuts on Haight St. for the breakfast after First Fridays' Mass. I could take her, or any of the Sisters, to funerals or doctor appointments, which was the only time nuns could leave the convent. Yet I was with Sister for only a few minutes, when I realized something was different. She laughed too loudly and talked too rapidly. When at last we were alone in the small pantry off the kitchen, a place that held memories of our intimate moments, I proudly shared the news about my driver's license. She smiled, saying that was wonderful, but when in my enthusiasm, I tried to hug her, she stepped back and gently took my wrists.

"What is it?" I asked, surprised.

She perched herself on the rickety stepladder and held my hands. "Listen, Jude, in August I had the most wonderful retreat and it came to me that it would be best for both of us if we didn't . . ."

"Didn't what?" I interrupted, frowning.

"If we didn't touch each other."

"What? That's crazy! We love each other," I almost screamed right there in the nearly empty cafeteria.

"Of course, we do, Jude. I'm not saying we don't. It's just that self-denial would be good for us. It builds character. You know you're special to me. I don't have to prove it over and over, do I?" I wanted to yell at her: *Yes, you do! Damn right, you do! I can't live without your touch.* "You know those chats we had about you possibly entering the Novitiate, now this will give you the opportunity to offer a real sacrifice to Jesus, like Nuns do."

I wanted no part in any stupid sacrifices. Then I noticed something different: on one finger she was wearing a shiny silver ring with a cross on it. I held up her broad hand, asking, "What's this?"

"Isn't it wonderful, Jude? I made my Final Vows at a special Retreat at the end of summer."

Final vows, retreat--those were the events that had changed her! For days, I pleaded, argued, pouted, but she was adamant: no touching. To make it even worse, she started teaching this special Consecration to the Virgin Mary according to some saint, Louis Marie Grignon de Montfort. I'd never heard of him. Another screwy idea she got during that retreat. She formed a small after-school group that met in the cafeteria. They studied from these little booklets and Sister promised the group that when they were ready, they'd make their Consecration to Mary in the convent chapel. Of course, Della was part of the group, but I refused to join. I didn't want anything to do with this new piety; I wanted her.

Feeling dejected and rejected, I often went home after school and hung out with Vicky, the girl across the street who was a year older than me. We'd walked to St. Monica's for years together and now she was our student body president. Though she was popular, unlike Tessie, she was sweet, irreverent and funny. She joked about keeping up with her older sister at Cal Berkeley where she was in one of the best sororities. I loved talking with Vicky about sororities, rushing and boys. Sometimes she had friends over--popular seniors, and she often included me. They seemed so sophisticated, chattering and joking about boys, dates and what they'd do after graduation. I could barely keep up with their conversations, but l loved being in their company.

Meanwhile my friend, Eva, hoping to meet boys, had started going to St. Agnes teen club. The parish was only a few blocks from our high school and the group met Friday evenings once a month in a room in the back of the church. Yet I had my doubts because I wouldn't know any of these teenagers, yet she insisted I'd like it. She was so dogmatic when she thought she was right that I gave it and decided to go to a meeting. I carefully selected a lime-colored cashmere sweater that was a little bit tight and a long plaid skirt and black suede shoes. I'd recently gotten new frames for my glasses that were more stylish and my too-curly hair was cut short. I'd bleached my bangs to look more interesting, though I still evied the girls with long straight hair.

The Moderator, Father Henley, a handsome, charismatic priest, welcomed all teenagers, even from other parishes. After leading us in a prayer and setting out simple refreshments, Father Henley, himself, would put on lively music and encourage us all to 'get up and move.' Often he was the first on the dance floor, grabbing a girl's hand, moving in a free swing and that got many of us out on the floor. To my surprise, I was soon asked to dance by a hefty boy who went to St. Ignatius High and who lived up on Twin Peaks. Several of his friends who were there, lived in the same affluent neighborhood. They were polite and well-spoken. In time, they all asked different girls to dance.

When we danced, we no longer moved to the formal steps of our parents era, but moved in a loose swing or jitterbug steps. I caught on quickly as we danced to *Rock Around the Clock* and *Shake, Rattle and Roll* but also to a few slower ones like, *Hey There* and *Mr. Sandman.* However, there was one guy, Patrick, charming and handsome. All the girls wanted to dance with him, but he was a rogue, a "man on the move," never settling on one girl. My hefty dance partner, John, asked for my number and I gave it to him. We danced at most of the teen club evenings. Once he asked me to a pops concert that was lovely and, though I enjoyed his company, I wasn't drawn to him. He was sweet and didn't ask more than a simple kiss at the end of the evening, but I wanted someone handsome and exciting. I went out with a couple of other guys, all Catholic and polite, but it was always just one date with a simple kiss or two at the end of the evening. Being with Sister Maureen was far more rewarding as our relationship was intense and personal. Being with her was so much more fulfilling. Boys couldn't come close to our intimacy.

At school, I still saw Sister between classes and often carried her books, but I wouldn't stay after school while she was still holding to her crazy rule of no touching. Yet one afternoon I gave in and stayed for clean-up after her cooking class. I saw her go into the tiny room off the kitchen to hang the wet towels on a drying rack next to the furnace. I picked up several damp towels and followed her. She had her back to me. Daringly, I put my arms around her waist. Last year she would've turned, hugged me and perhaps we might have kissed. But now she scolded, "Ah, ah, Jude, remember, no touching" and pulled away from me. I threw the damp towels on the rack, stomped out to the cafeteria in a fit of anger, grabbed my books and, hoping she'd call after me, I headed to the locker room, but she didn't. I took the bus home, but nothing made me feel worse than having a falling-out with Sister.

At home, I couldn't eat or concentrate on my homework or be civil with my family. I only wanted to make-up with Sister. After dinner I called the convent, but the nun at the switchboard said that Sister wasn't answering her call bell. I thought that possibly she was over at the school doing something in the cafeteria. Now that I had my driver's license, Mom would let me take the car after she came home from work. Sometimes I ran errands for her, but often I just cruised by the convent and school. I told Mom I was going to the drugstore, but instead, I drove straight to the high school, about fifteen minutes away.

I parked and sat in the car for a few minutes. No lights were on at the school. Then I crept into the garden between the high school and the convent. On the second floor of the convent, I saw a light at Sister's window. Long ago she'd told me which room was hers. If I could just talk to her for a few minutes, it would erase my pain. I threw a small pebble at the window, and then another. The shade and window sash shot up and a nun's face appeared. In the back lighting, I couldn't tell if it was Sister Maureen or not. "Pssst Sister," I whispered from the garden.

All of a sudden the sister started screaming, "There's someone out there! Help, help! Somebody's in the garden!" Instantly, lights started going on in other windows. A porch light came on and threw a glow on the garden. I panicked and dashed around the bushes, heading for the gate that now seemed a million miles away. High voices seemed to be following me as doors opened and nuns called out, "Who's there? Speak up!" Then I saw Quasimodo, the weird janitor, coming from the direction of the school. I jumped over a hedge and scratched my knee and bolted for the gate. Outside, I raced to car, gunned the motor and tore down Turk St. like an outlaw. Why hadn't Sister told me there was more than one nun to a cell or that she had changed cells?

The next day when I confessed to Sister what I'd done, she blanched. Shaking her head solemnly, she said, "Judy, Judy, whatever will I do with you?"

That day a large order of canned goods was delivered for the school lunches. If there was any job Sister disliked, it was to unpack those huge No. 10 cans of tomatoes, green beans and peaches. As a concession for the trauma I'd suffered, Sister agreed to let me come alone on Saturday to help her unpack the order. The warm Indian summer days had faded, daylight savings was over and the days were growing chilly. I was alone with her and we worked most of the afternoon in the cold pantry, hoisting the heavy No. 10 cans to the shelves. By late afternoon she was so tired, she nearly fell off the stepladder. I put my arms up to steady her. She stepped down slowly, deliberately turning into my arms. She rested her head on my shoulder and I thought she might cry. I could hear her breath quicken. Ever so slowly our lips pressed together, then again, hungrily. The days of sacrifice were over.

In the weeks that followed, we snuck embraces and kisses often in every private space. I reveled in being special to her again. The after-school group that Sister had formed had already made their Consecration to Mary in the convent chapel and no longer met in the cafeteria. I joined Della and another new freshman groupie, Annie, a sweet girl, helping Sister after school with her endless chores.

One day after school, the three of us were cleaning the cafeteria, the kitchen and the nuns' private lunchroom. Students were never allowed in that lunchroom. Sister, wearing her white starched apron with her habit pinned up, went into the private room. I followed her. Sister didn't scold me, she just kept brandishing a wet sponge over the long table. I moved along behind her, drying the table with a dry towel. I kept looking around to see what was so special about that lunchroom, but it was quite ordinary. When I got close to her, I gave her a playful kiss; then hovered over her. "One more, please." She frowned but obliged. Then she picked up a tray of sugar bowls to be refilled and headed to the door. "Just one more, please." I stood in front of her, arms outstretched, blocking the door.

"What is wrong with you today? Della and Annie are right outside," she hissed. She tried to pass, but I wouldn't move. Grudgingly, she brushed my lips with her chapped ones.

"That makes two hundred-fifty," I whispered, pulling a scrap of paper from my blue uniform jacket.

"Two hundred-fifty what?"

"Kisses we've had," I hissed. She arched her eyebrows, rolled her eyes in disbelief and bolted out, letting the door slam on me. I smiled.

In spring we had our annual three-day retreat where each day started with Mass in the Little Theater. Classes were cancelled and silence was expected all day, though there was whispering when the nuns where not around. We attended lectures by the Retreast Master, a witty, handsome Jesuit, who spoke from a lectern on the stage of the Little Theater. He went through the usual retreat topics--the Sacraments, leading an exemplary Catholic life, resisting temptations, purity, charity toward all, but he saved his special talk on vocations for the last day. He said the call to serve God in religious life was not for everyone, but to resist the calling, if one had a true vocation, would put one's soul in peril.

For as long as I could remember, I'd had thoughts about becoming a nun. I admired many of my teachers--powerful, kind and mysterious, but with my feelings for Sister Maureen, I felt a stronger calling. According to the learned retreat Jesuit, the requirements were simple: "If in your heart you feel an honest desire to serve God, are of legitimate birth and the Religious Order of your choice accepts you, then there is no doubt you have a vocation. What is required of you is great generosity to become a Spouse of Christ." Sitting in the darkened Little Theater, I heard Tessie remark, "Won't get me in any convent unless they admit boys." Shaking my head, I ignored her. "He may be waiting for you to answer His call," Father concluded. Then he made himself available for confession or personal questions in a makeshift confessional. Many girls made a beeline to wait their turn to speak to the priest, but I had an appointment to talk with Sister Maureen. I was feeling apprehensive as we settled on a secluded bench in the garden. The day was spring-like, not unlike that day, eons ago, when I'd confided to her my thoughts of transferring to Lowell and she'd spoken intimately about hoping I wouldn't.

Sister sat up straight and spoke in an unusually formal way about answering The Call. She was sure I had a vocation and the first step was an appointment with the Mistress of Novices. I wasn't ready for that step. I had to put her off for a while.

"Sister, I want to tell you that after praying and searching my heart during our retreat, I have to say I'm feeling a calling, but I'm still considering the Sisters of the Holy Names, you know the ones who taught me at St. Monica's. I want to be sure I'm not entering just to be with you, but for Jesus."

Sister's face collapsed to a dark-cloud look and she said in a hurt voice, "Judy, why on earth would you do that? Don't you love my community?" Then she took both my hands and squeezed them tightly, saying, "You can't imagine how often I've prayed that you'll become part of my religious family."

It was enticing to think of being part of Sister's family and I said, "It would be wonderful to be part of your family and I'll pray hard about this."

With a smile, Sister pulled an envelope from her pocket and slipped it into my jacket pocket. I waited until I was at home to read it. In her usual turquoise ink she'd penned:

> *Dearest Judy,*
> *I hope this retreat is full of grace for you. I am keeping you in my prayers daily and I cannot wait until the time when we are true sisters in Christ.*
> *Lovingly in J.C.,*
> *Sister Maureen*

Not long after our retreat, Vicky asked me over to her place across the street. We were sitting on her bed, exchanging bits of gossip when she said, "Now Judy, I'm going to share something, but you have to keep it secret, don't tell anyone!"

"No one," I promised.

She said, "Judy, its weird, but think I 've heard a call from God!" She giggled and blushed, then continued, "I'm going to apply to enter the convent to be a real nun."

I almost fell off the bed. Beautiful, fun-loving Vicky, a nun? She continued saying she decided to go to the Sisters of the Holy Names of Jesus and Mary, the Sisters from our grammar school who had a Novitiate attached to Holy Names College in Oakland, instead of to the Presentation Sisters who taught at our high school. I couldn't believe what I was hearing. Vicky had everything: beauty, brains, popularity, boyfriends, and even wonderful parents. Whatever would make her want to enter the convent? Then it struck me like a thunderbolt! I was witnessing a true calling and she was answering. I marveled at this momentous event. It made me feel special that she would share this news with me. It would be hard to keep it a secret. Amazing, my good friend Vicky, a nun!

Late one afternoon in May, Mom was surprised to find Father Flynn from St. Monica's parish at the door of our flat. Mom was still sporting her pastel suit that she wore as vice principal, but had already taken off her heels and was wearing her slip-on sandals. She loved company and immediately invited Father to settle into the big easy chair in our living room and in minutes was fixing a bourbon for both of them.

Steve, who would finish eighth grade in June, sat fidgeting on the piano bench. Curiously, he was wearing a clean shirt and his hair was freshly combed. Mom sat on the couch facing Father while I sat on a stiff chair I'd dragged in from the dining room as I didn't want to miss anything. After a bit of coaching from Father, Steve, a young man of few words, blurted out the reason for Father's visit.

"Mom, I wanna go in the sem after eighth grade, ya know, in September."

Father Flynn laughed a hearty laugh, louder than seemed appropriate to me.

"To the seminary to study to be a priest?" Mom asked, smiling weakly, attempting to conceal her astonishment.

"Yes, isn't that wonderful," crowed Father Flynn, raising his half-empty glass of bourbon to clink glasses with Mom. "To Steve."

I sat in stunned disbelief. Steve, my thirteen-year-old brother, who lived for sports, who was at best a passing student, who had girls following him home from school, who'd never pass up a fight, now had decided to pattern himself after this soft, non-athletic Irish priest who took him out for an occasional hamburger. How had I missed the spark of piety? For a short time he'd been an altar boy, but at eleven, Steve was already tough, darkly handsome and looked more like a candidate for the Mafia than the priesthood.

At this moment, agitated by this sudden attention, he sat on the piano bench, nervously beating a single low note on the piano until Mom told him to stop. I knew he was wondering when he could leave and go down the block to throw a few baskets with his friends. Mom got up to fix another short one for Father. I followed her into the kitchen.

"Mom, do you think Steve really has a vocation to the priesthood? Wait 'til they see his grades. They'll never let him in, unless they want a good basketball player."

Mom shrugged. " I don't know, Judy. It won't hurt him to go down with Father Flynn and take a look at the seminary. I think it's only in Mountain View." She poured herself a double bourbon and returned to the living room wearing her brightest smile. Typical of Mom, she assumed her new role as easily as Ingrid Bergman---playing the good Catholic mother, blessed with a son who would become a priest. I knew she would miss the man of the house. I wondered if Steve left home, would she consider letting me go to the convent next year?

Often in the chilly evenings I would drive to my favorite spot, the cliffs above China Beach in the lovely Seacliff neighborhood. I'd park the Studebaker and sit watching the sun slip into the Pacific, leaving salmon streaks creasing the grey horizon. Below the breakers raced up the solitary sands. I'd get out and walk to the top of the steep path to the beach and look out the to the Pacific ocean and dig at the sand with my shoes. To the woman walking her poodle this evening, I was only a teenager, staring out to sea, most likely dreaming about her boyfriend.

I recalled the summer after eighth grade when I was with friends on the beach below and I daringly plunged into the icy surf and swam beyond the breakers. Could I do that now and keep on swimming and not have to make any decisions about my future? The nuns taught us we had free will, but then in the next breath, they'd tell us: God knows what you are going to do before you do it. So on the one hand, our actions are predestined, but on the other hand, they taught us that our prayers could be answered, as if we could change God's Mind. We would have even more influence on Him if we did a penance, like giving up chocolates for Lent. Yet if you asked too many questions, they'd say: Have faith. Faith-always the same answer. Now I wondered if God was willing my love for Sister Maureen so that I'd become a nun? I felt so confused. I prayed:

Jesus, I don't know what to do. Do I have a real vocation? Should I enter Sister Maureen's Order or the Holy Names to serve You? And never see Maureen again? I need Your guidance.

Yet I 'd often thought of becoming an artist. I was the best artist in the school, but I didn't know any real artists. Where did one go to be an artist? My father's family, all seven, except for Aunt Irene, had gone to Cal Berkeley. When they talked to my Mom, they encouraged her to send me there. If only uncle Hube hadn't died. He knew everything. He'd gone to Cal Berkeley, too. A tear trickled down my cheek. Angrily, I brushed it away. My junior year was nearly over and Sister would go to college classes in St. Paul for summer. Her absence would leave room for thinking about other things. In truth, I was hoping for something different, something wild and wonderful to happen this summer.

After a month's escape to the Camp Fire Girls camp, I came back to the foggy city unusually restless. I put on records and practiced jitterbug and bop in our living room, sometimes even dancing with Ellen, four years my junior. I went out and bought a gorgeous, turquoise bathing suit. But nothing was happening and I was irritable and bored.

Then in August, Mom unexpectedly booked a vacation cabin in Lake County where we'd been several times in earlier summers. Against the triple outcry of we three kids, she insisted on inviting Ray to join us. But Mom let me invite Della, too. Forest Lake Resort had dancing every evening, yet sadly Della and I, dressed in full skirts and peasant blouses that we wore off the shoulder, were wallflowers lost among the tanned, blond beauties who had real make-up and deep-cut sundresses. If we wanted boys to dance with us, we'd have to import them. On Thursday, I called Jack, the boy from the teen club that I'd dated a few times. Yes, he could come up and he'd bring a friend and stay for the weekend.

On Saturday morning, Della and I anxiously waited outside the cabin. We had put on clean shorts and bright sleeveless shirts. When they pulled up and parked, I introduced Della. Jack introduced his friend, Don Reilly. He had even features, dusted with freckles and reddish hair that he slicked back and combed often. He talked out of the side of his mouth as if he wasn't sure he wanted anyone to hear, but the remarks I caught were funny. I liked him immediately. We changed and went to the pool where the boys showing off their dives with Della and I appplauding. I whispered to her that it had been a good idea to import our own dates.

However, it was at the dance that night that Della and I hoped we'd have the most fun. Yet we only danced a few stiff turns around the floor when the boys wanted to go outside to puruse their preferred activity, ping-pong. Della and I suffered withering defeats in several games with them. We went back to our own cabin and sat on the screened porch sipping cokes. The warm night held a promise of a moonlit walk with maybe a kiss or two.

All of a sudden, we heard a crash and a scream from inside the cabin. I gasped as I saw a drunken Ray brandishing a knife over Mom while she cringed behind a overturned chair in a corner. Jack and Don were on Ray instantly, struggling for the knife. Steve appeared and pummeled Ray in the back. When Della picked up the chair, I eased Mom into it. Ellen was crying and hid her face in Mom's lap. When Mom moved her hand from her face, I saw an ugly red welt where Ray had struck her. I wanted to kill Ray, but the boys were dragging him out of the house. "Hey, hey, boys, take it easy. Please, please let go of me." Even when drunk, he persisted in being overly polite.

The boys hustled Ray, who was taller than both of them, across the street to small, unused swimming pool, slimy with algae where they shoved a drunken Ray, fully clothed, into the green water. When I got to the pool, Jack, his cheeks flush with excitement, put his pudgy arm around me and said, "We'll take care of this bastard!" The boys guarded the sides of the pool shouting, "Sober up, you sonna-of-a-bitch," pushing Ray back in the slime whenever he got near the sides. In slurred words, Ray continued to plead to be let out of the pool. It seemed as if it went on for hours but finally, Ray got to the ladder at the far end and the boys let him go and he disappeared.

In the cabin we sat around the kitchen table drinking cokes, each retelling some part of the story. Jack had his arm around me and I was sure he was having the best date of his young life and I was wishing that it was Don's arm around me.

Mom remarked with her usual tolerance, "Ray just gets insane with jealousy, especially when he's had a few."

Ray was crazy. There were no other men around Mom, though she had the kind of personality that drew everyone to her. Late Sunday the boys went home. Indeed something wild had happened, but it wasn't the fantasy that I'd envisioned.

In late August Mom received an unexpected invitation for us to spend a few days at the Russian River with our neighbors. Luckily, there was no Ray. As Mom drove north to the teenage mecca, I thought of Don Reilly who's family had a cabin on the river. After we arrived, I hurried to a phone booth to boldly call Don, but when he answered, I could barely speak. Shyly, he invited me over to his cabin, right on the river, for a swim the next afternoon. I leapt in the air as I left the phone booth. I finally had a date with someone I liked!

Most beaches along the Russian River were jammed with families and kids, but in front of Don's cabin it was remarkably private and the metal bridge cast shadows that turned the water to emerald velvet. As we swam, his mother waved from the porch. Don was rather shy and I suspected it was she who encouraged him to invite me in return for our weekend in Lake County. We raced, dove and romped like puppies. I didn't wear my glasses in the river so the experience was like an out-of-focus film. After swimming hard, we rested, facing each other with our arms on the sides of the large inner tube, our legs entwined. It was the best afternoon of my whole summer.

After the swim, I was invited to stay for spaghetti dinner with the four boys and their mother. Don couldn't get in a word over the jabbering of the older brothers. After the meal, we all went to the local resort for dancing. Don and I moved in an awkward two-step as the band played, "Hey, There, You With the Stars in Your Eyes." I loved the feel of his reddish hair, still damp from the shower. After the dance we got in the back seat of his brother's car where he and his date snuggled close in the front seat. In back I moved as close to Don as I dared. Sadly, the ride only took minutes. Don walked me to my cabin door and planted a timid kiss on my lips. I kept my lips in place for another, but he was gone, with a simple, "See ya." The next day, slathered in Sea and Ski, I baked by the River, hoping Don would call me or come around. He didn't and I was miserable. I tried to rationalize that it was because of his male loyalty to his boring friend, Jack, with whom I'd had several dates. Once back in the City, I drove by his house on Roosevelt Terrace numerous times, but I never caught sight of him.

On the last weekend in August, we loaded Steve's luggage into the Studebaker, along with a picnic lunch, and headed for St. Joseph's Seminary in Mountain View. The building was scuffed and plain, like one of Steve's old Keds, but fortunately, it was set among lovely mature trees and green lawns. We trekked up to the second floor to find the room that Steve would share with another freshman. The rooms had twin beds, two desks, two chairs, but no curtains, no pictures—just squares and rectangles, browns and tans, sparse and functional. Soon Steve found some boys he knew and there was the usual shouting and punching—boys' ritualized way of communicating. One of the seniors helping the new boys get settled asked us if we needed assistance. He was the handsomest boy I'd ever seen. He had light auburn hair, green eyes and a sprinkling of freckles. His body moved easily in his dark suit. I stood staring at him while Mom thanked him and said we were settled. I asked Steve to find out his name. I knew it would brighten up our once-a-month Visiting Sundays to see him again. Steve shook his head and censored my interest with his most disgusted look.

On the manicured lawn under tall trees, we settled with our picnic lunch. After lunch I took out my Brownie camera and snapped the family photo. Steve appears serious; he was nervous, leaving home at only twelve. Ellen, wearing a bandana, smiled giddily; Mom in her light coat, a thermos of coffee at her elbow, looked directly at me with a smile, but there was a tightness around her eyes as she was finding it difficult to lose the man of the house. We three drove home. Summer was over. Our family would never be together in this same way after this day.

CHAPTER FOUR

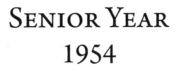

SENIOR YEAR
1954

IN SEPTEMBER I returned to school, a mighty senior. I splurged on a new camel's hair coat and sported white buck shoes. I bought a new dark red lipstick to flaunt a confidence that I didn't feel. In truth, I was a blob of wants. I wanted to be Sister Maureen's favorite; I wanted to be Sodality president; I wanted to be the best artist in school and I wanted to date Don Reilly. I couldn't forget our good times together over the summer. There was a St. Agnes teenclub autumn dance coming up. For days I thought of asking him to the dance. Finally, on a Friday afternoon, I went into the tiny school chapel and prayed. Kneeling in front of the painting of Our Lady of Good Counsel I implored the Virgin: *Please, make him say yes.* For privacy, I went to the phone booth located right outside the school. I was sweating. I dropped the dime. I dialed the wrong number. I had another dime and dialed again. Don answered. We chatted briefly about school. How are your classes? Are you doing any sports? Then I blurted out, "You know, there's a dance coming up and it's in your parish. I was umm, just wondering, like maybe you'd like to go to the dance with me?"

"Oh geez, I already asked someone to go. You might even know her--Sue Collins. She's a freshman at your school."

"You're going with a freshman? No, I doubt I know her. I don't hangout with freshmen."

"She's kind of cute and a little loud, but she's really fun to be with."

He preferred a lowly freshman to me, a senior! I didn't know this stupid freshman, but I was going to find her and stash a poisoned apple in her locker. When I looked her up, I found she was short, loud and brash. She even had curly hair like me. Jesus! I felt crushed and angry.

Soon I noticed Della wasn't coming around Sister after school. For three years she had been a daily presence, an adoring fan completely committed to Sister. She didn't even ask me to share a locker and never stayed after school. At first I felt relief; I'd worn down the competition. Then I began to miss her humor, her camaraderie. Had she given up hope of winning the prize—being first in Sister's affection? Or worse, did she doubt its value?

"What happened to Della?" I asked Sister as we worked on the usual chores around the kitchen and cafeteria.

Sister shrugged, "I really don't know."

"Did you two have an argument?"

"Don't be ridiculous." She went on writing the menu for the cook.

"Have you talked to her?"

"For a minute," she replied, her face expressionless.

Sheer devotion from Della, then instant divorce? It didn't make any sense. I got right up next to her, demanding, "What did she say?"

"That she had a nice summer. That's she's going to run for Sodality president."

"That's it?" Sister's nonchalance was driving me crazy. "Did she tell you about the awful episode with Ray and my Mom this summer?"

"No, she never mentioned you. Why would you bother her?" she said rolling her eyes in mock sarcasm.

"She's competed with me for years. Why would anything change?"

She stopped writing the menu and turned and faced me, "Judy, will you just drop it. Della might want to get into doing other things," she said with her perfect eyebrows knit in a frown. She sounded like my Mom: 'Calm down, Judy. Take it easy. Drive more slowly.'

The next Monday after school, I saw Sister and Della walking in the ball court and I gave them a wide berth. I knew Sister's feelings were hurt by Della's absence and now Sister would find out what Della was thinking. I knew Sister was hoping Della would enter the convent at the end of our senior year. Now every time I saw Della, she was with Sherry, a popular, petite girl with bouncy curls and an Irish freckled face. With their difference in height, they looked like a 'Mutt and Jeff' twosome. I heard the girls gossiping about this new companionship. Sherry's former best friend walked between classes with barely disguised hurt feelings. In days, Sherry would be elected class president. Della and Sherry were now inseparable. It was a mystery to me.

To my surprise, when the Sodality elections were announced, Della and I were the only two competing for president. I had never lost an election, but when the votes were counted, Della won! It was the most miserable, embarrassing day of my life. After school, I sat alone on a bench far out in the ball court, trying to grapple with the truth: I was a loser.

Sister came 'round a hedge looking for me. She sat right next to me and for a while neither of us spoke.

"It hurts, huh, Jude?"

"Yes, it does, it really does!"

"It's not the end of the world," she said putting her hand on my knee.

"Do you think I'm a real loser?"

"Of course not. By the way, I helped count the votes; it was a very close, but, Jude, that's how life is: sometimes you win; sometimes you lose. Do you remember you told me that your Uncle Hube took you to the horse races when you were young? He bet on the horses, right? Life is a bit like a horserace. You try your best, but you don't always win."

I smiled because she remembered my uncle Hube as she slipped her hand into mine, discreetly drawing her habit over our locked fingers. Even though we didn't speak of it, I knew she felt that she'd lost too; she lost Della. We sat together in silence for a long time, absorbing our losses.

One Saturday morning at Mass in St. Monica's church, I spent more time than usual in prayer after Holy Communion. I was getting up early now and going to Mass at St Monica's every day. Only a few parishioners, mostly older women, attended on weekdays. I prayed for guidance: *Jesus, what do You wish for me? Should I dedicate my life to You?*

Once I'd thought of going to Cal Berkeley, but that seemed remote. I wanted too much to be with Sister Maureen, to be like her. Was my love for Jesus as strong as my love for her? Should I consider entering the Holy Names Sisters who'd taught me here at St. Monica's? I loved our choir teacher, Sister Edward, but the only time I saw her now when I sang at choir on special Sundays.

Jesus, are You are calling me? I'm ready to be Yours. Please, give me guidance, even a sign.

When most of the parishioners had left, I knelt in front of the life-sized statue of my favorite saint, Therese, the Little Flower of Jesus, a Carmelite nun, who had died young, suffering a slow and painful fight against tuberculosis. I knelt on the padded kneeler and gazed up at her. She and I were old friends. At seventh grade Confirmation, I 'd chosen her name to add to mine. I was Judith Ellen Theresa Lyons. Now I prayed for insight, for guidance. As I knelt looking up at her beatific face, I was sure I smelled the scent of the roses she held in her arms. and I began to feel at peace. Yes, I think I was smelling her roses! This was surely a sign that she was pleased with my decision to be a nun, a Bride of Christ. Yes, I would enter. I would go to the Presentation Sisters, Sister Maureen's convent. Now I felt peace, but I didn't feel any excitement.

Saturday afternoon I spent helping Sister Maureen and she soon noticed I was pensive. "You've got something on your mind. Shall we sit and talk awhile, Jude? It's about entering, isn't it?"

I nodded.

"If you're ready, I can speak to the Mistress of Novices. She'll set a date for an interview with you and your mother. She'll have to approve of you but I know you and your mother will charm her."

"You can tell her I'm ready but I don't want the interview right away." She gave me a long, tender hug.

I believed I was on the right path but now I was concerned about aunt Margaret's call to Mom. She had asked if I had applied to Cal Berkeley yet. All seven, my father and his siblings, graduated from Cal Berkeley and I knew I was going to disappoint them. Fortunately, Mom spoke evasively and said she wasn't sure what I wanted to do. That was the truth! I needed more time to sort out my own feelings before I met the Mistress of Novices.

I was ready to tell Mom of my decision to enter the Novitiate, the first step on the path to beginning a nun, but it was complicated by the fact that I knew it annoyed Mom that I spent so much time with Sister. Yet she didn't confront me; she hated confrontation. She also was dealing with her own disappointment with Ray. After the summer incident at the resort, she knew how dangerous he could be and fortunately, he wasn't coming around now. In fact, she learned he recently crashed his M.G., though he wasn't badly hurt, probably just drunk. I was grateful Mom wasn't with him. If only she could meet someone nice. She had many decent suitors over the years and it would've been better if she had remarried, but uncle Hube lived in the flat above us and they got on well and he was always helping with us kids. Now with Steve in the seminary, it was likely she would be unhappy when I said I wanted to go in the convent.

For my seventeenth birthday, Eva was planning a party. It was supposed to be a surprise, but I knew about it. Lots of girls from school would be there there and a few boys from the St. Agnes teen club. Wistfully, I was hoping Don Reilly would arrive, but only Jack came. He gave me a a thoughtful gift, a fake fur collar and, though it wasn't my style, I pretended I loved it. Meawhile I had decided that my birthday was the day that I would tell Mom of my decision to enter the convent. When I returned home from the party, I stole into Mom's bedroom where she was asleep. I waited a moment wondering if I should wait 'til tomorrow, but then, I shook her lightly. Mom blinked and propped herself up on her elbow, hoisting the strap of her silky blue nightgown. I smelled a faint whiff of bourbon.

I whispered, " Mom I have something to tell you."

"An accident?"

"Oh, no, nothing like that!"

"Can't it wait 'til morning, Judy?"

"No, I want to tell you on my birthday." I got down on my knees next to her and said, "Mom, I want to enter the convent. I want to be a nun."

"What? When?" she asked, slowly sitting up.

"Right after graduation," I said.

She showed no emotion--no anger, no joy, no surprise. She simply murmured, "Wouldn't you rather try a year at college? You have the grades."

"No, my mind is made up. I feel God is calling me."

Mom shook her head, slipped back onto the pillow and I heard her mutter, "I bet Sister Maureen is happy."

When I left the bedroom, I didn't feel joy but rather a disappointment that she didn't say 'we have to talk about this later' or 'I'm going to insist you try a year of college first.' Deep down, I hoped she'd fight me, try to change my mind. Maybe she'd even have prevailed. Wasn't I worth fighting for? Yet the truth was I was so addicted to Sister that I no longer had my own free will. Mom seemed worn down with recent events: Steve had gone to the seminary, Uncle Hube was dead, Ray showed up erratically. In addition, she had her full time job as Assistant Principal. Maybe she didn't have the strength for a confrontation but I was secretly disappointed.

During my senior year, I did not have Sister Maureen as my teacher for any class, except for study hall where sixty students sat in a huge room with the desks jammed close together and each row rising toward the back. Standing in front at the wide desk, Sister appeared diminutive and she always wore her dark-cloud face to maintain order. For many students study hall was 'goof-off' time. Girls slouched in their seats, passed notes, whispered, and often dropped books loudly.

I should've had better sense, but the temptation to be at Sister's side was too great. I often got up to ask for help with particular problems from my advanced algebra class as she was a whiz at math. Yet the sight of a senior trotting to the side of the youngest faculty member for help invited whispers of 'Sister's pet' and 'kissy' sounds. After a few weeks, I grasped the stupidity of my actions and no longer asked for her help, but two brassy sophomores continued to hound me in the hallway, making kissy sounds and calling out "Hey, teacher's pet, on your way to carry Sister's books?" Instead of standing my ground and confronting them, I dashed away like a frightened rabbit. Now, I had to be on the lookout for these girls, who were only sophomores. Feeling like a hunted animal, I would take a different staircase or duck into a bathroom to avoid them. It was humiliating. Ironically, one of these girls entered the convent and thankfully, she was in the group below me, and I did not have much contact with her.

Since Della was no longer coming around, Sister Maureen and I had wonderful weekends together. We talked, hugged and frequently kissed while we worked on her many chores. I was tired of hanging around the cafeteria after school as many kids from the cooking class always stayed to help. I also noticed many seniors were getting after-school jobs and a few worked at nearby hospitals. I thought it would be good experience to have a job and to earn some money. One afternoon I went up to St. Joseph's Hospital which was perched on a hill above the Haight-Ashbury, where there was a nursing school as well as a hospital. Soon I was seated across from Sister Agnes, the Administrator, in her neat office. I answered her questions and was astonished when at the end of our interview, she hired me on the spot. I would be working in the Nursing School, not the hospital. Then I realized I really would have to leave Sister Maureen after school. My hours at the nursing school cafeteria were 4:30 to 7:00 p.m., Monday through Thursday. This would be harder than I thought.

My job was simple: set out the prepared food in big metal trays, keep them filled while the student nurses were coming to dinner in the cafeteria, then take care of the dirty dinner dishes. I worked with three older women who'd been in these jobs for years. With lined faces, graying hair caught in nets, they moved slowly through their tasks. I fit unobtrusively into their routines, but I wondered how they could tolerate these boring, repetitive jobs for a lifetime. It made me realize how important it was to get a good education. When the student nurses finished their meal, I stacked their dirty dishes into a dumbwaiter and send them to the basement. When the meal ended, I went downstairs and operated the huge dishwasher by myself. It was the only time I was ever alone. I could sing aloud, dance, fart, and do anything. If I broke a dish or two, I didn't take it upstairs as instructed. I just smashed it into smaller pieces and let the garbage disposal gobble them up, shielding myself as a few slivers were regurgitated ain the noisy process. In return, I got a small paycheck every two weeks.

After about a month, I noticed that Sister had attracted two new fans—sophomores Debra and Dottie, best friends. Debra wasn't the usual type that hung around any nuns. She wore tangerine lipstick applied above her lip lines and wore a size D bra that severely strained the buttons of her uniform blouse Yet after school, she entertained Sister with lurid accounts of her dates. "Sister, last Friday night I went out and I really wanted this guy to kiss me. Then when he did, he started using his tongue, but I didn't really go for that, Sister," she giggled. "'Cause I know French-kissing is a mortal sin." She went on and on about kissing and petting, then confessing her sins each week before Sunday Mass.

Next it was Dottie's turn. Thin and wiry, with a slight lisp, she spouted a constant stream of humorous remarks and stories. Sister would laugh that loud braying laugh, as if the film comedians, Laurel and Hardy, were entertaining her. Soon I realized Sister loved their attention. I hated going to work and leaving Sister with those two clowns. During the day, I followed her from class to class, carrying her books, hounding her with my jealous remarks. "You never laugh like that when you're with me. Why don't you go home right after school today? Do you think Dottie or Debbie is material for the novitiate? I don't think so. You're just wasting your time." Later, to my surprise, Dottie, the thin one, did enter the Novitiate.

Between classes Sister navigated the crowded hallways, ignoring my remarks. It was maddening. I was so fed up with Debra and Dottie that I felt I needed to talk to someone and on a Friday after school, I went up to the third floor to find to my friend, Marilyn, who was as usual, helping Sister Joseph. The biology lab smelled of formaldehyde and I spied Marilyn wearing a black rubber apron, making a weird face while she held the leg of a dead frog that she was trying to stuff into a jar. I knew Marilyn absolutely detested anything icky or smelly.

"Whatever are you doing, Marilyn? Stop, I've got to talk to you."

"Oh, Judy, Toots had lab today and a couple of kids were absent so we have to save their dead frogs." 'Toots' was her code name for Sister Joseph. I giggled watching her revulsion as she quickly put the lid onto the jar. Then we both started laughing at ourselves realizing for how crazy we had become and that we would do more for our adored idols than we would ever do for our moms. Out in the hallway, we roared with laughter until the tears rolled down our faces.

"Oh, Marilyn, I need to talk to you. I can't tolerate those two clowns, Dottie and Debbie, that are hanging around Sister all the time."

"Judy," her voice dramatic, "you are so spoiled! You've had so much of Sister Maureen's time, especially since Della isn't around. Look in there!" She pointed to the biology lab. "Toots' has hordes, just hordes of girls helping her!" I looked inside and saw a horde of girls doing many jobs: washing petri dishes, putting away microscopes, wiping the black topped lab tables, and in the midst of it all, was the beautiful, dark–eyed Sister Joseph, wearing her lab apron, smiling, answering questions, guiding girls in their tasks. Marilyn had a point, but it didn't make me feel better.

At Christmas time Mom was happy that Steve was home for two weeks. He didn't appear particularly eager to return to the seminary and cute Dolly Mapa from around the corner, hung around our house more than usual. On Christmas morning as we opened our presents and ate warm coffee cake, I felt a sadness that this would be my last Christmas at home. Even singing in the choir at St. Monica's, I felt nostalgic. I did not confide in Sister Edward, our beloved choir director, of my decision to enter the Presentation Sisters. I didn't want to hurt her feelings since I wasn't going to the Holy Names Sisters. When I was at St. Monica's I loved her, especially when she gave me piano lessons and asked about my family and all. I know she hoped I would enter her Order. However, now I only saw her on Sundays when I sang in the choir.

Suddenly, it was January. Only six months more with Sister! I wanted to spend every free moment with her so I quit my job. Sister

Agnes said she was sorry to see me go but I told her that the Senior Jinx was coming up--this giant production in which every senior had a part. I said I had to paint scenery as well as be part of a dance act, which was mostly true, but my main intent was to fend off the 'Laurel and Hardy' sophomores.

I was hanging around the cafeteria again and it felt like a personal set back, but those two sophomores irritated me no end and I wanted to 'guard my territory.' Meanwhile, Sister Antoine, the art teacher, had assigned me to work on a certain set for the Senior Jinx, but my passion for art was overcome by my obsession with Sister, so I had put it off.

Adding to my distractions was the presence of a senior, Joan Beatty, in the art class who got so excited about her little oil paintings of flowers and stuff that it made me want to puke. But I felt a bit competitive with her. However, it is noteworthy that after graduation she enrolled in the San Francisco Art Institute on Chestnut St. and the next year married artist, William Brown. Soon Joan Brown was solidly into the San Francisco art scene and became the well-known Bay Area artist and teacher that I should have become.

Sister Antoine liked Joan's enthusiasm but she was peeved with me because I neglected to help paint the Senior Jinx scenery and instead hung around Sister Maureen. One day Sister Antoine was so upset with me that she barreled down from the third floor art room, stormed into the cafeteria and, ignoring Sister Maureen, she leveled her wrath directly at me. "You get yourself over to the gym right now and do your part on the scenery!" she barked, then turned on her heel and left.

Sister Maureen furrowed her perfect brows and commanded, "Judy, go now! Do whatever Sister Antoine wants!" I knew she was mortified that another faculty member was scolding me for being with her, rather than doing my job. Red with embasrrrassment and without any comment, I grabbed my books and ran to the gym.

With Dottie and Debbie hanging around Sister every afternoon, threatening my special status, I wanted even more proof of her affection-- kisses stolen any place that offered a moment of privacy. One afternoon, in the interval between the last two periods of the school day, Sister and I had a short time to get paper cups from a cupboard for a meeting that evening in the cafeteria. We stepped into a dimly lit, large storage room right near the cafeteria. A small classroom was carved from one portion of this large room with a six-foot temporary wall defining that space for the Home Nursing class. On that side, girls were streaming in, gossiping under the bright fluorescent lights, while Sister and I were on the other side in the dim light of the storage room getting paper cups for an evening event. After we took a load of cups out of the cupboard, I slipped my arm around Sister and tried to kiss her. "Not here," Sister hissed.

"There's no one in here," I whispered and holding the paper cups in one arm, I moved to plant a kiss on her lips. Reluctantly, she gave in, but at the moment I kissed her, the door to the storeroom opened and Sister Paula walked in, halting at the sight of Sister and me kissing. "Oh, dear God," she cried.

I spun around and saw Sister Paula's face as red as a Heinz tomato, her eyelids blinking rapidly. "O dear God," she exclaimed again, backing out like a wind up-toy, lips sputtering. She flew into the Home Nursing classroom.

Sister Maureen froze, visibly paled and whispered, "Oh, no! Judy, get out of here now!" Eyebrows knit and head down, she bolted from the storage room. I'd like to have run the film backwards, edit the scene and leave it on the cutting room floor, but it was clear: Sister Paula had discovered us kissing.

Once out of the store room, we raced in opposite directions, mingling with the flow of girls moving to their classes before the bell rang. However, the nearest classroom belonged to Sister Andrew and as I left, I noticed her standing in her class doorway. Later I feared that Sister Paula may have shared the shock of her discovery.

The last period of that day was agony and I didn't hear a word of the economics lesson from Sister Bernadine. I agonized about the unknown consequences of our discovery. When class was over, I dashed to the cafeteria where Sister, ashen-faced, was packing up her books, getting ready to bolt to the convent.

"Let's talk," I wailed as I trailed her through the crowded atrium. Sister only furrowed her brows deeper, waved me away as she pushed through the crowd of girls and dashed across the garden to the convent without a word. In a daze, I boarded the crowded bus, but surrounded by jabbering students jostling me it was impossible to think.

Once home, I put on Chopin's Polonaise and lay on the couch, flinging my arm over my face, sighing and ignoring my Ellen's query as to why I was home early. I kept seeing Sister Paula's red face, sputtering lips and blinking eyes. With my temples throbbing, for the first time I began to wonder if what Sister and I were doing was wrong? I now was feeling a new shame but why did I feel this way only now that we had been discovered? I knew kissing a nun wasn't ordinary, but Sister and I loved each other fiercely. It didn't feel wrong. In fact, our physical expression of affection seemed natural. Was it Sister's vow of chastity that made it more complicated? Once Sister had told me about a rule in the convent that forbade Particular Friendships among the nuns. P.F.s she called them. Did this Rule have anything to do with me? Was I a particular friend?

I'd heard about men who liked other men. Mom called them fairies or queers and Mom didn't dislike these men. In fact, she was one of the two teachers in her school who stood up for a man, a fourth grade teacher, who'd been called queer. In the uproar, she'd invited him to our home one afternoon. He was blond, clean-cut and handsome. I liked him. Mom interceded for him with the school principal as Mom didn't think he should be dismissed. However, I think he was fired.

Yet what about women loving each other? I had no knowledge of that, no answers. Even if I did, I could no more stop loving Sister than I could stop breathing. I leapt off the couch and turned up the sound on the record player. Recently, I'd seen the film, "A Song to Remember." Cornel Wilde played Chopin and Merle Oberon, George Sand. Chopin understood passion. He poured it into his music. He'd understand me. I sunk below the surface of his music.

When Mom came in from work, she too, was surprised to find me home early, lying on the couch and wondered about the blasting piano concerto. I only sighed. I just couldn't talk to Mom about what happened. She knew nothing of my true relationship with Sister. I was scared that at any moment, Sister Marci, the principal, would call Mom and ask to meet with her to answer for my behavior. Would I be expelled? Would Sister be sent to a different school? I was frantic with worry. Everything we held between us as sacred and secret would be exposed. I was in a stupor of fear. I pretended I didn't hear Mom when she asked me to set the table for dinner.

For two days I moved in a trance, feeling as if I had the flu, evading Sister Paula and Sister Andrew. Once or twice a day, I yanked the strained Sister Maureen into any private cranny, quizzing her, "Anyone say anything yet?"

"Nothing, nothing, go away!" replied Sister irritably. I was sorry I had put her in this difficult situation and what if it had repercussions in her convent? Had the Superior gotten involved? But worst of all was that Sister would barely speak to me.

Finally it came: the summons. Sister was in the cafeteria with a group of girls and the scene appeared normal. Only I noticed that she laughed too loudly and worked on tasks too quickly and she wouldn't even look at me. One afternoon a sophomore pranced in through the swinging cafeteria doors and with great importance, presented a folded note to Sister Maureen. Sister Marci, the principal, wanted to see Sister Maureen in her office immediately. Sister tore off her white apron and told the other girls to go home. She took my arm, shaking it, her blue eyes pleading, "Judy, please, go home now!"

However, I hid in the tiny school chapel across from the office and from time to time, tiptoed out and peered through the amber glass of the principal's cubicle. Sister Maureen's silhouette was visible across from Sister Marci, who was poised at her desk like a bulldog. I knelt by the painting of Our Lady of Good Counsel and bargained with the Virgin: *I'll say a rosary in your honor every day; I'll never miss a day of Mass, I'll say the Stations of the Cross once a week. Please, dear Virgin Mary, let this mess be resolved without harm to Sister or to me!*

I wondered would Sister ever come out of that office? Finally, I left the chapel and stationed myself on an obscure garden bench in the Senior garden where I could survey the path that led from the school to the convent. I waited, shivering and drew my worn navy jacket tighter. Shabby jackets were a signature of seniors, who were all dying for graduation, except for me. The weak sun did nothing to warm me and the wind went through my uniform. After an eternity, I heard the crunch of gravel as Sister, head bowed, was marching down the path,

"Psst, psst, Sister!" I called from behind a bush.

"What are you doing here?" she sighed with frustration.

"What happened?" I demanded, brazenly trotting alongside her and putting my hand on her arm to slow her down.

"I can't talk to you!"

"Tell me what Sister Marci said!"

"Go home!" She scolded.

"Tell me what she said," I demanded. She wrested her arm free and muttered, "I'm never to be alone with you. I'm to have a group of girls around me all the time."

"It could be worse. It could be the rack or Siberia!" I called after her retreating figure.

I boarded a crowded bus and, once home, collapsed on my bed. For nearly three and a half years, Sister was my first thought on awakening and my last thought at night. I'd become known as a sister's pet. I was no longer invited to parties; I'd quit my after-school job. I was hounded by two sassy sophomores who mocked me. I'd sacrificed everything for Sister. Now being alone with her was being denied me. I had never felt so sad and confused in my life.

The next morning in desperation, I rose early and went to Mass and Communion. I reminded Jesus that I was going to be a nun, that I was trying to love Him as much as I loved Sister and now I needed His help. But praying didn't make it any better.

Moping like a sick puppy, I hung around after school with Dottie and Debbie and a few others. Sister tried to act normal, almost pretending I wasn't there. On Friday, she let it slip that Debra and Dottie were coming to school to help her tomorrow, Saturday. Saturday was my day, but now I was forbidden to be with her. She was replacing me with this Laurel and Hardy act! I wanted an explanation right now. I tried to corral Sister into the pantry but she ignored me, gaily prancing around the cafeteria, cleaning this and that. She remarked over her shoulder that I was being silly. What would it hurt to have Dottie and Debra helping her on Saturday?

Silly? She thought I was being silly! I began to tremble. A sudden volcanic rage rose from deep inside. I had to get out before it erupted. Brushing by Sister, I grabbed my books and bolted from the cafeteria, but when I hit the swinging door that led to the locker room, I hit it with such force that the small window in the door shattered like a gunshot! Sister raced out to see what happened. Angrily, I glared at her over the pile of broken glass. A gathering crowd of stunned girls and a few nuns streamed to the door of the cafeteria asking what happened.

"Just an accident. Guess I better turn myself in," I said nonchalantly, my eyes riveted on Sister, who was motioning Debra and Dottie to clean up the mess of broken glass.

"Jude, what is this about?"

"I can't believe you don't know! I'll just go upstairs and turn myself in to Sister Marci." I said with sarcasm and ignoring the crowd, I marched upstairs to the principal's office. I tried to make it sound like just a silly accident to Sister Marci, but she seemed suspicious. With her bulldog look, she glared at me across her desk.

"Really, Sister Marci, we girls were all fooling around in the cafeteria. You know how much fun Sister Maureen can be and it just got out of hand. I got pushed too hard into the door and the glass just broke. I'm sorry, really sorry. I'll try to pay for it."

Sister Marci eyed me, exhaling a little 'humph,' as if waiting for the real truth, but in my rage, I met her glare without flinching. Finally, Sister Marci said, "The window has to be replaced. You are going to have to pay for it." I nodded and left. I spent the loneliest Saturday of my whole life, imaging 'Laurel and Hardy' entertaining Sister.

On Saturday evening I called the convent and in a stroke of good fortune, Sister came to the phone. I quizzed her about her Saturday with D & D. Then out of the blue, she surprised me by saying she could meet me the next day, Sunday, at noon at school. Was it the window incident or that she, too, was feeling the loss of our intimacy? Sister devised a daring plan. Since it was Lent, she said, she would pretend to be fasting and could miss lunch without raising suspicion from other sisters. We could meet at noon while the others were having lunch in the convent refectory. Daringly, Sister chose new territory for our tryst, the school roof.

I arrived a bit before noon, darting up the three flights of stairs like a thief, pressing my body into the shadows whenever I heard a noise. I entered the blackness of the last short flight to the roof, but the metal fire door wouldn't open even though I pushed as hard as I could. Finally, heaving against it with my whole body, it gave way. The sun's glare on the white gravel of the roof nearly blinded me. I tiptoed across the gravel and hid in the shadow of the elevator, the only shade on the roof. After long minutes, the door opened. I held my breath. Sister stepped out, blinking in the sun. In a stage whisper, I called, "Over here."

We huddled together in the shady square behind the elevator shaft. In the starkness of that landscape and the sheer folly of our situation, Sister's restraint disappeared. She welcomed my embrace. When her stiff white guimpe nearly cracked from the force of our hug, she unfastened it and tossed on the gravel. Without her white bib, I could see the white of her neck and the delicate depression in her neck. Boldly, I kissed it. I could feel her breasts against mine. She never wore a bra. I could feel her nipples stiffen. Oh, the softness and the fullness of her! We held each other tightly for a long time. Then we sat on the gravel with our backs against the elevator shaft and talked and cuddled in our old familiar way.

"Judy," she said, I just don't know what to do with you?" and affectionately, she hit the tip of my nose with her finger in our old playful way. After that day, we threw the rules to the wind and became like outlaws, always avoiding Sister Marci, the principal. Gone were the days of mellow afternoons. Now we abandoned our old ordinary haunts, the kitchen and the cafeteria. Brazenly, we met often on the roof, kissing, hugging and giving into the passion that consumed us both. We discovered that the small third floor room where the school paper was assembled, was empty for days after the issue was completed. In that tiny room, she first let see what was under her habit.

"If I'm entering, I should know what I will have to wear." I was sitting on her lap as she sat sideways at a student desk. "Please let me see." Slowly, I lifted the long black habit; then, the black slip, which came to mid-calf; then the short white cotton slip. Finally, her soft white thighs were revealed with white garters holding up the black stockings. She wore white cotton pants over her cream-colored corset.

"Let me see your corset. Why do you wear that thing?" Her lovely, soft body was encased in stiff stays and ties.

"We just do. We call it 'a fence'," she giggled.

"A fence? Why?"

"It's just a little joke we have."

"Can I see your legs? Do you shave them?" I knelt and unfastened one of her garters.

"No, why would I?" Carefully, I rolled down one of her thick black stockings, revealing her pure white leg with black hair.

"You have fat knees," I said, laughing. "I love fat knees." I kissed her knee. She giggled again.

"Seems like an awful lot of clothes to wear."

"You get used to it." She reached down and slowly pulled up her stocking, carefully refastening her garter. I knew I would keep shaving my legs, even under the habit.

"I wish the Novitiate was still here at the Motherhouse instead of in Berkeley. It will be so hard to go through the Novitiate without seeing you." Sitting back on her lap, I hugged her with the desperation of lovers destined to be separated.

"Hopefully I'll get assigned to teach here and we can be together," I dreamed.

With a short time left until graduation, we sought any private space as a trysting place-the newsroom, the music studios, the school darkroom and the roof. Moments were tense; hiding became routine. We were constantly on the alert for footsteps. In our secret moments, she held me tightly or she'd let me sit on her lap and we'd talk about the Novitiate and what it would be like. I never tired of hearing about it.

"Tell me about entering one more time."

"First, you are a postulant for six months where you'll learn about our religious life. You'll wear a black dress and a black net veil."

"Will I have to wear black stockings too?"

"Yes, of course!" I wondered if I couldn't buy shearer black stockings, something like the Can-Can girls in "The Moulin Rouge" film. She continued, "After six months, you'll be received as a Novice. You'll wear a real wedding dress as Jesus will become your Spouse that day. During the ceremony, you'll receive your black habit and white veil. I'll be there that day and, if we're lucky, Mother will let me help you change from the wedding dress into the habit. Then you'll return to the chapel to make your promises to Jesus. I'll be watching you with so much happiness."

"I don't know how I will make six months without you," I moaned. Even now I could hardly go a few hours without seeing her.

CHAPTER FIVE

LAST PART OF SENIOR YEAR

ONE MORNING BEFORE classes began, Sister greeted me with an enormous smile.

I fell in step with her through the atrium on her way to the cafeteria.

"You have a date," she said.

"With you? Always!" I said

"No, with Mother Colette for your interview. Next Saturday at 1 pm." The Mistress of Novices, Mother Colette, had given Sister Maureen the date for an interview with Mom and me. Mother would have to approve of me before I would be allowed to enter the Novitiate.

"What?" I stood still as girls hurried past us to classes. "For real?" This news brought my decision too close to reality.

"Isn't this wonderful?" she replied.

Suddenly my dream was becoming a reality and I felt queasy. "What will she want to know?" I asked testily.

"I thought you'd be excited," she said with annoyance.

"I'm just nervous. Can't I be nervous?"

"There's nothing to be afraid of. She'll talk with you and ask a few questions."

"About what?" I said, irritably.

"She'll ask about your grades, how often you go to Mass, things like that. I know you and your mother will charm her," she said.

"Is Mother Colette nice?" I asked, gritting my teeth and inhaling nervously.

"Of course, all the Sisters are nice," she said.

I hated it when she lied. Now I had to tell Mom we were going to the novitiate interview and I hoped she wouldn't get all emotional about it. I myself was tense about my new reality getting so close.

The novitiate recently relocated from the San Francisco Motherhouse to a rambling complex in a parish in Berkeley, not far from the University of California. On the appointed Saturday, Mom and I drove to the novitiate now housed in a former girls' boarding school attached to St. Joseph's convent, a large wooden structure that housed the Sisters who staffed an elementary school and a girls' high school across the street. Trying to appear mature, I wore my lime green suit and low black heels, but when we approached the convent my palms became sweaty. As we turned up the tranquil tree-lined street, I said, "Mom, I'm kind of nervous. Are you? I've never met this Mistress of Novices, Mother Colette."

"Oh, Judy, You're a good student, a wonderful girl; I don't think there's any reason to be nervous."

"Mom, Marilyn, had her interview here last Saturday and she said Mother Colette was nice. I hope she was right." I rang the convent doorbell that was so ear-splitting that we nearly jumped. We stood outside at the huge door for a long time. "Shall I ring it again?" I asked, though it felt pleasant standing in the sun, suspended in time. Mom shook her head. She, too, seemed to be relaxing in the peaceful garden with its stately palms. "Now, Mom, don't absentmindedly take out a cigarette when we're inside," I admonished.

"Don't be silly, I would never." Finally, the huge door swung open and a shy, white-veiled novice ushered us into a formal parlor. We perched on ornate chairs in the high-ceilinged-room, where dark-green, velvet drapes eclipsed most of the light coming in the narrow windows. Mother Colette, the newly appointed Mistress of Novices, entered with a restained smile and shook hands with Mom, then nodded to me. She sat erect, without letting her back rest against the chair while a shaft of sunlight pierced the gloom, illuminating her triangular black shape. She was an intimidating presence as she carefully folded her hands and peered at us with serious grey eyes magnified behind thick lenses. In contrast, Mom, thin and angular in her smart, grey suit, her shapely legs crossed, looked quite worldly. Mother Colette began by inquiring about Mom's job as a San Francisco school vice principal and she expressed admiration for Mom, a widow, who supported our family with a full-time profession. I could see she was pleased when Mom told her that my brother, Steve, now thirteen, was studying in the seminary to become a priest.

As they chatted, I imagined myself living in the mysterious cloister beyond the heavy closed doors. I would wear the starched white veil of a Novice and become one of the holy ones and hopefully, see Sister Maureen often. Then Mother Colette asked a question that brought me back to the reality of the conversation: "Is she willful, Mrs. Lyons?"

If Mom spoke the truth, she would say: *Yes, she's a willful, stubborn daughter who has deserted our family to spent all her time with Sister Maureen.* "Not at all," replied Mom. My head jerked up. How could she lie so easily? "She has good grades and never gives me a bit of trouble, do you, honey?" She reached out and patted my knee. I exhaled, but before I could recover, Mother turned her attention to me.

"And tell me, Judith, why do you want to enter our Order?" Her grey eyes bored into me, demanding the truth.

I swallowed and uncrossed my legs. If I spoke honestly I'd say: *Because I'm completely under the spell of Sister Maureen and want to spend all my days with her.* But I said in a trembling voice, "Mother, I believe

God is calling me to Religious life and I want to serve Him." I paused. "I've prayed about it and I go to Mass and Holy Communion daily."

Mother Colette held my eyes for a long time. "And you've been recommended by Sister Maureen?" Her eyes narrowed. She uttered this as half question, half statement. Was my passion for Sister Maureen already apparent to her; the love that she would work diligently to eradicate once I was under her supervision?

"Yes, Mother," I murmured. I tried to hold her gaze, but faltered. It seemed she might ask me another question, but with a gracious smile she stood, grasped Mom's hand and put her other hand over it. They seemed like old friends, but I couldn't wait to escape.

Outside the sun was blinding. Mom and I walked toward the street on the path underneath the huge Canary palm. Mom immediately lit a cigarette, cupping the flame in her hands even though there was no breeze. As she exhaled, she stopped and remarked, "Judy, I think that Mother Colette is the finest nun I've ever met. There's something so special about her, don't you agree? I feel you'll be in good . . . hands." Her voice broke and she started to cry. "I'm sorry, Honey, I know you hate to see me cry but I'm going to miss you so much." She put out her hand and tried to pull me close to her. I moved stiffly, embarrassed at her outburst. Mom was like that lately: fine one minute, then weeping the next.

"You get in the car, Mom. I'll drive." I held open the passenger door of our Studebaker. Hopping behind the wheel, I turned on the ignition, but before pulling away from the curb, I glanced again at the large convent, stately in the expansive, formal garden. Soon, it would be my home. I was ready, well, almost ready.

For minutes we drove in silence, broken only by Mom's sniffling. As we approached the bridge tollbooth, she rummaged in her purse for a quarter and for another cigarette that she tapped on the dashboard. As she lit it, she said wistfully, "You know we brought you here to the World's Fair." She gestured toward Treasure Island attached to Yerba Buena island like a bright floating pancake at mid-span. Inhaling deeply, she settled back and continued, "Your father and I wheeled you around the Fair in the Taylor-tot for hours. He adored you. That Fair was so beautiful—all fountains and lights."

She never talked like this. I lapped up the details, striving to bring my dad alive in my imagination. "When he got that awful with stomach cancer, they were so good to me at St. Mary's. They gave me a bed so I could spend nights with him. Gram would bring you up to his room and, in your excitement, you'd jump on him. I knew it caused him pain, but he wanted you there."

"As soon as uncle Phil knew his younger brother was dying, he flew in from Indianapolis where he was working at that time. He and your dad were the closest of the five brothers. Right away he asked Frank if he could get him anything. He surprised us. 'Champagne,' he said. Times were hard. It was the Depression and no one had champagne. Undeterred, Uncle Phil went out and bought the most expensive bottle he could find. He popped the cork and poured a small amount into one of those thick hospital glasses for Frank, but he could barely manage a sip.",

"Champagne? Dad's final request was champagne?" I slowed, grasping the steering wheel tightly and glancing over at her, "Jeez, Mom, didn't he want to see a priest or get the last Sacraments?"

"Oh, of course, it was St. Mary's hospital, and there was always a priest around, but your Dad hadn't tasted champagne. After he died, your Uncle Phil came around for awhile and I think he was kind of in love with me, but he was already married to Henrietta." She took a long drag on her cigarette. "So he returned to back to Indianapolis."

"Then what happened?"

"First, I continued working evenings as the secretary at Commerce Trade School. We had air raids; the wardens would roam the school making sure all the lights were out, even cigarettes. I hoped I wouldn't go into labor during an air raid." She waved her cigarette, smiling at the memory. "But then Gram got sick and died of pneumonia in November. That was hard. She'd been taking care of you and Steve and

I was still pregnant with Ellen."

"How did you even go on, Mom?" The ashes on her cigarette were threatening to fall on her skirt; not a moment too soon she tapped the ashtray. Was she comparing my convent entry with death, talking about my dad's death from stomach cancer and Gram's death from pneumonia? She'd been heroic in tragedy but now she seemed so vulnerable. How dare I leave her?

"I had to think of you and Steve. Pearl Harbor was bombed. Then a week later, Ellen was born." She looked out the side window at the distant San Francisco skyline.

"Mom, is that when I stayed with aunt Irene and uncle Ed? I think I remember they made a huge fuss one day; it must've been Pearl Harbor."

"I think so. Hmm, you know, tomorrow I'm going to take down the curtains in the bedrooms and get them cleaned." Her tone was clipped. She'd shut off the memory stream.

Even though Steve was now in residence at St. Joseph's minor seminary, Father Flynn continued to be a visitor in our home. The priest would drop by in late afternoons, unannounced, saying he was just in the neighborhood. He'd sit in the easy chair, telling stories and laughing too loudly. Mom, ever the gracious hostess, would fix a short one-bourbon with Seven-up or on the rocks. When she went into the kitchen to fix another round of drinks, he'd pat the armrest of his chair, inviting me to sit there. When I sat down he'd put his arm around me and start this phony horseplay, trying to pull me into his lap all the while asking me about school, about my grades. His attention startled and confused me, yet I didn't resist.

One evening when he was at our home later than usual, I encountered him moving down our dark hallway after using our only bathroom. He was staggering and bumped right into me and then he threw his arms around me and pulled my head against his chest and his clerical clothing felt smooth and cool. He only needs a moment to steady himself, I thought, until with a chuckle, he clapped both his hands firmly over my butt and began to nuzzle my hair. What was happening? Doesn't celibacy forbid fondling women? Yet this wasn't really sex. Maybe I was special. No other men or boys had treated me this way. I mean this was a holy man of God and he liked me? I was more puzzled than offended.

After this happened several times, I decided to go see him in the rectory when I knew all the other priests were hearing confessions in the church. I didn't know what I expected, I just had an urge to be alone with him. I drove the few blocks to the rectory, but as I parked, I saw a very attractive girl from the class below me going up the steps. Why was she going into the rectory? I was stunned and realized I was not his special one.

I never spoke to Mom about these incidents, but they happened with regularity. I didn't discourage him because I felt flattered, but I did not have similar feelings for him. He continued to visit, have drinks, and if I was around, let his hands wander over me until the time I left home for the convent.

For the first time ever, I skipped singing in the choir on Good Friday for the three-hour service commemorating Christ's crucifixion. I was set on buying my convent shoes before Easter. Mom told me to park near Geary and Van Ness and take the bus downtown to avoid a lot of traffic, but I ignored her direction and drove way down to Mission St. and found a parking place. It was an easy walk to the Emporium on Market St. where I went straight to the shoe department on the first floor. I was wearing my best skirt and new nylons and a pair of black suede flats. Before I took a seat, I looked around to make sure no one I knew was in the area. The salesman acted as if he believed me when

I said I was going to buy two pair of black low-heeled oxfords for my grandmother. "She wears the same size I do, 6A."

The salesman smiled and his grey brows rose but he slid a metal foot measure against my foot. "You could take 6 AA."

"Do you carry the Red Cross brand?"

"Sure do," he said. He brought out three pairs of sturdy oxfords. Even shiny, new, smelling of fine leather, they were dreadful. I longed for my high-heeled red platform shoes. When I walked to the mirror wearing the squared-toed pair, I noticed two women trying on the latest styles, staring at me. Loudly, I called to the salesman, "I'm sure grandma will love this pair." I decided on two pair, the ones with the shinier toes for Sundays and Feast Days and the squared-toed pair for everyday. That's exactly what Sister Maureen wore.

"Fourteen dollars for the square-toed pair, sixteen for the one with the ones with slightly higher-heels," he said. "I'm sure your grandmother will be mighty pleased." He grinned as I handed him some twenty's that Mom had given me. This was my first purchase on the list of things that was sent from the Novitiate, along with my letter of acceptance. I was dying to get home and show Mom my new shoes.

It was Easter week and Steve was home from the seminary and that made Mom happy. Traditionally, Mom bought Ellen and I new shoes and hats, sometimes a whole outfit, that we would show off at Easter Mass. Afterward we'd go out for Easter brunch, often to the lovely Claremont Hotel in the Oakland hills with Mom's older sister, auntie Mabe, and their brother, uncle Emmett and his family. Later, they'd come back for Easter dinner at our house where there'd be drinking and dancing. Before she married Emmett, a pharmacist, my aunt Helen had been a chorus girl. Once married, she became a nurse. She was blond and lively and taught us the Charleston, the Black Bottom and our favorite, the Beer Barrel polka. Recently we'd got her to join us for the Bop and Jitterbug.

Unfortunately, auntie Mabe hurt her knee so we couldn't go to brunch with the extended family. After Easter Mass our family sat in our breakfast nook, eating warm coffee cake from Wirth's Bakery. Steve was swinging his arms, demonstrating how he and other seminarians used tennis rackets to chase bats from their dorms. Mom was smiling at Steve's antics while she savored a second cup of coffee. The fact that I didn't buy anything new for Easter was puzzling my sister, Ellen She knew how much I loved new shoes and she asked, "Judy, why didn't you get any new shoes like I did?" She swung her feet out from under the table to show me again her patent-leather shoes. I saw this as a perfect time to model my new shoes. I dashed to the bedroom, tore off my red platform heels and put on the shiny, ugly, black oxfords and returned to the family.

"Look at my new shoes," I announced, prancing up and down in front of the table. Steve barely noticed and went right on stuffing coffee cake in his mouth, but Ellen stopped, looked at my feet, and burst into tears.

"Oh no," she cried, "You're not going to the convent! You're not going away!" I nodded, shocked at her reaction. She ran to our bedroom and slammed the door. Steve remarked, mouth full, "Oh, is that what you're going to do. I thought you just bought some really weird shoes."

While Mom sat quietly sipping her coffee, I went to comfort Ellen. As I sat on the bed with my arm around her, I told her she could have all my cashmere sweaters but still she kept crying. I then realized how hard it would be for her to be alone with Mom. Steve would return to the seminary, I'd be in the convent and she'd be at home with Mom and her increased drinking. For the first time, I felt guilty about leaving home. Somehow Mom's drinking never seemed to affect her job performance yet now she was having several drinks each evening. That made Steve and me uncomfortable and we referred to it, with some as irritation, as her *slow time* because she moved and talked very slowly and didn't always make sense. We had no idea what to do. Where was

Uncle Hube? We needed him. I hated to think of it, but I suspected it might get worse and I didn't want to be around when that happened.

As the end of the school year grew near most seniors were excited and giddy, but I felt only dread. I wanted to spend every minute with Sister. I think she had similar feelings. One Sunday morning, even though it was her silent retreat Sunday, she agreed to meet me in the school for a short time. She would leave the school kitchen door unlocked. I snuck into the eerily quiet kitchen and in minutes she came in through the atrium. As soon as I saw her face, I knew something was wrong. I could always read her. She took my hand and led me into the pantry off the kitchen and closed the door.

"Honey, I have some bad news," she began. "This morning I received my summer assignment and I've got to be at college back in St. Paul's on June 9."

"Noooo! My graduation is June 11th. You have to see me in my cap and gown, getting my diploma and my art award! Why are they doing this to us?" I desperately wanted her to be at the Mass at Holy Cross Church, the parish nearby where our school held its formal graduation each year.

"Honey, the summer session starts early. That's all it is," she said. She sat on top on the stepladder and pulled me close. I laid my head on her shoulder and clung to her. We both held back tears. "I don't want to leave early, she whispered. "It makes me want to cry, too" After a few minutes she said, "Wait here. I'll be right back." She returned carrying a metal tray with two cartons of milk and some butter cookies.

"Eat something. You'll feel better. I'll eat some too."

"But you're not supposed to eat in front of me; I'm still a secular."

"Then turn around," she said playfully. We stood there back to back, rear ends rubbing, munching cookies, downing the milk and giggling.

"I have a surprise for you," she said. From the depths of her habit pocket she pulled out a small white box with a red ribbon. With a big grin, she handed it to me. "A little surprise. Happy Graduation!" she exclaimed. In the tissue was a leather rosary case with double lacing. I unsnapped the case. Inside it was lined with soft black suede.

"Oh, Maureen, its beautiful. Thank you so much." It would hold my new black rosary to which she'd attached my Sodality medal of Our Lady of Good Council.

"Oh, Judy, don't look too closely. I slipped when I was attaching the snap and I made a tiny slit in the leather near the snap." She looked embarrassed. Everything she did was perfect.

"You can hardly see it," I said, looking at the tiny imperfection. "I love it," I hugged her and we finished our cookies.

On the very last Friday before school ended, Sister would fly to St. Paul's. On Thursday she and I finished her chores in the cafeteria and kitchen. When everyone else had gone home, she took my hands and said solemnly, "Judy, I've something to tell you." I knew from the way she spoke it was more bad news. To insure our privacy, I pulled her into the pantry.

"Okay, now what?" I said sullenly.

"Judy, now I don't want you to get upset, but Della has asked to see me. She's going to come on Saturday."

"You gave away our last Saturday? I can't believe it!" I felt as if she punched me in the stomach and from deep inside, I could feel my rage rising. I spun around in anger and marched out through the empty atrium toward my locker, but Sister followed me.

"Judy," she called after me, "She deserves some time too."

"Why don't you talk to her after school. She hasn't done a thing for you all year," I called over my shoulder.

"Judy, you know she's entering the Novitiate. She needs some time to talk over a few things," she said following me. I stopped and turned to her. "See this," I held out my arms widely like a mother might do for a child. "I love you this much, but look at this." I made a tiny cube with my fingers. "In this this little box I have pure hate for you!"

"Judy, don't be like this!" she said.

"I can't help it. I'm just furious!" I reached in my jacket pocket and pulled out the rosary case. "See this case you made for me? You know how you slipped and made a tiny tear when you were putting on the snap." I held the case up in front of her face. "This flaw will always remind me of you, loving me; then, when I least expect it, hurting me!" She looked as if she might cry. I knew I'd hurt her and I was glad. "Can you wait here a minute? I have to get my jacket out of my locker." I stalked away.

In the inner locker room, I dialed my combination, pulled open my upper locker, stuffed in my navy uniform jacket and grabbed my camel's hair jacket, but it caught on the hook inside. I pulled harder. Still stuck. Impatiently, I jerked it hard. The coat held fast. Angrily, I yanked forcefully with both hands. All of a sudden the entire upper set of grey metal lockers began to topple over on me. Sister had come to see what was taking so long, and she dashed forward and raising both hands against the falling lockers. With a huge heave, she thrust them back against the wall. When I realized how badly I might've been hurt, I went into shock and started shaking. She grabbed my hand, led me into the nearby empty bathroom with a long row of stalls and over to a basin and ran the water. I started to cry. She pulled me into a stall and held me tightly. Now I was sobbing, great heaving sobs. At last we emerged, holding hands and in a subdued mood. Outside, we walked the garden path toward the convent.

"See ya," I said softly. "Have a good day with Della." We walked a few steps away from each other. She turned and called, "Judy, come here." I raced back. "Della is coming at 11 a.m. She won't stay all day. Why don't you come at 2:30? Wait out in the ball court and I'll come get you."

"Yessiree, whoopee," I exclaimed. I could hear the bell tolling to call the nuns to Vespers. She turned, picked up her habit and dashed toward the convent. It wouldn't be long before that bell will be calling me, I thought as I sprinted toward the bus stop.

We spent our last Saturday afternoon alternating moments of intimacy and sadness, already feeling the parting. Then Black Thursday arrived, our very last day. The next morning, Sister would fly to St. Paul, Minnesota to start her college summer session. Mechanically, I went through my school classes, but I was sinking into an abyss, the black hole of life without her. After school we snuck into the Sister's lunchroom off the cafeteria. We sat across from each other at one of the tables.

"Here you are." I handed her a box tied the box with a red ribbon. Inside with each item was wrapped in tissue paper. "I hope the Superior will let you keep some of these things." The box contained Yardley's English lavender soap and talc, stationery, a bottle of turquoise ink and a pair of black gloves. I knew she'd lost one last year. I bought her a pair when I bought a pair for myself, an item on what to bring to the novitiate list. She opened her box, exclaiming over each item. Then she came around the table and hugged me tightly. We solemnly walked toward the convent for the last time, but we had agreed on one more daring rendezvous.

That night I got in bed, but underneath the covers I wore my shirt and jeans. Every few minutes, I looked at the luminous dial of the clock. At eleven-thirty I rose, careful not to awaken Ellen, who was snoring, lips askew, in the other twin bed. I crept down the hall, lifted the car keys from Mom's purse. She was asleep in her own bedroom. In minutes I was speeding toward the high school.

The streets, ghostly empty, gave me an eerie feeling that I was the only one left in the world. I parked on the street and crept down the dark alley, tiptoeing past the small apartment where the weird janitor,

Quasimodo, lived. He often appeared at unlikely times with a leering grin. I was relieved to hear the muffled sound of his TV. Sister agreed to leave the kitchen door unlocked and I was praying Quasimodo hadn't noticed and bolted it. I felt the doorknob turn under my sweaty grip and I tore up the dark three flights to the chemistry room with its unfriendly, acrid odors. For our last meeting we agreed that this was the safest place, this remote storeroom at the back of the chemistry lab, a location far from the convent. I snuck into the unfamiliar lab with its long tables of sinks, Bunsen-burners and chemicals and crouched behind one of the black topped tables. The minutes dragged. Then I heard faint footsteps. I listened for the rattle of her large rosary dangling from her cincture. Uh-oh, no rattle. A figure entered. I squinted, trying to see in the dark. Was it Sister Marci, the principal? Had she somehow intercepted Sister Maureen? My heart beat loudly as the figure rounded the lab table. Relieved, I saw it was Sister Maureen and saw she hadn't worn her large, noisy rosary.

"Maureen, over here." We made our way to the tiny back room and sat on the floor by rows of brown bottles holding acrid chemicals. We held hands and talked of immediate things---her escape from the convent, my flight from my home, her upcoming flight to summer school. Then, she pulled out two items wrapped in tissue paper. In slow motion I pulled back the paper, revealing a leather cover for my St. Andrew's Missal, but the real surprise was the second item--a Breviary, the book of psalms called The Hours. The Sisters recited the psalms together morning and evening and I couldn't imagine how she'd gotten a new one. It had purple edges with a beautiful leather cover that she'd made. I handled it lovingly, turning it over in my hands, imagining myself in the chapel, reciting Vespers as she did. I marveled she'd found time to stitch the covers without my discovering them.

"Thank you so very much! You are a wonder," I gushed, hugging her, long and hard. She removed her stiff, white bib while I spread my coat on the floor and we lay down together. She held my head against her breast and stroked my hair. I knew her smell, the curves of her body, the feel of her close-cropped hair under the black serge, the feel of her oft-chapped lips. I traced my finger over her features for the last time. We kissed in the dark. As the minutes flew by, my panic rose began to rise like a threatening tidal wave. My chest felt tight and tears began to flow.

"Ah now, don't start that." She dried my tears with her hanky and stuffed it in my pocket, a treasure with her scent, never to be washed.

"Listen, Maureen," I sniffled, "I've got the car at the curb; we could run away tonight. Be together." The thought of it made me light-headed.

"Don't tempt me, sweetheart," she whispered. She hit the tip of my nose with her crooked finger as she'd done so often and held me tighter. As the black outside the tiny window faded to grey, a bird started chirping and I could hear cars driving on the street below. It was the end, not only to this night, but to our four tumultuous years together. I wondered if she might be relieved. Our fierce unrelenting love had filled many days with tension, secrecy and my unfounded jealousy. I looked forward to a time when we'd both be Sisters and dreamed of the day we'd live in the same convent.

"It's time, sweetheart," she whispered, holding her pocket watch to the light. "I've got to rise with the other nuns in fifteen minutes. I'll see you on your Reception day, only six months away." A fierce embrace, one long kiss. With arms around each other's waists, we went down two flights of stairs.

"So long," we whispered. We'd agreed never to utter the words, good-by. The last touch of our fingertips slipped away. At the end of the first corridor, silhouetted against the light of the glass door, she turned and gave a wave, then disappeared. I hurried down one more flight and out through the kitchen, already a place of the past, filled only with memories. I raced to the car with tears streaming down my face and sped home. I couldn't know I wouldn't see her again for three long years, then only for a few minutes.

On my graduation Sunday, I marched in my white gown trimmed with light blue with my two hundred and twenty classmates into our places in the church. As the organ swelled, our voices rose in the "Panis Angelicus" but I was holding back tears. She wasn't here. I tried to compose myself when I walked into the sanctuary to receive my diploma.

"Judy Lyons, Life Member in the California Scholarship Federation, Special Award for Art." My heels clicked on the marble floor as I stepped to the podium. I took my diploma encased in blue leather, but it meant so little without her to share it. After the ceremony, the parents and students went back to the school for breakfast in the school gym, but every corner reminded me of her. I kept imagining, I might see her pop in. "Surprise she'd say. I'm back." It was torture. I couldn't even taste anything I was served. The other nuns were smiling, moving about, gracious with their large sleeves that they wore on special occasions. After breakfast, everyone went into the garden for pictures. I stood watching the smiling groups. Mom had forgotten the camera and I was glad. No one asked me to join their group, but I watched Della pose with many groups. It was the loneliest day of my life. At the edge of the garden, Mom was enjoying a cigarette. She exhaled slowly.

"Mom, let's go home."

"Don't you want to stay and get into some of the pictures with your friends?"

"No, I don't, Mom. I just want to leave." It was such a stark contrast from my freshman year when I was voted class secretary; now I didn't belong. I'd abandoned everything for Sister and she wasn't here. As we were walking towards the gate, we ran into a group surrounding Sister Joseph. Marilyn was in the group with others trying to get their photo taken with Sister Joseph. As I caught Sister's eye, I gave a little wave.

"Congratulations on your graduation, Judy," she called as the shutter snapped. Then Sister Joseph walked over to me and said, "I know Sister hated missing this day, Judy." Tears spilled out of the corners of my eyes. She took my hand and said, "Oh, don't cry, Jude. I know its hard, but just think, it won't be long till you are one of us." I smiled wanly and walked with Mom to the car. My high school days were over.

Sister Mary Theophane

Ellen, Judy, Mom, Steve

Uncle Hube

PART TWO

CHAPTER SIX

THE NOVITIATE
BERKELEY, JULY 1955

AFTER THE NIGHT Sister Maureen and I parted in June, I moved through the days in a fog, but now on this warm July day, I was ready to follow in her footsteps. We piled into the Studebaker- me, Mom, Ellen and Steve, who was home from the seminary for the summer. We left the fog of the Richmond District in San Francisco and headed across the Bay Bridge to sunny Berkeley. All my things were packed in a compact trunk. Cousin Alice, who was a San Francisco school principal, gave me two expensive, soft St. Mary's blankets, one pink, one blue. I would need that color in my bed to comfort me on long lonely nights. They were packed in my trunk now being delivered to the novitiate by Marilyn's dad, along with hers.

Families arrived and small groups were moving toward the novitiate entrance. Mothers were dabbing their eyes with handkerchiefs; dads were stoically bringing in the suitcases. We moved into the cool, high ceilinged parlor of the novitiate, housed in the large Berkeley convent. Mother Colette, herself, was at the door when we arrived and greeted Mom warmly, "Mrs. Lyons, it's good to see you again. You know, I so admire you for making this sacrifice of your oldest daughter. God will bless you." She grasped Mom's slim hand in her pudgy one.

"This is a big day for Judy," Mom said and put her arm around Ellen as if to protect her from any thoughts of following me. Out of the corner of my eye, I saw Marilyn giving her mom a hug, while her brother and dad shifted uncomfortably in this formal setting.

"She'll be in good hands here," said Mother Colette. With a single hand motion, Mother Colette summoned a tall, white-veiled novice. Mother turned to me, "Sister Amata will be your Angel." I understood that Mother was trying to make this parting brief. I gave Ellen and Steve a hug. Mom started to cry. I kissed her soft wet cheek and whispered, "No tears now. I'll see you on Visiting Sunday." I was actually thrilled to begin my new life. Sister Amata, the novice, swept upon me like a white crane, her starched white veil flapping like wings; her lips pecked at the air near my cheeks, her lids fluttered rapidly.

"Welcome, dear sister," she whispered. "Come this way." She opened the large oak door just wide enough for me to squeeze through. My red platform heels violated the silence as I crossed the threshold. In place of the Oriental carpets and polished hardwood of the parlors, the floor was plain linoleum. Through an open door, I saw novices hunched over old wooden desks. As I followed my Angel upstairs, past niches with statues of saints with offerings of fresh flowers, I felt a bond with Sister Maureen. I'm here, I called to her, though she was hundreds of miles away. This was the first step toward being together again.

On the third floor, my Angel flew into a low-ceilinged dormitory where there were two long rows of single beds covered in tan bedspreads and a long aisle between them. Next to each cot were a chair and a modest three-drawer dresser. A simple crucifix hung above each bed, but not a single personal item was in sight. At the second to last bed in the dormitory, my Angel released the opaque yellow privacy curtains that were drawn back and tied at the corners. Now they formed a cubicle called a cell. Like a mime performer, Sister Amata motioned for me to put on the clothes that were set out. Except for my bra and white garter belt, everything else was to come off. In the next cubicle, she fluttered about waiting for me. Her cell was last in the row, next to the open window, the cell I would have once Sister Amata professed vows and moved to the Motherhouse. I would come to cherish that cell with its view of the garden, the smell of the flowers, dry grasses and the fog that swirled in the evening that gave some variation to the sameness of my days.

As I put on white cotton underpants and a white short-sleeved un-dershirt with three buttons at the neck, I noticed there was a laundry number, #230, sewed on each items. I pulled on the thick black cotton stockings, wishing for sheerer ones. Fortunately, there was no corset with stays like Sister Maureen wore--the undergarment she called her 'fence.'

Opening the curtain, I pointed to the remaining garments and asked Sister Amata, "These things too?" Pained that I was breaking the silence, she moved her head up and down rapidly.

I slipped on a knee-length white cotton slip and an ankle length cotton black slip. It was such a warm day and I felt hot already. Next, over my head went a collarless, long-sleeved pleated rayon dress that came to my ankles. Lastly, I put on the new shoes I 'd purchased ages ago at the Emporium. When I stood up I felt like a stuffed teddy bear. Then my Angel came in and wrapped me in a short black cape, her long fingers snapping the stiff white mandarin collar. She quickly pushed back the yellow curtains and tied them at the corners.

I whispered, "Where should I put my real clothes?" She put her finger to her lips. Efficiently, she folded my blouse, pants, slip, camel's hair suit and nylons and topped the pack with my red platform shoes, scooped them up and motioned me to follow her. She raced to a bath-room and pointed out the four stalls, a sink that had #230, the number sewn on my new undergarments, as well as another number, taped above it. I would be sharing this low sink that was originally designed for the young boarders that had occupied these dorms, with another sister.

"For your use," she whispered, pointing to a set of striped towels that I happily recognized as the ones I received at a shower before I entered. They'd been sent ahead in my trunk. Now each had #230 sewed on an edge. We went down to the second floor where she opened another door to reveal four large claw-footed tubs each in its own wooden cubicle.

"Baths are allowed three times a week. Be sure to scrub the tub after use." She pointed to the sponge and can of cleanser. At last she ushered me into the high-ceiling, airy community room and disappeared with my clothing. Large windows were thrown open to the garden and with relief I smelled lilac and roses. As other girls from my senior class entered the room, we grinned as if laughing at ourselves in these costumes. The stiff white collars gave the impression that our heads were merely resting upon them. When Della came in, tossing her hair and looking confident, she gave me only a nod.

Marilyn came in with red eyes. She'd never been away from home or at camp as I had. I motioned her to stand next me. We looked wide-eyed at each other when Carolyn, who had directed and performed in our senior class production of the Jinx, entered the room. What was she doing here? In addition to an amazing voice, she had flawless Italian skin and dark hair and moved across the room with the grace of a performer. How long would she last, I wondered? I counted fourteen of us, nine from my class, one a year ahead of us, and four that I didn't recognize. I thought fleetingly this might even be fun, like camp.

Mother Colette, standing with her hands hidden in her large sleeves, announced, "When you're all assembled, sisters, Reverend Mother will give you your postulant names and your veils."

Then the novices glided in with flowing starched veils, graceful like mobile sculptures. We heard footsteps, a hush of anticipation and the Mother General entered.

"Good afternoon, Reverend Mother," the novices chorused, making it sound like a cheer. She had a scrubbed open face with high cheekbones. The expression in her dark eyes was so intense, it seemed she might know divine secrets. Mother Colette was attentive to her every motion.

"Good afternoon, Sisters. What a fine group of postulants God has sent us. What a pleasure to see you on this happy occasion." Fixing her eyes on us, the Mother General continued, "Dear postulants, today you've taken a step the world will not understand. You've left family and friends, donned a black dress, symbolizing your death to the world, ready to live for Jesus alone. Come to me now, children. I will give you a blessing and a new name." Mother Colette held the chair as Reverend Mother seated herself at the head of the table. Next to her was a stack of neatly folded black net veils. I waited expectantly for my name to be called.

"Judith Lyons," Reverend Mother called. I knelt, felt her hands warm on my head, "God bless you. You shall now be called Sister Judith Marie," she said with a hint of a smile. It was comforting to retain my own name. Marilyn was now Sister Miriam; Della was Sister Laura. The beautiful Carolyn was now Sister Gloria. My friend Connie was now Paula. Names assigned, veils attached with bobby pins, Reverend Mother stood, her piercing eyes surveying us.

"Sister postulants, you are starting a journey into religious life. The Lord will be testing you, but He'll be there with the grace you need. You will be happier than ever before. Do you know why, Sisters?" Her piercing eyes examined us. "Because you are now living under the same roof as Christ in the Blessed Sacrament. Imagine sleeping in the same house as Jesus himself." I'd have never thought of living with Jesus, but I would now take measure of it daily.

Then we clunked through the long dark halls to the chapel, clumsy in our new oxfords and black outfits, not stylish enough to be real dresses, nor graceful enough to be habits. Awkwardly, we filed into the front pews of the chapel while the novices alighted like lovely white doves in the stalls that lined the sides of the chapel. Large statues of the Virgin and St. Joseph graced the sides of the altar and a large crucifix hung over the tabernacle that was draped in white. Candelabras with tall brass-tipped candles sat on either side of the tabernacle. Two huge vases of red gladioli adorned the altar. At each postulant's place was a prayer book and candle. We stood to recite an Act of Consecration to Mary and we transferred the flame from candle to candle. Yet I wasn't thinking of the Virgin, but of Sister Maureen, wishing she could know my new name and see me in my postulant attire. In that far away college in St. Paul was she thinking of me as often as I thought of her?

After the Act of Consecration, we reversed the trek back to the Community room. By now Reverend Mother was already on her way back to San Francisco. With a rare smile, Mother Colette gave permission for the novices to greet us, some of whom I recognized from classes ahead of me in high school. They turned to us with pent up energy, grasping our hands firmly, pressing a cheek to each side, smiling widely. The starch of the novices' headgear, that tightly encased their faces, was harsh on my cheeks and soon my face ached from too many greetings and endless smiling.

Next the professed sisters filed in from their section of the convent to greet us. It was then I felt most keenly the absence of Maureen. I wanted so much to have her see me now in the Postulant dress and little veil. *Maureen, I greet you in my heart. Your Judy is now Sister Judith Marie, but you can still call me, sweetheart.* When the bell began to toll, the novices stopped speaking in midsentence and filed out to the chapel with hands clasped inside their large sleeves.

As the novices left the room, I thought we'd have a few relaxed moments. I couldn't wait to huddle with Marilyn and Della. However, Mother Colette stood at the head of a long table and motioned us to gather round her. Of all the surprises of that day, none was more shocking than the transformation of Mother, who exuded charm in the parlor, and now became a resolute disciplinarian. Immediately, she began her work on us. "Sisters, while the novices are at Vespers I will give you each your rank. Sister Denise," she motioned to a chair at the top of the table. "Sister Judith Marie," she indicated the opposite chair. Marilyn and the lovely Carol, my classmates and the four girls from

Los Angeles, two of Mexican descent, fell to lesser places. Although there seemed no rhyme or reason to our rank, we sat seven on each side of the table, in our assigned places. This rank was permanent and applied to every gathering as long as we were nuns.

Mother announced, "Sisters everything you do from this moment on will prepare you to become Brides of Christ, to take vows of poverty, chastity and obedience, to enter a state of perfection." One of the girls from L.A. began to fiddle nervously with the veil that was sliding down her glossy, black hair. "Sister Guadalupe, you can fix the veil later. Please rest your hands in your lap." The postulant murmured apologies and bowed her head. Mother continued, "Sisters, all your movements must be marked by dignity and humility. You will never sit with legs crossed nor walk with arms swinging. When seated you will keep your arms folded under your capes." Several of us slipped our arms under our capes. "Keep your minds occupied with thoughts of our Divine Lover. You must learn custody of the eyes, the windows of the soul. You will elevate your thoughts to the Lord, repeating ejaculations such as I'm Thine alone, dear Jesus, or a favorite of mine, Mary, meek and mild, make me your humble child."

Sister Guadalupe was now making a grating noise and clearing her throat. Mother folded her hands and waited in silence with her eyes fixed on the postulant from Los Angeles. The postulant dropped her head and fell silent.

"A fertile silence feeds spiritual growth. Sisters, you will not speak except during the recreation hour. To utter even a single word in the chapel, cells or refectory is strictly forbidden. At nine in the evening the Great Silence begins. No word is to be spoken anywhere until after Mass in the morning."

Silence all day? We were used to spending hours on the phone or listening to the Burgie Music Box. If I closed my eyes, I could hear Rosemary Clooney singing, "Hey there, you with the stars in your eyes." Why didn't Maureen tell me about this? How will I ever do this? And we can't even cross our legs?

"Sisters, to gain practice in the vow of poverty and curb worldly desires, you will remember that you own nothing and the community owns everything. All things here are merely on loan to you. You will ask permission for everything you use. You will refer to nothing as mine, but instead, follow the community custom of referring to things as ours. It is our apron, our bed, our habit and so on and you will not borrow any item from another sister." Della and I were familiar with this odd use of the pronoun, our. We often teased Sister Maureen about carrying our books and brushing chalk dust off our veil, but the way Mother spoke drained it of any humor. Marilyn was biting her fingernail when our eyes met and she rolled her eyes.

"Sisters, we will meet here each day and learn the ways of religious perfection. We want to say like Saint Paul: It is no longer I that live, but Christ lives in me." Our transformation was now in progress, we awkwardly traipsed the dark halls after Mother to the chapel with arms under our capes, eyes cast down. *Sister Maureen can you see me? I'm becoming like you.*

After prayers in the chapel, we descended the narrow winding stairs to the dark, low-ceilinged refectory. For a moment, I felt my body hit an invisible wall. I couldn't go forward into this dark, gloomy room. My Angel, Sister Amata, sensing my reluctance, took my elbow and guided me to a place near the top of one of the long, narrow monastic tables where seating was only on one side.

At the head of the refectory, Mother reigned from her own small table. Behind her, stood a life-sized crucifix. The postulants' places were set with simple white dishes and silverware. A grace book lay at our place setting with a little rectangle of plastic so that one's thumbs would never leave so much as a smudge on the clean pages. Gingerly, we held the grace books and followed along as Mother and the novices recited a lengthy grace. Then in a dreadful scraping of wood on wood, forty chairs were pulled out and in again. When Mother tinkled a bell, the novices opened the drawer in front of them and removed white dishes. Again Mother rang the bell and a novice, sitting on a platform with a lectern, began to read aloud:

As I put the cloth napkin on my lap, Sister Amata picked up a starched oblong bib and fastened it to my cape with straight pins. Across the room, I saw Marilyn with her bib and she was starting to giggle as she did when she was nervous. A glance from Mother Colette censored her giggling. Marilyn and I locked eyes. I read her look: What have we gotten into? I wanted to bolt from the room and call Mom and say, come and get me now! I've fallen into the Dark Ages.

Then the swinging doors from kitchen opened and two novices, wearing long white aprons, wheeled in a large metal cart. Platters of meat and bowls of vegetables were passed to the head of each table. The meal was simple and hearty: green beans, mashed potatoes and slices of meatloaf. My Angel whispered, "Take a serving of everything." After passing the food, servers came around to offer hot tea, which, if we nodded, was poured into our mugs. They collected the empty platters, then the dinner plates. Dessert, squares of red and green Jello was our last course.

The novices devoured the meal with astounding speed while we postulants ate carefully. At the end of the meal, the two servers passed huge metal pitchers of hot water to the head of each table. Each novice filled her mug with hot water and, along with Mother herself, began to wash the silverware, plates, and then empty the water into metal basins that had been placed on the table. The dishes were dried with one's cloth napkin. Then the napkins were folded and draped over the mug and left out to dry 'til the next meal. When Mother rang the bell, drawers flew open and the dishes were stored until another meal. Fortunately for this first meal the servers removed the postulants' dishes.

Why hadn't Maureen shared this bizarre custom? Soon We'd be instructed to keep these practices secret from our families, practically under pain of death. Each letter we wrote home would be scrutinized and sometimes, had to be rewritten two and three times before all the secrets had been exorcized, leaving only a bland sentence or two to our families. I could only handle this because Maureen had done it before me.

After dinner, I caught up with Marilyn as we walked across the courtyard to the novitiate. "Is this what you expected?" I whispered. She tried to speak but tears started. We gathered in the large senior study that opened out to the garden. She grabbed my arm and dug her nails into it whispering, "Judy, I've got a big problem. They don't have full doors on the bathrooms. I can't go. I just can't go to the bathroom without a full door! What am I going to do? Doesn't it bother you, Judy?"

"No, I've had too many summers at camp. You'll have to talk to Mother. She'll . . ."

Mother's appearance cut me off.

"Sister Judith Marie, we do not take it upon ourselves to begin to recreate until the bell has rung and we've said our prayer," Mother scolded. My cheeks flushed and I murmured an apology, but now I was identified as a talker.

After the Hail Mary, Mother assigned two novices to each postulant and we began the walk around the large garden in threes. I was happy to be in the company of one of the novices I'd known in high school, but disappointed that we spoke of only of superficial topics.

"Wasn't it lovely to see Reverend Mother today? Didn't she look well?" remarked that novice.

"Aren't we fortunate to have such a fine group joining us?" replied the other. In truth Reverend Mother had cancer and would be gone in three years, but her condition was not yet known. Then breaking the monotony a novice said, "Did you know, Sister Judith Marie, we have a resident owl in that large Canary palm? Occasionally it swoops out and makes great circles above us." After thirty minutes of walking in threes in the garden, we gathered in front of a grotto dedicated to Our Lady of Lourdes. Lavender wisteria hung in fragrant spirals, framing the statues of Our Lady and Saint Bernadette. A novice turned a hidden handle and water flowed from the rocks near Our Lady's feet, trickling down in a stream to re-create the miracle of the Blessed Virgin's appearance at Lourdes. Mother began *The Evening Hymn to the Sacred*

Heart in her high soprano and the novices chimed in. The singing was unbearably innocent.

Suddenly, there was a commotion in the Canary Palm. Though not a single novice altered her gaze, we postulants looked up in time to catch sight of a great owl circling above us. I envied that owl, flying freely. As I listened to the sweet sopranos, I knew I didn't belong among these innocents. I harbored a secret passion for Sister Maureen, not for Jesus. I was a sham, an imposter. How long before I would be discovered?

At the end of the hymn a novice asked, "Mother, may we have your blessing?" In a flap of starched veils, twenty-five novices dropped to their knees on the gravel. We, postulants, awkwardly bent one knee or crouched down. I had seen priests give blessings, but never a nun. She gazed over the group and said solemnly, "God bless you and good night, Sisters." This was a powerful woman indeed.

In silence, we filed up to the stuffy dormitory. As I undressed in the cubicle enclosed in yellow curtains, I felt angry with Maureen, far away in her comfortable college. As I put on the long cotton nightgown, I ranted at her: Why didn't you tell me about Mother and all these strange customs? Were you afraid I might not have entered if you told me the truth? You betrayed me. Kneeling at my cot, reciting the prayers as Mother had instructed, tears streamed down my face. Once in bed, I felt some comfort with the soft blankets from my cousin Alice, but it was so hot that July in the low ceiling dormitory that it wasn't long before I pushed the blankets off and slept only under the white sheet. As I drifted off that first night, I recalled Reverend Mother's words: You will be happier under this roof than ever before, as you are sleeping under the same roof as Jesus in the Blessed Sacrament. Would that be true for me?

At five-thirty I awoke to an ear splitting clanging, wondering for a few seconds where I was. "Benedicamus Dominum" called the bell ringer after the tolls.

"Deo Gratias," answered soft voices from surrounding cubicles.

Around me I could hear the thud of bare feet on linoleum. As Mother had instructed the night before, I knelt to kiss the floor three times to begin my day with humility. On my first kiss, I got close, but didn't actually touch my lips to the floor. I glanced under the curtains, left and right, to see if other lips were touching the linoleum. Then on the last bend, my lips just grazed the floor, cold and unforgiving. By the time we were dressed and ready to leave our cubicles, only one novice remained. Unbelieveably, all the curtains were pulled back and all beds made. Like the Pied Piper, our angel novice led us on a journey to the chapel at least a half mile away, down endless stairs, out into a chilly courtyard, up more winding down stairs and through a long hallway. We arrived to find the entire chapel full of black-veiled professed sisters and white veiled novices reciting aloud the psalms of the Divine office. We clunked in, making awkward genuflections, and filling the front two pews of the chapel.

Soon a lanky parish priest appeared and strode down the aisle, his black cloth cincture so low on his hips it appeared it would soon slide off. He disappeared into the sacristy to don the liturgical vestments. A novice glided forward, picked up a long-handled instrument and lit the brass tipped candles high on the altar. This was as I'd imagined it: calm, beautiful, all praising God together. We stood as the priest came out wearing white brocade vestments. At the steps of the altar, he began chanting, "Ad altare Deum." (I will go to the altar of God.)

We all responded, "Ad Deum qui laetificat joven tutum meum," (To God Who gives joy to my youth). I knew the words by heart, but held tightly to my missal with the leather cover Sister Maureen stitched for me. I wanted to feel her with me as I began this first day of following in her footsteps.

Our first breakfast was eaten in silence while a novice read from the life of Pope Pius X. The server novices passed large bowls of green canned figs to each table. I took one, but gagged trying to swallow it. A novice server poured coffee. The novices downed hot coffee, dry toast and slimy figs at breakneck speed. Now began the dishwashing ritual. Metal pitchers of hot water were passed. I tried to pour the water carefully from mug, to cup, to plate but the water sloshed out, making puddles on the table. I wiped them up quickly before anyone noticed my clumsiness. Soon my napkin was soaking.

The novices and Mother sat with hands folded in their laps, eyes cast down. My Angel reached over, took my napkin, folded it and hung it over my mug. Then she unpinned my stiff bib. I felt as if I was being treated like a child. Mother tinkled the bell. Everyone stood. Had everyone been waiting for me to finish? My face flushed as I filed out of the refectory with the others.

After breakfast, we postulants gathered in hall outside the senior study and whispered among ourselves how difficult this was. I turned to Marilyn, "Isn't this just awful? Do you think it was like this for Maureen and Toots? Why didn't they tell us?"

Near tears, she just shook her head. Just then Mother appeared and scolded us, "Sisters, this is not a time for recreation. I will now assign each of you an employment--a section of the novitiate to clean. While you are doing this housework, I want you to elevate your thoughts to Jesus. Keep your minds free of frivolous and useless notions."

When it was my turn, Mother led me toward the senior study where Sister Amata, was racing around the desks and chairs in the Senior Study a large white dust cloth.

"Sister Amata, Sister Judith Marie will assist you with your employment." Then she moved on giving other assignments to other postulants.

Oh, not more time with the mime mute, I thought, and I picked up a white duster to help her, but she stopped me, whispering, "You first must offer this up."

"What?" I asked.

"Kneel and offer this work to God."

I dropped to my knees, my long blue-check apron spreading out around me and made a silent offering. Then at a frantic pace, eyelids fluttering, using gestures instead of words, she showed me how to dust every rung of every chair and desk and all the windowsills. I raced after her feeling as if we were actresses in a silent movie. When we'd finished dusting and sweeping, I took the dustpan and counter brush to sweep up the dirt, but Sister swooped upon me. "Wait, Sister!" Then she knelt and sifted through the dirt with her long thin fingers to retrieve a couple of paperclips and straight pins.

"What are you doing?" I asked.

"Poverty requires that we save everything useable," she whispered.

"You mean you go through the dirt everyday?"

She nodded her head, eyes blinking rapidly. I stepped back and let her go through the pile of dirt. Then she led me out the door to the garden and showed me the places where I could pick roses, daisies and gladiola to place in front of the large statues of the Virgin and St. Joseph that ruled the senior study. Outside it was warm and peaceful and I knew I'd be outside picking flowers for Mary and Joseph every day. By nine o'clock the entire convent was spotless.

All of us, postulants and novices, sat in desks in the senior study while Mother reigned from her desk on an elevated platform, peering down at us with eyes magnified behind her lenses.

"Sisters when I call your name, you'll come forward and receive your summer schedule." Each sister came forward, knelt at Mother's side and took her schedule from Mother's pudgy hand. When my name was called, I did the same, hoping there might've been a hint of a smile, but Mother seemed to be frowning. Glancing down at the schedule, I noted every moment, from 5:30 a.m. to 9p.m., when the Great Silence began, was regulated. When everyone received a schedule, Mother sat in silence, hands folded. As if reading her mind, the novices rose as a group, fell to their knees, white veils flapping like egrets, and kissed the floor. In unison they asked, "Mother, may we have the merit of holy obedience for all the activities assigned in our schedule?"

Solemnly, Mother replied, "Yes, Sisters, you may have the merit of holy obedience for all the activities in your schedule." As I sat surrounded by a sea of kneeling bodies, I was baffled. I thought I knew everything about Catholicism and much about the convent, but I was wrong, very wrong.

"Sisters," Mother continued, "the practice of asking for permission for our actions puts a sister in a constant state of holy obedience to God whose divine will is manifested through our superiors. Sisters, your summer classes will now begin. Promptness is a virtue. Therefore, you will be in your place at least three minutes before any activity."

Classes began right after we'd finished our employment and resumed after lunch. Like all postulants and the senior novices my schedule was full. It listed Religious Education and two college classes-European History and Spanish. In high school I'd taken four years of Latin so that as promised by our Dean of Studies, I'd never have to take another language. Languages were difficult for me. Here I was in a Spanish class taught by a short, pink cheeked nun whose first language was Spanish. Imitating her delightful accent, we were soon reciting together, "Arre, burro," trying to roll our 'r's and laughing aloud. Surprisingly, Spanish class became my favorite part of the day.

Our first full day of classes listed Collation in mid afternoon, a puzzling name for a course. After the history class concluded, we postulants whispered in the hall about the strange class. What could it possibly be? Where was it held? An amused novice led us through the courtyard to the Refectory. We discovered that Collation was a silent 'coffee break.' Two pots of coffee and one of tea, as well as fruit, were set on a metal cart. We sat in silence as we enjoyed the surprise. After classes the novices went to the chapel to recite the Office with the professed sisters while we postulants sat at the table in the Community room with downcast eyes. Mother Colette began our daily indoctrination into the ways of religious life.

CHAPTER SEVEN

LIFE IN THE NOVITIATE

THE FIRST WEEKS in the novitiate were a live drama—we postulants were the actors and Mother Colette, the director, prompting us in our roles. On stage we pretended to be nun-like, walking with downcast eyes, hands clasped under our capes, kneeling up straight in the chapel, feigning humility, going round the Stations of the Cross looking doleful. Once out of the director's sight, our teenage curiosity and enthusiasm resurfaced. We talked in the bathrooms, whispered in our cells, gazed out the windows and borrowed each other's blue-check aprons. We exchanged jokes at study hour and made faces at each other. If we were late, we ran across the courtyard, arms swinging wildly or we ambled slowly through the courtyard exchanging complaints about the endless silence, the brevity of mealtimes when we often stuffed half eaten morsels into our pockets. Marilyn whined daily about the short bathroom doors, saying she was so constipated and she didn't know what to do. However, a novice must have tipped off Mother as to our behavior because one afternoon as we postulants giggled our way across the courtyard, Mother stole up behind us.

"Sisters, this is a time of silence," she commanded. Her words struck instant fear. I stepped to the side with Marilyn, hoping Mother would move by us. Some hurried toward the novitiate door, but in front of our startled eyes, the beautiful Sister Gloria, ever the actress, dropped to her knees in the open courtyard and began to confess her fault. Mother immediately took her elbow and lifted her up, whispering sternly, "Sister, we do not confess our faults outdoors."

After that we were under constant supervision by a watchful novice or Mother herself. Daily I felt fearful of being corrected and wondered if Maureen's group had been under such scrutiny. In bed by nine, I'd hear children playing in the street and envy their freedom. At one end of the dormitory, the oft-corrected postulant from L.A., sobbed herself to sleep each night. In another cubicle, an older novice, with grey eyebrows, chuckled aloud as soon as she fell into a slumber. Then I'd recall Reverend Mother's promise: There is no greater joy on earth than sleeping under the same roof as Jesus in the Blessed Sacrament.

Yet away from watchful eyes, memories of Maureen taunted me. I heard her braying laugh, felt her soft cheek against mine. Often when I was nearly asleep, my fingers would touch my lips and for a fleeting second, it would be her mouth against mine. Then the tears would start. We were lovers bonded even through this inevitable separation and I told myself this was only an ordeal to be endured until we could be together again. I had a continual mindfulness of her the way mystics described their continual awareness of the presence of God. My wound, the amputation of Maureen, bled ceaselessly. To preserve my sanity, I would have to practice mind control like the character in the film I'd seen with Steve and Ellen, Winchester 73. In prison, a man played by Jimmy Stewart, was locked in a metal box in the broiling sun. He'd survived by mind-control, designing the Winchester rifle in his head. Since I couldn't stop missing Maureen, I had to control my mind. The minute her image arose, I'd slam my mind closed and reach inside my pocket to touch a holy card of Jesus, one where he looked like normal handsome man.

I held angry conversations with her--*Why didn't you prepare me for this life? How could you conceal the truth? This isn't at all what I expected!* The days were bearable only because I saw these hardships as helping me become like her and someday to be with her again.

One afternoon after lunch, Mother directed us to wait for her in the community room. On the second floor a special door separated the side where the professed sisters lived from the novitiate. Mother alone used this door. Its self-closing spring hissed, followed by a short bang-- sounds that were a warning: Mother is coming! As we waited in silence, I noticed that Della was late and knew that she would be in deep trouble. Hearing that hiss and bang, we all stood at attention. Mother entered, her face more serious than ever. She directed us to sit at the long table in our assigned rank. Della's chair was empty and so too, were those of the talkative blonde from San Jose and Reverend Mother's niece.

Seated at the head, Mother began, "Sisters we have lost three of our postulants. We recommend them to the Lord's care. However, we will not ever mention their names again nor will you discuss them among yourselves. Let us ask God's grace for perseverance for ourselves."

We bowed our heads, but I was stunned that Della left and angry that she didn't sneak a goodbye to me. She hadn't been here even a month. I recalled her complaints in whispered conversations: *Most of this stuff we're doing is ridiculous. We pray too much and my knees always hurt.* In her last year of high school, Della had gained status when she became a best friend to the popular senior class president, a student of status, instead of just one of the regulars that stayed after school to help a favorite nun. I imagined she thought this degrading postulant routine was now below her. Yet strangely enough, under Sister Maureen's influence, she would return in a year, but then she was in a lower group than I and we rarely talked.

Mother continued, "Today Sisters, I will read you a special section of our Holy Rule: *As the love and union of Religious should be founded, not on any human motive, but on God alone, and as their hearts should be united in Jesus Christ their Spouse, the sisters shall avoid particular friendships and factions, realizing that these are a source of discord and contrary to purity of heart, to charity, and to the spirit of religion."*

Mother explained that this meant we should avoid choosing companions at recreation that appealed to us, that we should love each Sister exactly the same, have no favorites, nor should we ever touch another sister. I knew about particular friendships, P.F.s, Sister Maureen laughingly called them. She'd told me if the Superiors ever discovered you had a P.F. with another Sister, never in all your days would you be stationed in the same convent. My only hope was to keep my passion for Sister Maureen hidden. She continued, "Sisters, we love Jesus first, then all our sisters equally. We do not touch each other ever, not so much as a hand laid on another's arm."

Maureen and I had touched each other daily; we kissed, we caressed, we were playful. Was that gone forever? I felt shame and confusion and realized if Mother knew my real truth, she would send me home immediately. I had to think, to pray on this, but my thoughts now turned to Della. She would see Sister Maureen at the Motherhouse when she returned next month from her summer classes. They would spend time talking and laughing while I was stuck here, unable to see or talk with her. I was sure Sister would try to get Della to return to the novitiate. The thought of them together gnawed at me constantly.

That night the demons of jealousy reigned. I recalled how entertaining. Della could be. Sister would love her company. Meanwhile, I was nursing my gaping wound of loneliness. But if I went home now, I could write her everyday, then see her in August. Yet, what would I do once I was home? Go to Cal Berkeley with Elena? Attend Lone Mountain College with many of my classmates? Mom would still be drinking. Steve was in the seminary. With my thick glasses and frizzy hair, I'd never have any boyfriends. If Don Reilly had shown any interest in me, instead of that nasty freshman, things might've been different. Now I wanted to be with Sister Maureen--to be like her. I wanted to serve God as she did. If I stayed here, some day I would be with her. I had to get control of my constant longing for her and the pain of her absence.

The next day in the quiet of the chapel, I turned to the crucified Christ for solace. I prayed with bluntness: *I need your help now! I came here to serve You and I don't want to think of Maureen all the time. I want to become holy and do Your Will. You have chosen me. You are just going to have to give me extra special grace now! Are You listening? Help me now!* When I stood to leave, I felt weak and sat down. I needed to stay a while with Jesus. I wanted to feel His presence. With my eyes on the crucified Christ, I began to feel a new strength. It felt as if Jesus was reaching out to comfort me. I heard Him reminding me that we, Jesus and I, loved each other long before I met Maureen. Perhaps He had used her to lead me to Him. Now He would help me love Him more than Maureen. I began to increase activities that would bring me closer to Jesus. I doubled up on my Stations of the Cross, I slept with the blankets on at night in the stifling heat, took my coffee black, served myself less dessert. If I devoted myself to suffering for Jesus, surely He would give me the strength to survive without Maureen.

On the next Visiting Sunday, I waited in the Senior Study for my name to be called to join my family in the garden for our two-hour visit. In the parlor I was surprised to see, not only Mom and Ellen, but also aunt Margaret and uncle Phil, my father's brother and sister. Aunt Margaret, a lawyer, always dressed fashionably and today was sporting a mink-stole, even though it was warm. My uncle Phil was handsome with a wonderful teasing humor. He owned his own food broker business. As ambitious and successful members of my dad's family, they expected I would go to Cal Berkeley as they did. I knew Grandma Teresa, my paternal grandmother, wasn't pleased that the oldest granddaughter was becoming a nun. Now Margaret and Phil were on a mission to survey my situation, and possibly, rescue me. As soon as I walked out to the garden, Aunt Margaret looked me up and down and scoffed, "Judy, why are they making you wear that ridiculous outfit?"

I flushed and tried not to show my hurt feelings. I protested it was only for six months, then I'd have the graceful habit and veil of the novice. I pointed to some of the novices gliding to benches with their families. My uncle Phil took my arm and we walked the garden path a few steps ahead of everyone. Under a tree, he slowed and pulled me close and whispered, "Judy, my car is right at the curb. We can make a run for it." He was half teasing, but I knew he would've taken me away in a minute if I wanted to go.

Margaret and Phil were now making their judgment clear to my Mom. They believed what I was doing with my life was, according to the achieving Lyons mentality, ridiculous. Thankfully, they didn't stay the entire two hours, but as they left, uncle Phil made one more attempt to whisk me off to his Lincoln. That was the last time they ever visited me. I felt sad that they didn't approve of me, but even more sorry for my Mom, who was often subjected to their views about how to become an achiever in life.

As part of our daily afternoon instruction held in the airy community room, Mother began teaching us to pray the Liturgy of the Hours, sometimes referrred to as The Divine Office or Canonical Hours or the Breviary. It consists primarily of psalms, supplemented by hymns, and other prayers. We used a prayer book referred to as the Breviary. Its origin in the early Church was to sanctify each hour of the day with prayer. In the chapel, mornings and evenings, together we recited the hours of Matins, Lauds, Vespers and Compline in all our convents. In the hand-stitched leather-covered breviary Maureen had given me, she had underlined all the parts of the First and Second Reader and of the Leader in different colors. It must've taken her hours.

Yet now Mother was going to spend a half hour each day reading aloud the lines to be underlined with different colored pencils. I fretted Mother would want to know who would go to the trouble of underlining the correct parts in over 100 pages just for me. Finally, out of fear of discovery, I showed Mother that my pages were already lined, trying to give the impression that Sister Maureen must have found a used one that was in good condition and given it to me. Mother's eyes narrowed. She looked at the pages carefully; they didn't look worn.

"All right, Sister Judith Marie," she conceded, "You just follow along page by page anyway." I winced at her words, but I savored this as proof of Maureen's love.

One afternoon I noticed a novice, Sister Johanna, pacing up and down in the garden in her manly way of walking, reading aloud. She smiled at me with her rabbit-like expression that her protruding front teeth projected. Odd as she was, one couldn't help but like her. Today she was practicing for her turn to read aloud in the refectory. During the reading, Mother would write down all one's mispronunciations in a little notebook and hand it to you at the end of the meal. Then you had to learn how to pronounce the words and repeat them correctly to Mother.

That evening in the refectory we finished the Grace and sat expectantly for the tinkle that initiated the reading, but instead, Sister Johanna was stumbling to Mother's side, whispering to her. We all waited with downcast eyes. Mother tinkled the bell, but the reading did not begin. Mother announced that Sister Johanna was going to confess a fault. This had never happened at dinner. The sister servers froze in their positions, holding the doors tightly closed. We all looked down at our plates. No one moved.

Sister Johanna made her way to the center of the refectory and knelt with head bowed, before Mother's table. She confessed aloud to the fault of forgetting the book for the evening reading. Then, as if that was not humiliation enough, Mother proceeded to scold her for denying us the spiritual thoughts the material would have provided. As punishment, she was to take this meal on her knees in the middle of the refectory. A novice tiptoed over with a wooden chair and placed it in front of the kneeling novice and set a place setting on the seat of the chair. It seemed a scene from the medieval Inquisition. Even the servers tiptoed around the refectory as they scooped small portions of food onto Sister Joanne's plate. I'd never witnessed anything so cruel and I could hardly swallow a morsel. The meal seemed to last for hours.

After the endless meal, we marched up to chapel reciting aloud the grace after meals. Soon the chapel emptied, but I couldn't move. I knelt with tears streaming down my face. I was having another angry monologue with Maureen, Why didn't you tell me it would be like this? The constant silence, the dreadful mealtimes, this cruel Mistress of novices?

Surprised by a tap on my shoulder, l was startled to find Mother Colette kneeling in the stall behind me. She put her face close to my ear and whispered, "What is wrong, Sister?" Unable to speak, I shrugged my shoulders. She knew that it was the scene in the refectory, but she asked again, "What is it, Sister?" I was silent. Was she going to torture me now also? "Sit down, Sister," she commanded. I sat, but looked straight ahead at the crucifix above the altar. When Mother leaned over my shoulder, I began to tremble. She spoke in a determined voice, "Sister, it is my solemn duty, as entrusted to me by this Order, to form novices that will become responsible sisters that will serve God well. Remember, Sister Judith Marie, God gives each person the grace to bear the cross He sends." Then she stood, genuflected, crossed herself and left the chapel.

Why did Mother feel a need to explain herself to me? I stayed in the chapel for a long time, watching the red sanctuary lamp flickering, reassuring me that Christ was in the tabernacleI felt an usege. I felt an urge to tell Mother that I had to leave, but I prayed, hoping He was listening to my plea: *Jesus, You will just have to help me!*.

CHAPTER EIGHT

THE UNBEARABLE

IN MID-AUGUST I was outside in the novitiate laundry yard cleaning my long black postulant dress that I'd hung on a clothes line. We had two dresses, one for everyday and one for Sundays and Feast days. I dipped my clothes brush into a pan of water I'd set down on the gravel and thought how good it felt to be outside in the sun. Instead of thinking of Jesus, I was wondering if Mrs. Waters would serve the leftovers of her wonderful tuna casserole. Lately my worst failing, one Mother couldn't see, was my constant obsession with Mrs. Waters' dishes. Recently hired to be the convent cook, this good-natured woman could cook circles around my Mom. I loved her strawberry shortcake, her Sunday pancakes, her tuna casserole and her tasty meatloaf. Then I heard footsteps on the gravel and I glanced over my shoulder, though I should have guarded my eyes, and see Sister Amata approaching.

"Sister Judith Marie," she whispered, "Mother would like to see you in her office this minute." She emphasized, this minute with a flutter of her lids, then hurried off, her white veil billowing, her matchstick legs moving like a crane in black stockings now faded to grey-green. Holding up her everyday shoes, she raced toward the shoe-polishing closet which was not unlike an outhouse.

From the moment I heard the word, "Mother," I began to worry. I untied my blue check apron as I crossed the courtyard and wondered if Mother had discovered that Marilyn and I whisper in the bathroom after breakfast when I serve as her scout to insure her privacy while she uses the toilet compartments that didn't have full doors. As I mounted the narrow wooden stairs I rejected the possibility that she knew I used the last toilet stall where I could read tidbits of news from the cut-up pieces of newspapers provided to wrap around sanitary napkins. All newspapers and TV were forbidden. As I walked the corridor to Mother's office door I was convinced she noticed that during recreation I sought the company of Sister de Salle, an older novice, a delayed vocation, meaning she had held a job in the real world before God called her. Sister de Salle would fall back and make hilarious critical comments that sent us postulants into spasms and we'd have to smother our giggles when Mother stopped at the Grotto of the Virgin and St. Bernadette and began the hymn in her sweet soprano voice.

I knocked gingerly on Mother's office door, grasping the brass knob with a sweaty palm. "You sent for me, Mother?"

"Come in, Sister." Mother sat silently behind her uncluttered wooden desk. Her grey eyes were magnified behind her rimless glasses, her nose hooked down toward her thin compressed lips. Her pudgy hands were folded. The room was hot and airless with the August sun beating against the weathered shingles. I knelt alongside her chair. My eyes were level with the windowsill and I could see a slice of blue through the curtains. Head bowed, I focused on the polished hardwood floor. I was feverish.

"Sister, I have spoken with Sister Maureen this morning and she has received a Mission for the coming year. Instead of returning to Presentation High School in San Francisco, she will be teaching at St. Charles Borremeo, our Mission in Albuquerque, New Mexico. She has requested a visit with you before she leaves." The mention of her name made my heart pound, but I kept my eyes lowered, concealing any emotion. Why was she being transferred? I waited to hear what day we would meet. Would I see her tomorrow, Sunday? Or would it be next week? Would Mother give us an hour or only a half hour? Ordinarily, the nun that guided you into the convent was always allowed the special privileges of visitation. At least for a short time we would be together, we would hold hands and she would tell me everything. Sister Maureen and I had often discussed my Reception Day and hoped she might even be allowed to help me to change from postulant garb to the holy habit.

"I have refused Sister's request." I reeled as though I'd been slapped. "I feel that you are settled here in the novitiate and her influence could be upsetting for you."

I could hardly grasp what she was saying. I wouldn't be able to see her? She was keeping me from my true love, not even allowing us a few minutes? I closed my eyes, my breathing became short. Suddenly, I saw myself rising, moving around the back of Mother's chair, reaching out and encircling her thick neck, beginning to choke her 'til her face turned bright red. Then she would change her mind.

I swallowed and pleaded, "But Mother, Sister Maureen is responsible for my vocation and now she'll miss my Reception Day in January, a day when the professed sisters are allowed to visit us." I continued, "Wouldn't it be fair that we have a visit now instead?" I emphasized the word 'fair.

Clasping her hands on the desk, she continued with a sigh, "You may not understand my reasons for refusing, but the dear Lord will give you the grace to abide by my decision. If you must know, Sister Maureen, herself, is quite annoyed with me. She doesn't understand my refusal. It would be easier for me to say yes."

I pleaded, my breathing quick and shallow, "Mother, please, this will be the only time I'll have to see her. What harm would a few minutes do?" The silence stretched out long and thin. *I see my hands tighten around her neck, her glasses fall from that hooked nose, the eyes bulge, her pudgy fingers tear at my tightening grip.*

"Sister, look at me," Mother commanded, annoyed at my persistence. I lifted my eyes and saw Mother's eyes asking me for understanding. The weight of her gaze crushed me. "God will give you the strength,"she said. Then sitting up even straighter, she continued, "Now Sister, listen to me! If you really want to see her, you may." She paused.

I let out an audible sigh of relief.

"But you'll have to leave this novitiate to do it. The choice is yours." She sat back in her chair and closed her eyes.

I began to tremble. I had no choice—I would have to leave; I had to see her! Maybe we could even go to New Mexico together. I could move down to the parish where she had been assigned. I remained silent, swaying on my knees. I felt it was time to strangle Mother. I had the strength to do it. Yet surprisingly, rational words came out of my mouth, "Mother, may I write her a note?"

"Yes, Sister, you may write her a short note that you will leave on my desk by this evening. God bless you, Sister."

I fled to the empty chapel. Soft light flowed in through the stained-glass windows, white gladiola adorned the altar. I slumped into my seat, too weak to kneel. I was a criminal who wanted to murder Mother. As I sat in pain, I devised a plan: I would leave right after lunch when I had more strength. I closed my eyes. Yes, I'll leave after lunch. I will have Mother call my Mom. It's Saturday so she's not at work today. She'll pick me up and be glad to have me home.

Then I envision Maureen, wearing her best habit, smelling of English lavender, smiling as she entered the superior's office at the Motherhouse. She asks permission to call Mother Colette to arrange a visit with me. The Superior smiles and grants permission. She likes Maureen. Maureen uses the phone booth on the first floor of the Motherhouse, the same phone I often used to call Mom to tell her I 'd be late coming home. Maureen's voice is eager as she speaks to Mother Colette. When she hears the words of refusal, her jaw tightens, but her voice softens, she makes her case persistently. After all, she reiterates, she is the one responsible for Sister Judith Marie's entering. Mother stands firm in her refusal. Sister ends the conversation, letting Mother know she is annoyed. Her face is a dark cloud as she goes right to her Superior to complain that Mother Colette is being unreasonable. She asks the Superior to intercede. The Superior says she will consider it. Sister Maureen will not take no for an answer. She'll find a way.

The chapel filled and we recited the Angelus and filed into the refectory for a silent lunch. As I went through the motions of eating, I continued to formulate my plan. I'd go back to Mother's office and tell her I'm going to leave. I'd ask her to call Mom and I'd demand the return of my camel's hair suit, nylons and the red heels that I'd worn on Entrance Day. I know they're locked away in some closet. I'd leave and right away go to see Sister Maureen at the motherhouse.

After lunch I decided to hide in the garden to think further on my plan. I stopped under the fronds of the ancient Canary palm that was home to the large owl, but I didn't see the owl. I walked to the farthest end of the garden. At this neglected end no roses, wisteria or daisies grew, only shrubs and pines near a moldering compost heap. I paced like a caged animal, then sat on dry pine needles, my black dress crumpled under me, pine needles prickling my legs. The tears started, trickling down my cheeks, then came great racking sobs. I could lie down and die here like an animal. No more pain. Or I will go right up to Mother's office, ask for my clothes and call Mom who'd take me home. I'd go see Maureen and we'd spend the whole day together and she'd hug me tightly and we would talk and laugh and kiss. And then--and then she would fly to her Mission in Albuquerque and I well…well, I would just be at home--a shamed, failed almost-nun with no other prospects in sight.

Gritting my teeth, I returned to the Senior Study, and ignoring the sisters who shot furtive glances at my red eyes and angry face. I stomped to my desk, took out a piece of stationary, slammed down the desktop and wrote:

Dear Sister Maureen,

I can't tell you how sorry I am we will not see each other on my Reception Day. I want to wish you the best in your new Mission in Albuquerque. It sounds exciting. You will do fine work out there.

The letter was short and formal, ending with the required, *Your loving sister in Jesus Christ*. I put it unsealed on Mother's desk at the head of the room. Of course the letter was written for Mother Colette, not for Sister Maureen. She would know that.

All during that hot August, whenever I heard the loud doorbell slice the silence of the cloister, I'd stop whatever I was doing, hold my breath, and believe Maureen had found a way to see me. Any minute a novice would come to tell me Sister Maureen was in the parlor waiting for me. But when August dissolved into September and I knew that she was far away in her Mission in Albuquerque, I resigned myself to the novitiate routine of praying, cleaning, studying and confessing my faults. Yet I wasn't prepared for what happened on September's Visiting Sunday.

On Visiting Sunday, the first Sunday of September, I was waiting in the Senior Study for my family. A novice tapped my desk--the signal that I could go to meet my family in the parlor and take them to the garden for my visit. I hugged Mom fiercely, inhaled her perfume, White Shoulders. I hadn't realized 'til that moment how much I missed her.

When I gave Steve a hug, he squirmed and grunted. "Hi ya, Jude." I ran my fingers playfully through his hair. He moved away and pulled out his comb. It was wonderful to hear his male voice, to smell the grease in his hair, to see his scuffed shoes. My sister was squirming, anxious for her turn. I gave her a hug and told her she looked cute. Her blond hair was short, her face eager. Fortunately, she would never enter the convent.

Steve and Ellen ran ahead and dragged two benches together in the warm sun. Arm in arm, Mom and I walked to the benches. Mom sat opposite me and began looking around as if she wanted to make sure no one was listening but not a soul was close enough to overhear our conversation. Was Mom going to ask me to come home or tell me Steve wasn't going back to the seminary or that Ellen wanted to go to a public high school? What news required such caution? Mom looked at me and said, "Judy, Sister Maureen called me and told me she is being sent to New Mexico?" Mom was puzzled. She was wondering if it was a promotion or a punishment.

"Did she sound upset, Mom?" I tried to speak causually.

"Not really, but I don't think she was thrilled. She said she was sorry she was going to miss your Reception Day. That's the day you get the white veil, right?" Mom crossed her legs and leaned toward me. "But she said something odd--that Mother Colette wouldn't let her see you. I don't understand why that lovely Mother Colette would refuse her."

Mom began fumbling in her purse. I hoped she wasn't searching for a cigarette. Instead she pulled out a square envelope. "Sister Maureen gave me this letter to give you." She held out a square envelope addressed in turquoise ink. I stared at it. To take this was forbidden. All mail had to go through Mother Colette but I hesitated only a moment, grabbed it and buried it deep in the pocket of my postulant dress. Though I was dying to open it, I had to wait. This was Mom's time. Steve was sitting on the edge of the bench, knees moving restlessly, bored by the conversation.

"Hey, Steve, tomorrow's the big day? Back to the seminary?"

"Yeh, back to the grind." I couldn't tell if he was happy or not but Mom's face tightened. She wasn't anxious for Steve to return. I thought of home with only Ellen and Mom left and Mom drinking. I shuddered and changed the subject.

"El, are you ready to start high school? Got your uniform and books?"

"I'm ready, but I hope I don't get that 'I know your big sister routine' from the Nuns. I'm having a really good vacation. Diane and I bought new 45's yesterday. We're going to have an end of summer party. You should hear this new Elvis record, *Heartbreak Hotel*. It's really neat."

"Elvis?" He was the one the nuns always told us to avoid with all that gyrating when he was singing. I smiled. Ellen wasn't like me. She was going to have fun. Mom had already begun her school year as vice principal and was feeling confident that it would go well.

She said, "You know, Judy, Miss Jamieson went to Presentation. Of course, that was years ago but she's so impressed that you've entered the convent of the same nuns that taught her long ago. Your being in the same Order will make my school year easier. You know, what a fuss-budget she is."

I started laughing. "I'm so glad, Mom, that there's something positive for you in my being here. Do you know what Sisters actually taught her?"

"She mentioned a Sister Canius, who taught Latin. She just adored her. Didn't you have her for something?"

"In high school I did, but she's old now, Mom, not anyone's favorite, yet she still teaches Latin. Tell Miss Jamison, she's still at it." We went on talking, but I could feel the envelope burning my thigh through my pocket. When it was time for the visit to end, I hurried Mom to the front door through the crowd of families leaving. I gave her a quick peck on the cheek and moved her toward the large convent door. Today I didn't want a crying scene. I flew up the three flights of stairs and into the last stall in the bathroom. It smelled of disinfectant. I sat on the lid of the toilet and with trembling hands tore open the envelope. I read the words written in turquoise ink.

My dearest,

I couldn't leave without a word of goodbye to you. It breaks my heart to miss your reception day, the day we had so long counted on seeing each other. I guess the Lord has other plans. I 'm grateful to your dear mother for delivering this. Mother Colette wouldn't let me visit with you although I asked her twice. She thought it might upset you and that is the last thing I want to do. I'll be praying for you, especially on the day of your Reception. This fall will be a lonely time for both of us but we will be united in Him. I'll be thinking of you everyday.

    Your loving sister in Jesus Christ,
    Sister Maureen

Though I wanted profound declarations of love, at least she admitted she would be lonely too. This daring act of smuggling in the letter was proof of her passion. Was there a place I could keep this that it wouldn't be discovered? Our drawers, everything was subject to unannounced examination. Then I felt a stab of guilt: Would Jesus punish me for accepting this forbidden letter?

As I sat on the toilet seat rereading it, tears began to blur her words. When I heard the bell tolling for Vespers, I sat a moment, then I stood over the toilet, paused, and slowly tore up her note, threw the pieces in the bowl and watched the turquoise ink blur, before I finally flushed it away and raced to the chapel for prayers.

In the following weeks, I made daily deals with Jesus. I needed His help with the phantom pain in my heart where I felt the loss of Maureen as an amputee feels the ache of missing limb. When she came to mind which was often, I would silently recite the spiritual invocations Mother had told us to use.

We were required to do spiritual reading for at least fifteen minutes daily and Mother always chose the book. In the novitiate library, I discovered a biography of St. Therese of Liseaux and when I told her St. Therese was my favorite saint who I had taken her name at Confirmation, she allowed me to read it. St. Therese was a French Carmelite nun, who endured unbearable suffering from undiagnosed tuberculosis and offered her daily pain to Jesus.

She wrote:

Suffering stretched out her arms to me from the first and I grasped her hand with love . . . Here we are wanting to suffer generously, greatly. We want never to fall. What does it matter if I fall often and in that instant, in my weakness, I see a great opportunity for Grace.

As the days grew short and the rains came, my wound began to harden with scar tissue. Agonizingly, bit-by-bit, the edges of Maureen's features blurred. When I spoke to her, I wasn't sure she heard me. Did my voice carry as far as Albuquerque? Was she talking with new girls? I surrendered Maureen for my new lover, Jesus.

CHAPTER NINE

THE VEIL

IN MID-DECEMBER MOTHER Colette called us Postulants together. She stood next to her desk looking solemn as we took seats in the Senior study Would this be a collective scolding? Fear of reprimand was always present. Mother could instantly ruin the funniest conversation in the refectory or the most exciting moments of recreation. If someone slipped with a wrong word, a laugh that was too loud, her stern words would assault the offender. What would it be now?

"Dear Sisters, I'm pleased to tell you that Reverend Mother has accepted your written requests to become novices in our Order. Your Reception Day will be January 8, 1956, a Saturday, at the motherhouse in San Francisco." A rare smile graced her face. "Congratulations, Sisters."

We grinned at each other. Eleven of us survived of the original fourteen. One Sister spontaneously exclaimed, "What good news, Mother!"

"Please, Sisters, it is not yet time to recreate." She continued, "Sister Miriam will not receive her veil at this time." I gasped. This was completely unexpected. Why wouldn't Marilyn take the veil? I was forbidden to question her.

"I'm so happy for you, Judy, I mean, Sister Judith Marie," she said as she opened her huge eyes even wider, smiling nervously. I searched her face for an answer but I couldn't read anything.

A few days later we were given black serge material and with the assistance of the petite perfectionist, Sister Anastasia, we began the daunting task of cutting out and stitching up our own habits. One afternoon when we were sewing, Marilyn was sitting in the corner, darning her faded cotton stockings. I gave her a quizzical look and she plied her needle even faster. When Sister Anastasia stepped out of the room, Marilyn looked around nervously, then beckoned me to follow her. We went across the hall and into the last bathtub enclosure. As we stood next to the large claw-footed tub, her eyes darted nervously as if expecting we might be discovered at any moment. She clutched my wrist, looked straight at me and said, "Judy, about the Reception, don't worry, it's my choice." For a moment, I felt the old intimacy we shared in high school.

"But why, Marilyn?" She was far more scrupulous than me. Did she feel that she wasn't worthy? How would she explain this to her beloved Sister Joseph who had sponsored her entering?

"Judy, I can't tell you!" She looked agitated and trapped.

"Did you do something? Is this a punishment?"

"No, no, Judy. It s just that . . . I'm not ready."

"Marilyn, do you feel unworthy? Is that it?"

"Judy, I just can't. Not yet."

I grabbed her wrist and demanded, "Why?" She squirmed uncomfortably.

"Mother said not to tell."

"You tell me now!"

"It's the boys."

"What boys?" I asked, squeezing her wrist hard. No boys visited us. In fact she'd only two blind dates in high school for our proms. As long as I knew her, her only passion was for Sister Joseph. Puzzled, I asked,

"Any boy in particular?" Then we heard the dreaded sound—the hiss and bang of the door that Mother Colette used. She was right outside the bathroom. I dropped her wrist; the color drained from her face. Then nothing. Mother had passed on to another part of the novitiate.

"I'm afraid I'll get professed and be out there, like at summer school at U.S.F. and I'll see some boys, and I'll want to be with them." The words tumbled out urgently. "I had to tell Mother Colette and Reverend Mother how I really felt. They said it was a temptation from the devil and it would pass. They want me to take the veil, but I want to wait another six months until I'm really sure."

"I think you're making mistake. This sounds crazy to me. Maybe it is the work of the devil."

"Judy, I just can't go ahead now. Not a word of this to anyone; Mother would kill me if she knew I told you."

We snuck back into the room where the others were still sewing. We lived in a place without men, except for the priest that said daily Mass and heard weekly confessions. Christ was our Man. Boys? What a ridiculous thing to worry about. Neither she nor I had had any real relationships with boys. We never would. We both wore thick glasses. Our hair was too curly and we weren't pretty enough.

One day Mother called me to her office. As I climbed the stairs, I wondered what had I done now. Looking solemn, she said, "Sit down, Sister. I have something to tell you. It's about your brother."

I braced myself for the terrible news. "It looks like you won't have a priest in your family after all. Your mother called and told me your brother has left the seminary."

She paused so I could digest the tragedy, but I didn't feel sad. I was sure Mom was annoyed that Mother wouldn't let her speak directly of the news to me. Mother was relaying this news as if Steve had died, but

I was sure Mom was glad to have the man of the house home again, even though he was only fifteen. I tried to look sad, but when I left her office, I smiled and mused about Steve. I wished could know him better. He was only twelve when he went to the seminary. We had fought a lot growing up as I was the oldest and he was the boy. It was always a power struggle. Now I wished he and I could visit alone as I'm sure the seminary had changed him in a good way.

On Christmas Eve, a cold, rainy night, Mother made a surprise announcement. That evening the parish choir would come to the convent to sing carols for the professed sisters and we would be able to join them--a rare event. We gathered in their Community room with its old linoleum floor and dark wainscoting, sitting in silence on folding chairs while the professed sisters chatted among themselves. The choir filed in wearing scarves, knit hats and heavy overcoats that smelled dank, like a school coatroom on a rainy day. They huddled close to the piano, shifting into groups: sopranos, seconds and altos. Some of the men were bearded; the women looked pleasant but plain.

I wondered how could any singing compare to our Gregorian Chant. The pianist removed his damp pea coat, adjusted his music and his glasses and then struck the chords for *Adeste Fideles*. The voices rang out with great gusto and I was startled by the power of the men's voices in this sanctuary of sopranos. I looked over at Marilyn, but her face was implacable. They sang old favorites with zest and harmony and then began a song I hadn't heard before, "Go Tell It on the Mountain. Over the hills and everywhere . . ." Their voices rose strong with a quality of longing, like the Advent psalms of Old Testament prophets longing for the Messiah. The men's voices continued to echo in my ears as I climbed to our cold dormitory. I thought fondly of our dedicated coed choir at St. Monica's.

At midnight we were awakened and surprised by soprano voices of the novices singing *Silent Night* right in our dormitory. We tumbled out of our beds, dressed and filed down to Midnight Mass. The altar was ablaze with candles and stacked with poinsettias. In a bank of firs the once empty crib, now cradled a statue of the Infant. Sister Cecelia pounded the organ and our voices rang out: Gloria in excelsis. I felt it was a true celebration of Christmas. After Mass, we filed to the refectory for hot chocolate . To the surprise of us Postulants the formal refectory tables adorned with sparkling with small metallic Christmas trees on lengths of red ribbon. At our places were thin gold-rimmed plates instead of our heavy crockery. The novices watched our faces, hoping their hours of work would be rewarded with our smiles of delight and they were not disappointed.

On Christmas morning, while we were at breakfast, Mother had a novice go upstairs to our cubicles and distribute the gifts that our families had sent. After Mass and breakfast, we went to our cubicles, closed our yellow curtains and in private, opened the gifts that were on our beds. As I picked up the first package in Christmas wrapping with a bright red ribbon, I thought of our living room with a tall Christmas tree topped with crooked star and the red felt stockings hung over our fireplace. Mom, Steve and Ellen would be opening gifts and eating coffee cake from Wirth's Bakery.

I teared up as I opened my presents, wishing more than anything that I was home. Was Sister Maureen sitting with gifts in her cell in New Mexico? As instructed, I piled the opened gifts--a small silver pocket watch, (nuns didn't wear wristwatches), stationery, soap, a box of See's chocolates and a black sweater-vest my Aunt Alice had knit herself---in a stack. Obediently, I carried the gifts to Mother's desk where I left them with a small paper with my name. Some of the things might or might not appear on the chair in my cell next week.

On Christmas, visitors would arrive at one, rather than two o'clock and I was surprised when just before 1 p.m., I was called to the parlor.

Mom and Steve were coming in, smiling and carrying two huge white bakery boxes. Ellen trailed behind with her usual smile. To my amazement, the boxes contained ice cream snowballs, coated with coconut, topped with holly and a candle and packed in dry ice. Mom made much ado about the dessert—how it needed to be removed from the freezer fifteen minutes before serving and that each snowball should be served with the candle lit. She couldn't know that I had no control about how they were served, or even if, they would be served. A novice from Los Angeles who had no visitors helped me rush the boxes to the faraway kitchen where Mrs. Waters, our cheerful cook, received them. We sat indoors, small groups crowded into the two large parlors. Mom wanted to know how I liked my gifts. I told her everything was lovely, but I couldn't tell her that they were sitting on Mother's desk and that I didn't know if I'd ever see them again. Steve and Ellen talked of the presents they'd received, but the big gift to both of them was a stereo for the living room. They interrupted each other trying to tell me about this amazing new way of listening to music. Ellen was telling me how great Elvis sounded singing *Blue Suede Shoes*. I just couldn't imagine it. When I walked them to the door at the end of the visit, I wanted to keeping walking right out with them. I tried to peer out the door to see our Studebaker.

At dessert time that night at our Christmas dinner, a novice suddenly dimmed the lights. I smiled when the server wheeled out a cart with the dessert and each snowball with a lit candle and the sisters oohed and ahhed. Mother Colette announced, "This special dessert is a gift of Sister Judith Marie's mother. Let us remember her in our prayers after dinner." I felt teary again because I knew that my Mom, a widow, working full time, was being honored for her generosity and her creativity.

On Christmas evening, we sat in the circle in our community room singing carols and munching chocolates. Then the senior novice stood up and announced: "Santa has been here!" Two giggling novices passed a gift to each sister. A card with a little rhyme gave a clue to the contents. Each gift was a spoof on the sister's mannerisms or personality. My card read: With these you can see and peer--without your specs, Sister dear. Inside a velvet jewelry box, were two glass inserts from the tops of coffee percolators: my present--contact lenses! Years later when I was offered free contact lenses by my optometrist who said I would see better with them, Mother Colette instructed me to refuse. A nun wearing contacts would be a sin of vanity she declared, but that night we were young and enjoyed these childlike things.

On a grey January day, Mother Colette and the ten of us postulants, piled into three cars and crossed the Bay Bridge to the Motherhouse to rehearse the ceremony for our profession of vows. As I entered the huge doors, nostalgia overwhelmed me. As we passed the switchboard, an eager young high school girl was operating the equipment. I saw in her a version of my younger self--giddy and idealistic. Countless times I'd been here with Sister Maureen. Now we went to the chapel on the second floor and I glanced down the corridor that into the cloister, wondering which cell had been Sister Maureen's.

In the chapel for our practice, Mother stood in the sanctuary in place of the priest and asked: "Sisters, what do you desire?"

"Father, I desire the grace of God and the holy habit of religion," we answered in unison. As we knelt, Mother moved along to each of us, pretending to place a folded habit in our arms. Sister Agnes Ann struck a chord on the organ and we rose and proceeded to the spot where we would prostrate ourselves in an act of humility during tomorrow's ceremony. Mother Colette, herself, knelt in the aisle and demonstrated how to hold the large sleeves of her habit which we would have tomorrow and how to slide gracefully onto the hardwood floor for the prostration. Collectively, we held our breath. Would Mother actually prostrate herself on the floor? It struck me as incongruous that she felt it important for us to look graceful in this act of humiliation. But then, she stood without prostrating

The next day when we returned for the real ceremony, Mother led us upstairs to the library where Reverend Mother would give us our new religious names. We had each been allowed three suggestions. I had submitted: Sister Judith Marie, Sister Steven Marie and Sister Maura, after Sister Maureen. I was hoping Mother would choose the latter. As we sat on either side of long wooden table, Reverend Mother entered the library, her face scrubbed shiny, her piercing, dark eyes surveying us. Mother Colette held out a chair for her. She gave us a hint of a smile like the master of ceremonies drawing out the suspense. First, Sister Denise, senior of our group, was called. She knelt, receiving, Charles, as her religious name as she had requested. It was her father's name. Then it was my turn. I knelt by her chair with a dry mouth and bowed head.

"Sister Judith Marie, in religion you will be called Sister Mary Theophane."

I swayed. Did I imagine one of my fellow sisters gasped when she spoke? Was this a punishment for daring to ask for Sister Maura, a choice similar close to Maureen? I murmured, "Thank you, Reverend Mother," but I was in shock at receiving this difficult name and I listened with envy as the others received names they requested, names of fathers, brothers and mothers. Their 'thank yous' reflected their genuine pleasure.

Reverend Mother stood and began moving among us, enjoying the delight and thanks of my fellow sisters. I could see them my examining my face, looking for signs of shock. I had to feign joy and forced a smile as Reverend Mother moved toward me. She smiled as she remarked, "I thought we needed a 'Theophane.' It is such a beautiful name."

I swallowed hard and murmured, "Thank you, Reverend Mother and asked, "And my patron saint is Saint Theophane Venard, the martyred French priest, a favorite of St. Therese?"

"No, Sister dear, you are named in honor of the Epiphany of Jesus, often called, Little Christmas. That day was a theophany, the Greek word for a manifestation of Christ. Your feast day, January 6, commemorates the day Christ was presented to the Wise Men." It didn't change my name but it invested it with a deeper meaning.

Now it was time for us, Brides of Christ, to change into our wedding dresses. Downstairs in a large parlor, a chosen few novices were waiting to help us change. In my corner Sister Sean was waiting. She was my favorite novice because of her sense of humor that often made difficult things bearable. She grinned and looked at me with her intense blue eyes. As I sat on the couch and began to take off the black cotton stockings, she winked as she handed me the beige nylons. In minutes, I was in my wedding dress.

Once Mom dealt with the shock that she would have to buy a brand new wedding dress that would be worn only a few minutes in this ceremony, she started shopping. She had found a dress with a tiny lace bolero that covered the shoulders as required but the buttons were now difficult. When she had delivered it in December, she said, "Judy, I had a devil of time finding a dress that covered the shoulders. I hope this will do. You're marrying Jesus. Is that it? All of you are marrying Jesus?" Mom queried. She would never grasp the mysteries of convent life.

" Yes, Mom, that's the way it is. We are Brides of Christ."

At this moment Mom was waiting in the chapel, sitting in the uncomfortable stalls with my sister, Ellen, Auntie Mabe, Mom's sister, and their brother, my uncle Emmett. Without a mirror I had to believe Sister Sean when she said I looked beautiful as she placed a tiara with simulated pearls and a long net on my curly brown hair. Slipping on white heels and long white gloves, I answered Mother's summons, "Sister Mary Theophane, you're next."

In the second parlor, Sister Clara, a large nun with a kindly face waited with her view camera mounted on the tripod. I stood against the wall in front of two arc lights while Sister Clara gave directions, laughing as she spoke, enjoying her task.

"Look to one side, clasp your hands in front of you, now smile. No, not that wide, no gums showing." The shutter clicked as Sister pushed the cable release. The camera was always my enemy, reflecting light off my thick lenses. However, the chuckling Sister Clara got me to relax in front of the glaring lights. I recalled that memorable day in the sewing room when I was a sophomore and Sister Maureen and I were sewing up tiny shirts for the Missions. Sister Clara had come in and Sister Maureen started that awful baby talk she sometimes used. Sister Clara had laughed at her antics. Would she mention her today? At that moment she said, "Judy, I mean, Sister, it's too bad Sister Maureen can't be here today. Oh, I think you moved. Let's take another shot."

As soon as Sister Clara started talking about Maureen, I wanted to say to her: I'm not the silly girl you knew in high school. Don't you know how hard I've worked to kill my passion for Sister Maureen for the love of Jesus? Today I'm going to be a Spouse of Christ but I was silent and stood still while she snapped the shutter again.

Our practice in the chapel the day before was as a rehearsal in a dark theater. Now it was lights, candles, music and the audience--our families and nuns who had been our teachers. Women's perfumes mixed with the scent of the flowers and beeswax candles. On both sides of the organ, Professed Sisters gathered, singing, "Veni, Sponsa Christi," Come Spouse of Christ. The excitement was palpable as we glided to our places in our wedding dresses. Out of the corner of my eye, I spotted my family and I could hear their excited whispering as I moved to my stall, trying to suppress a smile.

The priest, in his brocade cape, blessed and sprinkled the folded habits with holy water as well as the white veils that sat on a table in the sanctuary. As each of us approached the altar railing, the priest handed us our habits. We left the chapel and entered into the whirlwind of changing quickly from wedding dress to a habit and veil while our families whispered and squirmed on the hard stalls.

To change into the habit that I was now carrying, I was assigned to large cell on the second corridor where three cubicles were divided by curtains. In the cell nearest the window, Sister Sean and the older novice, who laughed in her sleep at night, awaited me. They helped me remove my wedding dress and veil. They slid my one-piece hand-made habit over my head. I changed from beige nylons back to my black stockings. They wrapped my waist with a leather cincture from which a large rosary dangled. Then came the critical part of putting on the white veil and all the starched under-parts.

While Sister Sean draped a towel around my neck, Sister Redeemer came at my hair with a sharp scissors. Suddenly, I wanted to be shorn like a real nun. I knew Sister Maureen's head was closely shorn. At that moment something tore loose deep within me and I wanted to reject everything worldly. It was almost a physical thirst for my new life of penance and mortification.

"Cut it short, Sister," I said.

"Mother said only trim it," she said, almost apologetically, as my brown curls fell to the floor.

"Sister, cut more. I want it really short," I commanded. Sister Sean started laughing. Sister Redeemer picked up the clippers to cut the hair at my temples so no stray hairs would stick out of the veil.

"Just keep clipping," I said.

" I don't think I should," she protested meekly. Now it was her will against mine.

"Yes, you should," I instructed.

Suddenly the curtain snapped back and Mother Colette's frame filled the opening. "Sister Mary Theophane, Sister Redeemer has her instructions from me. You are not to open your mouth again. Do you understand?"

"Yes, Mother." My cheeks reddened, my eyes filled up, She had never spoken so harshly and it was more painful because Sister Sean and Redeemer were witness to my humiliation. The space was now silent and tense. A small white skullcap was placed on my hair, followed by the complicated starched pieces that were the underpinnings for the white veil, and the bib-like stiff guimpe that covered my chest almost to the waist. Sister Redeemer's hands shook as she tried to put in the last pin that held the white linen to the bandeau at my temple.

Mother came in, "Everyone is ready, but you," she scolded. She pushed Sister away and took the pin and gave it a jab. It pierced my temple but she didn't seem to notice. As I joined the others in the corridor outside the chapel, my temple throbbed and I bore invisible welts from Mother's tongue lashing. When the organ music began, Mother motioned us forward into the chapel and our procession moved slowly down the chapel aisle. I could feel the heat of the lights and the smell of the wax of the candles. Huge bouquets stood in tall vases on each side of the altar. I heard Mom whisper to Ellen, "Here comes Judy." I hoped they wouldn't notice my face was now sad and solemn.

After reciting in unison our vows of poverty, chastity and obedience for three years to Jesus our Spouse, we all prostrated in the aisle, sliding forward on the large serge sleeves, while the choir chanted the long *Te Deum*. Lying face down on the polished floor, I recalled the words of the poet, John Donne: *Take me to You; imprison me, for I, except You enthrall me, never shall be free, Nor ever chaste unless You ravish me.*

After the ceremony, I was pulled from the line of new novices that was headed toward the high school where we would visit with our families and friends. Mother took me into the library and motioned Sister Sean to follow. Something was wrong with my headgear. They reassembled my veil and bandeau one more time. Again Mother stuck the pin that anchored the veil at the side of my head, right into the skin of my temple. I winced, but offered this pain to Jesus and tried not to believe it was purposeful.

As I left the library Sister Clara took my arm, pulled me aside and led me down to the convent parlor. There was Father Flynn waiting for me. As a priest, he was given the deference of a private visit before I went to my family. He stood and grasped my hand and laughed in that old familiar way. I was puzzled but flattered that he left the parish and came to the Motherhouse for my ceremony. As he rambled on, making little jokes and small talk, I felt restless. I wanted to be with my family but I forced a smile and wondered if he still stopped by my house for drinks with Mom. Then I remembered his hands on my body when I was a teenager. I wanted him to leave.

Finally, I escaped to the high school and my assigned a classroom so I could visit with my extended family and friends. Ironically, I was given the one where once Sister Maureen had held strict study hall. It sloped upwards and had a platform desk at the front where my Mom reigned, trying to keep the restless crowd entertained. Entering, I stared at the huge crowd of friends and relatives chattering while awaiting me in the tiers of desks of the lecture-stle classroom. Immediately Mom hugged me, but gently, so as not to disturb my unfamilar habit and head dress. If she could have been pouring a few bourbons, she would have had a fine Irish party.

"Mom, I'm so sorry I kept you all waiting. It was Father Flynn."

"Father Flynn? Where is he? Everyone has been waiting for you here. Oh, never mind. Tell me, Judy, how do you pronounce you new name? Attention, everyone!" Mom's principal's voice rose over the buzz, I'd like you to welcome Sister Theopain." I winced as she went on trying to say my new name correctly.

In the front row, squeezed into one of the desks, was my old grandmother in her familiar black dress and lamb's wool coat. Grandma Teresa was my dad's mother. and she despised the Church because her own mother had left her fortune to the Church to save her soul after divorcing her husband. This left Teresa, a young widow, to raise eight children on a fireman's meager pension. I knew it didn't please her that I was becoming a nun and that made her presence, a momentous healing family gesture.

I left my Mom's side and went to hug Grandma. She rasped, feisty as ever, "Theophane, harrumph, sounds like cellophane to me. Sister Cellophane, that's what we'll call you, easier to remember."

Other relatives and friends immediately repeated her remarks and soon the whole room was enjoying the joke. Embarrassed, I smiled uneasily, but Mom skillfully orchestrated the crowd of well-wishers and preserved my dignity by saying, "Judy, I mean Sister Theophane,

I know your name has special significance. Why don't you explain that meaning to everyone?" I was grateful for her finely honed social skills and talent for disguising her real feelings.

The next hour was a blur of smiles and hugs. Too soon Sister Sean came to the door and told me it was time to return to Berkeley. I felt badly that I had so few minutes with my Mom but I could tell she was proud that so many had to come to see her daughter become a real nun.

When we returned to the novitiate in Berkeley, the older novices that hadn't attended the ceremony were eager to greet us and know our new names, but I was feeling sorry for myself with a difficult name and the worst headache of my life. Then out of the corner of my eye, I saw Marilyn, self-conscious, pudgy, now the only one left in the dreary postulant dress. Then I felt pride in my new status and I could bear any headache.

After we new novices greeted the older novices, Mother Colette called me aside to inquire why I had kept my mother and guests waiting so long. I told her I'd been in the parlor with Father Flynn who'd come to visit me.

Mother said, "Sister Mary Theophane, you are not to offer me excuses for your behavior. You may kneel and repair this fault." She seemed tired, but she was never one to shirk her duty.

I knelt at her feet and kissed the floor and began to repair my fault. "Mother, I accuse myself of being late and inconveniencing my family. For this, and all my faults, I am sorry and beg a penance from you."

As she gave me a small penance of saying a rosary, I tried to take it in the spirit of St. Therese as her words came back to me: *Suffering stretched out her arms to me and I clasped her hands with love.*

CHAPTER TEN

LIFE AS A NOVICE
1956

IN MY FIRST year as a novice, I felt a new sense of belonging to the Order. I learned to love prayer and meditation and felt I was becoming a spiritual person, only interested in unworldly topics. On Visiting Sundays, in my new zeal, I rambled on to Mom and Ellen about the sacraments and spiritual topics. Mom crossed and recrossed her long legs. She was visibly bored and I knew it was all she could do not to light up a Lucky Strike.

As novices we were now initiated into community penances, such as taking ones breakfast kneeling in the center of the refectory with a plate and silverware on a chair or kissing the feet of the other novices as they ate breakfast. I often said my rosary kneeling in the corner of the chapel with in the penitential gesture with arms extended. I obtained permission to make a holy hour at three in the morning, praying in the dark chapel, lit only by the red glow of the sanctuary lamp. I dared to imagine I might soon be favored with the gift of mysticism

Another initiation into the long-standing monastic tradtion, was the Chapter of Faults. Every Saturday afternoon while our high school contemporaries were at ball games, picnics and birthday parties and listening to Elvis and Johnny Ray, we were participating in this strange ritual. In our second floor Community Room, we knelt in two long lines while Mother sat up front at her desk as we took turns confessing our faults. Initially this ritual seemed humiliating, but when the recitals became similar week after week, it lost its terror.

At your turn one began, "I confess all my faults, but especially . . ." Then we identified one or two of our own failings, such as speaking unnecessarily or talking after The Great Silence or being impatient with another sister or failing to wear our black apron to the refectory or skipping one's time to help in the laundry.

Some sisters were more prone to trouble than others. Everyone listened carefully when they confessed. They would say: "I squealed like a pig "or "I ate the priest's remains,"(referring to sweet rolls and orange juice that the priest left behind after breakfast in the parlor); "I spilled the beans;" I smashed Jesus' head--a crucifix knocked over; I burned the ears (a starched part of the headgear)." With these confessions, the room would rock with smothered giggles.

Every six weeks, we would be assigned a new Employment. Often Sister Gloria and I were assigned together as a team. Since I was senior in rank, I would be in charge. Sister Gloria had been our high school social director and responsible for many large musical productions, but now through fate, I was in charge. Though Mother never showed favoritism, I sensed she put her faith in my sound judgment. I would listen to Sister Gloria's suggestions that were often good, but at other times, extreme; yet somehow we were usually able to compromise and get the work done well.

One of the most difficult tasks we were assigned together was that of sacristans. We knew this was the most important Employment we would have because it had to do with the sacred rituals and also because the professed sisters would be watching us. They would report any obvious mistakes we made to Mother. We were in charge of the altar, the priests' vestments, the candles, the incense, the flowers, the altar cloths, everything.

Many things could go awry. We might set out the wrong color of tabernacle veil or incorrect color vestment for the priest. The huge candelabras had tall candles that were topped with brass tips to prevent dripping. These tips had to be cleaned and polished constantly. The altar cloths had to be ironed and hung perfectly straight. On feast days, huge bouquets of flowers were to be arranged, but the worst that could happen was that we would let the sanctuary lamp burn out. One day Sister Gloria noticed the sanctuary lamp was burning very low, but we were in the midst of reciting the psalms with the Professed sisters. Subtly, she got my attention. Now neither of us could focus on our prayer, but kept a constant eye on the low flickering light. If it went out during the prayer time, we would both be scolded and punished. As the prayers ended we started to file out to the refectory. Sister Gloria started a coughing fit that allowed her to step out of the line filing to the refectory. Dramatically, she kept it up and Mother passed by her with an annoyed glance, but didn't insist she join the line. I sighed with relief because I knew she would dash back into the chapel and replace the dying candle with a new eight-day candle avoiding a severe scolding and a command to repair the fault in the refectory. Finally, we finished our six weeks without any serious mishap and were glad to move on to a new Employment.

Next, we were assigned the refectory together and this brought a different set of challenges. Every spill had to be completely wiped up, every serving apron had to be clean and starched, a pitcher of slightly sour milk was unacceptable, an un-defrosted refrigerator was a sin, and the days of big feasts took untold hours of thought and preparation. We would have to be imaginative in the decorations for the table and be sure the fine china was ready. Then pray that Mother would find our choices suitable. As we were both artistic, we outshone the previous novices, though Mother rarely paid us a compliment.

The laundry was the biggest test for us. We novices did the laundry for the professed sisters of the elementary and high school, as well for the novices and postulants. Every Monday between 5 and 5:15 am an old professed sister would lumber over to the laundry, a small wooden building across the courtyard from the novitiate. She would fire up the huge washer and make a fresh batch of starch using the old one like starter dough. She would set the mixture under steam to simmer like porridge while she trudged up the stairs to the chapel for meditation and Mass.

When Sister Gloria and I were given charge of the laundry, we rotated weeks to learn the process from Sister Wilhelm. When it was my turn, I dressed in five minutes, forgoing washing my face or brushing my teeth and flew down to the laundry where I followed Sister Wilhelm around. She slurred her words so that her speech was completely unintelligible. So I had to learn by imitation. Somehow I got the huge washing machines running and the hot starch percolating by pushing levers and buttons that I hoped were the same ones that Sister Wilhelm pushed. Then I raced to the chapel and knelt breathless in my stall at the last toll of the bell.

After breakfast Sister Gloria and I would spend the whole day in the hot laundry, leaving only to say a few prayers and eat an early lunch. It was our job to assign each novice a different task in the laundry with rotating shifts. In the morning with burning fingers, I would hand press the hot starch into the bandeaux-the white rectangles we tied around our foreheads to hold up our veils. Some sisters we assigned to the large steam press where the bandeaux were pressed until they were as stiff as cardboard; others went to iron the long altar linens until they were perfectly stiff without a wrinkle. Any pieces that were not perfect were done over. Six sisters were assigned to the large mangle where they pressed the endless sheets and the starched white veils; others folded the laundry.

A laundry number was sewn on every garment so that the finished items went into proper cubbyholes that resembled large mailboxes. Sister Wilhelm would come in occasionally and grunt approval. Sister

Gloria and I secretly prided ourselves on running the laundry more efficiently than the last two novices. Mother never praised us but we joyfully turned off all the big machines, the mangle and the presses on time to enjoy recreation, the best hour of the day

Mother had to fill the position of choir mistress after Sister Amata, a true musician, received her black veil and moved to the motherhouse. Though a talented novice in the group ahead of me would be the natural candidate, she had a dominating personality that Mother was trying to subdue, therefore she didn't give her the job she obviously coveted. Yet Mother's judgment failed when she chose me to be choir directress. She misunderstood my enthusiasm for singing as aptitude. When I protested I was not right for the job, she said that God always gives us the grace to do our assignment. However, grace was no substitute for my lack of ability.

Every Sunday morning we assembled in the classroom with the piano. We prided ourselves on being able to learn complicated music, sing three part harmonies, master new hymns easily. In terror I stood in front of the assembled novitiate and tried to direct pieces sung in a three-part harmony. When I raised my hands to conduct, everyone knew I was faking it, but there was an unspoken code of support among us. I was always a soprano, I couldn't tell whether the altos or the seconds were on key. I brought the strongest singers to seats up front and they understood that it was up to them to get it right.

When we had to learn a new piece, my eyes would plead for help from Sister Robert, who was the accompanist. She sat attentively at the upright piano to my left and knew I was dependent on her. She'd begin playing strongly and the voices would follow her lead. Mother sat at the back of the room and interrupted whenever she didn't think it was going well. Yet no amount of grace could compensate for my lack of ability but the real torture began in the choir loft on special feast days when I had to direct what I hoped we had learned. It was only through the kindness of the other sisters that I got through my time as conductor. Finally, without explanation and to my great relief, Mother turned the job over to the feisty, but far more competent novice, Sister Louis, who should've had the job in the first place.

One morning Mother called us into the Senior Study before we started our Employments. Ordinarily, after breakfast the convent was alive with novices cleaning, sweeping, scrubbing every corner of the novitiate. Now we sat in desks curious as to the nature of this gathering. Mother came in took her place at her elevated desk and then announced, "Sisters, the Order has made a decision to move our novitiate. In two weeks you will continue your training in a new site in the Santa Cruz Mountains." A ripple of surprise went through the room. We didn't know how to respond to this unknown adventure. We didn't know that many Orders were moving their bulging novitiates to that area and that even the Jesuits would be just down the road.

I worried if my family would still visit me. Mom had been going to visit Steve at the seminary in Mountain View to visit Steve once a month. But Steve had left the seminary and was now attending St. Ignatius high school in the City. Mother had called me into her office and told me that news as if she was announcing a death. I had pretended I was sad, but I knew Mom would be glad to have Steve home. Would she find her way to the distant Santa Cruz Mountains on Visiting Sundays?

On a sunny Saturday in June, 1957 in charged silence, thirty of us novices piled into a big yellow school bus while Mother supervised the loading of the boxes that held our belongings and chatted with the uniformed driver, a Black gentleman, who wore his hat at jaunty angle. As he loaded the boxes, he remarked to Mother, "Well, Ma'am, looks like you got quite a family."

As he called her Ma'am, we knew he wasn't Catholic and must be given the greatest courtesy as that's how converts are made. When he saw a different name on each box, he continued, "You mean this is all each one of these girls owns? Why I just sent my oldest daughter off to college. I needed a van to bring all her stuff down."

By the time Mother boarded the bus, we'd fingered through a distracted rosary on the beads that hung from our cinctures. Her face resumed its chiseled solemnity, discouraging any levity. She moved down the aisle, grasping her own rosary carefully, so that it wouldn't bang any seats. Sister Gloria insisted that I, senior in rank, should enjoy the window seat. As we drove down University Avenue in Berkeley to the freeway, Mother Colette began the Litany of the Blessed Virgin. "Mother Most Pure, Mother Undefiled, Tower of Ivory, House of Gold."

"Pray for us," we responded in a strong chorus after each title of the Virgin.

We sped past the industrial section of Oakland, passed a Milpitas auto plant, and skirted Fremont. Most of us hadn't been out of the convent in two years but nothing looked different. Then a red convertible zoomed ahead of the bus. I heard a blast of music and caught a glimpse of the teenage driver with one hand on the wheel and the other hand around his girl. Her head was snuggled against his neck, her blonde hair was dancing in the wind. I couldn't take my eyes off them. What did it feel like to race with the wind with a strong arm protecting you? I let the question linger before I murmured a prayer for their safety and her purity.

When the bus left the highway and began the slow ascent into the Santa Cruz Mountains, the temperature rose and the smell of pines and redwoods was intoxicating. Finally Mother spoke. "Sisters you may converse quietly for the remainder of the trip."

We began talking, careful to address each other as Sister and to speak in full sentences but my heart was pounding. I never dreamed I would experience the joy of the mountains again. It was like going to camp! As the bus heaved around the last hairpin turn, we couldn't believe our eyes. A lake welcomed us, the sun playing on its surface, a breeze whistled through the trees and ducks quacked a welcome. On the property were several buildings. One was designated as the professed sisters' convent. Smaller cabins were scattered about the large property. Our restraint failed and we squealed with delight as the bus pulled up in front of a large, pink stucco Pueblo-style dwelling with outside ladders to the second story. It had been the Montezuma School for Boys, but we were about to turn it into God's training ground. We stumbled, almost pushing each other out of the bus, while the driver reached up and gave us a hand. Mother led us into a great living room with the huge stone fireplace and timber beams in the ceiling. Uncharacteristically, she was smiling, enjoying our delight.

"Sisters, let us kneel and ask God's blessing on our new home and on the benefactors who have made this possible." As there was no crucifix or statue to turn to, we fell to our knees around Mother, rosaries and crucifixes banging on the black and pink tile floor. Mother began the Magnificat: "My soul does magnify the Lord and my spirit has rejoiced in God my Savior." Our voices rose in genuine thanksgiving. Mother then pulled out her list and began to call names, then giving us the number of our cell.

" Sister Mary Theophane, number 23."

"Thank you Mother," I replied and went off down a corridor. The inside walls were the same as the outside, pink stucco, and rough timbers held up inside walkways. It was so unconvent like, I began to giggle. I hoped for a remote room on the second floor but #23 was the first room off the inside courtyard. Inside were two beds with new striped bedspreads. I chose the bed with the small outside window above it. I threw myself down on my back. I could hear birds chattering a noisy welcome. The other bed would belong to a postulant who hadn't yet arrived. For the first time in my life, I would have a room to myself. Then I went out to the corridor and discovered that the bathroom was only steps away and had showers of pink and black tile. I wouldn't miss the claw-foot tubs. Directly opposite the door to my cell, was another door that opened to the outside; trees and flowers grew right outside. It was beyond wonderful.

Under Mother's supervision the first two weeks were dedicated to domestic decisions of women in a new home: brooms and mops into closets, books into old fashioned glassed bookcases brought from Berkeley which looked anachronistic against stucco walls, dark clocks hung oddly on the bright pink walls. In the refectory and kitchen, housed in a separate building a few steps below the main novitiate, we unpacked new unbreakable dishes and huge shiny, stainless steel pots. A Professed Sister was assigned as cook, but I knew I would miss Mrs. Water's recipes.

One morning, Sister Gloria and I were assigned the strenuous job of hanging the heavy opaque curtains that would divide the rooms into two cells. The track had already been installed into each ceiling. She would hold the curtain, while I stood on the stepladder, feeding the casters into the track on the ceiling. We saved my cell room 'til last. I was fretting because soon there would be a new postulant rummaging around on the other side of the curtain, making noise, perhaps snoring. I hated cutting my room in half but I was glad the single ceiling light would be on my side.

Suddenly, I lost my balance and fell backward off the ladder, grabbing onto the curtain, I landed on my back with a scream. I had dragged the curtain out of the ceiling track and now Sister Gloria was underneath the fallen curtain. With her flair for drama, she began to cackle from under the cavern of the curtain and recite lines from Macbeth. I began to laugh hysterically as I tried to extricate her from under the curtain. When she emerged, her headgear was over one ear. We giggled uncontrollably. Suddenly Mother's frame filled the doorway.

"Sisters, what is going on in here?" she demanded.

"Mother, I fell off the ladder," I said nervously, dropping my hold on the curtain.

"Sister Theophane, that is no reason for this juvenile behavior."

" Of course not, Mother." I fell to my knees, untying my apron. Sister Gloria, her headgear crooked, knelt next to me. We looked down at the floor.

"And you, Sister Gloria, I don't know how many times I have spoken to you about your lack of self-control. When will you ever learn?

Now Sisters, you may repair your faults."

"Yes, Mother," we replied in unison, "Mother, I most humbly accuse myself of all my fault especially for . . . " Here we paused. Sister Gloria let me speak first. "For laughing and acting in a juvenile manner," I declared. Then kissed the floor again.

"For laughing, acting silly and losing control of my emotions," confessed Sister Gloria. She kissed the floor. Together we continued, "For these and all my faults, we humbly ask forgiveness of God and penance of you, Mother. " We awaited sentence.

"Sisters, just because we are a little unsettled here is no reason to forget the Rules. Silence in the cell is our Rule." She paused letting her words sink in. She continued, "For your penance, Sister Theophane, I want you to work an extra hour in the kitchen. You, Sister Gloria, will help in the laundry. That will be all, Sisters." Then she was gone.

"Sorry," I whispered to Sister Gloria.

"My fault," she replied. Chastened, we quickly got the curtain on the track.

Corrections were a part of our life here but no matter how many times I was reprimanded, I never got used to it. Mother's words felt like blows, raising welts that lasted long afterward. Humiliation, I tried to rationalize, was good for me; it made me stronger. I'd become attached to having a cell of my own, even for the short time before the new postulant arrived. The Lord was reminding me that I didn't own anything, not even my own space.

After a few weeks in the new building, our lives settled into a routine: prayer, housework, classes, and recreation. It was easy to praise God in the cool of the morning in the low-ceilinged meeting room-turned chapel. During meditation, birds chirped outside the windows. One bird made a distinctive call, two whistles and a trill. The sight of the bird eluded me, but when I heard that piccolo trill, I took delight in imagining it was calling to me. Another consequence of the move was that my thoughts of Sister Maureen were few. I was in a new country setting, a place not associated with her in any way.

After our early morning meditation, one of the Jesuits from their nearby college, would say Mass in quiet Latin tones. At nine o'clock our summer classes began. With other novices, I hurried the quarter of a mile to a hayloft above an old barn now converted to a classroom. The main floor had been converted to the dining hall for the professed sisters and for visitors. In silence we sat at Formica desks awaiting Sister Fidelity who would teach us English literature. After so much time with the serious Mother Colette, Sister Fidelity appeared as a natural comedian. A few minutes after nine she'd bustle in, breathless, asking how everyone was. As she turned her head, birdlike from side to side, eyes bright, eyebrows raised, she'd mutter funny asides to herself. Then she'd begin. "All right, Sisters, who will read from our first selection?"

As one of her favorite authors was James Thurber, we read *The Catbird Seat* aloud. Next we read *The Night the Bed Fell*. Ordinarily, we were only allowed to read spiritual books. In our literary desert, James Thurber was an oasis. We laughed uproariously, enjoying the act of laughing. Later that summer we read Masefield's play, *Riders to the Sea*. Sister Gloria read the part of the bereaved mother with such feeling and an authentic brogue that we were spellbound. That summer our English Lit class became our movie, our TV, our entertainment.

As June slid into July, the temperatures rose into the 80's and 90's. The sun baked the gentle hills into crisp brown loaves and we were serenaded with the sound of buzzing insects. No fog eased the heat that penetrated the pink stucco and poured in through the skylights. Our black habits were magnets for the heat. At noon when we left the hayloft classroom to return to the novitiate, heat waves shimmered off the blacktop and my heels made soft prints in the asphalt. The bounce was gone from my steps; sweat ran in rivulets down my forehead and neck, wilting the starched pieces of my headgear. In the chapel the air was motionless. I elevated my thoughts to Jesus and offered up this discomfort, but it sucked my strength and dried my brain. I longed for four o'clock recreation. So when Mother finished the psalm, a sister would pull out a box of old tennis shoes and we'd each find a pair that fit well enough, pin up our habits, take off the starched white bib and start off in groups of threes to circle the lake.

With white veils flapping, habits pinned around the hips, tennis shoes flopping, we looked like a group of geese waddling to the lake. Sometimes we took a longer walk down to the creek. When we reached the gurgling water, Mother would start a song, frequently *Green Cathedral*, an appropriate selection as we rested under the redwoods. After recreation, forty tolls summoned us to Vespers. We stood in the hallway until Mother intoned, "Let us go into the house of the Lord."

"It is right and just to do so," we responded. Then we marched into the low ceilinged chapel where the heat was the worst. We were crowded together on thinly padded kneelers and, even though the windows were open, it was at least 100 degrees, unbearable for a San Franciscan who grew up in summer fog.

CHAPTER ELEVEN

THE MOVE TO THE MOUNTAINS

IN THE MIDDLE of July, a miracle occurred. Mother announced at the beginning of recreation, that the swimming pool repairs were complete. A new eight-foot wall now surrounded the pool and bathhouse for privacy. After the psalm, a smiling Mother handed each of us a white towel. Wrapped inside was a black bathing suit and white cap that Mother had ordered from a catalog. They reminded me of the suits that rented for ten cents apiece at Sutro Baths in San Francisco in the '40's, as when I was very young and had gone there with my parents. After handing out the towels, Mother actually giggled as she asked, "Anyone for a swim?"

In an enthusiastic chorus we replied, "Yes, Mother." But then Mother became serious. "Sisters, before we go to the swimming pool, I want you to know the rules: Silence will be observed in the bathhouse; there will be no sunbathing. This is your exercise. After you change, go directly to the pool; when you leave the water, go directly to the bathhouse and get dressed." Then with a rare smile she said, "So let's try out that water, sisters"

I found an empty cubicle in the bathhouse, pulled the muslin curtains over the opening. I sat on the cold bench, removed my oxfords and black stockings. I reached up with one hand under my domino and veil, searching for the two strings that were tied at the back of my close-cropped hair. If one did it correctly, the whole thing would come off in one piece and hang on a hook, but one false move and the headgear would fall apart. Off it came. I felt ten pounds lighter. I pulled the serge habit over my head; ten more pounds gone. I untied the black half-slip, took off the white cotton slip, the cotton pants, the white garter belt, the cotton shirt, the white bra. Now standing naked on cement in this strange cubicle, curtains barely covering the opening, I was feeling uncomfortably exposed. I hurried to pull on the suit with its short skirt, high square neck, and wide straps. I pulled on the swim cap over my close-cropped hair and then looked down at the sizable dark growth on my legs and my white thighs. Oh no, I couldn't go out there. Get hold of yourself, Theophane. You're not at the country club! Get going! I wrapped a towel around myself, pulled back the curtain, and hurried out of the bathhouse. I wanted to run, to jump in with a huge splash, but I walked slowly to the pool. I smiled at Mother Colette who sat on the cement bench in the shade. Carefully I removed my thick, rimless glasses, noting their exact location so that I cold find them when I got out. I dropped my towel, strode in the shallow end and plunged toward the deep end.

Several of the sisters already in the water, were only blurs to me. Without my glasses, I moved in a world of my own. By the diving board, I squinted to view the scene. Bodies, so long in bondage for the Lord, were hanging out of loose suits: white legs, arms, backs, the outline of nipples, bottoms where the loose suit caught in the crack. A few hung on inner tubes. It made me laugh. Then I broke into a crawl and the smell of the chlorine and the feel of the water brought back memories of summer days, even of that lazy afternoon at the Russian River when I swam with Don Riley. If he'd really liked me would I be here today?

"Sister, want to race?"

" Is that you, Sister Gloria?"

"No, its Mother McCrea."

"Don't get smart with me, Sister. I can't see much but you're on. Freestyle!"

We took off swimming hard. I bumped into a few bodies, 'murmuring "scuse me," hoping Mother didn't see me touch anyone. When I reached the end of the pool, Sister Gloria wasn't next to me.

"What team were you on? You're too good for me," she panted.

A new blur on the other side of me, challenged, "Got your breath? I'll race you."

"'Is that you, Sister Eleanor?

"Yes, are you ready?"

"All right. When you say, go."

Holding my breath, kicking hard, I went the length of the pool again. When I touched the side, the blur that was Sister Eleanor was ahead of me.

"You're good," I said.

"Get out, Sister Theophane. I'll give you some tips."

Sister Eleanor, a quiet, competent novice, was a year younger and from my same grammar school. She had a compact body, almost like a young boy. We stood at the end of the pool, and even though I was feeling self-conscious in this loose fitting black suit with my hairy legs exposed, I took her instruction. She showed me how to chop the water with powerful strokes and how to kick my legs just below the surface. I also noticed she had shaved her legs. Suddenly, Mother approached us. We tensed but she surprised up by taking great interest in the lesson. Mother encouraged others to join us. Soon Sister Eleanor was teaching a whole group of novices.

The next day we advanced to the diving board. Some jumped, a few did belly flops, others did passable dives. Then Sister Eleanor went to the end of the board, sprung high and executed a perfect jackknife.

"Teach me how to do that! " I screamed.

Sister Eleanor was two inches taller than me and her body was perfectly proportioned under the loose suit. "Do it again," I yelled. "Mother, watch this."

Sister Eleanor, red-faced at the attention, ran to the end of the board and sprung high. In a flash of glistening legs and pointed toes, she was in the air, bent, touching her toes, then, opening and slicing the water with barely a splash. We clapped. I wanted to do it just as she did.

"Isn't that great," I called to Mother who was enjoying our antics. It seemed that once away from the Berkeley convent Mother eased her constant correcting of us. She wasn't under daily scrutiny of the professed sisters who taught at the parish schools. To our surprise, she loved watching us at the pool.

Sister Eleanor took my hand on the board and paced off the exact number of steps, marking the place to put all one's weight so the body would spring high. My first dives were miserable; however, by the end of the week, I had it. I thought of my brother, Steve with his half gainers, his twists, and his cannon balls. If only he could see me now. Since he'd left the seminary, he was probably with my family at a summer resort and I wondered if they missed me.

After that day it was Eleanor and I competing, pounding the board, springing higher, never tiring of it. Fortunately, Mother Colette who sat in the shade, nodded like an approving Southern matron, encouraged our performance She took pride in everyone's progress.

After I mastered the jackknife, Eleanor did a forward somersault, spinning round the air in a tight ball then opening up, slicing the water with pointed toes.

"Teach me," I cried. She tried, but I in my fear I held back and often landed with a stinging slap on my back. Yet I didn't give up. Soon I could do a passable somersault. I practiced in my sleep, even at evening prayer. I could feel my back and legs muscles tighten as if they were on the board, but I was never as good as Sister Eleanor, a natural athlete.

On rare occasions, Mother asked the professed sisters, who lived in another building on the property, to come and watch the novices swim. To our surprise, Mother called on Sister Eleanor and me to perform our dives. Now we were center stage! Never had my body performed so well.

At the end of summer, a program was being organized to show what we'd learned in our English class. The event would take place in a large outdoor amphitheater nestled in the pines by the lake. We'd each recite a selection aloud. During class Sister Fidelity went down the aisles stopping at each desk, pad in hand, asking what selection we chose. I loved the English poet, Francis Thompson and my favorite was his *The Hound of Heaven*, which narrates a mystical journey. God is the Hound who pursues a soul who flees Him, hiding in every possible pleasure. But God advances with the persistence of a hound in pursuit during a hunt. To choose just one stanza broke up the narrative, but the poem was several pages long. Sister Fidelity, pad in hand, stopped at my desk and leaned over, "What have you chosen, Sister Theophane?"

"I 'll do the *Hound of Heaven*, Sister."

"Which verse have you chosen?" She looked over my shoulder at the English book. Not looking at her, I sucked in my breath and replied, "I'll do them all."

"What, Sister dear? It's several pages! Do you think you can do that?"

"I'll try, Sister." She raised her eyebrows and said. "Let me know if you change your mind" as she jotted my selection in her pad.

After lunch I sat in the study area staring at the poem I loved. It portrayed God as a persistent Lover and that excited me. It was one of the best prayers I'd ever read but then I panicked when I realized the program was a little more than a week away. How could I memorize this long poem with so little free time? I devised a method. I wrote each verse on a tiny piece of paper and pinned the first verse on my sleeve. Now I could memorize it while doing my housework, standing in line, making my bed. As soon as I mastered one verse, I pinned on the next one.

On Friday we walked to the amphitheater by the side of the lake.

My mouth was dry and I was overcome with nervousness. Soon I was alone, center stage and the words were flowing;

"In the rash lustihead of my young powers, I shook the pillaring hours and pulled my life upon me. Grimed with smears, I stand amid the dust 'o the mounded years—My mangled youth lies dead beneath the heap."

It was going well, but suddenly I couldn't remember the next line. Panic. I repeated the last one and then the next one came to me.

"My days have crackled and gone up in smoke, Have puffed and burst as sun starts on a stream. Yea, faileth now even dream the dreamer."

I sped toward the end, embarrassed that I had stumbled over one line. There was a burst of applause. I nodded and left the stage, but my cheeks burned as I berated myself for that one failure.

Now Sister Eleanor was onstage. She began: Once upon a time there were three little pigs...She proceeded to tell the whole story as if reciting for a group of school age youngsters, stamping her foot at the knock on the door. We were mesmerized. We laughed, clapped. I felt envious. Why hadn't I chosen something so entertaining? It didn't matter that at the end of the program Sister Fidelity came and congratulated me, as did Sister Eleanor, but I protested, "Didn't you hear my mistake?" No one seemed to recall it. In spite of my success, I was still intolerant of my failings, demanding unrealistic perfection. I had always strived to be at the top maybe to compensate for inferior feelings. I got nearly all straight A's for four years in school and my way with Sister Maureen was beyond competitive. Perhaps after my dad died I didn't get enough praise at home. Whatever it was, it would have served me better to be tolerant with myself.

Once the pool opened, that summer was one of the happiest in my life. But in late summer a serious challenge to that arrived: organ lessons. I can not imagine who cajoled the talented Mr. Havorka, the director of the choir of St. Ignatius Church attached to the University of San Francisco, into driving sixty-five miles from San Francisco to the novitiate in Los Gatos to teach singing to a group of novices and to give organ lessons to two of us. Even more mystifying, was why I was chosen as one of those novices.

One day Mother called Sister Gloria and me to her office and announced that at 2 o'clock we should go to the organ loft in the professed sister's convent to meet Mr. Havorka. In the Berkeley convent some of us had taken piano lessons from old Sister Reginald and in a final program Sister Gloria and I had played a duet, each on our own piano. It sounded impressive, but she played the complex parts, while I played a repetitive bass. I wanted to say to Mother, "I know my limitations and this is a huge mistake." But one didn't speak to Mother that way." Holy obedience ruled. I wondered if I could I act under holy obedience my entire life. Reluctantly, I trudged down the road to the intimate chapel of the professed sisters and up to the small organ loft. In a thick Russian accent, Mr. Havorka introduced himself. He was short, in his late fifties with a wart on his nose.

When Mr. Havorka gestured to the organ bench, I whispered, "Sister Gloria, you go first," As Sister Gloria sat down, he placed a sheet of music in front of her. "Play," he said.

She began to laugh nervously. "I really don't know how to play an organ" she protested.

"Try," he encouraged. When she began playing, he said, "Slide, slide, don't jump from note to note. This isn't a piano where your fingers can jump around. This is an organ." Then he motioned for her to get up from the bench and he sat down to demonstrate the technique. Sister Gloria sat down again and her long fingers slid from key to key.

"Wonderful. Now you," he said, pointing to me. My fingers were damp as memories surfaced of my tortured piano recitals at St. Monica's. Even when I practiced for hours, I could not play the simplest tune in front of people. As I sat down, I murmured to my fingers, "Play, you devils or I'll cut you off." They landed on the correct notes, but they jumped.

"No, glide, glide!" Mr. Havorka sat next to me and played the same notes an octave higher. I glided, after a fashion.

"Will you girls practice now? I'll see you next week."

Oh, how I practiced! The organ had switches where one could add flutes, violins, and other instruments or tremolo or super-tremolo. I added accompaniments and tremolos with every piece. It sounded wonderful, but when Mr. Havorka came, there were no fancy extras. We simply played the organ. He made me so nervous that my fingers would start toward a key, then back off, then hit it lightly and try to slide over to the next. He paced the tiny organ loft shouting: "Hit it, yes, hit it! No, not that note, the E flat." In frustration he stood with his back to me, looking out over the chapel. After a few minutes of torture, he'd command, "Up, up, up get up! Let me show you." As he played, he closed his eyes and hummed and swayed. He took great pleasure in a piece well-played. I was so unsure of myself, hesitating over every note that soon he dubbed me, Sister Stutter. Sister Gloria found this quite amusing and with each lesson, she got better and I worse.

Then he started on the complicated foot pedals. He showed us how to slide our foot from note to note. Coordinating my hands was difficult enough, let alone my feet, but not for the taller Sister Gloria with her long fingers and legs. When she sat at the bench and spread out her legs to reach the pedals, even though her body was covered by the habit, it seemed so sensual that I was embarrassed to watch. Her body melded with the organ, producing beautiful sounds. Mr. Havorka was transported, humming and swaying as he sat next to her and often providing a duet. I wanted to flee the scene in the chapel.

One day as Sister Gloria finished her turn and I was crawling onto the bench, Mr. Havorka began some small talk, most likely to postpone the agony of my turn. He was standing with his back to us, gazing out over the balcony as usual. Then he asked a question neither of us understood.

"What do you think of Sputnik?" He pronounced it "spootnik."

We looked at each other, puzzled. Repeating the question, he turned toward us. We looked at him blankly. "Girls, you know, Sputnik, the Russian satellite?" Seeing our void expressions, he asked in astonishment, "You know nothing of Sputnik? It's in the papers, the TV, everywhere! Everyone knows about Sputnik." He sat down on the organ bench and began to describe this wonder with his eyes wide. Finally, he jumped up, shaking his head, went down the narrow stairs of the loft, forgetting about my lesson and muttering in disgust about our ignorance.

Sister Gloria and I sat on the organ bench and talked in conspiratorial tones about this revelation. "Do you think Sputnik is really that important?' I asked.

"Of course not," she laughed. He's making a big fuss because he's Russian."

"Ah, You're right," I agreed. As I walked up to the hill to the novitiate, I never gave another thought to Sputnik. We lived in our own world and at this moment I was enjoying the delight of escaping my lesson.

November 1st is All Saints Day, a holy day, and it was the last day that our novitiate pool would be open. The day was sunny, but crisp and not all the novices wanted to swim, but Mother allowed Sister Eleanor and me and a few others to go to the pool for recreation without her supervision. We donned our suits, now faded to grayish green. One last time Eleanor and I did favorite dives, the jack knife, excelling our own previous performances. We raced and, laughingly, agreed it was a tie. After one last somersault, we raced out of the pool, frantically donned our habits and tore off to Vespers in the chapel. That day we both sensed something was coming to a close. Winter was coming. In January, I'd make my vows and transfer to the Motherhouse. By the time Sister Eleanor would arrive at the Motherhouse, I 'd be assigned a Mission. We'd formed a warm friendship without any guilt. Through our diving, we'd come to care for each other, and in a way, we had a forbidden particular freindship, though we never put it in words and it occurred right in front of Mother's eyes.

As the bell began to toll for Vespers, we ran from the pool to the novitiate building, one last time, laughing, tightening our cinctures, large rosary beads flying and hoping Mother wouldn't see us running. As we crossed the open space, a cool wind swirled brittle leaves around our ankles. At the last toll of the bell, we knelt, breathless, at our places in the chapel and began to recite the psalms.

Winter was upon us and it brought an unwelcome guest. Without warning, the Asian flu invaded our ranks. One morning, when I was the senior server in the refectory, I realized I had a fever, but I was determined not to give into my body. Too many sisters were already sick. I bustled around the refectory, passing the mush, the soft boiled eggs, the toast. I collected the empty dishes, but I thought the meal would never end. At one point, I felt faint and steadied myself by holding on to the end of one of the long monastic tables. Unfortunately, Mother Colette observed my behavior. When she rang her bell, signaling that the meal was over and the Sisters began filing out of the refectory, I took my place at the door, holding it open until the last Sister left. I was hanging on tightly to the knob to steady myself. Mother was the last one to leave and she stopped and looked at me.

"Sister, what is wrong with you?"

For a moment, I thought I might get sympathy. "Mother, I don't feel very well."

"Why are you playing the martyr, Sister Mary Theophane? Go to your cell immediately and remain there."

Slowly, I removed the long white apron, folded it and went to my cell. I didn't bother to eat breakfast and left the other two servers alone, silently crunching their cold toast. Soon Mother came into my cell and took my temperature. She didn't share with me what it was. "Get in bed and stay there," she commanded. I was burning up and my throat hurt.

My meals were brought on a tray by Sister Noreen, one of the novices spared the flu. She was Sister who was frequently reprimanded for breaking the silence; she just couldn't keep anything inside. She spoke rapidly, breathlessly and constantly. No matter how often Mother Colette corrected her, she couldn't change. However, this epidemic would reveal her valuable qualities to Mother. Her large frame would barge in the door of my cell, swish round the curtain that divided the cell in two, a tray in her pudgy hands and announce, "Here you are, Doll, breakfast! How ya' feeling this morning? Better?"

"Noreen, I'm dying."

"Gee whiz, you don't look that great. See look, what I brought you? Real orange juice! I snitched it out of the pitcher they keep for the priest's breakfast. Here, sit up. Try it."

"Thanks. Just leave it. Right now I can hardly swallow." For days I lay there. Three times a day forms would pass the opaque window in my cell that let in light from the corridor. The novices were going to the refectory so I knew Sister Noreen would be coming with a tray.

"Listen, Doll," she told me in a stage whisper as she set down the lunch tray, "Everybody's getting it." She wore glasses that magnified her large dark eyes. They opened even wider as she said, "Three more down today. Only five of us left at breakfast! You should've seen the server running between tables, big gaps everywhere. It was a riot, but Mother never cracked a smile. I'll be back later. Got ten more trays to go."

A few days later, Sister Noreen, dinner tray in hand, confided, "Theo, Doll, I've been so frantic running trays up two flights that I've got a whole cupboard of broken glasses and dishes." It was the custom whenever we broke anything to go straight to Mother, to kneel, show her the broken pieces and confess the fault. "Don't know when I'll ever tell Mother. Maybe just hit the garbage can? Ya' think she checks that?"

I started to laugh 'til tears came, but it hurt too much to laugh, yet her humor was healing. Through the little window above my bed, I caught a glimpse of a bare tree shoving its branches at a gray sky. Some days it rained. Next to my bed was a small radiator that was on more often than off. I was burning up, but I had no control over it. Yet three times a day, every day, Sister Noreen came with food and humor. Only once did Mother Colette come in. She stood away from the bed, looking worried. I smiled weakly. I was glad to see her.

"How are you feeling, Sister?"

"I just went across the hall to take a cold shower because I'm so hot. I'm just burning up," I replied.

"Sister, that is not a good thing to do. You could make yourself worse! Do not do that again." Then she was gone. I didn't care. I was dying.

Sister Noreen barged in with a lunch tray, talking as she put it next to me. "Listen, doll, its been raining like crazy and there's pots all over the place catching the water. Everything leaks. Hardly a pot left in the kitchen."

A few days later she said, " Can you believe it, Doll? Now the water is out. Mother's set up a brigade with the few of us left standing to carry water from the bathhouse."

Just before Christmas, I tried to get up. I had to direct the singing for Christmas as the more competent novice director had professed vows and moved to the Motherhouse. I told Mother my throat was raw.

"We need you. Gargle with warm salt water," she commanded.

Somehow I got through it all, the flu, the sore throat, even the singing and Christmas, but I would always feel a deep gratitude to the dedicated Sister Noreen.

After Christmas, Mother called the seven of us senior novices to the Community room. Her face was unreadable. It was a cold gray day and the convent smelled of dampness. In the huge alcove where there could've been a blazing fire, was placed a life-sized a statue of the Sacred Heart. Mother stood in front of it. "Sisters, you have all received permission from Reverend Mother and her Council to profess your vows. The date is set for January 18th. I will make a time to speak to each of you individually in my office."

A ripple of excitement went through our group. We were the seven survivors of the original fourteen! We each had our own scars, but now we were headed to the Winner's Circle. During the two and a half years of the novitiate, Mother made the road to perfection appear difficult, but uncomplicated. Every detail of our lives was bound by obedience. How could we possibly fail? I felt a quiet peace, but I was surprised I didn't feel joy or excitement. Slowly, doubts began to arise. At my appointed time, I entered Mother's small office, furnished with a desk, bookcases and two chairs. Mother allowed me to sit across the desk from her, rather than kneel at her side. I looked directly at Mother, who displayed a rare smile. We discussed spiritual reading and meditation, but I was biding my time. I needed to ask the hard question that had been percolating below the surface. At a pause in our conversation, I spit it out.

"Mother, do you really think I have a vocation?" The words hung like a disagreeable presence in the room. Nervously, I watched Mother's face. Her expression didn't change.

"Sister, I haven't a doubt in the world about your vocation, not a single doubt." Her words were strong and affirming, overpowering the ugly beast of uncertainty that prowled the room. I took a deep breath and shrugged away the doubts that had invaded my meditation as of late. I took Mother's words as if Christ, Himself, spoke to me. Yes, I would make my vows. I would give my life to Christ with no inkling of how much that gift would demand.

Our Profession ceremony, where we received the black veil of the professed sister and made our vows for three years, was held in the intimate chapel of the Professed Sisters' convent where I'd suffered through organ lessons in the choir loft. It was down the road from the novitiate buildings. One side of the chapel was a large picture window that looked out on a valley of evergreens making the chapel seemed larger than it actually was. Ours was a private ceremony, attended only by our Sisters. Father McGill, thin and wizened, said Mass and delivered his usual sermon, reflecting his experience as a skid-row priest, which seemed to color his view of everything. I wished one of the Sisters who knew us could have delivered a joyous sermon, but it was unthinkable to have a woman in that position. At the end of the Mass, we moved to the altar and in turn each pronounced our vows. I said in a clear, unwavering voice,

"I, Sister Mary Theophane, do vow and promise to God, poverty chastity and obedience for three years."

At the altar railing, Mother deftly unpinned the white veil and headgear and carefully slid on the black veil that had been blessed with holy water. Proudly we stood, professed sisters at last. In the loft a choir of professed sisters sang the *Te Deum*. While they sang, I thought I heard a familiar voice. Could Sister Maureen possibly be in the choir? My heart started racing; old emotions began to stir. No, she's not here; she's in New Mexico! How could I know that during my novitate time, she'd been reassigned to a school in the Bay Area?

After the ceremony, I was standing in the crowded vestibule where Sisters were hugging and congratulating each other. Suddenly, I looked up. Sister Maureen was coming down the steep stairs from the choir loft! I froze on the spot. She seemed as if she was descending in slow motion. Then I caught her eye and she smiled widely. At the bottom of the stairs we hugged eagerly. Now I had a black veil and our two veils fell forward and formed a little cave, obscuring our faces. My breath was short, my palms sweaty, my heart beating wildly. We gazed at each other, communicating with our eyes. She was still so beautiful, her lavender scent the same. We savored each other in the way lovers do that have endured a long absence. I hadn't seen her since that night in that tiny room on the third floor of the school at the end of my senior year. I wanted to race up the hill with her and catch up on the years apart. Did she still feel the same passion for me? I felt she did, but now I had to release her and move on to greeting other sisters, to pretend I wasn't still in wildly in love. My two and a half years in the novitiate did not serve to erase my passion for her from my heart!

In the afternoon, our families came to visit and somehow Maureen and I managed to have our picture taken together by my Mom. I was wearing my new serge habit that was so heavy it cut my shoulders. I'd gained weight so my cheeks were chubby. Maureen looked exactly the same: blue eyes under perfectly arched brows, wide smile and straight white teeth. She still had that same quality that captivated me at four-teen--a vitality, a love of life. She held my hand tightly. I spite of the vows I had just made, nothing had changed. That passion for her still owned me!

CHAPTER TWELVE

MOTHERHOUSE
SPRING/SUMMER 1958

ON A RAINY January day, the seven of us, proudly wearing our new black veils, said teary good-byes to the novices we were leaving behind. I squeezed Sister Eleanor's hand and whispered, "Do a few dives for me this spring." She winked and nodded. I got behind the steering wheel of one of the two cars and the sisters piled in. We headed down the mountain and after we reciting the Litany of the Blessed Virgin with its endless titles, we rode in silence for the two and a half hour journey to our new home, the motherhouse in San Francisco.

A smiling Sister Thaddeus, newly appoionted as Mistress of Junior Professed Sisters, greeted us at front door of the motherhouse. She was tall and regal in her bearing with a prominent thin nose and deep blue eyes under heavy dark brows. "Welcome, Sisters! Just leave your suitcase here in the vestibule and follow me upstairs." We clopped up the narrow wooden stairs to a room newly dubbed, The Juniorate. This would be our own gathering place, separated from the professed sisters, most of whom taught at the high school across the garden and had the large community room across the hallway.

"Sisters, welcome. I'm happy and honored that I will be your guide for the next three years. I'll meet with each of you soon and never hesitate to knock on my office door if you have a concern." I could see already her style was quite different from Mother Colette. Reprimands would be few, but good manners and proper etiquette would be important. It was a welcome change. She led us on a quick tour: the huge refectory, a chapel with monastic stalls, stained-glass windows and a mighty organ, a library and the large community room. As we toured, I was always thinking of Sister Maureen. Now I would be living in the exact same places she lived when we first fell in love.

The sleeping arrangements were compact. The cells were long narrow rooms divided by curtains into three cubicles. Bright yellow curtains hung from metal rods that were bolted to the pine floor. A small passageway was left at one side of the room so that the first two cubicles were accessible without passing through each cell. The one near the window, the largest, was occupied by a sister who taught at the high school. The seven of us juniors were assigned the cubicles in the middle or near the door on the third floor. Every cough and snore would be a shared experience.

When I was assigned a cubicle, I wondered if it was one that Sister Maureen had slept in. The cell furnishings were simple--a metal frame bed, a small desk and chair. In the shallow closet, I hung my Sunday habit and robe. On the right, was a compartment with an ancient cold-water basin and a shelf for a glass and toothpaste. Between the closet and basin was a cupboard with two low compartments where I placed in my towels, underwear and stockings. A clean set of white sheets was already inside. The top surface of the cupboard served to store one's rosary and cincture at night and the detachable parts of my headgear. All very compact.

The majority of the sisters who lived at the motherhouse taught at Presentation High School across the garden where I had fallen in love with Sister Maureen. These sisters were an efficient group who greeted us warmly the first evening in the community room, but soon they were bustling about involved in school activities. They were happy to have us do the laundry, the heavy cleaning and the waxing of the hardwood floors, but they didn't hesitate to report to Sister Thaddeus any infraction they noticed in us. In a short time, we seven formed a small nucleus of our own where we supported and cared for each other as we began a full semester of college classes. Education and English classes were taught by older sisters right in our Juniorate, but each of us had one class at the Jesuit's University of San Francisco, within walking distance from our motherhouse.

Though this was an all male campus, our Dean of Education, with great foresight, had made an arrangement long ago with the Jesuits to allow our sisters to attend their all male university. I was registered for philosophy/cosmology and was surprised to find Sister Amata, my Angel of postulant days, who now taught Latin at the high school, was also in the class. The instructor was a tall, gangly, enthusiastic scholar who often abandoned the textbook and brought in copies of the original works of Heraclitus, Aristotle and Plato. He led us in discussions of ancient philosophies. Here was a realm where no Superior had control. One could participate in the class and marvel at the wisdom of the ancients with no censure. I loved the class and studied hard, but my competitive spirit was dampened when I earned only a B, while Sister Amata received an A. Yet being at U.S.F. that spring, my first time on a real college campus was a great joy. I loved my classes and the freedom away from the convent. In June our spring classes ended, but we continued to live at the motherhouse during summer and continue our education at U.S.F.

As summer session began, I wondered if Sister Maureen would be taking any classes at the University of San Franciso. After the first week, I was in the library at the card catalogue and was startled when I glanced up and looked straight into her blue eyes as she stood on the opposite side of the catalogue. It was forbidden for us Junior professed sisters to speak to the final professed sisters, yet when she saw me, she exclaimed, "Judy!" She didn't even use my nun's name. We whispered by the catalog for only a few minutes, but I felt as if I was being tossed high by a wave, backwards in time. Suddenly I was an adoring adolescent again. That night at the examination of conscience at night prayers I tried to get hold of my emotions. I noted in my exam book that I must exercise restraint. Yet every day I was on the alert, hoping I might see her. When I did see her, we spoke only a few words, but our eyes spoke volumes. I ached to follow her, to find a place where we could catch up on our time apart, but we both exercised control.

Then came the Fourth of July film. As a treat for the Sisters that were taking classes on campus, the Jesuits ran a movie in the old auditorium. I was down in the front, socializing with the other Junior Sisters before we went to our seats. I glanced up and saw Sister Maureen in the doorway of the balcony. Without any hesitation, I raced up the stairs to be at her side.

"Hi Maureen", I whispered. "I'm loving my classes here. How is it going for you?" It didn't matter what either of us said, we really were communicating with our eyes, our smiles. As we stood there, I realized she still had a passion for me. I was short of breath and worried that someone would report me for being with her, yet I couldn't go back downstairs as I should have to sit with my group. The auditorium darkened, the film began. Jimmy Stewart was on screen in *The Man Who Knew Too Much*. Finally, in the dark, we stumbled to seats together. When something in the film amused her, she gave out that high braying un-nun like laugh and slapped my knee in that old familiar way. "Did you catch that, Judy? I mean Theo?"

"Shhh," whispered a nun of another order. We grinned at each other like silly schoolgirls. Partway through the movie, while Doris Day sang on 'Que Sera, Sera,' our knees touched and we squeezed hands in the folds of our habits. I exhaled deeply. My old feelings for her rose to the surface, and in the joy of touching her again, nothing else mattered.

At night prayers' Examination of Conscience, I acknowledged my fall. I noted in my Exam book: *The demons have been uncovered. Jesus, help me!*

Yet she and I found several occasions to have conversations in nooks in the large university library. She seemed to enjoy our conversations as much as I did. Each time I spoke with her, I noted my failure in my Exam book at evening prayers, but I could not let go of her.

An unusual event occurred early that summer. Sister Thaddeus called us into our juniorate room on a Saturday morning and said she had a surprise. We were all going to learn folk dancing. One of the professed sisters had relatives who taught folk dancing professionally and they proposed teaching us nuns to dance for our recreation and exercise. Sister Thaddeus agreed and said it would make us more graceful in our movements. Every Sunday afternoon for the rest of summer we junior sisters marched in pairs across the garden to the high school gym and formed a huge circle. Soon Mr. and Mrs. Patton would put on a record and we learned to twirl, doesy-doe, spin, sashay, brush, pivot and more. The gym floor creaked under the bodies with twirling veils and habits. Some sisters loved it, others tolerated it, and a few hated it. I partnered with Sister Sean, my friend from the novitiate who hated it and muttered hysterical complaints under her breath. I, however, loved it.

When summer school classes were over we eight would receive our first Missions. Finally, we were summoned to the community room where sat in rank in two lines facing each other. The superior of the motherhouse would deliver to each of us a white envelope that contained God's will for the coming year. When my name was called, I knelt, received the envelope and followed other sisters to the chapel to discover my fate. At my stall, I read:

Dear Sister,

It is God's Will that you teach first grade at St. Anne's Elementary School, San Francisco for the school year 1958-59. God bless you, Sister.

Oh dear God, after all the classes in philosophy and logic at U.S.F., why was assigned to teach first grade? No, it couldn't be right! I was terrified of little children and had no idea how to speak to them. How could I possibly handle this Mission? Looking up at the crucifix hanging above the altar I prayed: *Dear Jesus, give me the grace to do Your Will. I imagine You think my pride needs taming after philosophy and logic classes where I tried to excel. I know I'm going to need an abundance of grace for this Mission.*

I wondered about Sister Maureen's Mission and imagined she'd return to St. Joseph's, our Berkeley high school, where she was teaching biology. I knew we'd never assigned to the same convent, but now that we were both at schools in the Bay Area, I hoped we might see each other at community gatherings

PART THREE

CHAPTER THIRTEEN

———∾∾———

FIRST MISSION
SAINT ANNE'S OF THE SUNSET
SAN FRANCISCO 1958

SAINT ANNE'S WAS a well-established elementary school in San Francisco's Inner Sunset district where the parish was led by the colorful Monsignor Moriarty who took great pride in the parish's annual celebration of Saint Anne's feast day with a nine-day novena in July. This included a parade with students and teachers marching around the parish complex with a full brass band. This July we young nuns reluctantly had to participate. We followed the band, led by the Monsignor who waved to the parishioners who lined the sidewalk, while we held tight to our veils and stiff white guimpes as the day was foggy and windy, typical for San Francisco summers. We hated being in the parade as it made us feel like we were on display while we were blown apart by the wind. Now in September I'd be teaching in this very parish.

Most of the sisters at Saint Anne's elementary school had taught there for years. Only in the lower grades were new sisters assigned. However, this year the position of Superior/Principal was newly appointed, a conservative high school teacher. Four of us newcomers were juniors--we hadn't taken final vows. The older sisters were set in their ways and had peculiarities and penchants that the Superior felt should not be imitated and she did her best to shield us from them. One was their habit of watching T.V. sit-coms in the community room in the evenings, a practice unheard of in the motherhouse. To shelter us from this scene, the Superior would send us young sisters to our cells soon after dinner, telling us to use the time for class preparations. I often read poetry that had nothing to do with my lessons, but was a passion of mine. It was my TV.

I inhaled deeply as I entered my first classroom. No help was offered me to get ready to teach my fifty first graders. The classrooms had been painted during the summer so all the school supplies were stored in the basement of the convent. The other first grade teacher, Sister de Salle, who was so humorous as a novice, beat me to the basement and selected the most desirable supplies for her class, leaving me with the remainders. It was a difficult not to be angry with her.

I also had the challenge of decorating the bulletin boards in my classroom. Since I was artistic this was a challenge I'd enjoy. I made a jolly clown, holding balloons, each a different color with the color name on each balloon. I put it up on the largest bulletin board at the front of the class. When the Superior, a reserved woman, came in the next day, she called me over.

"Sister, I'm sorry, but I can't let you have that clown on the bulletin board. It will excite the children. They are only first graders, easily stimulated, and I want order in here."

"Yes, Sister Superior, I'll remove it," I said, trying to keep my disappointment out of my response. I put up printed words on colored paper and saved the clown for another time.

Luckily, my fifty had attended kindergarten at this school and they understood the basics, lining up, raising their hands, how to play and share at recess, how to find the bathrooms. Most were from well-educated middle class families and learned quickly. They were like the children I went to school with in my Richmond district school. They were delightful and funny and smart. I liked them immediately.

I xeroxed endless worksheets and did my best to teach them to read and do basic math, but my favorite part of the week was our art lesson and I praised the students for imaginative work. One young boy did such a wonderful rendition of Ichabod Crane that I secured a spot in the library to display his work for all the school to enjoy. Since I had no experience on how to conduct a class, I was sometimes unorthodox in my ways. One little boy always lagged behind at recess for a few more minutes of play, instead of lining up. One day I decided to pull a prank to teach him to come in on time. All the children had come into the classroom except Billy. I instructed everyone to get under his or her desks; then I held the door closed tightly, ducking down low. When Billy got to the door, he couldn't open it. When he peered in the window of the door, it appeared the classroom was empty. He burst into tears. The class gave out a collective sympathetic sigh. I opened the door and the whole class emitted a cheer for him but I hoped this would make him to come in on time.

In December, when our own Supervisor of schools, Sister Brian, visited my classroom, I was happy that she was taken with the originality of my advent display. I'd put up a special bulletin board that ran the length of the classroom above the blackboards on two sides of the room. There was a wonderful blue sky and clouds and then I added cutouts of Mary and Joseph with their donkey that I moved incrementally forward each day in their trek from Nazareth to Bethlehem. Sister Brian was the nun who started our mission in Albuquerque, where Maureen had been sent the year I entered the convent. She said my display reminded her of the bright blue skies of New Mexico. I was glad that she shared her enthusiasm with my conservative principal.

Another afternoon, the young assistant priest, Father Shanahan, stopped me as I made my way across the schoolyard toward the convent. As soon as Sister Superior noticed him talking to me, she rushed to join us. He said he had visited the family of one of my first graders, a lovely blond girl. She had told him, Sister said 'Mary and Joseph are on their way to Bethlehem and Baby Jesus is coming soon.'

"Well, Sister, you've got your first graders converted. Sister says it and its gospel! You're right up there with the Holy Trinity, Sister Theophane," he laughed. I blushed but I felt grateful to him as it was rare to receive compliments.

In an unusual move after Christmas, the other first grade teacher, Sister de Salle, was replaced with an experienced teacher, Sister Kerry. She was a tall, smiling nun who gratefully taught me how to bring organization to my class. Prior to her instruction, I had let all the children go into the coatroom at the same time. Most of the little jackets and sweaters were on the floor, lunchboxes everywhere. From her, I learned to call row by row, to stand at one door to supervise the activity in the coatroom and the classroom. I was shown how to set up three reading groups and to bring them together around my desk to read in small groups. It made my teaching and classroom organization far more effective. I was so grateful to her generous ways.

In this convent, one of the older nuns was particularly flamboyant. Sister Clarinda was a wiry, thin woman with a face dominated by black brows and piercing dark eyes. She was originally from Belgium and had an accent and a trigger temper. She'd explode at the least provocation, anytime, anywhere; she loved attention. I'd received a sketchbook as a gift from Mom and the superior gave me permission to keep it. One day at recreation, I made a sketch of this nun. To my surprise, she was delighted with it and of course, I gave it to her. After that she was pleasant to me, almost flirtatious. For me, lonely and new to the convent, I was thrilled with her attention.

One day she asked the Superior if she could go to the de Young museum in Golden Gate Park to visit the Van Gogh exhibit and take me as her partner. It was a special outing. As we walked through the park, she prattled on about her early life and acted as if Van Gogh was practically from her 'neighborhood.' The paintings were stunning, though she insisted on making distracting comments thoughout the exhibit. It was a wonderful day; indeed, she could be charming. Later I wrote her a note, thanking and praising her and slipped it under her cell door. However, the note seemed too familiar to her. She was off to the Superior with the note, claiming I was treating her with too much intimacy for a young nun. The Superior called me to her office for a reprimand. I was deeply disgraced. I believe it surprised the Superior that anyone would be fond of this problematic nun, but the rest of the year was difficult for me as she became abusive and sarcastic in her remarks to me.

In the meantime, the ailing Mother General died. Mother Colette, my former Mistress of Novices, was elected to complete her term. In that capacity in late spring, she visited all the convents. When she came to our convent and I had my private visit with her, as did each nun, I asked her to give me a change of Mission. I had upset the entrenched sister and living here with her was now difficult. Mother spoke more kindly than I expected. She said she would keep my request in mind. I was glad to see the school year end and return to live at the motherhouse and take another summer of classes at the University of San Francisco.

CHAPTER FOURTEEN

EAST LOS ANGELES
AUGUST 1959

THE DAY OF the Missions, the most long-awaited day of the year, finally arrived. In our twenty-two convents, at the same hour, the sisters would receive their Missions for the coming year from the hand of the superior At the motherhouse, Mother Colette would distribute the envelopes. The tension was palpable as we sat in rank in the community room in rows of chairs, facing each other. When my name was called, I knelt at Mother's side and with a trembling hand took the small, white envelope that contained God's Will for me. I followed other sisters to the chapel to discover my fate. At my stall, I tore open the envelope.

Dear Sister,
    It is God's Will that you teach first grade at our Lady of Lourdes, Los Angeles for the school year 1959-60. God bless you, Sister.
    Mother Mary Colette

This was a real Mission! I was excited but very nervous. I had never lived anywhere but the Bay Area. Looking up at the crucifix above the altar I prayed:

Dear Jesus, Thank you for this real Mission. Give me the grace to do Your Will. Stand by my side as I do Your work.

Mom was not going to be happy I was going such a distance, but I felt it was a challenge. I wondered about Sister Maureen's Mission. It was likely she would return to teach biology at Saint Joseph's, our Berkeley high school. I would be far away and wouldn't see her 'til next summer. That was best. I returned to the community room and when the envelopes had all been distributed, Mother broke the silence with a warm greeting,

"Good Afternoon, Mother," we answered in chorus and jumped up and began inquiring where God was sending each of us. Some sisters held back tears as they discovered they were not returning to a favorite convent. I sidled up to my friend, Sister Dominic, who was a year ahead of me.

"Lourdes!" I said.

"Welcome. This is great! You'll love it." In one of her rare displays of emotion, she hugged me. "The Superior is a kick, not like you know who." She gave a slight turn of her head toward Mother Colette.

Two other nuns, a few years ahead of me, who were also returning to Our Lady of Lourdes came over and we chattered and laughed. I was glad I was going to a place with some younger nuns. Mother mingled, glad to see smiles about her choices. All summer she'd been at work on this plan trying to get the right mix at each convent--strong principals who could deal with difficult pastors, a mix of old and young, excellent teachers and those with lesser skills, one or two sisters who could drive. Every convent had to have someone to take the sisters to doctor's appointments and grocery shopping. I was proud to be one of the few who had a driver's license. When she came to our group, I grinned and said, "Thank you so much, Mother."

With a smile, she replied softly "I'm sure you'll do very well at Our Lady of Lourdes."

Too soon the forty tolls began. The voices hushed and we lined up in rank in the corridor, pulling on our long sleeves, heads bowed and slowly moved into the Chapel to recite the Office Hours of Matins, Lauds and Vespers. I tried to pray, but I was distracted. Could I really handle East L.A where the population was nearly entirely Hispanic? Yet, this Mission could be an adventure and an education, if only God would give me the grace to teach these little ones.

Sunday, August 9th, was my last visit with my family before I left for L.A. Mom, well dressed as always, was followed by my brother, who'd just finished his senior year at St. Ignatius College Prep High School and was now looking for a job, and my sister, Ellen, who was starting her last year at Presentation High. She was far more fun loving than me. She was tall and attractive and fortunately didn't have to wear glasses. She'd have boyfriends. She made me smile when she told me she was thinking of going to modeling school. We sat on overstuffed chairs in one corner of the large parlor in the Mother House and chatted. Mom wasn't happy to learn that I was leaving the Bay Area but she imagined the Mission to L.A. as a promotion. She had recently been promoted from teaching fourth grade to assistant principal in a more disadvantaged area near Chinatown. She loved her job. However, Steve and Ellen, who thought it quite tedious to sit through the two hours each month on Visiting Sunday, were delighted I had a Mission. They talked about how they'd come to L.A. to visit and how they'd like to see Hollywood. Mom and I held back tears as we said good-by, giving each other a long embrace. I'd miss seeing her every month and hearing stories of her new job. As she got to the front door she advised me, "You just get in there and be a fine professional teacher, Judy. We'll get down to see you." Then she turned quickly, took Ellen's hand and went down the wide steps.

Two weeks later I was waiting with the thin Sister Dominic and the heavy Sister Zita at the Los Angeles airport to be picked up by sisters from Our Lady of Lourdes. Soon our black suitcases were in the trunk and we three were tucked in the back seat with me in the middle. The sky was ochre under the blanket of smog and a trickle of sweat ran down my back under my serge habit. I wanted to ask questions but after the Litany of the Blessed Virgin we rode in mandatory silence. We passed fine homes with palm trees and manicured lawns but now came endless rows of shabby pastel houses, punctuated with an occasional tall skinny palm. Then I saw it--the white stucco convent with its red-tiled roof, the finest structure in the neighborhood. Adjacent to it, rose the lofty bell tower and spacious white stucco church, Our Lady of Lourdes, my new home.

As I pulled my suitcase from the trunk, a battered black Ford drove by leaving a trail of grey exhaust and loud Latin music hanging in the air. New songs in a strange land. As I moved toward the steps I noticed something scrawled in dripping red paint on the fence between the school and the convent, Little Valley Termites rule. My face must have reflected my concern because Sister Dominic, laughed and said, "That's just a little gang staking out their territory."

Sister Zita chimed in, pointing to the alleyway behind the convent. "Oh, there was a murder down there last spring but nothing to worry about. Everyone loves the nuns." This was indeed a Mission.

Sister Superior, herself, opened the door and waved us in. "Don't just stand there. Come in out of the heat. You'll fry like eggs." She was an energetic Irish woman with a broad freckled face and I could easily imagine a mop of red hair under her veil. Only five foot, one, she was the shortest among us, though she wore oxfords with higher-than-regulation heels and the sheerest of stockings. In the cool interior,

Sister Superior parceled out quick embraces, instead of the traditional community greeting of cheek to cheek.

"Welcome, welcome, Sister Theophane," she clucked as she gave me a quick hug. I followed her through the convent as she babbled information so quickly that I only grasped half of what she said. "Workroom here, ditto machine there, at the end of hall, the chapel."

Looking out the windows, I saw the convent was built around a lovely courtyard with remarkable flowers that I couldn't yet name. Ascending the stairs, she said, "Right here, Sister Theophane, this is your cell."

She left me standing by the open door, holding my suitcase. The cell was simple, furnished with bed, bureau, desk and chair. The window looked out to the street and during many nights, I'd hear gunning motors, Latin music and an occasional gun shot, reminding me I was in a new land. Yet the most amazing feature was a small bathroom with a tub all to myself, luxurious after the shared accommodations of the motherhouse and the novitiate.

The next morning Sister Superior walked me over to the school to show me my classroom. Chatting non-stop, she nearly pranced across the hot asphalt. The schoolyard was bleak without a trace of greenery and the one story elementary school was old and dingy. My classroom was the last one in the long row of low-ceilinged rooms. A blast of heat struck me as Sister Superior opened the door. The ancient desks were on wooden runners, three in a set attached to each other with a useless ink holes in the corners. They'd been pushed to one side to allow for polishing of the floors. At least the linoleum floor was shiny.

"Well Sister, I'll leave you to get started. The books are all packed away in the back closet."

I sat down at the teacher's desk and studied my class list. Sixty children! Dear God, how will I manage? No aides, no mother's helpers. This will be a challenge. I started shoving the desks into rows and began thinking of ideas to enliven the room with colorful displays on the bulletin boards. Sister Zita, who had second grade in the next room, stuck her head in and in her booming voice said, "Doing all right? Let me know if you need any more "shalk" or "shairs."

"What are shalk and shairs?"

"You know, shalk, she made as if to write on the black board, and shairs." She pointed to the teacher's chair at the desk. "That's the way the kids say it, Shalk and shairs and shickens." She flapped her arms. "And one more thing, don't smile 'til after Christmas. You've got to keep order."

Her remarks only added to my anxiety, but by noon I had the place in the semblance of a classroom and I returned to the cool, dark convent chapel for the prayer of the Angeles that we recited together at noon. Kneeling at a wooden stall in the soft light from the stained-glass windows, gazing at the crucifix above the tabernacle, I prayed: *Jesus, are You sure you got the white envelops right? You are going to give me the grace to do this job?* Then I recalled Mother Colette's words: Sister, God always gives the grace to do His Will, no matter how difficult it may appear. Was this really true?

Only old Irish Sister Peter, who'd taught the sixth grade here for years and Sister Laurentia, who was sinking into senility, came to the chapel. We three stood and recited the Angeles together. I was surprised that the others arrived only to go to the refectory for lunch.

The next few days were spent getting ready for the first day of school, unpacking books, pinning up lively decorations--a clown I'd made, holding balloons with letters on each spelling out its color. Around the top of the blackboard, I put up the alphabet, made cards with each child's name that went on the desks in alphabetical order. Of the sixty names, only one was non-Spanish sir-name.

The other first grade Sister was new to the school, but an experienced no-nonsese first grade teacher. She was short and with an intimidating manner. She decided the primers were too old and worn and then she made a huge fuss with Sister Superior about ordering the newest version. Sister Superior resisted, but the sister told Sister Superior that these disadvantaged children with poor English skills deserved the best. Reluctantly, Sister Superior gave in. No one even considered that a set be ordered for my class.

In the convent while I made lesson plans and dittoed worksheets, I'd hear laughter coming from other parts of the convent and know that Sister Superior was in the Community room, telling another funny story. Silence was the rule in the novitiate and Motherhouse and I wondered how she'd made it though her novitiate with that constant gift of gab. But then, she didn't have Mother Colette as novice mistress, but the easy-going Sister Gertrude that Mother Colette had replaced.

Suddenly, I longed to be back at the University with the wonderful discussions we'd had in Logic and Philosophy classes. With a smile I thought of my favorite professor, the white haired, Mr. Brusher. I'd often sketched his portrait in my notebook. On the day of our final exams, I'd slipped one of my pencil sketches into my Blue Book when I turned it in. I wondered if he liked it. Already, I was looking forward to returning to university classes next summer. I felt the same loneliness as in the first weeks in the novitiate. I wished I could talk with Maureen but she was teaching biology in our Berkeley high school. I wondered if she was finding other students to adore her.

On Monday morning, a few days before my twenty-second birthday, I crossed the schoolyard where it was already warm at eight-thirty. As the first graders streamed in, I tried to look welcoming, rather than terrified. The boys' grey uniforms made them look like five-year-old prisoners; the girls faired better with white blouses and plaid jumpers. Shyly, they moved into the classroom while the parents gazed at me anxiously with hope in their eyes.

Over and over I said, "Welcome," but I recalled only a few words from my Spanish class. With hand shaking and smiling, I tried to make the parents feel as ease. They were the lucky ones who'd had their child accepted into the only Catholic school in this neighborhood. As they looked at me, I felt the burden of their dreams for their children. I'd very much need God's grace to fulfill their aspirations. Cautiously, the children's brown eyes met my blue ones, staring at me like some mysterious Madonna who'd escaped her pedestal.

Unfamiliar names rang out in the airless classroom: Gilbert Sauceda, Maria Salizar, Miguel Ruiz, Roberto Gonzalez, Ricardo Magallenes, Maria Elena Garcia. As I was seating the children alphabetically, I had to interrupt the roll call several times to chase after little Alberto. He fled the classroom every time I took my eyes off him and ran into the arms of his grandfather who sat in the schoolyard on the bench under my classroom windows. I soon realized that this new teacher wasn't to be trusted with his precious grandchild.

"Boys and girls, sit down, sienta-se," I repeated over and over at the moving sea of five-year-old bodies. I feared Sister Superior, who was also principal, would descend upon this uncontrollable scene and realize I was unfit for this assignment. Through the vent from the second grade room, I heard Sister's Zita's booming voice organizing her class. I recalled her advice: Be sure to keep them in the room or you'll hear it from Sister Superior. Also: wear a scowl and don't smile till after Christmas.

As squirrelly Alberto was making his fifth dash for freedom, Sister Superior appeared at my door. Fortunately, she understood the problem was with *el abuelo*, the grandfather. Out she went to the schoolyard, took Alberto under her arm, and escorted grandpa out of the schoolyard.

When all sixty were finally seated, I introduced myself, slowly saying my name and pointing to it on the blackboard: *Sister Mary Theophane.* However that year no child or parent ever called me anything but 'S'ter.' We stood and slowly made the Sign of the Cross, "In the Name of the Father and of the Son and of the Holy Ghost. Amen."

And so began the long school year. It was weeks before Alberto stopped running from the room each morning. Rudy threw himself on the floor in a tantrum whenever I expected him to do his work. Michael poked everyone around him with a pencil that he was constantly sharpening. Danny still pouted at the smallest slight. Handsome Eduardo was often absent as his mother was grooming him to be a child star. Still lessons needed to be taught.

At midmorning, I was grateful it was time for recess and in the hallway I attempted to get the boys in one line with a parallel line for the girls. Few had been to kindergarten so the concept of lining-up was unfamiliar. We marched down the hall, an unsteady mob, moving toward the bathrooms. Just as I'd sent them into the lavatories, Sister Superior appeared. "Everything under control, Sister?" she asked, as she watched the last of the girls straggle into the bathroom.

"Oh yes, Sister Superior," I lied.

"Ah, Sister, you've sent all the girls into that lavatory?"

"Yes, Sister Superior."

She burst out laughing, as she watched the boys coming out of the other bathroom, struggling, needing help with the new zippers in their uniform pants.

"Sister, dear, you've sent the girls into the boys' bathroom."

As confusion reigned, I tried to hide my own embarrassment by announcing, "Boys and girls, follow me." Like a Piped Piper, I led them into the fierce sunlight of the playground. To my surprise, the little girls surrounded me, grabbing handfuls of my serge habit, clutching my large rosary that dangled from my waist, others gripping the tip of the back of my veil. I could scarcely move. The children at St. Anne's in San Franciso never acted like this. I surveyed the the crowd of first and second graders in grey uniforms, moving around the black asphalt, surrounded by a chain link fence. It had the feeling of a prison yard, rather than a schoolyard. Some of my boys had climbed on the jungle gym, pushing and screaming, "S'ter, look at me," as they fought each other to the top.

"Hey, S'ter, look. I'm the highest," yelled Gilbert. In the crush of bodies, Gilbert fell off the structure and cut his elbow and was bleeding all over his new, grey shirt. Sister Superior came striding toward the scene and led away the injured Gilbert, dabbing at his bloody arm with her white handkerchief, calling over her shoulder, "Five more minutes, and you can take them inside."

In the midst of this confusion, trapped under this smoggy, yellow sky, with sweat pouring down my back, I wanted to dash back to the convent chapel. I needed urgently to speak to Jesus: *Where is that grace You promised? I need it this very minute. Is it possible you got those white envelopes switched? I'm mean, are You noticing, I'm really in trouble here?*

By three o'clock dismissal, I was exhausted and anxious to escort my students into the arms of waiting parents or older siblings. When I returned to the classroom, I found one little boy still at his desk, head down on his arm, sobbing.

I couldn't understand his mumbled response. I bent over and asked again, "Danny, what's wrong?" With his lisp, I still couldn't grasp his problem. Then, quite irritated, he yelled something about a lion. I leaned closer, putting my hand on his shoulder, my head near his mouth.

He was furious that I couldn't understand him and he shouted at me, "You tweat me like a lion! All day when I try to come up to you, you shout, sit down, go back! You act like a lion tamer." Then he broke into sobs. "I can't even get near you."

"Forgive me, Danny, I'm really sorry." I knelt next to him, put my arm around him. I continued to comfort him as we walked to the door together. Soon I'd realize that this sensitive, lisping child, the oldest of nine, needed more of my kindness than the others might.

Yet, others needed my attention also. It was weeks before Alberto stopped running from the room; Rudy threw himself on the floor in a tantrum whenever I expected him to do his work; Michael poked everyone around him with a pencil that he was constantly sharpening; Danny still pouted at the smallest slight; Handsome Eduardo was often absent as his mother was grooming him to be a child star.

Still lessons needed to be taught. I began with numbers, counting, and simple addition. The boys had a surprising aptitude for math, quickly excelling the girls, calling out the answer to sums on the blackboard with amazing speed. Reading the antics of Dick and Jane and Spot, the dog in the old primers, held little appeal. So after a page of reading, I'd have one tell a story of his or her pet and I tried to keep it lively.

One of the favorite events of the week was Show and Tell. On this particular day I'd agreed to let the shyest girl in the class bring her pet to school. Maria Elena came in, her scrubbed face beaming as her father followed her, holding a large scarlet blanket. Suddenly at the side of my desk, he threw open the red blanket and a huge iguana, like a small dinosaur, blinked its yellow eyes and sent out a flicking tongue.

For a moment this shy girl was a star of the class as she announced to the children, "This is my pet and his name is the Jose, after Jesus's father."

Though I was terrified of this thing out of the jungle, the children excitedly gathered around the iguana. I didn't let the father take one step away from the animal who was still flicking its tongue at us. I couldn't wait for Show and Tell to end.

The heat was unbearable until December. We taught with the doors and windows open. After lunch, it was easily 100' in the classroom that smelled of sweat and tortillas and bananas. Perspiration streamed down under my habit. I had the children put their sweaty heads on their desks for rest time. I walked between the aisles, scowling, to keep order, while I passed out the lined paper and the fat pencils to begin printing the alphabet that was printed on cards above the blackboard. I noticed so many peeking up at me with adoring, pleading eyes, hoping for my approval. It was then that I ignored Sister Zita's admonition not to smile till after Christmas and I broke out in a big grin, realizing that we'd all have to work together to make it through, one day at a time.

After school, we sisters hurried to the convent community room, the only room with air conditioning and sat at long tables correcting papers and working on lesson plans. Often Sister Superior, sitting at the head of the table, broke the quiet with some anecdote that occurred during the day, racing through the account with snorts of laughter and so fast that it was difficult to grasp the details. This wasn't recreation hour and she made it difficult to concentrate on lesson plans for the next day. Yet Sister Superior's moods were as unpredictable as summer storms. Some days she'd start on a rant about the pastor. "He's got to stop interfering in my school," she'd declare. "None of those priests know anything about education."

On another day she'd say, cheerfully, "It's just too hot. Let's all go in the refectory and have ice cream." Then the sister in charge of the kitchen would race ahead to the freezer, hoping she'd bought ice cream that week. But on the days when she was quieter than usual, I knew to beware. Whoever approached her would be subject to a remark that would leave the sister stunned. When Sister Zita asked her a question, she only replied, "Sister, I heard you shouting all the way down in my office. What's the matter with you? Don't you ever have control of your class?"

The first or second week of school Sister Superior decreed the monster heat as she called it, would be with us 'til Christmas.

"Sisters, I've decided that we'll recite the Office in the community room with the air conditioning." In her brogue old Sister Peter protested with little bleats, "No, no, Sister Superior, in the chapel."

"Now Sister Peter, don't give me that. You've done your purgatory all day in the classroom."

The Office--the recitation of the Hours of Matins, Lauds --was recited at five o'clock in the chapel in all our convents. This was a monastic ritual that required bowing, kneeling and sitting. I knew that Mother Colette would say that we should pray in the chapel and offer up the discomfort. Now it would seem strange, bowing and kneeling to an air conditioner, instead of the crucifix.

In the refectory, the monastic tables were arranged in U-shape with Sister Superior presiding at the head table, the center of the U. At the most flimsy excuse, Sister Superior would tinkle the bell after the Grace and begin a 'talking meal,' instead of listening to the spiritual reading that accompanied most convent meals. It was a rule that at each meal, a sister should make some contribution to the conversation that was directed solely to Sister Superior.

As the youngest, I sat at the end of the refectory where I found it difficult to make a contribution, to address the Superior who sat at the far end of the refectory at a head table. Over and over the Sisters related tales from their classrooms, stories of the parishioners, and anecdotes from last year. I'd open my mouth but nothing of merit came out. Could I say I felt bad because Danny called me a lion tamer or that the heat was unbearable or that last night I was startled and screamed when a cockroach shot out of the faucet while I was in the bathtub? Could I complain that the seventh grade teacher was always using the Xerox machine and I couldn't get copies made for my class?

In the refectory, I was seated in rank next to Sister Zita, who was a year older than me, a clumsy, heavy woman with a booming voice and a matching appetite. Too often she related the story of the first time she read aloud in the huge motherhouse refectory. Afterward Sister Superior told her to turn down the microphone. "But," she'd protested, "it wasn't on." Most of the sisters obliged her with a laugh.

The platters of food that started with Sister Superior would arrive scraped clean by Sister Zita who, absentmindedly, handed me the empty platter. She didn't seem to notice or she forgot our rule that she was to call the attention of the Sister Server to the empty dish. One couldn't ask for food for oneself. So I often sat silent and starving. Finally, I remarked to her, "Did you expect me to eat the plate, dear Sister?" Later I made remorseful entries in my Examination of Conscience binder about my rudeness.

Soon the repetition of anecdotes of the summer and stories of last year grew stale and boring. Still Sister Superior, who was quite a talker herself, dawdled over coffee, dragging out each dinner endlessly while I was anxious to get to my chores—the breakfast things set out, lessons to be planned, worksheets to be dittoed before night prayers. I prayed for silent meals.

At Sunday Mass in the parish church, where the statues of the Virgin, Saint Joseph and the other saints had real hair and intensely painted features, we nuns each knelt with our own large class. While old women edged up the aisles on their knees, clutching rosaries, murmuring soft Aves, we kept the restless children in line with fierce looks and whispered threats. I noticed that many children kissed their thumb after making the Sign of the Cross and the parishioners did the same. In response to my query, Sister Succorra told me that this custom was a holdover from the time of religious persecution in Mexico when all crucifixes were destroyed; the faithful Christians made a cross with their thumb over their forefinger and kissed it after making the Sign of the Cross. I was indeed in a new country.

Each convent was assigned at least one sister with a driver's license, and here, I was the designated driver. Often I'd hurry from school to take different Sisters to doctors or dentists appointments. Sister

Superior would carefully explain the routes in L.A. and I was always relieved when I successfully completed the mission. One of my recurring duties was to take Sister Agnes, who managed the kitchen, to do the weekly food shopping. Every Friday after school, I met her in the kitchen along with Mrs. Hernandez, a cheerful woman who cooked for us five nights a week. Over six feet tall, Sister Agnes towered over my five foot, four frame and the diminutive Mrs. Hernandez. Trying to remember any last additions, Sister would peer at her list through her thick glasses, even thicker than mine. She would check again with Mrs. Hernandez and then announce, "Theophane, let's go!" At school and in the convent, Sister Agnes, who taught seventh grade, was taciturn, scholarly and meditative but to this job, she brought a childlike exuberance.

In the car as I was pinning my veil back behind my head for clearer vision, she'd begin the Litany of the Blessed Virgin-" Tower of Ivory, House of Gold, Refuge of sinners." After each title of Our Lady, I answered as in one word, 'Prayforus.' By the time we finished the Litany, we would have arrived at Albertson's Supermarket at the edge of our parish. Following her long strides down the aisles, I wheeled the grocery cart as she efficiently pulled items from the shelf, muttering and chortling to herself.

"Monday, Lima beans. They won't like that." In would go two cans of lima beans. "Applesauce for breakfast. Thank God we finally finished those Kadota figs. For Friday--enchiladas. They love them." In would go two cans of Las Palmas hot sauce and packs of tortillas. and a large pack of hamburger.

"Let's try Rice-a-Roni next week. What flavor what do you like?"

Before I could get close enough to see the choices, she'd tossed in a couple of boxes. "I bet you like carrots or should we have broccoli?" She'd already be choosing the vegetables, peering through her thick glasses at the prices. "Oh, look at that eggplant. I love it, but no one else would eat it and Mrs. Hernandez wouldn't know how to cook it. Not carrots again. Let's have zucchini and frozen peas. Theophane, would you run back to the freezer and get two packages of frozen peas."

Then with a huge grin, she'd declare, "Theophane, let's see what they have at Van de Kamp's." As I wheeled the loaded cart toward the blue windmill display with the baked goods, Sister Agnes would already be at the counter. "Oh, we have a feast day. Shall we have a yummy chocolate cake or lemon one?" Reaching into the display, she picked a boxed chocolate cake. "Now what about Sunday?" She ordered six bear claws and several strawberry Danish from the woman behind the counter. She clearly savored the power of these decisions. I, myself, hadn't been to a supermarket in years and I was content to take in the sights and smells and leave the choices to her. At checkout, she'd watch the checker to make sure each item was rung up correctly and then pull out the checkbook and her black fountain pen from the depths of her pocket. She'd fill in the exact amount on the check that was previously signed by Sister Superior.

On the way home, oblivious to the rule of silence, Sister Agnes pondered aloud how sad it was that the students wrote and spoke such poor English; what a shame it was none of us, other than Sister Succorra, spoke Spanish; how difficult it was to teach in such heat. Still, she loved this Mission and wouldn't want to be anywhere else.

At the convent I helped her carry the groceries to the pantry. She began conversing with the tiny Mrs. Hernandez, discussing the week's menu. I scurried off, past the empty chapel, to recite the Office with the Sisters in the Community Room. It was unlikely I'd speak with Sister Agnes again until next Friday, but I loved our outings as it was interesting to see real people out shopping.

Sister Succorra was kind and thoughtful as well as funny. Often she asked me if I needed help with small things, especially when it was my turn to cook dinner on the weekend. I began to wish that she and I could be special friends. I felt I was becoming dependent on her. Once when Sister Succorra and I were both working in the sewing room, mending our habits, I blurted out, "Sister, I so wish we could be really good friends, me being new here and all."

Gently she replied, "Theophane, we were both trained by Mother Colette. Sometimes I feel like she's still watching me. Mother often said having a special friend was a sin against charity, as it excluded others. You know she taught us to treat every sister the same. I feel bound to try to live up to the things she taught us, don't you?"

I was embarrassed I'd spoken but tempted to reply: Don't you notice how Sister Superior treats you as special?

In time, it became apparent that Sister Superior had a favorite among the faculty. Yet Our Rule stated: *A Superior must be distinguished for her virtues and for her fidelity to the obligations of the religious life.* In another chapter it said: *the Sisters shall love one another equally.* The object of her favor was Sister Succorra, a nun of Mexican-American descent, who had attended this school as a youngster and the only one among us who spoke fluent Spanish. Sister Superior often called on her to be a translator in the dealings of school and parish. I'd see them laughing and talking in the parlor or chatting together at recess. It was easy to understand why Sister Superior liked her. Everyone did. She was a stocky nun, who carried herself with unusual dignity and often poked fun at herself about her weight. She had wonderful expressive dark eyes and her sense of humor often provided the only relief at our dull dinners. She taught the eighth grade and was the only one who could handle the schoolyard fights. At dinner she'd relate tales of her day.

"Sister Superior, today I made Spike Rodriguez and Rudy Lopez kiss and make-up in the school yard. You should've seen the girls screaming."

"Oh, Sister, you didn't?" Sister Superior replied gleefully.

"I sure did. I'd warned them this punishment after their last fight."

I was so grateful that dinners were enlivened with her stories. This Mission was far more difficult than I'd imagined; the convent life was a round of boring dinners, petty arguments and hidden jealousies. Yet, I was not without blame. Recently I'd had a nasty disagreement with another sister over who would use the three dimensional gold letters on their bulletin board during the Open House for the parents. She and I were both artistic and knew the gold letters made class displays more attractive and there weren't enough in the gold set for both of us. As we each reached the closet where they were stored at the same moment, I happened to get my hands on the box first. Tall and imposing she asked, "Are you going to use all of those, Sister?"

Of course, I wanted them all and I took the box out and made as if to leave. She called after me. "Come right back here, Sister!" After some negotiation, we split the set, but with only half a set, they lost their effectiveness and there weren't enough vowels.

In time, we younger sisters discovered that the way to get a special treat, such as playing volleyball for recreation, was to get Sister Succorra to ask Sister Superior. When the date for the first school band concert grew near, we began to ask among ourselves: how could we get Sister Superior to let us attend? Four afternoons a week, the band practiced in the auditorium adjacent to the school and the Latin beat invaded even the sanctity of the chapel.

First, Sister Dominic made several overtures, but Sister Superior remained noncommittal. We decided Sister Succorra, Sister Superior's favorite, would have to ask, but she acted annoyed and wondered aloud why we wouldn't ask for ourselves. Naively, she said, "Sister Superior's no more responsive to me than to any of you." Yet at dinner on Friday night, she said, almost coyly, "Sister Superior, what time shall we be ready to go to the concert?"

"Who said we're going to the concert?" snorted Sister Superior. With raised eyebrows she looked round at us, as if she suspected a conspiracy. Yet at eight o'clock, Sister Superior led us out the gate and across the yard to the brightly lit auditorium. We sat at the rear, a black silent phalanx behind whispering parents in riot of colored cottons.

The lights dimmed; the spots highlighted the students as they sat behind their music stands dressed in newly pressed pink shirts and charcoal grey pants and skirts. Under the direction of the balding band teacher, Mr. Garcia, they began. Serious and proud, the boys caressed the brass mouthpieces with tender lips and poured out their souls in "Tijuana Swing" and "La Bamba" and other Latin tempos.

My feet began to move and my toes tapped in my square-toed oxfords. As the tempo increased, my body swayed slightly. When the boys stood tall with saxophones moaning, trumpets blaring, I closed my eyes. Inside me a woman, lean and bronze, began to click her heels. Her scarlet dress swirled, revealing firm thighs; her long hair fell over the low-cut dress, golden earrings flashed. She stamped her feet to the music. Suddenly, Mother Colette appeared, her eyes emanating blue-white light to the sound of dentist's drills whirring and drowning out the music. Mother's eyes became searchlights, dissolving everything; the gypsy woman evaporated.

I opened my eyes and sat up upright, gripping the cool metal of the folding chair. *Jesus, what was I imagining?* Yet, I didn't want the evening to end as I loved the Latin flavor that was rubbing against our tidy lives.

As many of us hadn't completed our college studies, the Dean of Studies sent correspondence courses for us to complete during the school year. One day after school, with a gleam in her eye, Sister Superior called the four of us youngest nuns to the Community room.

"Surprise from the Dean of Studies, " she announced, handing each of us a packet. "Now Sit down, sit down and open your packets." She watched while we opened the material. Sister Zita got a physics course that she hated; Sister Dominic, an advanced math course which she could handle easily; Sister Paulette, a geology course that she would enjoy. Then to my great surprise, I received a correspondence course in art: Basic Drawing and Painting, from the University of California. My hand went to my mouth to stifle a cry of joy. I knew it was Mother Colette, now the Mother General, who had influenced the Dean of Studies in my favor; otherwise I would've had geology or another science.

Since I never had family visits, this was a wonderful way to combat the loneliness of the weekends. I spent hours in my cell completing each assignment. It might be to draw and paint one's foot or a study of one's hands. I'd send the assignment off and anxiously await the next one which was returned with a grade and yet another assigment. One assignment was to paint a self-portrait in something that distorted one's image. I asked Sister Superior if I might borrow the tall coffee percolator from the special dining set that was reserved for priests or visitors. The resulting painting may have made the U.C. professor grin.

In my self-portrait, I elongated my face which was framed in the black and white of the habit and accentuated the thick lenses of my glasses. When he returned it with an A+, I was pleased.

After Mass one Sunday, Sister Superior who was impressed with my artistic talent, introduced me to the pastor, Father Lawrence. He was a handsome man, fortyish with a bit of grey hair and much admired for his sincere dedication to the parish. As soon as I was introduced as 'our Sister artist.' He immediately asked if I could do a painting of his church. This was a flattering, but unnerving request.

The next Saturday, I perched on a low stonewall across the street from the Church with my sketchbook. The Church was a beautiful white stucco Spanish style structure with a red tile roof, a striking bell tower and arched doors. Curious stares came from passer-bys who peeked over my shoulder as I made my sketches. From my drawings, I painted the church against an intense cobalt blue sky with billowing white clouds, ignoring the dense yellow smog. The Pastor was pleased with the result and had it framed and hung it behind his desk.

Then he made another request: Could I make a simple sketch that could be used for the weekly parish bulletin? Again, I went to work. This was an easier task. When Sister Superior delivered the finished work, she put it to immediate use as the heading in the weekly parish bulletin. This work brought me some respect among the Sisters, but to me, it seemed only by chance that the work turned out well. I was never confident I could repeat what I'd done.

One afternoon, I walked into the community room while Sister Superior was opening the mail. She began reading aloud sections of a letter from the motherhouse.

"Sister Agnes Ann is making a remarkable recovery after surgery, thanks be to God. Oh dear, Sister Euphemia fell and broke her hip and listen to this! Our dear Mother General, Mother Colette is celebrating the twenty-fifth anniversary of taking her vows. There'll be a grand celebration at the Motherhouse. All the sisters in the convents up north will attend the celebration Mass followed by a buffet luncheon in the gym. I bet every convent is making special things for this occasion."

She stopped, thought a minute, and then and gazed at us. "I think we need to make somethings too. Sister Helene, do you think you could make a set of thank-you cards with your fine calligraphy and Sister Dominic, would you knit a couple of baby jackets? Mother loves to gives those to our benefactors." Then, she looked at me. "Sister Theophane, could you possibly paint a nice landscape or two, something suitable for a doctor's office? She'd love that kind of gift."

Nervously, I nodded. Then she went back to the letter. "Uh, oh." Her voice dropped. Had someone had died? "Sister Paula won't be renewing her vows. What a shame!" Looking up at me she said almost with accusation, "Sister Theophane, isn't she one of your group?"

I nodded. A weighted silence spread over the room. One of my own was leaving. What terrible thing had my friend, Connie, now called Sister Paula, done? True, she was overweight and her habit was always spotted and her veil often crooked with a few stray hairs escaping her headgear, but those things weren't grounds for dismissal. She was very smart and most likely doing a fine job of teaching fourth grade. It was unthinkable that after only two years of teaching, she could be leaving of her own will. Our mothers were friends and I knew how disappointed and embarrassed her very Catholic mother would be. What shame would come with leaving, turning one's back on Jesus? I slipped out of the room and went to the chapel. I knelt at my stall in the gloom, craving more details. Could it be possible she was asking to leave? That would take great courage. My head began throbbing and it was impossible to think clearly or even to pray. Could it be possible I envied her?

After several days of depression, I tried to put the subject out of mind. I went to Sister Superior and told her I had to go to the nearest library to get some art books. With "How to Paint Watercolor Landscapes" and a new set of watercolors, I began to teach myself to paint landscapes. In time, I had four decent landscape paintings. When I showed them to Sister Superior, she was enthusiastic.

"Really good work, Sister. We'll send these to the motherhouse for Mother Colette's feast day." I left them on the community table for a couple of days and I was suddenly elevated to 'talented artist.' I felt this was undeserved but the attention delighted me.

Yet in a few days I noted in my exam book at our nightly examination of conscience in the nights prayers to note the faults of the day.

Jesus, I am sorry. I took too much pleasure in Sister Superior's comments. I seek to be humble around my artwork.

Jack Kennedy was the first Catholic ever to run for President and I devoured articles in *Newsweek* about the Kennedy clan and the exotic Jacqueline. Sister Superior read it first and never kept it longer than one night; then she put it out on upstairs the community table. We'd never had any worldly magazines in the novitiate or at the motherhouse.

Eagerly, I watched for it. Suddenly, the magazine disappeared. It wouldn't arrive on the table for days. Through careful sleuthing, I discovered that Sister Superior was slipping it under the door of Sister Succora's cell. Angrily, I complained, not to Sister Superior, as I should have, but to Sister Succorra, informing her that I wasn't the only one who resented her being Sister Superior's favorite. Hurt and bent on setting things right, she went directly to discuss the incident with Sister Superior.

Of course, the *Newsweek* reappeared, but overnight the mood in the house changed. A chill permeated the convent. Sister Succorra was silent and pale; her freckles stood out darker than ever. Sister Superior went round with a sour face and razor tongue. She scolded me sharply for not contributing to the dinner conversations. I fell to my knees and kissed the floor as we were to do when corrected, but I felt an irresistible urge to yell at her about favoritism. I felt personally responsible for the loss of gaiety in the house and berated myself for my petty jealousy. Then my thoughts turned to Sister Maureen. How would she have handled this same situation? I knew she had a way of charming her superiors, a skill I lacked. Now she seemed so far away from the land of East L.A. and I had so many challenges, that she receded from my mind.

At night prayers, I wrote in my exam book of my sins of impatience, of thinking badly of Sister Superior, of my jealousy of Sister Succorra's special position in the convent, of my complaints when I was given extra work to do in the convent or school. Unhappily, I wasn't a good, charitable, patient nun. Each morning at Mass I prayed:

God give me strength and grace to accept this situation as it is. Let me do your Will every day without complaining.

CHAPTER FIFTEEN

THE WILD RED POINTSETIA

ONE MORNING IN December as I left the convent for the school, I noticed that overnight, the wild red poinsettia bush had blossomed on the white convent wall. It crawled as high as a tree in a huge profusion of red flowers. I'd only seen poinsettias in little pots at Christmas. This explosion of beauty lifted my spirits. That same day Manuel marched into my heart, this lively six-year-old child who gazed at me from the second row. That day when I put my hand over his, to help him print his unsteady alphabet, he looked up at me with limpid, brown eyes and and at first, I thought I was imagining the thrill that ripped through me, but we both were blushing For a moment, I felt as if it was just the two of us in the room. When I came back to reality, I acted sternly, addressed the class impatiently, trying to hide my own emotions. I felt as if I had butterflies in my stomach. With his neglected teeth, hand-me down uniform, and wearing pants already too short that revealed his scuffed, high-top brown shoes with broken laces, he was an unlikely suitor. When I returned to the convent that afternoon, I spent minutes observing the wild red poinsettia, climbing ever higher on the white stucco. It seemed to represent my own raw feelings with Manuel. I felt stirrings that I hadn't felt since I was with Sister Maureen.

Whenever Manuel stood next to me in the reading circle and my hand grazed his thin arm, my pulse quickened. The other children began to protest, "Manuel was next to you yesterday. Seems like he always gets to be next to you." Reluctantly, I'd make room for a different child. I reflected it wasn't uncommon that a child would be enamored with his teacher, especially a child with many siblings, and Manuel was the fourteenth in his family. The mystery was why Manuel aroused delicious sensations in me when I touched him or he was near me. I told myself this would soon pass, but instead, the attraction grew. Each morning, I could hardly wait to see him.

"Did you do your homework, Manuel?" I'd ask.

"Yes, S'ter," He'd reach in his back pocket and pull out a smudged paper folded many times and open it. "I wrote all my spelling words." However, if he didn't have his homework, he'd shuffle his feet and lower his eyes and mutter, "Didn't get time to do it, S'ter."

First , I'd scowl, as if he disappointed me; then I'd smile and a pat his shoulder. I might reach out and push back a few hairs just to touch his warm face. He'd pull back, self-consciously, and push his stray hairs, just so. As the youngest of fourteen children, it couldn't have been easy to find a quiet place to copy spelling words or do addition. Off he'd go, often tripping on his untied laces as he dashed to his seat. He was well liked by his classmates and talked animatedly with the boys around him until the bell rang. To have him to remain after school, I gave him the coveted job of cleaning the board erasers at the end of the day. He'd go out to the schoolyard and bang the erasers together. Soon he'd present the box of cleaned erasers for my inspection with chalk dust in his hair and clinging to his long lashes.

I'd ask, "Do you want help with your reading?" He'd grin, grab his primer and stand next to me at my desk. Soon his sturdy body was listing toward me until it pressed against my warm thigh. He'd read, stumbling over the words. When I'd slip my arm about his waist, it would be as if lightening shot through my body. He'd blush and stumble even worse than before. His reading was atrocious but he when looked up from his primer with those innocent eyes and asked, "Am I doin' good, S'ter?" I always nodded. He'd quickly tire of reading and in his poor English, tell me of the goings-on in his family, who was in trouble with his mother, who was doing poorly or well in school. Wide-eyed, Manuel whispered that his mother would lock his brother, Michael, who was in seventh grade, in the large aviary when she left the house so he wouldn't cause trouble. I was captivated by his family life.

After he left, I walked across the steamy asphalt of the schoolyard with a fullness in my heart, but also flustered and confused. Mother Colette had instilled in us a commitment to Christ our Spouse so deep that the thought of loving this child seemed sinful. What would she say if she knew I delighted in the slightest contact with Manuel?

One Sunday at the children's Mass, I met Manuel's mother. I watched her slightly stooped figure as she shooed her children down the aisle to places with their classmates. I'd been intrigued to learn from other nuns that she'd once been a nun in Mexico. After the government disbanded her convent, she had married and borne fourteen children, two sets of twins among them. Kneeling in a back pew, she seemed quite ordinary in her faded print dress, a net veil on her head. I wanted to have an intimate conversation about her life and her children, but it would've been unheard of for me to speak to her with such familiarity.

After Mass I greeted her," Mrs. Alvarado, I'm so happy to meet Manuel's mother. He's such a charming child and tries so hard with his school work." I shook her hand.

"I sorry, Sister, that he's late sometimes, but its big job getting them all of to school. Bless you, Sister," she said and went off surrounded by her children, hitting and chasing each other, almost tripping her. Manuel glanced back and gave me a little wave. I watched until they disappeared around the corner. I wished I could've gone home with them, instead of back to the sterile convent

Each morning in the sacred moments after Holy Communion, I asked Jesus, with the anguish of an unfaithful wife, to help me eliminate this consuming affection for Manuel. Each evening, during the examination of conscience, I wrote exhortations in my exam binder.

December 5: *How foolish to waste affection on creatures when you should be loving You, my Lord. Forgive me.*

December 20: *Manuel on my mind constantly. I will give up dessert this week, Jesus, will You give me the grace to forget him?*

January 8: *Terrible to have this love for Manuel. It is like a disease. It torments me. O Mary, help me to love Your Son.*

Yet each day when Manuel would greet me with his cheery, "Morning, S'ter," or sidle up with a mangled daisy, my resolve would vanish. Manuel played hard at recess and would dash up to me grinning before mounting the jungle gym, "S'ter, watch me climb higher than Jose." Of course, I couldn't take my eyes off him. In time, Manuel realized his special status and began to use it to his advantage. He'd turn around in his seat and whisper or act silly or get up to sharpen his pencil and stay too long away from his desk. Impishly, his eyes would catch mine, daring me to correct him. I'd be lenient, then, feel guilty when I bellowed at Miguel Ochoa, who was constantly jumping out of his seat.

One night at the dinner table when the conversation was particularly dull, I opened my mouth and before I could censor myself I said, "I love Manuel Alvarado." Suddenly, everyone was staring at me. I blushed, then hurried to add, "I love that Manuel has become one of my best readers." The puzzlement on their faces gave way to amazement because there were six other Alvarado children in school, most of whom were notoriously poor students. Several sisters commented that I must be a very good teacher and they were glad he was getting a good start. I smiled and dreamily took an empty platter from Sister Zita, without even noticing it was empty.

When we sat in the community room watching Jack Kennedy's news conferences on T.V. with half the sisters making giggly remarks about his good looks, I would close my eyes and see Manuel's crooked grin and brown eyes. While we watched Sister Superior's favorite, The Lawrence Welk Show, I found myself like a lovesick teenager, doodling Manuel's name in the margin of my lesson plan book. At times, the lure of play was too strong for Manuel and after school he hurried out with the other boys Through the long afternoon, I'd been anticipating moments alone with him and when I'd seen the last child out and returned to an empty classroom, I was astonished at the depth of my disappointment. I went to the convent like a spurned lover and took consolation by saying my rosary in the courtyard amid the beauty of the Birds of Paradise that ran riot next to brilliant Hibiscus. What was wrong with me? I asked myself? I had no answers, only a yearning to be close to him, to experience that delight that came with his look, his touch. I wanted to squeeze him. I had no insight into these emotions, only the certainty that they were wrong. Yet, I was incapable of breaking our bond.

One afternoon, while I was on yard duty, a ball shattered the second grade window. Neither Sister Zita nor I saw who threw the ball. Little fingers were pointing and blame was being assigned every direction. I questioned the boys in my class. Sister Zita quizzed her boys. No one admitted blame. Sister Superior marched into the cluster of children swinging her yardstick.

I stepped in front of my boys and said, "Sister Superior, none of my boys threw that ball. I questioned each of them. Certainly, it was someone in Sister Zita's class." She believed me. When recess was over, my class lined up and filed into my classroom but as they were gathering for the reading circle around my desk, I noticed the boys whispering and giggling and focusing attention on Gilbert, a handsome, athletic boy. Outside, Gilbert had protested great innocence, but now wore a look of bravado. Suddenly, I realized that out in the schoolyard I'd been deceived by my own students. Indeed, Gilbert did throw the ball that broke the window. My anger rose as I sat steaming in the midst of the reading group, listening to the boys struggle with the escapades of Dick and Jane, Spot and Sally. Then, I looked around at them and an unexpected wave of sympathy overcame my anger. I saw the eagerness and the cleverness of these street-wise man-children, clustered around my desk, grabbing their primers, trying their best. At that moment, I crossed the line over to their side. I realized we were all struggling together to make it work in this harsh land, called East L.A.

I had others things to distract me as in early December, Sister Superior assigned me the enormous task of teaching both first grades and second grades--two hundred and forty children--three songs for the Christmas pageant since the other Sisters protested they were incapable of teaching singing, leaving the duty to me, the youngest. Though the school band was the main attraction, the little ones would sing *Santa Claus is Comin' to Town*, *Silent Night* and *Away in a Manger*. I began by going to each class for twenty minutes to teach the children the songs while that teacher would mind my class.

Sister Superior called all four classes with sixty children each, to march into the auditorium with their own teachers for a practice. Sister Superior spoke briskly, "Good afternoon boys and girls. We are going to have a Christmas pageant and you'll all be a part of it by singing these wonderful Christmas songs." The children smiled and squirmed. "Now Sister Theophane, I'd like you to arrange all of them on stage in three rows according to height."

I called a group of first graders forward. "You girls, start by lining up at the front of the stage. Now boys, go right behind them. Please, boys, stop that pushing. You, come forward. No, not you, the boy with the dark hair." They all had dark hair. I was at a disadvantage, not knowing their names, except for those in my own class. "You, please file in behind and now you, make a second row. You, in the back with the pencil, stop poking that girl in front of you. Sister Zita will you take that pencil away from him." It was a quite a trick to get them to stop at the correct spot on stage so that they weren't all bunched up at one end.

"Jose, let go of that curtain! Sister Zita, will you pull that boy out of the line? Yes, that one. He's pulling on the girls uniform in front of him." It went on and on.

The next day we tried to repeat the feat in a more organized fashion. Each Sister was standing to the side, looking stern to help keep order. Sister Superior was offering suggestions. We were all awaiting Father Vincent, the parish priest who would be the accompanist. In swept Father Vincent, painfully thin and wiry under his belted black cassock. He was a caustic, witty, impatient man, but a talented musician, who played the organ like a master. He skipped the 'Good afternoon' formalities and slid on to the piano bench.

"Ready, Sister?" His back was straight as a ramrod, his greying crew-cut stood at attention, and his attitude, *lets get this over as soon as possible,* was clearly visible. On the piano, right below the stage, he struck up a lively introduction. I stood at the front of the children with my arms raised and after Father's musical introduction, I gave the signal to begin singing.

Father and I joined in loudly, "You better watch out, you better not cry." Only half the children even opened their mouths. They were staring at Father, mesmerized by his banging out a tune on a real piano. Most hadn't seen one before. We tried several more times, but the children could not start together. Father was not amused. I went over to consult with Sister Superior who stood at the back. She went up to Father. "May I suggest just a starting chord, no introduction?"

"That's not the correct way to do it, Sister," he insisted "Oh, we'll give it a try anyway."

Standing below the stage facing the children, I would hum loudly with Father's sustained chord. Then we'd try to sing all together. "You better watch out, you better not cry…" It was me who wanted to cry as the children sang very slowly. On the piano, Father was way ahead of them. I looked back at Sister Superior with a helpless look. Sister Superior clicked to the stage with her higher than regulation heels, put her hand on Father's shoulder and purred, "Father, can we try it once more? It's coming along nicely."

Father snapped, "They've got to keep up with my tempo. This is not a funeral!"

The tension rose with several more attempts and the children's voices trailed off at the second verses. Father turned to Sister Superior and demanded, "Are we going to have second verses?" Sister Superior turned to me. "Sister, did you teach them the second verses?"

"Yes, Sister Superior, I did. They just don't seem to recall those verses right now."

"Sister, we don't want to waste Father's time. I suggest you practice the songs back in the classroom."

Father was heading for the door, his cassock flying. He called irritably over his shoulder, "Learn the second verses!"

It went on like this for at least a week with no marked improvement in the children's singing or Father Vincent's patience. The week before the performance, I got a terrible sore throat and before the week's end, it had blossomed into laryngitis. I'd come home from school and go to bed drinking hot lemonade and honey, but the practices dragged on and on, even though I was voiceless.

One afternoon Father Vincent strode in briskly, plopped down at the piano and in a tone that intimated it was he who was waiting for me, said, "Ready, Sister?" Miraculously, we got through the first two songs with only a minimum of stop and start, but during Away in a Manger one of them boys in the last row bounced a tennis ball down the stage. A boy in the first row scrambled to get it. In a flash, Sister Zita pulled the offender off the stage.

For Father Vincent, it was the last straw, final proof of the folly of my efforts. He stood up and announced to me, "Sister, you will never get this together by Friday. I suggest you scrap the whole thing!" He strode from the auditorium, cassock flying. Later I told Sister Superior what occurred. She muttered a few words about tempermental musicians and brave woman that she was, she marched off to the priest's rectory to confront Father Vincent. We practiced the rest of the week without any sign of Father Vincent.

On the evening of the performance, the auditorium was filled to overflowing. Excitement crackled in the air. Sister Superior and the Pastor sat in the first row. The children lined up in the back stage, dressed beautifully and whispering nervously. Father Vincent arrived on time. As soon as they marched onstage, they received a terrific burst of applause. Father gave a nod to the audience, sat up ramrod straight, looked up at the children, hit one long chord, then he played at a moderate tempo. The children sang well, although the second verses weren't sung confidently, yet no one seemed to care. The applause was loud; audience loved the children. Sister Superior and the Pastor beamed. I was too exhausted to savor any joy. I was only glad it was over.

Two days before the concert, I received permission to renew my vows. This was not unexpected, but it was my feelings that concerned me. I noted in my exam book:

Dec *16 Permission given to renew vows. Desolate. I feel I wish I wasn't given permission.*

A few days later:

Dec. 19 Lord, I'm sorry I'm having thoughts of leaving You. You know I love You. Please give me strength and grace.

Dec. 29 *A day of retreat. Father reminded us that the just man lives by faith. Put your future in God's hands. Sometimes it might be hell. That's implied when you take your vows. You give up your will. Now all is for Him.*

The life of a teaching nun was rigorous; submitting my will to my superiors was painful. I tried to tell myself it was tolerable because I was serving my God and reaping a reward hereafter, but my thoughts kept turning to Sister Paula. She was home now, no longer a nun; most likely looking for a teaching job. I wondered whether she was asked to leave or had bravely left on her own. Her mother was a dedicated Catholic and a teacher at a public school. Her father had a good job. She could go home. My father was dead and my Mom, even though she was a principal, was drinking more. My sister still lived at home with Mom. I didn't feel I had any welcome home to which to return.

A few days later, I renewed my vows of poverty, chastity and obedience for two more years at the end of our Mass in the convent chapel. The priest and the Sisters in the convent were the only witnesses. I wanted no fuss, no celebration, just to get on with the school year.

I simply noted in my exam book:

Jan. 3 I renewed my vows today. Sister Paula is gone.

In the spring, Manuel grew taller and more confident. He played hard at recess and he didn't stay after school often. He got on well with the other boys and I tried to take pride in his growth. Yet I felt a terrible void and was often irritable with the children. In the convent I grew weepy with sadness, knowing the day after school closed, I'd be on a plane bound for San Francisco for our annual eight-day retreat at the Motherhouse.

I wrote in my exam book:

June 15 I've made a mess of this year.

June 16 So hard to say good-by to Manuel. After he left, I went to my cell and sobbed. It must be wonderful to be his mother.

The next day as I was driven to the airport with two other sisters. I gazed out the window as the pastel houses and palms trees flew by. I was trying to hold back my tears as I left this strange land called East L.A. that I had come to love.

CHAPTER SIXTEEN

MOTHERHOUSE
SUMMER AFTER EAST L.A.

FOGGY SAN FRANCISCO was a sepia film compared to the wild Technicolor of East L.A. In the motherhouse chapel our annual eight-day retreat was beginning. In moments I would bare my soul in confession to the Jesuit Retreat Master. Noiselessly, my soft rubber heels propelled me to the line outside the confessional at the side of the chapel, a place stale with the guilt and body odors, yet which held a promise of forgiveness. As a sister came out, I entered the box and knelt on the worn step facing the grille where the priest sat between the two small chambers. A high muffled voice told me the sister, kneeling on the other side of the confessional, was confessing to the priest. I was perspiring, asking myself: would Father be scandalized, lecture me, or worse, insist I discuss it with my Superior? The partition behind the grill slid open. With a deep breath, I began with the ususal form. "Bless me, Father for I have sinned. It has been several weeks since my last confession. I've been impatient with my Sisters, had uncharitable thoughts about my Superior, gave into to my love of chocolate and took too many pieces at recreation." I paused.

"Is that all, Sister?"

"No, Father. I have more, but it is difficult speak of it."

"My confessional is the right place, Sister."

My fingertips pressed purple against the grill. The words came out in a rush. "This year while I was teaching first grade, I got attached, well, actually I fell in love with one of my students, a little boy."

"A student, Sister? And how old was the boy?"

"S-s-six," I stuttered.

"A six-year-old? I see. Did you touch this child, Sister?"

"Sometimes I touched his forehead to push his hair out of his eyes and I put my arm around his waist when he was reading, but I really wanted to hold him." My voice quivered. "I thought about him all the time. I didn't think about Jesus. I was fixated on him and it wasn't fair to the other children." With the release of the burden I'd carried many months, my sniffling gave way to sobbing.

"There, there, Sister, no need for tears."

"If only I'd someone to talk to, but the Superior was not easy to confide in and, even if I confessed, I knew I'd fail again. I loved him, but now I'm away from L.A."

Through the grille Father's voice was gentle. "Sister, dear, God has given us all the capacity for normal affections. We wouldn't be human otherwise. With your vow of chastity you promised God to remain celibate, not to de-humanize yourself. The vow is meant to free you from caring for a family, so you can devote yourself to loving and teaching many children. Often one will be more appealing than another and we can't help our feelings any more than we can help having blue or brown eyes. I don't believe you have committed any sin, Sister."

Tears of relief streamed down my face. My thick glasses fogged up. I fumbled for my handkerchief.

"For your penance, Sister, say five Hail Mary's and during this retreat ask the Blessed Mother for the grace to become a teacher that will act as if each child were a favorite."

The festering guilt was lanced! As I moved to my stall, I glanced about at the well-scrubbed faces of my peers. Only six of us are left out of the original fourteen who entered that hot day in July of 1955. We, survivors, had bonded like soldiers who've done battle together. That summer of '55, while our classmates crammed theaters to see Jimmy Dean in *Rebel Without a Cause* and ate fries at Mel's Drive-in where the jukeboxes blared *Rock Around the Clock*, we'd sat with downcast eyes at the feet of Mother Colette while she revealed the steep path to holiness. The Sisters now reflected a serenity that I envied. Are they approaching the goal of holiness Mother Colette urged us to strive toward? Am I the only one with a straying heart?

I opened the book to begin my spiritual reading. A photo slid to my lap. Manuel grins up at me. I'm standing behind him in the school-yard, hand on his shoulder. I doubt I've asked the necessary permission to have my picture taken. I can't recall who took the photo. Perhaps Manuel's brother, Michael, who sometimes came to pick him up, curi-ous to see the teacher Manuel babbled about at home. Manuel seems smaller than I recall, his head just above my waist. If I was truly re-pentant, I'd tear up the snapshot, but I thrust it deep in the pocket of my habit. Could my love for Manuel have been a substitute for Sister Maureen? For years I'd tried to root that passion from my heart and I didn't think of her often when I was in L.A. but next week we begin summer school at U.S.F. and I'd likely I'll encounter her on campus. How strong would I be?

My stall was near an open window, the wind whipped in and it was cold. *Good*, I told myself, *you deserve this penance.* I closed my eyes and repeated a favorite prayer: *You, Yourself, O Christ, are my all. For You I keep myself chaste and holding aloft my shining lamp, I run to meet You.*

In summer we, junior professed sisters, filled every available bed in the motherhouse and the overflow slept in cots in the third floor high school classrooms across the garden. None of us had yet com-pleted a B.A. degree or even had a Teaching Credential when we started teaching. It took years to get the degree and credential. A few days before summer classes started, we received our class assignments at the University of San Francisco from the Dean of Studies. This stocky red-faced nun, her thick glasses perched half-way down her nose, emerged from her cluttered office in the North Hall with slips of paper, muttering names and commenting on courses. When I received my slip of paper it stated I was to take the History of Education, a normal choice for an education major, but the second class was unusual--lab biology. Why was I, a first grade teacher, enrolled in that class?

On the first day at U.S.F., I found the science building and climbed to the third floor with its strange antiseptic smells. I found myself a high stool where I perched nervously and discovered with dismay that I was the only nun in the class. Dr. Kessel, famous for his research with Platypezidae (flat-footed flies), paced in his white lab coat as he outlined the course. Then peering over glasses perched low on his nose, he flashed a wicked grin and promised plenty of lab tests. I learned during the summer that he really knew his subject and had an impressive collection of insects on display at the auspicious California Academy of Sciences in Golden Gate Park. When I discovered that the other students--men and woman--were all in nursing or premed, I knew I was in the wrong place. I would never do well. Recently, the Jesuits had allowed women in the School of Nursing to attend the university. In addition to nuns, they were the only women on the campus. Certainly, the Dean had made a mistake. I wanted to get out of this science class, yet I knew the Dean would never change her mind. It would be: *God will give you the grace.*

When I left the lab on the third floor and started down the stairs, through the high window, I spied Sister Maureen walking away from the building. Even from the back, I knew her walk. I flew down the three flights, trying to catch her, even though as a junior professed, I wasn't supposed to speak to the final professed sisters, but by the time I got outside, she was gone.

That night I noted in my Exam book:

June 28: *Biology will be difficult. With Your help Lord, I can do it. Saw sister Maureen today. Would like to have talked to her, but I didn't have a chance. Thank you, Lord. I must be careful of contact with her. Must not stir up old feelings.*

At lunch time, we nuns walked in twos, as required, the short distance from the campus to our high school, adjacent to the Motherhouse to eat lunch in our school cafeteria. There was no need to sit in rank and or have a silent meal. Grabbing a tray, I got in line behind Sister Dominic, my friend who I taught with in East L.A.

"So how was biology, Theo?"

"Terrible. I'll never pass. What am I doing in that class?"

"Why don't you complain to the Dean?" she said with a grin.

"Very funny!" She was as always calm and confident as I was fidgety and anxious. We took seats together and compared notes on classes. I knew there was no getting out of biology.

At the end of the first week, I was walking out of the cafeteria when I saw Maureen coming toward me. As soon as I saw her, my breath quickened. She was with her real sister, Sister Danielle, also a nun, two years her senior, but they looked like twins. As she got close, the air around us seemed charged. We stopped in front of the door to the storeroom where so many years ago we'd been caught kissing and had been reported. My stomach turned at the painful memory!

"Hello, Sister." I hugged her in the community way, but her giggle in my ear, the feel and smell of her was magnetic. I wanted to pull her away and talk for hours. Then, I remembered my manners and gave her sister a similar greeting.

"What classes do you have?" asked Maureen.

"I'm taking biology," I said, now proud that I was taking something other than education classes.

"Are you? How interesting! I took a great biology class at Loyola in L.A. last summer. Now I have morning classes at U.S.F., but after lunch I study in the university library or in an empty classroom here in the high school." I knew this information was an invitation. As they walked away, I sighed and felt an envy that her real sister could spend time with her and never be accused of a particular friendship. Unfortunately, I still had strong feelings for her.

Back on campus, I roamed the stacks of the library. On the third floor, I spied her sitting at a table alone, secluded among the high stacks. For a second I hesitated: *Suppose I'm seen with her and someone will report me?* Still, what harm to study at the same table? Of course, neither of us could concentrate and soon we began whispering together, talking for nearly an hour. That evening guilt overcame me. When I had an opportunity to talk to the Mistress of Juniors, Sister Therese, I confessed I'd spoken at length with Sister Maureen. I knew this went directly against instructions--juniors sisters were not to speak with final professed sisters. Fortunately, she did not know my history with Sister Maureen and spoke gently about doing small mortification to reinforce are sense of obedience without a lecture on the evils of particular friendships.

The following week at U.S.F., I had my first biology quiz. To my surprise, I got an A- and I understood, if I studied hard, I could actually pass the course. In my excitement, I wanted to tell Sister Maureen. At lunchtime back at the high school cafeteria, I caught sight of her going upstairs to an empty classroom to study. I thought I'll catch her right after lunch. A short time later, I bounded up the stairs, trying to find the classroom where she was studying. I hungered for a good conversation, maybe even a long hug. When I opened the door of the second floor classroom, I was stunned. Sitting close to Maureen was a younger nun, the one I'd heard had been devoted to Sister Maureen when she taught at our Berkeley high School, St Joseph's. Under the direction of Sister Maureen, she had entered our convent. As I stood in the doorway, scowling, unmoving, I noticed, this younger nun was quite attractive.

"Theophane, I have an appointment now. I will see you tomorrow."

"Not tomorrow. I'll be back in fifteen minutes," I growled, reverting to the jealous high school student I often was.

"I will see you tomorrow, Theo. Do you understand?"

My fists clenched. I refused to move, but Maureen stood by the side of the young nun, shaking her head. I glared, I shook my head, I stomped, and, finally, I gave in and left, not for any rational reason, but for fear that the young nun would spread word of my jealous rage. That evening I wrote in my exam book:

Dear Jesus, half the day I struggled against my old enemy, jealousy. My spirituality is crumbling. How You must love me, Jesus, to give me this difficult test.

Then I prayed with the words of a John Dunne poem I'd learned in the novitiate:

Batter my heart, three-person'd God, for you

As yet but knock, breathe, shine, and seek to mend;

That I may rise and stand, o'erthrow me, and bend

Your force to break, blow, burn, and make me new.

I hadn't cried for a long time, but that night in bed, I sobbed. I loved Maureen far more than she loved me. 'It's time to let go, Theo,' I told myself over and over. But each morning as I headed to campus, I wondered if I'd see her that day. If I didn't catch sight of her, I'd fall into a depression. I felt I'd sell my soul to Satan to be free of her, but he already owned part my heart.

On the July Visiting Sunday, excitedly, I paced in the hall near the front door as I waited to see my family. I hadn't seen them since last August just before I went to East. L.A . When the door bell rang, I saw Mom was alone and soon I noticed she wasn't her usual self. First, she was late, then, she came alone, mumbling that Steve and Ellen were busy. When I gave her a kiss and a hug, her response was careful, like a person who has been sick and guards their body. She was taller and thinner than I, and had always moved confidently. Today she seemed bent and her face was puffy. What had happened this year? She'd written newsy letters about her job as new principal of Ulloa in the Outer Sunset. It sounded as if she was doing a great job as principal.

As I led the way to the large parlor, I held out my arm, but she ignored it. Though I wanted to ask what happened, I sensed it was best not to ask too many questions. Intuitively, I knew the answer: It was the drinking. It was worse. But why? When I started chattering about Our Lady Of Lourdes, of the large classes, and the heat, I could see her relax. She interrupted my chatter: "Judy, can we go somewhere where I can smoke?"

"Of course, Mom. Lets go out to the ball court." I led her out a side door and we began to pace in the sun. She inhaled deeply, apologizing for her needing a cigarette.

"Judy, when can you come and see our new house?" When I'd been sent to East L.A., Mom had sold the flats in the Richmond district and moved to a newer three-bedroom home in the Sunset district near the Stonestown Mall. "The garden is wonderful and I planted all kinds of flowers, especially roses. You should see my prize, a sterling silver rose. The house is beautiful too, except for Ellen's room. She calls her mess, a conversation piece."

"Mom, the Rules haven't changed. I can't go home unless you are on your deathbed. Why don't you bring me some pictures?"

"I really don't know why that nice Mother Colette wouldn't let you visit our new home?"

"Mom, she doesn't make the Rules; she enforces them." I wanted to know more about her drinking, but Mom hated conflict; she'd never talk about it. I wasn't any better; I couldn't think of her as an alcoholic. In truth, I saw it coming when I was seventeen and ran away from it. Now was time to face the truth. At the end of the afternoon, she seemed more relaxed, but I was worried.

The next day, after walking on the second floor in front of Mother Colette's office door four or five times, I screwed up my courage and lightly knocked, though I knew I should have an appointment. I'd never been in this inner sanctum office since she'd become the Mother General.

"Come in, Sister." Mother Colette sat behind a desk so large it almost dwarfed her, but the severity of her features surmounted that impression.

"Mother, may I talk with you a minute? It's about my mother." She scrutinized me, weighing my request. Then her face softened. "Have a seat, Sister Theophane."

"Mother," I began to cry. "She's drinking... rather heavily. I feel helpless." Mother let me cry. Her face softened, she leaned forward and when she spoke it was with genuine compassion. "These things happen, Sister. I have always admired your mother. She is a fine woman and her life has not been easy. It's very hard when we cannot help someone we love. It sounds like you need a family conference. Talk with Ellen and Steve. See what you can do together."

I loved that she recalled my whole family and I realized this nun I so feared was also the person on whom I could depend to be understanding. I left feeling that her empathy was as strong as her sternness.

When I got ahold of my sister, Ellen, she told me, flatly, without emotion, that Mom drank everyday. She sounded annoyed at my ignorance. She said she had no idea what to do. I sensed she was angry at me for leaving her with Mom. The next evening, I called Steve, who, now married, lived in a flat in the Richmond district. He responded matter-of-factly. "Judy, I'm trying to get her to go to the doctor. She'll never go to AA because of her position as a principal. It would be too embarrassing, she says. She falls frequently, has lots of bruises and she's banged up her car."

I could hardly believe what I was hearing. "Oh no, Steve, are you worried she'll lose her job?"

"I doubt it. She never misses a day of work. She just wears dark glasses. She has a great secretary and assistant principal and I think they cover up for her. She may even keep a bottle of bourbon in her drawer."

" What can be done, Steve?"

"Ellen and I are trying to get her to a doctor, but she resists."

That night I hardly slept at all. What were we going to do? What could I do? I felt guilty that I'd left the family when I suspected her drinking would get worse. Now I was helpless and could do no more than pray. I began saying an extra rosary each day and pleading with the Virgin to help us solve this as there was little else I could do.

At U.S.F., I began to enjoy my biology class with Dr. Kessel, partly because I had a lab partner, John, with whom I shared a microscope. He was a shy, young man with sandy hair and he teasingly called me a 'DAR'.

"What does DAR mean, John?" I asked

"Don't tell me you don't know!" His light eyebrows raised and his blue eyes opened wide with surprise. "Don't you know that we refer to you nuns as Damn Average Raisers?"

"What?"

He continued, "You nuns study too hard and raise the class averages. The rest of us hate all you nuns for that." I laughed, imagining I might be considered competition in a class that held so much fear for me. At first, I studied for my two classes with equal zeal and at midterm I was rewarded with the only A+ in my History of Education class. The teacher, a handsome, lively Jesuit, strode down the aisles, announcing as he returned our Blue Books, "We've got one hot shot in here." He tossed my book on my desk with a red A+ on the cover. I was shocked and turned the book over immediately so that the older nuns, some seasoned school administrators, wouldn't see it. But later I boasted of it to Sister Dominic.

That evening I wrote in my Exam book:

July 20 *So boastful. Sin of pride. I must confess.*

Soon the demands of the interesting biology took precedence over the education class. Endless slides were to be identified–samples of bacteria, yeast, molds; bottles of sea animals to be identified—sea cucumbers, jellyfish, squid; then Dr. Kessel's favorites, the insects, trays of them, poised midair with thin black pins through their abdomens. They were to be identified as to genus and species. Now I was calling beautiful butterflies, Lepidoptera and beatles, scarabs. There were hundreds of names to master. I looked forward to talking to John each day and he, too, seemed to enjoy my company. One day at the end of class, John and I walked downstairs together, comparing answers on our lab test.

"Sister, what did you put for that purple slide with those funny shapes on it"

"That'a a strepticoccus bacillus,"

"Oh jeez, I put some screwy thing. How do you remember all that?"

As we headed toward the cafeteria together, I spied some nuns of our Order approaching. I walked slowly, hoping the sisters might notice us. I tossed my head, my veil flipping in the wind, like a silly teenager tossing her hair. We entered the large cafeteria together and John stopped at a table, dropped his books and held out a chair for me. "How do you take your coffee? Black, I bet," he grinned.

I bit my lip and paused. "John, I'm so sorry, but I have to go behind that partition. Nuns can only eat with other nuns."

His face flushed with embarrassment as he jammed one hand in his pocket. "Jeez, I didn't know that. I'll see you tomorrow back in class." He loped off toward the coffee stand.

I walked behind the partition where nuns were drinking coffee and eating snacks and sandwiches they'd brought in waxed paper. I frowned at them and plopped down alone, simmering, hating these rules.

That evening in a moment of retrospection, I wrote in my Exam book:

Jesus, forgive me for my worldliness with John. Let me raise my thought often to You.

One afternoon my sister, Ellen, surprised me with her arrival at the U.S.F. campus. She had come to talk about Mom. My sister was tall and slender and was working as a secretary at a radio station downtown. She seemed sophisticated and worldly. As the morning fog had lifted, we comfortably strolled around the campus in the shadow of the magnificent St. Ignatius Church, modeled after St. Peter's in Rome. She told me that Mom had gone to see a doctor and was cutting down on her drinking and Ellen was feeling hopeful.

"I hope to God this helps, El. I know how hard it's for you to live with her and that drinking." After we walked a bit I said, "Would you like to see the biology lab where I spend a lot of time?"

"Sure, why not?" My class was over for the day, but many students were sitting together to study. I introduced Ellen to John and the others. John said something funny and we all laughed. As we walked downstairs my sister commented, "You seem to be the belle of the ball in there? Are any of those boys hitting on you?" I stopped and made a face, as if I was scandalized. How could she make such an observation? But in truth, I was amused. The reality was that in suffering through this difficult class, an unusual cameraderie developed between me, the only nun, and the other students.

Toward the end of summer, a picnic was arranged for all of us at our Novitiate property in the Santa Cruz mountains. Our Mistress of Juniors gave us the extraordinary permission to socialize, within reason, with the Final Professed sisters. I loved returning to this place of my novitiate days. As I got out of the car, I inhaled the scent of pines and dry grass and felt a sudden freedom. I ran toward the lodge, hoping to find Sister Maureen. When I saw her near the doorway, I said, "Hi there, what a great day!"

She turned with a broad smile and said, "Oh hi, Theo, it is a fine day. Tell me how are you doing with your biology class?"

I shrugged. "Pretty good. Can I entice you to take a walk with me so we can talk?"

"Maybe after lunch. I'm waiting for my sisters." It annoyed me that she always spent these free days with her real sisters, leaving little time for me.

After a generous buffet lunch in the big dining hall, a sister put on the dance records. We pushed back the tables and chairs. Immediately, a few pairs of sisters moved on to the floor. The next record began: *It had to Be You.* I sidled up to Maureen and put out my hand. "Please, do me the favor?" She smiled. I took her broad hand in my slender one and we began sliding, turning, dipping. When we danced, she always led. The next number was *Tammy*. I couldn't resist asking for another dance. As we moved around the floor, she sang snatches of the words, "La, la, la; la, la, la, Tammy's in love..." I adored dancing with her and we were easily the best on the floor. I wanted to have every number with her, but we were already a scandal by dancing two numbers together.

Fortunately, the Mistress of Juniors and Mother Colette were too busy to attend the picnic. But there were spies. The next day I was called in by the Mistress of Juniors, Sister Thaddeus, to explain why I'd spent so much time with Sister Maureen. Fortunately, she didn't know our long history and gave me only a small scolding and a simple penance--to say the Stations of the Cross. I had loved dancing with Maureen and it was worth the scolding and I realized my feelings for her would never change.

Summer school was coming to an end. We were cramming for finals and I felt sad that my biology class was ending because I'd miss the fun I was having with John. Our Dean of Studies never shared what grades we achieved in our summer classes, but Dr. Kessel, with drama and flourish, announced the class grades as he returned our final tests. I smiled broadly as he returned my test, saying, "Congratulations, Sister, you've earned an A." John made a funny face at me and said, "See, Sister, you are a DAR!" (damn average raiser). He was happy with his B+.

In August, summer school was over, but we Junior sisters were still living at the Motherhouse awaiting the day the Missions would be distributed. Anxiously, we walked past the second floor office of Secretary of the Mother Colette, the Mother General, because it was she who typed our assignments. We walked very slowly. Was she typing? Yes, but was she typing even after dinner? That would be more telling. We were like children, aching for Christmas morning.

At last the day came and as the bell tolled, we hurried to the community room and sat in rank in two long rows. If you received a square white envelope it meant you had a new Mission; if you weren't called, you would return to last year's Mission. Mother Colette didn't call my name. I inhaled through my teeth. I didn't want to go back to Our Lady of Lourdes in East L.A. I couldn't bear another year under the unpredictable Superior and endure a seat in the refectory next to the thoughtless Sister Zita. And, more importantly, how would I deal with my attraction to Manuel? A fresh start would've been best. How could I show any joy when in moments we'd stand up and share our Missions? Yet with God's help, I did get through another year in the land of East LA without any entanglement with Manuel, who then was in another class.

CHAPTER SEVENTEEN

―――∽∾∽―――

TEACHING
MOTHERHOUSE, SAN FRANCISCO
AUGUST 1962

ON THIS FREEZING cold day, typical of San Francisco in August, the sidewalk resembled a sailing regatta as sudden gusts of wind billowed our veils and rotated our large bibs, revealing our white necks above collarless habits. Our large rosaries caught on suitcase latches and 'good-byes' and 'God bless you's' competed with the traffic noise.

I heaved my heavy suitcase to the sidewalk in front of the Motherhouse. Today was moving day, when every Sister went to her assigned convent for the coming school year. It was four years since the spring that I'd lived here as a Junior Professed Sister, and a year since I'd left teaching in East L.A. for two years and then been assigned to teach first grade in one of our San Jose convents.

Now after my San Jose Mission, I was coming to teach at the high school. Three weeks ago we received our Missions, and I was certain that I'd have another year teaching first grade in San Jose. I was stunned to discover it was God's Will that I teach at Presentation High School in San Francisco. Me, going back to teach where as a student I'd fallen in love with Maureen? In this amazing promotion, Mother Colette was showing great confidence in me. The Sisters who taught at the high school were the most respected in the Order.

"Goodbye, Sister Superior. Thanks for everything," I said as I gave Sister Superior Alicia our sisterly embrace. Her cheek barely touched mine, but she was never demonstrative, yet I wanted to hear her say: I'm going to miss you, Sister, but she simply said, "Goodbye, Sister Theophane." As I grabbed my suitcase from the trunk, she called to me, "I don't know what challenge you'll have teaching high school, but you need a challenge and keep up your art." She gave me that funny, jerky smile that lasted only a second before her face settled into its immobile folds. She pulled the car from the curb and I watched until it was swallowed in traffic.

She was glad that I had been given a Mission so she wouldn't have to deal with the tangle of jealousies that had surrounded her in our San Jose convent this spring. After two years in East L.A., I was assigned to teach first grade at our upscale school in an affluent parish in San Jose. The children were well-prepared with scrubbed, shiny faces and full lunch boxes. They read almost instantly, learned math easily and I loved teaching them. Initially, I got on well with the Superior, a tall, reserved, creative soul of few words. She chose me as her partner on nearly every errand or outing. The other sisters were easygoing and everyone got along. However, mid-year, Sister Felicity, a thin, domineering, older sister was sent to teach seventh grade. Immediately our harmony was disrupted. She wanted Sister Superior's complete attention and was jealous of the close relationship Sister Superior and I had established. Whenever she could arrange it, she'd try to enlist all of us to do her bidding. Soon the convent was filled with tension, but that year was now over.

In a unprecedented shake-up, Mother Colette appointed six new sisters to teach at our all girls San Francisico high school, where, until now, the same staff had taught for years. At twenty-four, I would be the second youngest and with God's help, I would be able to handle the challenge ahead. With a deep breath, I turned and faced the mother-house as if seeing it for the first time, surveying the three-story build-ing that was the color of stale cream with its impressive steps leading to a wide porch graced with tall Greek columns. Atop the three stories was a small bell tower. A swath of lawn surrounded two sides like an emerald ribbon. Hoping to spot another newcomer, I walked toward the front steps lugging my suitcase. At that moment, Sister Jacqueline, the youngest of the new staff, emerged from a car and bounced up the stairs like a fluffy terrier. I resisted the urge to join her. She was imma-ture and giggled constantly. Still standing at the bottom of the steps, I heard someone ask, "Is that you, Sister Theophane?" I turned and looked into the denim eyes of Sister Loyola. She puffed up behind me and banged her suitcase into the back of my knee and nearly knocked me off balance.

"Oh, I'm so sorry. Did I hurt you? This has been such a day, Theophane. You wouldn't believe what happened to me this morn-ing. I put all my clothes in the washer, but no one mentioned that the convent dryer went out yesterday; so I arrive at my new Mission with a plastic bag of wet laundry. Can you imagine greeting the Superior with this dripping mess? She sent me around to the side door and straight to the laundry, but I left my suitcase here at the front stairs. So how are you? What are you going to teach?" She swept me along in her private whirlwind. Though I only knew her from our summer vacations, I liked her. She always seemed on the verge of breathless, but humorous disaster. When at last she took a breath, I said, "Biology and art."

"Art! Theo, How great. You'll be wonderful. I remember those wa-tercolors you sent up to the Mother General's feast day. They got raves."

"How about you, Sister Loyola?"

"I'm here to teach Spanish though the Lord alone knows why. We spoke Spanish at home, but that was eons ago. And Sister Andrew, our principal, wants me to take over the glee club and music appreciation from her. Imagine me trying to follow in her footsteps?" With a little snort, she rolled her eyes and on the energy of her humor, we sailed through the convent vestibule. Inside it was cool and dark with high ceilings and long polished corridors. We both shook the veined hand of the Superior, who was greeting the incoming Sisters. On the bulletin board on the second floor, we located the daily schedule and our cell assignments.

"Look at this, Theophane," Loyola said as she tapped the schedule. "We recite the Office together at 5 p.m. Vacation is over." She poked me with her elbow. "Got to shape up now. We're at the Motherhouse!" As she pointed, I looked with envy at her silver ring. I wanted so much to be friends, but until I got my ring at Final Vows, a chasm lay between us. It was the custom that Final Professed Sisters didn't fraternize with Junior Professed Sisters. I was counting--four more months until our group made Final Vows. Sister Loyola started for the third floor, tripped on her habit, let out a yelp, then clapped her hand over her mouth. She looked about in mock terror, as if expecting Mother Colette to emerge, scolding, from her office. I smiled. With her light coloring and her humor, she reminded me of the comedian, Danny Kaye. Indeed, Mother Colette, now Mother General, and her secretary did occupy a small kingdom here on the second floor.

Though Mother Colette had brought stability since she replaced the Mother General who had died in office, she also insisted on a rigor that counteracted a laxness that filtered in during the illness of the former Mother General. In time I would learn that not everyone was happy with her particular style of governing. Checking the board again, I saw that I had one of the few cells on the second floor, right next to the chapel. Even though it was convenient, it was too much in the thick of things. I had the middle cubicle of the three cells, separated only by yellow opaque curtains. I threw my suitcase on the bed, knelt before the crucifix hung in the recess of the cupboard and prayed:

Jesus, You know I am going to need all the grace you can spare to do this assignment. I thank You for the honor and trust You have put in me for this Mission. Amen!

As I entered the refectory for dinner, I saw that below the large, standing crucufix Mother Colette was seated at the head table surrounded by her Councilors and the Superior of the motherhouse, an intimidating group. For the first week, Mother dispensed with the usual silence at dinner and we enjoyed talking during meals. Ten of us, including the six of us newcomers, were guided to a wide middle table between the long monastic tables where the older sisters sat. Our voices were shriller and laughter more frequent, but still we sat in rank. I was disappointed to be seated next to a quiet, aloof sister, also newly assigned, but who rarely spoke to me. Across from me, sat the next youngest, Sister Jacqueline, and a few seats up, Sister Loyola, who kept up a continual stream of banter. I wished I could next sit next to her. In the first weeks, the Old Guard welcomed us newcomers with smiles and offers of help. They showed us where things were kept and assured us we'd all be fine. I scribbled in my nightly exam book:

August 30 : *So far it holds promise of an exciting year.*

The unquestioned leader of the Old Guard was Sister Andrew, the high school principal, with her chalk-white skin, wide mouth and pink-flared nostrils. A constant stream of words often flowed from her mouth like a long, trailing kite, but she seldom listened. When I'd seen her a week ago at our Community gathering, she'd lumbered by me and I had to grab her sleeve to stop her and tell her how pleased I was to be joining her faculty. When I asked her what I would be teaching, she rattled off four subjects: biology, art, religion and Christian Family Living. My heart nearly stopped. How could I possibly teach all that? When I expressed reservations. She'd replied, "Don't worry, Sister, I've assigned sisters to help you." She blinked and adjusted the glasses that were always sliding down her wide nose, flashed a half smile and moved away.

The vice principal was Sister Agnes Ann, who had been at the school forever and still monitored the school gate at 3 p.m., waving cars of boys to move on just as she did when I was there. Though in her late sixties, she walked with a spring in her step and added a dramatic flair to everything she did. She demanded special respect and she got it. A few more of my old teachers were still teaching, but none took a special interest in us newly assigned sisters. It was two weeks before school opened and I needed guidance for my classes, but it was difficult to come by.

Sister Esther was to assist me with my biology classes. When I was a student in the high school, she had taught sewing and made the costumes for the school musicals, but now she taught three classes of biology. I would teach the other three. I found her in the Community room reading the newspaper, bifocals perched on her long thin nose. The Examiner headlines read: *Kennedy talks with Khrushchev.* I walked over, timidly interrupting, I asked for her help. I watched her struggle not to be sharp with me.

"In about ten minutes, I can talk with you."

By the end of our conversation, it was clear she was a practical, no frills woman who did her job efficiently. I doubted that she had any more science education than I did and was unlikely to hover over me. During the year, she would order the movies and lab specimens--the amoeba, paramecium, earthworms, the frogs--and as well as the science movies for my classes as well as hers. At the end of our exchange, she peered at me over her spectacles and, sensing my anxiety, she patted my hand. "Don't worry, Sister, God will provide the grace the strength to do this. You know, Sister, I've been teaching more years than I want to count and whenever I received an assignment that was new, God gave me His blessing and was there to help me. Besides, I'll be here to answer your questions. They're nice girls. You won't have any trouble." Without a pause she asked if I played bridge. They needed a fourth at recreation. I shook my head, but she said she was sure I'd pick it up easily.

After dinner each evening, we would gather in the Community room for an hour of recreation. Thankfully we no longer had to sit in a one huge circle, addressing all the conversation to the Superior; now we mingled freely. Some sat at small tables for a game of Scrabble or to work on a puzzle; others found cards in the drawer. But the evenings I was dragged into their serious bridge game, were terrifying.

When the convent Employments were posted, I was stunned to find that I was assigned the sacristy, the most demanding, time-consuming task. Not only did it require full charge of the liturgy--preparing the vestments, altar breads, chalice and candles for daily Mass--but also meant keeping the sanctuary and altar clean, the linen cloths pressed, the tabernacle veil changed to the proper liturgical colors. Sister Dorothea's name was above mine which meant we would share the job. She was also the art teacher and Sister Andrew assured me she would guide me in the one art class I was assigned to teach. Certainly a camaraderie would develop between us as we worked side by side.

Each day after breakfast, I raced to the sacristy to fulfill my duties. My job was to mop the sanctuary, dust the altar and vacuum the sanctuary carpet while Sister Dorothea put away the brocade vestments, cleaned and stored the gold chalice. Whenever I asked her a question, she bit her lower lip and gave the briefest possible answer. Soon I realized she would have preferred another Employment, one where she wouldn't have to speak to me, nor make decisions about how to split the tasks. She often finished first and disappeared without a nod, leaving me wondering which of us would come in at four o'clock to change the tabernacle veil and set out the vestments for the next day's Mass.

One morning I finally felt the strength to inspect my school classroom, the biology lab. I walked across the garden, past the bench where once I sat dreaming of transferring to Lowell, where Sister Maureen had declared her affection for me and my plans changed. I pushed open the heavy door of the school atrium. Smells assaulted me- disinfectant, chalk dust, new paint. With a pang I realized that this was not a new assignment, but a return to a trysting place. At every turn, I was haunted by memories of Maureen: here we'd hugged; there we'd quarreled; in that storeroom we'd been discovered kissing. Instead of going up to the lab, I walked into the cafeteria and imagined I heard Sister Maureen humming *That Old Black Magic,* but now someone else was in charge of the kitchen, a portly Italian woman, who cooked lunch for the students and the nuns. It was no longer our place.

As I climbed to the third floor, I wondered what Maureen was doing now. In August she had been transferred to our Seattle convent to teach biology in a coed high school that was staffed by several different Orders of nuns. Sister Angel of our community had been teaching physiology at this coed high school for several years and Maureen would travel daily by car with Sister Angel to the high school. From my high school days, I knew that Sister Angel was difficult and even then, she had disapproved of Sister Maureen, perhaps jealous of her many followers and was particularly annoyed by me with my obvious crush on Maureen. Then Sister Angel wasn't popular with the students and rarely had helpers. How did Maureen handle being with her every day? Yet Maureen had a core that could overlook the disapproval of others and go self-confidently about her own tasks. I envied that trait as I worried what others thought and often needed approval. Now I willed away the memories. I was no longer that young girl with a crush on Sister Maureen. I clutched Mother Colette's expectations around me like a protective shield, determined to be the mature teacher she expected me to be.

When I reached the biology lab, I surveyed the room and could almost hear giggling coming from the small back room where the ghosts of Sister Joseph and Marilyn and sister's many fans lingered. For several years, Sister Joseph had been weaving her science magic in our Berkeley high school. Now this was my domain. I saw the black-topped lab tables needed paint. Rows of insects in thin drawers were still pinned in mid-flight, dusty stuffed birds stared down from top shelves. Rows of petri dishes and beakers were lined up next to the wilting plants and a King snake lay coiled in a terrarium. With only two science college classes in biology--one in entomology and one in vertebrates, I felt ill prepared. In the backroom, I found an autoclave and other equipment that I had no idea how to use. Suddenly a wave of panic arose, like vomit that rushes up, then recedes, leaving a burning sensation behind. With sweaty hands, I gripped a black-topped lab table, closed my eyes and prayed: *Dear Lord, You know I would never choose to teach biology. Please infuse me with enthusiasm and knowledge. I want to do Your Will. You have to help me!*

I didn't realize that the biology textbook would be my guide and, that in any case, I would know more than the students. After my assessment of the lab, I ventured down the hall to the art room. Art was always my true passion and I was glad I was assigned to teach one art class. Eager and full of questions, I opened the classroom door and called to Sister Dorothea. She peeked out from the small workroom at the front of the room.

"Hi Sister, this room brings back such memories. You know I took art here in high school and it hardly seems to have changed." I walked around the room, touching familiar objects--the old easels, the white plaster models of hands and fruit used for drawing exercises. "The place seems much the same. My friend, Marilyn, and I used to work here at these very easels, painting, jabbering." I didn't add that all Marilyn and I ever talked about was her passion for Sister Joseph and mine for Sister Maureen.

Sister Dorothea emerged wearing a bright smock over her habit. She said, "Sister, I've been in this room for over five years and it isn't the same at all. I've added something new each year. For years, only drawing and painting were offered. Now I have ceramics, mosaics and stained glass." Her eyes traveled around the room, proudly surveying her territory and waiting for me to acknowledge her authority. Her eyes rested on the large half completed glass mosaic of the Virgin, nearly eight feet long and four feet wide, a full figure in white, gold and shades blue. She picked up bit of blue mosaic glass. I admired her chiseled fingers that moved with the precision of a craftsman's hands. Her face, too, was chiseled with sharp angular features. She made it clear that I was to come to the art room only to teach my class as she planned it. Everything else, the other art classes, the large bulletin boards in the halls, posters, scenery, banners, decorations for various events, were solely her domain. Mother Colette told me I was to learn from Sister Dorothea. Had she forgotten to mention it to her? I was like a dry sponge, eager to absorb from her, but it appeared the well was dry.

"Oh, I see now you've done marvelous things here. I'm looking forward to working with you. You're busy now. Let me know when we can go over the details of my class." I darted out and back to the convent and straight to the chapel where I prayed earnestly for the grace to get me through the beginning of this school year.

The next week I spent becoming familiar with the biology textbook and putting the lab in order. I decided the scuffed blacktopped tables needed a new coat of paint and found black spray lacquer cans in the back. I had almost completed spraying the tables when I ran out of paint before I finished the last one. Impatiently, I shook the can and sprayed, but nothing came out. Irritated, I thrust a can opener into the bottom. Like a shot the can exploded. The noise brought Sister Jacqueline running from her classroom to the lab. When she saw me, her frame doubled over in laughter and tears ran down her chubby face.

"Theophane, I can't tell your back from your front, " she gasped.

"Would you mind helping me?" I asked icily as I removed my thick glasses and groped for the paint thinner. My face, glasses, teeth, my white guimpe, headband--everything was shiny black. She couldn't stop giggling as she dampened a rag with turpentine and began to clean me. Then I let go of my anger and we roared together. The cleaning process took a long time. I even used Ajax on my teeth to get rid of all the black paint, but when my eyes cleared, the classroom looked much better.

On the first day of school, bells rang, lockers slammed and girls shrieked greetings to one another. They wore plaid uniform skirts, navy jackets and white blouses and sported summer tans. Suddenly the silent school was infused with life and energy. I wanted to laugh aloud at the transformation, but I was careful to appear serious, lest my inexperience be discovered. I was afraid the students might notice I wasn't wearing a ring like the other nuns who had made final vows and they might ask me about it, but no one noticed. In my homeroom as instructed, I watched to see that no freshman had hair-dos teased too high or wore skirts that were too short. At the first faculty meeting, Sister Agnes Ann had told us that last year she'd made some girl take down her hair and a spider had crawled out!

In the biology lab, the desk was on an elevated platform and it was as if I had my own stage. Though at first, I felt stage fright, I soon rose to the challenge of the upturned faces, some eager, some daring me to teach them anything. Biology was a required class for sophomores, but not a subject that interested all of them. I usually began class with a humorous anecdote about my earlier teaching experiences in East L.A. or other places. I'd see them elbow each other as they laughed. Then I would launch into the topic of the day which might be photosynthesis, plant and animal classifications or insects and their patterns. It was fresh in my mind as I read the pertinent chapter only the night before and I was amazed at learning the way nature worked-- so intricately, so wonderfully. My enthusiasm was contagious and the classes were often buoyant, engaging even the poorest students who worked hard and asked for help. In spite of Sister Dorothea's coolness, I loved teaching my art class and envied the students their forty-five minutes to draw or paint, wishing I had time to paint, but my own tubes of watercolors were tightly capped in a box at the bottom of my closet.

On Friday after the first week, I walked into the school office hoping that I might share with Sister Andrew my elation that the first week hadn't held any particular disaster. She was in her inner office. Through the amber glass, I could see her laughing with a student. I waited. Then, ignoring me, she went out the other door and off to the convent for coffee with Sister Agnes Ann. In the hall, I watched in dismay their retreating figures.

Sister George came toward me with her white bandeau slightly askew and unsightly hairs straying out of one corner, calling, "Come with me, Sister Theophane. Sister Andrew wants me to show you your school Employment. Hurry, please, I've got to get right back to the bookstore. I sell more books and supplies in the first week than in the entire year."

We went to the backroom of the bookstore where she stopped at a stack of cartons. Her large freckled hands pulled out a penknife and she deftly opened the top carton. "These," she announced, "are sanitary napkins. It's your job to service the Kotex machines in the bathrooms on each floor." I stared at her. Why didn't Sister Andrew herself tell me about this? Wasn't she ever going to speak to me directly? I already had the care of biology lab and the sacristy in the convent. Beyond that, I needed every moment to prepare for my classes.

"Do I have to do this every day?"

"Every other day is enough. I found the best time to refill the machines and collect the money is when the girls are in class. You can do it in your preparation period. At the end of the week, I'll show you how to wrap coins for banking."

I muttered, "At my preparation period?"

"I could take a minute now to show you how to do it," she offered. I followed her plodding figure through the locker room to the bathroom amid a barrage of 'Good afternoon, Sisters' from the girls eyeing us while they teased their hair at the mirror where long ago Tessie had preened as she applied Revlon's Fire 'n Ice. Oblivious to the girls watching us, Sister inserted a small key in the white machine. She dropped several of the individually boxed sanitary napkins into the metal channel. "See, Sister, how simple it is. Now here's your key." She pulled the tiny key off her large key ring that was attached by a strap to her cincture and handed it to me.

"Do all your keys fit places in the school?" I asked.

"Yes, indeed," she said, giving them a jangle. "This one opens the side door of the school as you come from the convent, a real convenient one to have." I knew she had earned each key with hours of service. I dropped the tiny key into my pocket.

At the school lunch period, I was assigned to supervise the large atrium where the girls ate lunches they brought from home. They gathered round me and spoke about their problems with their mothers, their grades and their boyfriends. I listened sympathetically, but offered little advice as they seemed happy just to have someone listen to them. One day one of my biology students sidled up to me and asked, "Sister, have you heard Barbra Streisand?"

"No, I haven't. And who is she?"

"Oh, Sister, she's the most! You haven't lived 'til you've heard her sing. Tomorrow I'll bring you her latest album."

"Ah, Cheryl, where would I play it?"

"Don't you have a record player in the convent?" she asked wide-eyed

"No."

The circle of girls that had gathered chorused, "Oh, no!"

"Then, how do you listen to music?"

"You know we Sisters just sing Gregorian Chant." They laughed and tried to sing a few bars of songs they loved.

One afternoon I was in the sacristy pressing the long white alb that the priest wore under his vestment at Mass. Suddenly, Sister Dorothea marched into the sacristy, waving the tall red glass lamp containing the remains of the eight-day candle, screaming, "The sanctuary lamp has burnt out! Mother Colette just handed this to me! It was your week to change the lamp. I wish you'd take your responsibility seriously!" The candle glowed day and night in the sanctuary to signify the presence of Christ in the tabernacle on the altar. To let it burn out was akin to dragging an American the flag in the dirt.

"I'm sorry. I thought it was your week."

"It doesn't matter whose week it was. What matters is the lamp burned out and the Mother General had to call it to my attention!" With her heels tapping an angry staccato, she strode out to the sanctuary with the newly lit candle. I just kept ironing.

After school was my favorite time. I had two faithful helpers. Barbara, plump, blonde and humorous, and Janice, thin, dark-haired, quiet and sensitive. As we tidied up the biology lab, changed the bulletin board or corrected papers, they sometimes asked, "What would you do without us?" When I only smiled, they chorused: "You'd have to handle the King snake yourself!"

I reminded them it had escaped during the first week of school and, after several days, it was I who spotted it under the radiator and grabbed it with false aplomb. While all the girls were screaming, I threw it in its cage and fastened the top tightly. As they hung around laughing and joking, I was pleased that I felt no extreme emotional attachment to them. I imagined myself now mature and free of the curse of misplaced affections that had ruled my teenage life.

In October, the Second Vatican Council opened in Rome. The school celebrated this auspicious event with a special Mass. None of us dreamed of the enormous changes that would follow from this Council. At the Offertory, one student stood and made a petition that God would guide President Kennedy in dealing with Cuba. Another asked for the light of the Holy Spirit for the Bishops attending the Council. I asked silently for the grace to get along with Sister Dorothea. A student, passing out the song sheets interrupted my thoughts. Dimples creased her cheeks as she stood at my side in her slightly pigeon-toed stance asking, "Sister, would you ask the girls to pass along these the song sheets?" She kept grinning at me until I smiled back, as the students passed along the song sheets.

The next week we changed Family Living classes. I taught Art in the Home, which brought a new set of students every six weeks, and the same girl, Michelle, sat squarely in the front row, again smiling up at me.

After class she came up to me and said, "Sister, I've been so looking forward to this class. You know, we kids talk about you nuns, ...uh, I mean, I heard you were a really good teacher." Though her remarks were bold, she spoke in charming way, standing slighly pigeon-toed. She wore her uniform plaid skirt just a bit shorter than most, revealing knobby knees. Michelle began to ask to carry my books from one class to the next and this embarrassed me, though in these same halls only seven years earlier, Della and I had competed to carry Sister Maureen's books. Michelle began to stay after school and I welcomed this new-comer, though she was different than Barbara and Janice. When Michelle was part of the group, the tone was different. She behaved in a sassy, almost flirtatious manner. I found myself laughing at her jokes and favoring her.

The last Saturday in October was the eve of the Feast of Christ the King and I spent most of the day in the sacristy with preparations. While I was working, a sister brought boxes of gladioli that had been ordered from a florist. My work was done so I went over to the school to tell Sister Dorothea the flowers had arrived. I yearned to learn the secret of turning ordinary bunches of flowers into stunning displays that adorned the altar. In the art room Sister Dorothea, wearing her flowered smock, was humming to herself, absorbed in placing pieces of colored tile on the large mosaic of our Lady. The smock gave her softness, like catching a wife in her housecoat.

"Sister, I thought you'd like to know the flowers arrived-gorgeous flame gladioli, white carnations, shiny lemon leaves and fern stalks," I said enthusiastically. "I was wondering would you like any help in doing the arrangements?"

"No, no, I can take care of it. I hope you left the door of the workroom closed so the flowers will stay cool. You know flowers are expensive." Without another word, she turned back to observe her mosaic work with a critical eye.

As I walked across the garden to the convent, I felt a winter chill pass through me, even though it was a warm day with no hint of the damp winter that was coming. In the Community room, Sister Esther was reading the single daily newspaper and I could see in the headlines something about Kennedy and Cuba. I sighed and walked into the next room, the one assigned to those of us who had not made Final vows. Sister Jacqueline looked up from her Latin book.

"Hi, Theo," she beamed. I slumped into a chair opposite her with a nod.

"Guess what? My Latin textbooks finally came. I can stop using the duplicating machine for classwork everyday. I know Sister Hubert is happy too. She hated me in her business department every day. I was always getting the paper jammed and asking her to add more fluid." She rolled her eyes and giggled. "You know how she is, territorial and" . I looked at her with a grin, finishing her sentence, "and mean."

We both laughed. I knew she wanted to be friends with me, but she was the youngest of the staff and had that irritating giggle that erupted at the least provocation. I longed to be friends with the irreverent Sister Loyola, but she was a Final Professed and always busy and stressed with her classes, the glee club and its performances.

I got up and stared out the window at the traffic below. I'd just turned twenty-five, I was back in my beloved San Francisco, at the school where I felt as much my home as our flat on 22nd Avenue where I grew up. My classes were going well. I should've felt content, but I felt lonely.

One day Michelle came to school wearing a pikaki flower behind her ear. I should have asked her to remove it as it was against our uniform code and had it been another student, I would have, but today was school pictures day and I knew she wanted to stand out so I said nothing. Often she'd carry my books as I returned to the convent, but she'd walk too close to me, sometimes stumbling against my arm. At her touch, I realized there was an undercurrent of feelings going on between us. Emotions I thought buried, were coming alive, the way weeds spring up after the first rain.

In the evenings I began writing in my Exam Book:

Be careful of Michelle

Another night: *Don't let Michelle take over your affections.*

One afternoon I received a note from Sister Andrew that said she wanted to see me in her office after school. Through the frosted glass, I could make out her bulk as she talked to the student body president who was laughing. With the students, Sister was a great comedian. Finally, the student left. At the the doorway I asked, "You wanted to see me, Sister?" My palms were sweaty; my stomach in knots.

She cleared her throat, twisted sideways in her chair. "Come and sit down, Sister."

The chair was still warm from the departed student. "Sister, I'm unhappy. Do you know why I'm unhappy?"

"No, Sister."

"Because you're not on my team." I looked at her quizzically. "You are a team of one Sister with too many girls.

" I'm not sure what you mean, Sister"

"Whenever there's a job to do, and there are many in running this high school, the other sisters jump right in. They volunteer if there's an evening function; they stay till it's over. If they need girls to help, they rotate them. They don't gather a little clique around them. Now it's my observation, you have the same girls around you all the time."

The perspiration under my arms trickled down inside my habit. I was angry and hurt. She hadn't bothered to tell me that she'd changed the rules since I was in school with Sister Maureen when many nuns had the same girls around.

"I'm sorry, Sister. I didn't know, I didn't realize…." I sat with head down, near tears. I imagined her unspoken thoughts: *I will never trust you, because of your history with Sister Maureen.*

Her face softened. "I have my pulse on the school, Sister. I do know you're doing a good job in the classroom. The girls like your biology classes. As far as the art class is concerned, I realize Sister Dorothea is not the easiest person to work with, but she's under a lot of pressure and responsible for many things--these huge bulletin boards, the decorations for every activity. You just teach your one class and try not to hinder her work.

"I've offered to help her."

"She has her own system. She works best alone. Now in a couple of days we are having Father-Daughter night. I'd like you to greet the girls and their fathers as they come in.

"Of course, I want to be on your team. I'd love to help."

"Good, welcome to the faculty." Her phone rang. Grateful for the distraction, I escaped. The chapel was empty except for old Sister Julian mumbling her rosary, her beads clattering against her stall. I knelt in my stall, feeling beaten. Why did she wait so long to tell me her new rules?

Jesus, You have willed me to this Mission. Please give the the insight, the grace to do this well. I reached down and held my large crucifix to my cheek. "*Just help me!*"

The next day Michelle asked to speak with me privately. She said it was important, yet I knew it was a ploy to have time alone with me. I should've said no, but foolishly, I agreed. After school we found an empty classroom at the far end of the building where we wouldn't be disturbed, rather than using the biology lab where we would certainly be interrupted. The shades were already drawn and I by-passed the teacher's desk and sat in a student's desk and Michelle plopped down opposite me. We were on the same level.

As she began to pour out her story of a broken home, a divorce that forced her to spend part time with each parent, I listened sympathetically. Divorce was an embarrassment for any Catholic family. I recalled my own intimate talks with Sister Maureen when I was a sophomore and Mom began dating Roy, a younger man who drove an MG. Michelle's parents had divorced at least two years before and I sensed this wasn't as new and as painful as she was describing. Then abruptly, she talked coyly of a boyfriend. I had the odd feeling she was trying to make me jealous. She was a true seductress and, in spite of myself, I was succumbing. I felt envious of her ease with boys, an ease I'd never had.

I noticed the room was darker now. I looked at the clock and jumped up. "Dear God, I have to be in the chapel in five minutes. You have to leave this very minute." She was unmoved, but I took her arm. For a moment we froze, standing close, looking at each other, feeling each others quickening breath. One more second and we might've embraced. I pulled her forcibly to the classroom door. As she followed me down the hallway, she was slipping her arm into her camel's hair jacket, shifting her load of books from one arm to the other, moving too slowly. In a panic, I ordered, "Michelle, go now!" I pulled her to the least used exit, the furthest away from the convent where the nuns were now lining to up to take their places to recite the hours of Matins and Lauds.

"All right, I'm going. What is your problem?" As I opened the door, I heard the jangle of keys.

"Who's there?" It was the singsong voice of the vice principal, Sister Agnes Ann. Her huge bulk was barreling down the corridor toward us. Michelle just stood there, her lips twitching at the corners. Sensing the danger, she was drawing on the scene to bind us further. "Go," I hissed and gave her a shove.

"It's just me," I chirped toward Sister.

"Who is me?" she demanded, closing in on me.

"Me, Sister Theophane"

"Sister, you shouldn't be here at this hour. What are you doing at that door? Is someone with you?" Her hand shaded her eyes against the light, peering at me, then past me at the thick door slowly closing.

"I lost track of the time. I'm just letting one of my helpers out. I'm going to be late for prayers if I don't hurry." I scurried past her. She stalked me like a jailer with keys jangling loudly. At the garden, I could hear the convent bell tolling and holding up my habit, I sprinted like a runner. If I could make it in on the last toll, I would be safe.

A few days later it came, as I knew it would: the summons. To my surprise, it wasn't to the vice principal's office nor to the principal's nor to Sister Superior's but to Mother Colette's office, to her inner sanctum. The access to her office was entered through a dark maze. In her office the light was too bright after the dark entry. Blinking, I knelt at the side of her grand desk and avoided her eyes, magnified behind thick lenses. Mother knew my strengths, my flaws and she'd put her trust in me giving me this promotion. My mind flashed back to our encounters over the years: the day she told me solemnly, in the manner of announcing a death, that my brother, Steve, had left the priest's seminary; the worst day, when she forbade Sister Maureen to visit with me before she went to our New Mexico convent; the terrifying day she appointed me choir-mistress when I knew nothing of music; the time she'd gotten down on her knees with the brush and showed me how to scrub the toilets. Now this.

"Sister Theophane, what is this I hear? Such poor reports of you. Sister Andrew says you have the same students around you after school; Sister Dorothea says you ask much too much of her and that you are frivolous and talkative. Don't you realize she has her own classes to prepare? And now Sister Agnes Ann tells me you are staying late with one girl, so late that it was dark when you let her out of the school. What have you to say for yourself Sister?"

Humiliation washed over me. I wanted to cry out: "From that first evening in the novitiate garden when you led the novices in singing *The Evening Hymn to the Sacred Heart,* I knew then I was base metal among true carats, feigning love for Jesus, when in truth I was driven by my passion for Sister Maureen." I have tried to change, but now my weakness is exposed: I have a deep need for human love! My secret discovered, ironically, not with Sister Maureen, but with the youthful Michelle. Mother's deep gaze would surely see my desires, my hunger, my passion and she will remove me lest I contaminate others. As Jesus drove the moneychangers from the temple, I must be cast out. I bowed my head, awaiting sentence.

She repeated," What have you to say for yourself, Sister Theophane?"

My head falls lower. I have no words; my only answer, racking sobs. I would I leave wearing sackcloth and ashes, unworthy to live among God's chosen ones. No final vows, no silver ring and no betrothal to Christ.

"Can you explain yourself, Sr. Theophane?" she asked a third time with less patience. Still I said nothing. She commanded in exasperation: "Sit down, Sister."

I took a chair by the side of her desk, my eyes still lowered and for few moments, only silence. Then I peeked at her. Her head was turned as she gazed out the window at the large Canary palm filtering the afternoon light. Her face was more lined and her double chin more prominent than I remembered. Her hands were clasped tightly in front of her.

"Sister, I do realize this high school is not an easy assignment. It requires not only intelligence, but also tact and adaptability. I thought you capable of this. I am deeply disappointed in you. Sister, you must relinquish your pride, your self-will, your unruly nature."

Stunned that she wasn't focusing on the current incident with Michelle, I whisper, "Mother, I am so very sorry, but the high school Sisters are not easy to get along with."

She replied with a rueful laugh, "I realize that, Sister, but I want you to keep on trying. It is high time for some changes in that high school and I am counting on you to help me make that work."

Sweet Jesus, she is counting on me to help her? She, too, finds the Old Guard intractable. She wants me on her side? No, I cannot do this. My heart was pounding. Did she imagine she is Samson, using me like the jawbone of an ass to slay the mob? Suddenly, she sat taller, her face stern. She was indeed the Mother General with great responsibility on her shoulders.

"That is all, Sister."

A reprieve? No, no, this wasn't right. She should've carried out the execution. I leaned forward in my chair. "Mother, I heard that Sister Louis has been asked to leave." She was the nun, a year ahead of me, who commanded the singing in the novitiate masterfully after my failure.

Her brows furrowed. "Yes, Sister, that is true."

Only days before, a sister whispered to me that Sister Louis was asked to return to the world after six years of service. I was aware she'd committed an offense that might merit such a punishment.

During our ten-day vacation at the Order's property in the Santa Cruz mountains, she'd spent the night in the same room as younger sister. What actually occurred was never revealed, but it was easy to imagine the gregarious, self-absorbed Sister Louis talking long into the night and her companion laughing and giggling in a youthful, worshiping manner. When discovered, the two had been sent to separate cabins and confined to their rooms for the remainder of the vacation. The younger sister was gone by Christmas.

I said, "I don't think I'm any different from Sister Louis. Do you think it is wise for me to make final vows in January with the difficulties I'm having right now?" My words were urgent. In slow motion, her face rearranged itself and her head cocked to one side, puzzled, as if listening to my words as distant echoes: *So different from Sister Louis? So different from Sister Louis?*

"You are entirely different from her, Sister. I have never doubted your vocation for an instant!" Her eyes bore straight into my soul. Then she rose and moved from behind the grand desk. Hesitantly, I stood. Her arms encompassed me in a restrained embrace. How could she still believe in me when I, myself, doubted I had the stamina to continue? She opened the door, ushered me out. "God bless you, Sister."

I stood in the dark entry maze, puzzling over what just occurred. Then I headed to the chapel and knelt right at the altar railing. It was definitely time to talk to Jesus. I needed His Grace, a huge dose of it. Deep down in my heart, I hoped she would send me home, say that I was unfit. I felt troubled and trapped, but couldn't yet make the decision to leave on my own.

The date for our Final Vows was set for early January. The six other sisters in my group arrived the day after Christmas to spend the week in retreat, preparing to take vows of poverty, chastity and obedience for the rest of our lives. As soon as the sisters entered the gloomy vestibule of the Motherhouse, I raced to greet them. Brashly, we broke the silence, hugging and giggling.

Sister Robert, in her down to earth manner, held me at arms length. "How ya' doing, Honey? Just walking into this place gives me the creeps."

Before I could answer, Sister Gloria embraced me. I felt the heat of her long sensuous fingers right through my habit. With envy she asked, "How is it going at the high school? How's the art? Is it just wonderful?"

As ever, I was awed by Sister Gloria's beauty. and talent. She'd been our high school Social Director, putting on plays and complex musicals. Mother should have chosen her for this promotion. Now they closed in a circle around me, a shelter from eavesdroppers. "Tell us the truth! What is it like, really?" I wanted to hold each of them tightly, my precious fellow warriors. I only rolled my eyes. If I spoke, I would've sobbed. They nodded. They knew.

Eight days later after a silent retreat, we took the last step of initiation into the Order, final vows. The ceremony was simple in comparison to the ritual of first vows. After Mass in the Motherhouse with only the Community present, the six of us moved to the altar rail and in turn, pronounced our vows of poverty, chastity and obedience for the rest of our lives. The grey-haired priest, still wearing wearing the chasible, slipped a silver ring with a raised cross on each of our wedding fingers. Then he extended his arms and prayed over the six of us:

"O God, Who hast established Thy habitation in a chaste heart, look down upon Thy servants and may they receive by Thy consolation whatsoever they require in their daily trials, through Christ Our Lord."

As he the sprinkled Holy Water on our heads, we replied, "Amen." We were Brides of Christ for the rest of our lives.

CHAPTER EIGHTEEN

AFTER FINAL VOWS 1963

IN JANUARY I returned to school wearing my shiny new ring, symbol of my final vows. I thought of it as a shield, warding off my attraction to Michelle, but on my lunch duty in the cafeteria, she raced over and in the midst of all the girls' chattering and lunch trays banging, took my hand and gushed over my ring. I could feel myself blushing.

"Could I come to school and help you on Saturday afternoon, Sister?"

I took a deep breath and replied, "That's a generous offer, but I've no work for you to do." She made a face. She knew in truth: I would've liked to say 'yes.' Off she went dancing, skirt swaying and my eyes following her.

The next day I had to clean the biology lab and asked some students, including my faithful two, Janice and her good friend, Barbara to stay and wash the beakers and scrub the dissecting trays. Yet Michelle found her way into my third floor lab. She chattered and laughed and plied me with endless questions and acted as if she belonged in the biology class. Then she asked Janice to come out in the hall with her.

Later, Janice said to me, "That Michelle is a little weird. She wanted me to ask you if we could all, including you, play Hide and Seek around the third floor."

"That is silly, indeed," I said, but it brought back memories of my days where Sister Maureen, Sister Joseph, Marilyn and I played "Sardines. " It was a game where one person hid and the others looked for that person and piled in next to them. The loser was the last person remaining who hadn't found the hiding place. I recall trying desperately to find Sister Maureen first so I could squeeze in next to her.

Janice and Barbara often asked questions about the convent life. I saw the mystique of the nun's life held a similar fascination as it did for me when I was their age. Yet I had no desire to make my life appealing or mysterious. I simply answered their questions matter-of-factly and went on with the chores.

One afternoon as I was leaving school and starting down the path to the convent, I saw in front of me Sister Jacqueline and carrying her books was Michelle. The two of them were laughing and giggling. Suddenly, I felt as if I'd been punched. How could Michelle have changed allegiance so casually? I told myself, Jacqueline, still not a Final Professed, was going to find herself in trouble. To avoid them, I stole around to the side door and entered through North Hall. I headed straight to the chapel. I knelt there in soft light of the stained glass windows, twisting my silver ring and trying to suppress my feelings of betrayal. I told myself: This is Jesus answering my prayers. It's His way of helping me end this foolish attraction.

"Thank you, Jesus. Now I know you are listening to my pleas. I want you to be at the center of my heart."

Yet I was so hurt and angry that I avoided any contact with Sister Jacqueline for days.

One night just before the Great Silence at 9 p.m., Sister Jacqueline came to my cell, stuck her head through the curtains and motioned me to follow her to the library. What does she want at this hour, I wondered.

"Did you hear what happened?" she whispered.

"No, what?" I said.

"Michelle was discovered in the school at eight o'clock this evening. Sister Andrew and Sister Agnes Ann found her and another girl running around in the cafeteria."

"Who was the other girl?"

"I don't know. Sister Andrew called Michelle's mother, who hadn't even missed her at eight o'clock and wasn't worried. That made Sister upset with the mother as well as with with Michelle. Then she came to find me and asked if she'd had she been with me. Luckily for me, she wasn't!"

"You are very fortunate!" I replied.

As I returned to my cell, I felt a sadness for Michelle. Her home life was difficult and she wanted attention so badly that she was now acting recklessly. With Sister Andrew onto her, she'd have to leave school as soon as the bell rang. Was this God answering my prayers and removing temptation?

After Christmas, the nun in the sleeping cubicle next to mine moved to another location. Sister Vincent was, like me, new to the teaching staff this year. She came from one of our convents in southern California to teach chemistry and math. Tall, with a wide mouth and mobile face, her gift was as a comedian. As she was several years ahead of me in rank, she sat further up my table in the refectory. When she'd tell a story, everyone would lean in to catch the details and laugh loudly at her tales. At dinner, I was able to catch parts of her story. One night she was imitating Gina, one of her students, who always wore heavy purple lipstick and had a huge, teased bouffant hairdo, anchored with a headband. Sister had Gina's lisp down perfectly, imitating her pep talk to the students to give money to the Mission. Everyone laughed. She ended by stating, "Yet she is the best darn Mission leader and shames the girls into contributing."

Sister Vincent's antics were not limited to the refectory. When a nun in our infirmary died and as customary, her body was laid in an open coffin in the center aisle of the chapel, surrounded by four tall candlesticks. That afternoon a well-dressed woman came in to pay her respects to the deceased nun. She sat in a stall near the coffin. At five p.m. the bell began to toll, calling us to the chapel. The Superior began the recitation of the Hours of Matins and Lauds, a ritual that included turning, bowing, kneeling, as we prayed aloud, holding our purple-edged prayer books. The startled woman, imagining this to be prayers for the deceased, tried to follow the motions of our ritual, contorting herself in twists and turns without any prayer book to follow the psalms. Across the aisle, I caught sight of Sister Vincent in the stall behind the woman, mimicking her moves and confusion. I could barely stifle my laughter. All around me, sisters were shaking in silent spasms. Finally, the Superior came up to the woman, still in contortions, and instructed her to sit while we prayed aloud. I wondered if she'd caught sight of Sister Vincent's irreverent antics.

When Sister Vincent moved into the cell next to me, I soon discovered she had another side. She muttered and grumbled as she banged around her cell while I sat at my desk in the next cell, trying to master the next chapter in biology. One evening I heard her swearing as she shoved her books and papers around. I thought she might be embarrassed if she knew I could hear her. Loudly, I cleared my throat. Suddenly she yanked back the yellow curtains between our cells. With her hands on her hips she asked, "Isn't this place a bitch?" I couldn't help but laugh aloud.

Then in an unusual turn of events, the older nun in the larger end cubicle was hospitalized, leaving only Sister Vincent and myself in the divided room. In a serious violation of the Rule of Silence, we began conversing regularly between our cells. Sister Vincent's behavior would swing from angry rants, to moping depression, to exuberant hilarity. I gleaned from things she said that she'd been transferred from our high school in Los Angeles because she'd formed too close a bond with one of her students. Ah, a kindred spirit, I thought.

After school, I loved walking to the convent with her. Her wide mouth and large hands moved in synchronized motions as she told anecdotes of her day. She'd take giant steps in the low flat-heeled shoes she wore. I had to trot to keep up with her. I loved that we were becoming special friends.

Meanwhile, in school, evolution was a topic I was about to teach in my biology classes. In our convent library, in the spirit of the Ecumenical Council convening in Rome, more enlightened, advanced authors were made available for our reading material. I devoured Huns Kung and Bruce Vawter and other authors. It became clear that the works of the Old Testament was comprised of stories that had principles and morals with a spiritual message, but were not to be taken literally.

When I began the subject of evolution in my biology class, a student soon asked,

"Sister, wasn't the world created in seven days?" I explained that it was a story, meant to enlighten and show the power of Yahweh/God, but not a scientific fact. I went further, sharing with them that Adam and Eve, Noah and the Ark were not factual events, but metaphorical stories. As the discussion became heated, some girls were visibly shaken to learn that Old Testament wasn't to be taken literally. Cecile Herman stood up and shouted, "This is heresy, Sister." I tried to calm the class, but I knew they were thinking: what else in our religion might not be literally true.

That afternoon I was summoned to Sister Andrew's office. "Close the door, Sister." As I did so, she gestured to the chair across from her desk. She peered darkly at me through glasses perched at the end of her wide nose. "Sister, some of the sophomores came to my office today. They were upset about something you told them in your biology class." She leaned forward, glaring at me. "Are you teaching the theory of evolution?"

"Yes, Sister, I am."

"Well, the girls said you told them much of the Old Testament was fictional. Are you intent on destroying their faith?"

"Sister, its true that a student asked me if the world was created in seven days. I said that was a figurative story as were the accounts of Adam and Eve and Noah. Cecile Herman did get upset. In fact, one class got in quite an uproar, but Sister I've been reading an account of Genesis by an Old Testament scholar, Bruce Vawter. He holds that the stories of Genesis are myths to illustrate God's attributes. Unfortunately, this was the first time the girls heard this. It upset some of them. We were. . ."

She interrupted me, "Vawter, Fawter, I don't care about that! Sister Esther has been teaching biology for years and nothing like this has ever happened. I don't want you to teach the kinds of things that upset the girls. If this topic is discussed in any class at all, it should be in religion class, but don't you bring it up again."

"Yes, Sister."

"You stick to science, do you understand me? The Science Fair is coming up and I want you to focus on helping the students to do good projects. We will be having Open House for the parents and I want fine science projects on display. You put your energy in that, Sister."

"Yes, Sister, I will." When I left I was fearful that she give a bad report to Mother Colette who might return me to elementary school teaching. I liked teaching the girls in the high school and also the status that teaching at the highschool brought. Yet I was angry with Sister Andrew's viewpoint. It was thrilling to read of scholarly new interpretations of the Bible and I believed these views should be shared with the students. We'd been taught these 'facts' from the time we were small children, but now with Pope John XXIII convening the Vatican Council, throwing open windows, the Church was questioning itself. However, Sister Andrew was intent on holding the windows shut as long as possible.

The next day she called an assembly of the sophomores in the Little Theater to dispel the uproar that my teaching of a new interpretation of the Old Testament caused. I stood at the back, flushed with embarrassment and too upset to focus on the information she gave the students.

I had to zero in on the Science Fair. Before I was at the high school, the brilliant Sister Joseph had produced excellent Science Fair projects, year after year. Since Sister Esther had taken her place, the projects had lapsed into mediocrity. Fortunately, I had two or three brilliant students who, in spite of me, produced amazing science projects, two of which were entered into the citywide competition at the Science Fair in Golden Gate Park's science building. One was awarded a gold ribbon. Sister Andrew never said a word to me, but I knew she was not only surprised, but also pleased.

On a wintery day, I hurried to the convent after school. I wanted a hot cup of coffee, but knew it would be lukewarm because the Sister cook, a simple woman born in the Azores and in charge of the kitchen forever, always made the pot early. She set it out on the metal cart too soon and left the kitchen. The Sisters tried to explain the problem and she'd nod, but no one could change her routine. When I opened the door of the refectory, my mouth dropped. The long monastic tables had disappeared. In their place were warm wooden tables that seated six with matching chairs. I went over and pulled out a chair and noticed there were no drawers in the table. Where were our dishes? We always had our own dish drawer.

"Hey, Theophane, isn't this new stuff nifty?" Sister Vincent, who had followed me in, was smiling.

"Incredible," I whispered.

"They were supposed to be here before Christmas and now finally, they've arrived." She talked loudly though silence was compulsory in the refectory.

"Look what else!" She scooted to the end of the refectory in her broad, flat shoes. "Get a load of this! " She held up the cover of a portable dishwasher by the sink. "Isn't this great?" She pulled out a thick black hose and attached one end to the faucet. "No more washing dishes at the table!"

"I can't believe it." I looked with awe into the machine, smelling its rubbery racks.

"You know," she lowered her voice, her blond eyebrows furrowing over slate-blue eyes, "they already have these at our Novitiate."

"No way!".

"Yes, Mother John Mary pushed for them. You know she is light-years ahead of this Motherhouse."

"Wow, She got them for the novices? I've never met Mother John Mary."

"Theo, she was my Superior down south and she is a doll, an absolute doll." She lowered her voice, "Not like you-know-who." She poured herself a cup of coffee from the battered metal pot that sat on the metal cart.

"Who? Sister Superior?" I asked, while pouring myself a cup of coffee, startled she was speaking so candidly.

"No, the Big Cheese," She made a face, her wide mouth turning down in a frown.

"You mean Mother Colette?"

"Shhh, yeh."

The door opened. Sister Jacqueline came in. "Geez, wowee! I can't believe this!" she said moving toward us. Sister Vincent gave me a quick glance that meant, end of conversation. She stepped to the sink, washed her cup. "Gotta go back to school. Gotta a meeting." She scooted out the door.

Sister Jacqueline sidled up to me and whispered, "Isn't this great, Theophane? I can't believe we won't be washing our dishes at the table anymore."

"It is great," I replied, though I was annoyed that she'd interrupted the unusual conversation I was having with Sister Vincent. Since I'd made my final vows I tried to distance myself from Sister Jacqueline who hadn't yet made Final vows. I downed my coffee and left the refectory.

That evening Sister Superior stood at the door of the refectory. As the long line of Sisters filed in after reciting the Office in chapel, she said with an unusual grin, "Take any seat, sit where you like, Sisters."

Giddily, we stumbled to random seats after years of sitting in rank. I boldly took a seat at a middle table near the top of the refectory where a small table and assigned seat was still reserved for the Mother General and the Sister Superior of the convent. After the Grace, Mother Colette turned to us with a beaming face, "Good evening Sisters, do you like our new look?" She seemed genuinely pleased with this step away from the monastic shape of the refectory. "Yes, Mother," came the loud joyful answer.

"Mother," boomed Sister Andrew, "I had to take Sister Agnes Ann by the arm and lead her to a chair. She thought she was in the wrong convent." She patted Sister's arm affectionately. Everyone laughed. I thought ruefully those two are a regular 'Abbott and Costello' act. Wouldn't they be great in movies?

Mother continued, "Sisters I want you to know I've decided to substitute the evening hour of recreation with a recreation at dinner each night. There are too many evening functions at the high school where the sisters must attend and miss the recreation hour in the convent."

I wanted to cheer. No more silent dinners, no more turns at spiritual reading during the meal on the high lectern at the side of the refectory where the Superior would jot down any mispronounced words for one to correct, no more tense hurried serving of the meals.

Mother continued, "As you may have noticed, Sisters, we have two new workers at the end of the refectory." A grinning sister server held up the lids of the two new dishwashers. With a ripple of laughter, heads swiveled No more passing of hot pitchers of water and washing our dishes in place. Tonight was a startling step away from old monastic ways!

"And Sisters we will no longer use the long antiphonal Grace, but will use a short form."

"Whoopee!" cried Sister Vincent. Then clasped her hand over her mouth. "Progress at last," she whispered, lowering her head. Lately

Sister Vincent's bubbly manner was a bit diminished. I'd observed also that she too, had been called to Sister Andrew's office a few times.

One day after school, I walked from my biology lab down the hall to find Sister Vincent in her chemistry lab. She was decorating her bulletin board. I read it aloud: Now is the time to change the world. You are the hands and feet of Christ.

"Hi Theo, how do you like it?" She was on a stool pinning up the scroll she had penned in her fine calligraphy. Her large flat shoes we're practically at my eye level.

"It's beautiful. All your bulletin boards are wonderful and I love your calligraphy." She smiled with that broad grin and pinned up a pair of hands that she had drawn.

"You know down south, I'd have girls helping me with this. I tell you, Theo, I miss that place and Mother John Mary so much." Suddenly, a sob caught in her throat. She turned her face to the bulletin board. "Its completely different here, Theo. I can't explain it. It's just not the same."

The late afternoon sun was streaming in the window and it was peaceful here at the end of the third floor, away from the convent. I sat in one of the desks and listened to her babble. She changed subjects frequently and confessed she, too, had been warned by Sister Andrew not to have the same girls around her and never to have just one. I tried to tell her about my similar experience with Michelle. She listened briefly and as soon as I took a breath, she interrupted and continued with her stories. I didn't mind as I was grateful to have her as a friend.

One evening I went to the convent switchboard to take my turn at answering phones. I saw Sister Vincent hovering over something with Sister Hubert, who ran the business department with an iron hand. Even when I was in school, she lorded it over those rows of girls with their clacking typewriters as if she was an overseer of a plantation. Now clearly Sister Hubert was upset. Sister Vincent was nodding her assent. When I got to the door the conversation ceased. Sister Hubert strode by me, while Sister Vincent gathered up her papers and books.

"It's all yours, Theo."

"Thanks. Was Sister Hubert upset?" I put my books down as she removed hers.

"Yeah?"

"About what?"

"About Mother Colette."

"Why?"

"Now, Theo, I don't want you to repeat this, not a word. Hubie would kill me."

"No, I won't, absolutely."

"See, Hubie rode down to the novitiate in Los Gatos to see Mother John Mary. In the car were two other Sisters and Mother Colette. After they said the Litany, not another word was spoken; a two-hour ride in oppressive silence. Hubie says she'll never ride anywhere again with Mother Colette, Mother D.A. she calls her- for "Dark Ages.""

I was stunned. I'd never heard anyone criticize the Mother General. I felt ashamed I hadn't defended her, but I wanted so much to be Sister Vincent's confidant. That aloof Hubert, who wore her cincture high and tight as if to show off her breasts under her white guimpe, was now "Hubie?" What I heard was so troubling that I had a hard time concentrating on my biology class material of osmosis and the movement of materials across cell membranes.

On a Saturday afternoon Sister Vincent decided she wanted to go to a parish church for confession--a most unusual request. Did she imagine that in our confessional at the back of the chapel any nun, standing the customary five feet from the confessional box, could hear what she said? But she detested what she felt was the oppressive atmosphere of the convent and had an inexplicable paranoia about the motherhouse.

She needed a partner to leave the convent so she asked the Superior if I might accompany her to the nearby St. Ignatius Church, attached to the Jesuit campus of the University of San Francisco.

As we walked toward the church, I had to run to keep up with her giant steps. A fierce wind whipped our veils and twisted our white guimpes, but she scarcely noticed. She rattled on about the next General Chapter, a subject that had scarcely entered my mind. Every six years a General Chapter was held to elect the next Mother General and her counselors. Every Superior was a delegate, as well as one other nun elected from each of our twenty-two convents. If the incumbent was healthy, she was usually reelected. Mother Colette had been elected at an extraordinary Chapter when mid-term, the current Mother General died of cancer.

"We're looking down the road at the summer of '64, Theo. That's our chance."

I was confused. "Don't you think Mother Colette we'll be reelected?"

"Not necessarily. We have another choice." She shot me a distrustful glance to see if I'd challenge her view. "We'd like to see Sister John Mary elected, you little silly," she hissed. "She's wonderful, a real human being, not like that Mother Colette who acts like she's from the Inquisition" She paused to see the effect her words had on me.

" Sister John Mary?" I asked, "The one who Mother recently appointed Mistress of Novices?" I'd only met her once and my memory grasped for an image. What came to mind was a heavy-set woman with an Irish face and a determined set to her jaw.

"She's fabulous, Theo, simply fabulous." Her voice broke; she gave an enormous sniff and wiped her nose with her sleeve. I could see Vincent loved her. "We've got to find out where people stand before we elect delegates."

We reached the entrance of the cavernous church and I dipped my fingers in the Holy Water font. Inside, it was muted like a Botticelli painting. I knelt in a pew near the back pondering what I'd just heard. What about the direction of the Holy Spirit and God's will? Would this be a political event? True Mother Colette was much stricter as head of the Order than she'd been as Mistress of Novices. Some resented this. Yet a laxness had crept into the Community under the former Mother General who was ill during much of her term. I believed Mother Colette was now trying to restore the ideals of our Irish Founder, Nano Nagle and I cared deeply for Mother. In the motherhouse everyone seemed tightly coiled and secretive, but a plot to oust her? What about our Rule that forbids soliciting delegates? My own feelings were now at war: on the one hand, my loyalty to Mother Colette competed with my desperate need for closeness with Sister Vincent. I slumped against the pew while she confessed to a Jesuit she trusted to cleanse her soul. I wondered if I should warn Mother Colette. How would I say it? A plot to overthrow you is brewing?

As the days went by, I could see Sister Vincent slipping deeper into a world of anger. She was no longer in the mood for conversation with me. One Saturday night she didn't come into her cell and I wondered where she'd gone. The next afternoon I ran into her in the refectory at coffee break. Humming aloud, she seemed unusually serene. I sidled up to her, "I missed you."

She put her finger to her lips and furtively motioned for me to follow her into the pantry. "Don't tell anyone," she hissed, "but I've been to visit Sister John Mary. Oh, Theo, she's simply marvelous. I can't even tell you." She spread her wide hands with the nails bitten short. "This woman is spiritual but also very human. Do you know what I mean? She has vision and sees where our community needs to go."

A Sister peaked into the pantry, but when she saw us whispering, she moved away. Sister Vincent moved deeper into the recess of the pantry. "Now don't say a word, but she's got these two Jesuits, trained by that well-known psychologist, Carl Rogers, who are now teaching the novices. I got to sit in on one of their classes. You should hear those guys talk about being human, not all that garbage we were fed. They believe in friendships between sisters. Mother also discusses things with the novices and asks them stuff like: What would you like to major in? Blind obedience is out. Who knows if asked, I might've taught art, instead of chemistry and math. How about that? They even have sharing time and tell each other what good they see in each other. No falling on your knees and confessing faults! There's an atmosphere of love, not fear. Theo, we've got to get her in. Oh, Jesus, here comes Sister Andrew. Gotta go." She bolted off, leaving me dumbfounded.

One evening I heard Sister Vincent sobbing in her cell. I'd witnessed her in many states, but never crying. Cautiously, I parted the curtains and saw she was sitting on her bed, fully dressed; her eyes were red and swollen. She looked at me but didn't speak. Though we often chatted from cell to cell, I'd never stepped a foot into her space. Fearing I might be hit by a thunderbolt for violating this Rule, I tiptoed toward her bed. She put her hands to her face, crying harder. For a while I only sat next to her. Then I stretched out my arm to gently pull her head to my shoulder. I could feel the resistance. Suddenly, she relaxed and gave in to my comforting touch. I patted her head while she cried.

Then she sat up, spewing out fragments between sobs, "Everything's wrong, no one understands, I can't go on like this, this is hell, I don't know what to do." I felt a keen empathy for the vulnerability that she usually hid under her humor. After a few minutes, she stopped crying and pushed me away.

"Theo, I don't want you to see me like this. I'm okay now." She stood up went to the basin and splashed water on her face. She sat back down on the bed and bit her lip. I stood up and put my hand on her shoulder. I waited a moment, thinking she might confide in me as to what had triggered this outburst. She only stared ahead vacantly and waved me away with her hand.

I returned to my cell, confused about what happened. As I tried to fall asleep, I mused about our relationship. I loved being her confidant but she was older, a highly respected math/chemistry teacher in the community and I was afraid I wasn't the wise seasoned person she needed.

The next morning after our silent breakfast, I returned to my cell later than usual as it was my turn as Server in the refectory. When I came in, Sister Vincent had finished making her bed, had pulled back her curtains and was folding her blue-check apron.

"Hi, feeling better this morning?" I whispered.

She stood close to me. "Listen, Theo. I'm fine now. Just forget about last night. Don't ever speak of it to anyone, do you hear me? I'm fine, just fine, do you understand?" Her words and her tone tore into fragments any hope I had that last evening's episode bring us closer.

"Yes, of course. I'll never speak of it to anyone. I never speak about you."

"Good." She picked up her books and left the cell. A few minutes later, she came bursting back in. She drew aside my curtain as I was giving a last turn to my bedspread. I turned and smiled at her.

"Listen Theo, you just can't depend on me. That's all there is to it." Her tone was pleading, at the same time, threatening. "I'm just so mixed up that you can't help me and I can't help you. I want you to just leave me alone, will you do that?" She didn't wait for my reply, just bolted out the door.

When she left, the room seemed darker. What had I done? Had I asked too much? Was my own loneliness, hanging out like soiled laundry, scaring her? I needed her, but she wanted someone stronger, with more prestige and someone as angry as she was. I was low on the totem pole and I couldn't be of use to her. I didn't love her dear Sister John Mary because I didn't even know her. I tried to view her behavior objectively, but the hurt she'd just inflicted bled all over any rational thoughts.

After the event where Sister Vincent exposed her own vulnerability, she stopped speaking to me. She spent her evenings in the convent library, while I sat alone at my cell desk, feeling wounded, but trying to prepare for my own classes. As the days went by, the ice between us never thawed. Neither of us would even look at the other.

I noted in my Exam book: *Jesus my medic, where are You? Are You leaving me to suffer without anesthetic because I broke the Rules and I needed her too much?*

For several weeks she nagged the Superior to move her to a different cell, insisting she needed to study late and didn't want to keep the other two nuns awake. I overheard Sister Superior laugh and reply, "Sister dear, every cranny is occupied. If the Queen of England came to visit, I couldn't give her a room."

Ever resourceful, Sister Vincent discovered the garret, the unheated, unused bell tower with only room for a bed and a chair. A few days later, she went to Sister Superior and told her the garret would be fine for her. With much noise and haste, and not a word to me, she gathered her things and moved up into the tiny space. Though I was hurt, I pretended to scarcely notice she was gone.

One night at the dinner table the conversation centered on philosophy and free will. Sister Vincent and I got into a discussion that quickly turned into an argument. I prided myself on being conversant with the subject as I'd had more philosophy classes at U.S.F than most. I knew well Thomas Aquinas' arguments on the subject from his Summa Theologica. I countered the point she was trying to make with a caustic question, "I wonder where you ever got that odd opinion?"

Her face flushed with anger, "Odd, am I? You're calling me odd? You don't even know me!" She compressed her wide lips and glared at me. The heat of our anger shocked others at the table and they tried to shift the conversation to another topic; nothing was so foreign in the refectory as overt anger. I was fuming but immediately regretted my words, knowing that it would widen the rift between us.

One day a notice was posted on the bulletin board that announced the Dutch theologian, Hans Kung, would be speaking at the University of San Francisco. His reputation was that of a notable avante-garde thinker, almost a rebel in the Church. Next to the announcement was a sign-up sheet. Sister Vincent was walking away and I noted she had signed her name right under Sister Hubert. Undaunted, I added my name. The Dean of Studies, Sister Brian, walked up and as she took the pen from me, she said, "I bet I won't agree with him, but I want to hear what he has to say. I see you are going, Sister Theophane. Would you like to walk over with me and Sister Anna?"

"Yes, I'd love to, " I answered, surprised that this important and well-respected nun would ask me to accompany her and her secretary.

On Saturday, we found seats in the university gym that was jammed with nuns from other Orders as well as students and lay people. People were even hanging over the balcony. As Sister Brian settled in a folding chair next to me, she remarked, "Change for change sake goes against my grain, but I want to listen and learn. I don't want to be left behind like a dinosaur. I like to hear what you young sisters are thinking, too."

"Me, too," chimed in Sister Anna. She was a delicate nun who served as the Dean of Studies secretary, initially shy, but once she started talking, there way no stopping her. "Just the other day, I was saying to Sister Brian that . . ."

Out of the corner of my eye, I saw Sister Vincent and Sister Hubert slide into chairs not far from us. In my heart, I wished I could be sitting with them.

A Jesuit came to the podium to introduce Hans Kung. "He preaches a new message for our times," the priest said as Kung strode confidently to the mike, looked around at the huge crowd and said in his Dutch accent, "I am so happy to see all of you busy people coming to hear what I have to say." As I listened to his words, I wanted to cheer as he was positive and forward thinking. When he finished, there was a moment of dramatic silence, followed by a long, deafening applause. He took questions, recognizing a man with his hand up in the balcony who asked a long, convoluted question. How will he handle, this idiot? I wondered.

Hans was silent. Then in his strong accent he asked, "Shall I give my whole speech over again?" Magnificent answer, I thought. I marveled that this man, a rebel, who was at loggerheads with the old Church doctrine, was allowed to speak here at the Jesuit university in this city that had the very conservative Bishop McGucken at the helm of the diocese.

As we walked back to the convent, Sister Brian remarked, "What he said really made sense to me. I'm quite surprised at my own reaction." I felt a surge of hope. Here was this older nun in her prestigious new appointment as Dean of Studies willing to listen to us younger Sisters. That never would have been the situation with the former Dean. In September, Mother Colette had brought her from New Mexico where, as Superior and principal, she'd successfully opened our mission in Albuquerque. She was moving with restraint and grace into the new position, bringing as her secretary the slightly damaged Sister Anna.

Near the end of the school year, the faculty received an unusual invitation. We'd been invited to Alcatraz! One of our students lived on the island where her father was a prison administrator. The facility had recently been discontinued as a prison, but was open to a few visitors. For me any outing was welcome, but I didn't want to risk any unpleasantness with Vincent. To my relief, she didn't sign up. I noticed Sister Brian had added her name.

At Fisherman's Wharf, fifteen nuns piled out of the convent cars. As we walked toward the dock, our veils blew and our large rosary beads that dangled from our cinctures made a clacking sound. I was aware of tourists gawking at the procession of "penguins" as we were often called. I didn't mind. It was wonderful to be outdoors and away from the convent. A sturdy young man reached out a hand and assisted each of us across a plank on to a small boat used by the prison for transporting the personnel that lived and worked on the island.

As the small ferry rolled out into the bay, I looked back at the City growing more distant. It was chilly and the engines churned up the grey water that gave off an acrid smell of fuel. I shivered, but I didn't want to sit inside and talk with the others. I moved to the bow and clung to the railing. I felt a communion with the grey mist and churning sea and wished the ferry would carry me off to some distant place, never to return to the motherhouse. The school year was coming to a close and what I had hoped would be my best year, was my worst. I couldn't ever remember being in so much pain. In truth, the six of us who were newcomers to the high school faculty, all had a difficult time. How could I possibly teach another year here? In the end, none of us were sent back to the high school next Fall, except Sister Jacqueline. As we moved closer to Alcatraz, I even imagined that my circumstances couldn't be much worse than those in the prison we were about to visit. I stood at the bow like a Munch painting with my mouth open in a silent scream.

"Penny for your thoughts, Theo?" Sister Jacqueline asked, startling me.

"I'm afraid they are not worth a penny, Jac." Her veil was flapping wildly and her rigid guimpe blew up. I reached out and grabbed the tip and tucked it under her arm as I'd done with my own. She too, stared at the island with an expression more serious than usual.

"Hasn't this been a tough year, Theo? I don't know what I expected, but this wasn't it. I was on my knees being scolded even more than in the novitiate." She gave rueful laugh and leaned on the railing. "I know I got on your nerves sometimes and I'm sorry. I've seen how Sister Vincent hurt you, but we're still friends, right?"

"Right! I'm sorry I hurt you." I patted her chubby hand as if to say, hey, lets be friends again. "What did happen with you and Michelle?"

"Boy, what didn't happen? I got clobbered with scoldings from all sides for being with her. They came down on me and then on Michelle. You know after she got caught in the school around eight one evening, they banished her from hanging around any nuns."

" But you noticed what's happened between me and Vincent"?

"Yes, it's so obvious, but I can see she's very unstable. I mean, she can be funny, but she pouts if she doesn't get her way. Don't let it get you down." Suddenly, she pointed, "Look, Theo, now you can see the houses on the island. I wonder what its like to live in the shadow of the prison?"

As we climbed the steep road on the windswept island, I stared at the gun towers. We went into the main building where Mr. Harding, whose daughter was a junior at our high school, gave us a short informational talk before the tour. The prison was left much as it was as when the prisoners were moved. He told us stories of attempted escapes. One cell was left completely furnished with bed covers and he said we could see how it really looked. When we reached that cell, I stared at it. It was a bit larger than my own cell. It had a tiny sink, as did mine, but there was a toilet. The cot had an orange blanket, but there were bars, three stories high of cages. No privacy, no curtains around the space, no tiny closet, everything open to scrutiny. Suddenly, I appreciated my own private space, enclosed by light yellow curtains as never before. We saw the places between the cells where men had tried to gain freedom by digging with primitive tools. We went through the kitchen where the outline of each utensil was painted on the wall in black; anything missing could be detected immediately. The large shower room was concrete with single showerheads spaced evenly, not a shred of privacy. Then came the dark holes of solitary confinement, below ground level. Awful! The system was so degrading that it gave me the shivers. I felt pity for the men who had spent their lives here. This wasn't at all like my safe convent. They could never leave. Could I?

After the tour, we crowded into the small living room of the Bursar's home in the shadow of the prison. Mrs. Harding and her daughter, Kay, were serving hot coffee and brownies. I sat against the wall, out-of-the-way, glad to be warm. Sister Brian squeezed into a chair next to me. "Wasn't that an experience?" she exclaimed. At that moment, Mrs. Harding came round with a plate of cookies. I took one brownie, but she urged me to take another.

"Enjoy two, " encouraged Sister Brian, nodding at me. These small acts of caring made me tear up and I drew out my linen hankie and blew my nose.

By June, Sister Vincent and I had regained the barest of polite exchange. I was exhausted and fearful about next year. Gone was the naïve, hopeful nun who arrived in September. In her place was a woman who had created a protective shell around herself. Sister Andrew may or may not want me back and I really didn't care to return, but couldn't think of any where else I wanted to teach. For summer, it was enough to simply tend to my wounds while living with my peers in one of our smaller convents in the City while attending summer classes at the University of San Francisco. Sister Maureen was studying in Los Angeles so I would have a peaceful summer.

PART FOUR

CHAPTER NINETEEN

SUMMER 1964 SAN FRANCISCO

AFTER I'D FELT my own light extinguished following my disastrous first year at the motherhouse and teaching at the high school, my salvation came in the form of an unexpected Mission to our Seattle convent. I felt my rescue well-expressed in the last lines of my favorite Gerard Manley Hopkins poem, *God's Grandeur.*

> *There lives the dearest freshness deep down things; And though the last lights off the black West went, Oh, morning, at the brown brink eastward, springs—Because the Holy Ghost over the bent World broods with warm breast and with ah! bright wings.*

The Holy Spirit was sending me to teach biology in Seattle's progressive coed Catholic high school, unique in that it was staffed by several Orders of nuns, and even priests as teachers. Our community had two teaching slots. Initially, I was frightened of this Mission as it meant teaching with Sister Angel. I suspected it was her complaints about Sister Maureen, rather than God's will, that ended Maureen's stint in Seattle after only a year. Her popularity and vivaciousness likely irritated Sister Angel, who looked deceptively angelic, yet surprised one with her biting, righteous temperament. I'm sure she wasn't expecting me as a replacement.

However, I found I loved teaching at this school where the principal was an earthy, jovial priest, who reminded me of Jackie Gleason, warm and welcoming. It was marvelous to meet nuns of other Orders and wonderful to have no other duties except to teach my biology classes where many of the students were top notch. The other Sisters at the convent taught in the parish elementary school. It was a coincidence that Sister Maureen's oldest, real sister, Sister Karen, was also newly assigned. We quickly developed a warm friendship. She was motherly, funny, and gladly accompanied me on my painting outings when I was completing another art correspondence course. This successful year, far away from the motherhouse gave me a sense of confidence.

Now that I was back in San Francisco for summer classes at U.S.F., I felt like a visitor who could avoid being drawn into the Order's squabbles arising around this summer's election of the Mother General. Yet I was unprepared for the series of events that would occur like earthquakes as soon as I started summer school. A severe jolt occurred at exactly 9 a.m. on my first day back at the University of San Francisco when Dr. Millikan, Chief of Psychological Services, strode into the cafeteria where his popular class, Adolescent Psychology, was held.

"How's everybody this morning?" he bellowed.

The class roared back, "Fine!"

Scholarly, black-robed Jesuits or conservative professors in suits and ties or scientists in lab coats taught most of the classes I'd taken, but suddenly a Kodiak bear had slipped in among the Jesuits. With a thud, Dr. Millikan set his briefcase on the table, peeled off the tweed jacket from his burly frame and rolled up his shirtsleeves. His hair was a military cut. A pack of Camels jutted carelessly from his shirt pocket.

He hoisted a tree-trunk leg on the seat of his chair, leaned forward, arm resting on his thigh and surveyed the class with green eyes shadowed by dark brows that ran across his forehead like rain clouds.

The class was crowded with young men, and a few women in the nursing program. I chose to sit at a table alone. Dr. Millikan explained how he ran his classes. "We'll work on the text in the first half and after a short break, it will be open discussion." He usually started class by saying, "Good morning, everybody. Where did we leave off yesterday?" A few days into the first week, when he asked that question no one spoke up.

A young man with hair to his collar called out, "You were telling us about that lady."

"And what lady might that be?"

"The one who thought she had a dick." Everyone giggled and for a few moments, Millikan contemplated the tabletop, his hooded eyes unreadable. "Later," he retorted. The second half of class would be questions and discussion with no holds barred. I glanced at my notes to see what had been discussed yesterday. I'd missed much of it with everyone laughing loudly. I deciphered my scrawl: masturbation? orgasm? come? Would *come* be in the dictionary? I didn't know what these words meant. I wouldn't dare tell our Dean what was being discussed here; she'd transfer me to child psychology.

Millikan ran a hand over his greying crew cut and began dictating notes on the emotional characteristics of adolescents. Exactly forty-five minutes later he flipped his binder shut. "Okay, now who's got a question, a problem, hypothetical or otherwise?" He strode across the front of the class. "All life is related to psychology. If you have something on your mind, feel free to bring it up here."

I lowered my eyes. I had no questions to ask, at least, not aloud. The things discussed in class were beginning to intrude on my morning meditation and seemed more important to ponder than the gospels.

"So what about that lady with the dick? Did you ever cure her?" asked the persistent young man. I looked at my notes: dick = penis?

"She wasn't really sick," he replied. "See, this is the deal, some women have as good a dick as any guy, but sometimes it frightens them. Many women have real power, but most don't actually feel it between their thighs the way this woman did. That part scared her to death. She used to lie on the couch in my office and talk about her dick. She could actually feel it rub against her legs. It was embarrassing for her."

I shivered as I imagined what it would be like to lay on his couch, to bare my soul, to have him examine it. What would he see?

"After awhile, you see, she began to take charge of her power and she took to that dick; she enjoyed it. Now this didn't happen overnight, of course." I was spellbound, though he acted as if he was discussing something quite ordinary. Collectively, the class shook their heads as if wondering whether or not to believe him.

"So who else has something to say?"

A skinny, young man raised his hand. "I've got this girl, I mean, my friend has a girlfriend, who never has an orgasm--she's never come. Wha-da-ya thinks her problem?"

What did I need to know of these topics? Still I was curious and, in spite of my discomfort with these these discussions, I loved listening to my classmates.

"What makes you think it's her problem? Did you ask her what she likes? Anyone want to address this?"asked Millikan.

"Yeah let 'er alone awhile and let her try girls," a fellow shouted from the back.

"Okay, we have one suggestion. Let her experiment with her sexual feelings toward women. Who else has an idea?"

As the candid talk continued, Millikan never condemned or ridiculed the students. I marveled at the freedom of these discussions, the polar opposite of the superficial conversations we had at our recreational meals. The discussion continued, "Doc, if her brother was homosexual, don't you think she'd be gay too? I mean coming from the same parents?"

"Not necessarily, not at all."

"Doc, do you think homosexuality is inherited or do you get that way because of the way your parents treat you?"

"I believe it's mixed and I think it's a complicated deal."

The discussion was getting heated. A student nurse remarked to a young man with unruly hair, "I don't think you were listening to what I said!" Millikan moved like a rearing grizzly toward the young man who stammered something back at the woman. Then everyone laughed and I grinned, not because I caught the answer, but because Millikan himself displayed a rare grin. He seemed to understand what things meant below the surface. Could he possibly explain the restless yearnings that I was trying to banish to the darkest corners of my soul?

After a week of summer school, Sister Sean and I experienced another tremor. She discovered an early morning experimental Mass that was being held in the university's student lounge. In a conspiratorial mood we decided to attend, though we'd already been to Mass in our convent. The atmosphere seemed to crackle with intrigue and we secured the last two vacant chairs. A smiling nun with a shoulder length veil and a shock of exposed hair passed out song sheets in English rather than Latin. My veil fell to my waist and a white bandeau covered my close-cropped hair. As she moved down the rows, I stared at her knee-length habit and her varicose veins visible through thick beige stockings. My habit covered my black oxfords and was cinched at the waist with a leather cincture with large rosary beads dangling from one side. She looked like an imposter.

In strode the stocky priest, Father Gregory Baum, said to be in the avante-garde of the reforms coming from Vatican Council II. He faced the small group that stood in front of folding chairs, raised his hands in welcome and smiled at us over a makeshift altar. As he began the Mass he recited the words in English. The fake nuns began to strum guitars; one tapped her foot. I shook my head. The Mass I loved was recited in Latin and accompanied by Gregorian chant or hymns in Latin. At the Kiss of Peace, Father, extended his arms and said, "Peace be with you!"

I couldn't help but respond in Latin, "Et cum Spiritu tu tuo." Now those nuns were grinning, hugging each other and coming to embrace us. My head began to ache. Before Holy Communion, Father asked, "May I see a show of hands of those receiving Communion?" A few hands went up. He continued, "You may chew these whole wheat hosts brought to us today by the Sisters of St. James." For years we'd swallowed small white wafers that often stuck to the roof of one's mouth, but we dared not touch nor chew the Body of Christ. He was commanding, "Take and chew!" At the Kiss of Peace the fake nuns were hugging each other and coming toward us for embraces. My head began to ache. As soon as Mass was over Sister Sean and I dashed out to avoid chatting with the smiling nuns in modernized habits.

The sky had patches of blue now as the fog was lifting. College buildings appeared where earlier they'd vanished in swirling mists. A weak sun was breaking through.

"What do you think, Sean?" I asked as I ran to keep up with her lanky frame and long stride as she moved across the campus quadrant.

"Kinda feels like something's missing, not like a real Mass, you know what I mean?"

"Yes, more froth than substance. And those new habits--aren't they the worst? I hope we don't change our habit."

"Right! No short skirts for me!"

"Listen, Sean, could we go somewhere and talk, just for a few minutes?"

"No, no, I need to get to my class and take notes. There'll be tests down the road. You know I'm not the star student like you. I'll see you at lunchtime, Theo."

However, lunchtime in our high school cafeteria would be crowded, not conducive to intimate conversation. I wanted to talk to Sean about Millikan's disturbing class. I wondered what topics would come up today. Sean's response was spoken from habit: we do not deviate from the schedule. Our lives were run by rules, day in and day out, orderly and predictable, but now change was in the wind and it was making me uncomfortable.

One day after class I stopped at Millikan's desk and asked if he could recommend any other contemporary books in addition to the text as I was teaching high school now. I stood poised with pad and pen to take down notes as I'd expected he'd give me a couple of book titles. As he grabbed his jacket and briefcase, he said, "Follow me, Sister."

We went downstairs to the student bookstore. Inside, he took my elbow and guided me to the psychology section where he pointed out several books. "Sister, this one by Carl Rogers and that one by Abraham Maslowe, will put you in touch with current thinking." I was distracted by the nearness of his bulk. He grinned at me as if we were sharing some secret. I nodded my thanks. Then he was gone. I stood there, savoring the moment. Dr. Millikan, Chief of Psychological Services, had taken his time to walk me down to the campus bookstore. No one ever treated me as special. I didn't have any money. Nuns couldn't buy their own books, but basking in the glow of his attention, I picked them up and glanced through them as if I might make a purchase.

Often the discussions in class turned to homosexuality. I was not familiar with that word. Queers and fairies were the terms my family used when I was growing up. Did the wording in our Rule Book have something to do with homosexuality with its admonitions never to touch another sister, never to like one sister more than another? I loved Sister Maureen. Was I a homosexual?

Several days later, brooking the wind, I crossed the campus and headed for the library. It was my favorite building, gleaming with chrome and glass, so unlike the wood and wainscoting of our motherhouse. I was on a mission for information. First, I headed for the bathroom and washed my hands in warm water, a luxury absent in my convent cell. I stared in the mirror at the plump face encased entirely in black serge, with a stiff white bandeau cutting low across my forehead. Below it, blue eyes peered through unbearably thick, rimless glasses perched on a long nose. I pinched my cheeks. Too fat, I thought. No wrinkles yet but why did I feel old and yet naïve at twenty-six?

Many evenings during night prayers at the Examination of

Conscience I'd noted in my small Exam binder:
Unmortified appetite. Shouldn't have had second helping of dessert!

Up in the stacks, I sauntered down the aisles on my search, checking the call numbers. The only book on the subject of homosexuality on all four floors of the university library was "The Life of Oscar Wilde." I snatched the book off the shelf, concealed it in my large outer sleeves and found a sheltered cubby desk. I began to skim the pages. Oscar Wilde was a poet, a homosexual and jailed for that. This wasn't the information I wanted. I paged through the book again. I needed specifics. Frustrated, I shoved the book back in place. High up in the stacks, I sat and pondered my life. The few dates I'd had in high school, weren't satisfying except for Don, the guy I swam and danced with that summer at the Russian River. If he'd liked me, things might have been different. Yet Sister Maureen was my true passion. I'd never told anyone about the physical loving we had in high school. I was ashamed of it now, but I still cared deeply for her. Were we homosexuals? I wished I could talk to her, but she was studying at Loyola University in Los Angeles.

A few weeks into the summer session at U.S.F., another tremor was about to alter my world. Sister Sean and I were walking back to the high school for lunch. Instead of walking in the obligatory silence, Sister Sean couldn't help chatting. Earlier that morning the General Chapter, held every six years, convened in the motherhouse chapel. The first order of business would be the election of the Mother General.

"Theo, I think the voting for Mother General is going on this minute."

"Sean, you know I've been in Seattle and I'm out of the loop. Dare I ask are the delegates leaning a certain way in regard to the Mother General?"

"It's hard to know. There's been a lot of politicking and talk from L.A. about electing Mother John Mary. In fact, I'll tell you something very strange. Yesterday I saw Sister Vincent at lunch--you know how she always sits with her special crowd--but I was next to her in the lunch line and she whispered that tomorrow would be a special day. I asked what she meant, and she said, 'New boss tomorrow'. I looked at her quizzically. She continued, "You know, she's talking about Mother John Mary who's now the Novice Mistress, but she had been a popular Superior at one of our convents in Los Angeles."

"I know of her but I don't really know her."

" Sister Vincent is sure she'll be elected the new Mother General."

"Sean, no Mother General in good health has ever failed to be re-elected. Mother Colette has had only one term and she's healthy."

"I know, Theo, but that group of delegates from the Los Angeles' convents seem to want her out and John Mary in."

Sister Sean continued speculating, but my thoughts traveled back two years to memories of Sister Vincent who'd asked me to be her partner to walk to Saint Ignatius Church. She had talked animatedly about the election and said she was hoping to influence delegates to vote for Mother John Mary. Now I realized a real conspiracy to oust Mother Colette had gained traction. What about the guidance of the Holy Spirit?

When we reached the high school cafeteria, I moved down the lunch line. "Please not too much spaghetti, Mrs. Petrini," I said to the hefty woman in white uniform who stood behind the hot trays serving the nuns.

"Ah, you Sisters, watching your figures! For what? Vanity is a sin. My spaghetti's good for you." She heaped my plate with the steaming entrée. I saw a long arm waving to me across the cafeteria. Sister Gloria had saved chairs for Sister Sean and me. It was wonderful to have casual meals where we could sit wherever we liked and with any one. I blessed myself, said a silent grace, then asked, "Has anybody heard anything?"

Sister Gloria paused mid-bite, "Don't be silly. They only started this morning. I'm sure Mother will be reelected."

Sister Gloria was often overly optimistic. I envied her amazing beauty and musical talents, but in discussions, we rarely agreed on practical things. Yet now I wanted to believe her. At every table the speculation was the same: Would Mother Colette have six more years? I knew she'd have the vote of those Sisters who want to move slowly in implementing the changes coming out of Vatican II, but the liberal nuns who wanted progress now, would try to elect Mother John Mary.

After lunch, I walked across the garden to the Motherhouse, even though I knew it was forbidden to enter while the Chapter was in session. I wanted to retrieve my watercolors and brushes that I had inadvertently left behind in Seattle. My Seattle Superior was a delegate to the Chapter and she'd flown down last night and brought my art supplies with her. She said she'd leave my box at the Motherhouse switchboard. I knew I should've waited until the Chapter was over, but I was afraid my precious box of paints might get mislaid. It was cool in the high-ceilinged Motherhouse. The Grandfather clock marked the half hour with solemn chimes. The floor was buffed to a brilliant shine and I tiptoed through the corridor, clutching my dangling rosary so it wouldn't rattle. A luxurious, black overcoat hung on the rack near the front door. Apparently, it belonged to the Monsignor, a representative of the Bishop who was sent to oversee the election of the Mother General.

In the switchboard room, I spied my precious box marked with black pen: *For Sister Theophane.* I snatched it up and retraced my steps. At the end of the corridor, old Sister Patrice shuffled out of the bathroom, her hands red and raw from constant washing. She moved close to me and clutched my wrist. "Have you seen the Superior? I've got to find her.'" She ran her words together in her thick brogue. Her breathe was sour, her habit stained.

O Lord, deliver me from this fate of scruples and senility.

"Sister, She's in the chapel, but you can't bother her right now." I heard a door open and I tried to pull away, but her grip was fierce.

"Help me look for her, Sister." Footsteps approached and I heard the rattle of a large rosary.

"Sister, try the refectory." As the steps came closer, I tried to extricate my wrist and pulled my veil forward to shield my face.

"Sister Theophane, is that you?" Without turning, I could see the piecing eyes behind the thick glasses, the hooked nose, the compressed lips, the scowl. That voice often brought me to my knees. Now I was ready to beg: Please do not take away my box of paints and brushes!

"Sister Theophane, I'm so pleased to see you helping dear Sister Patrice." She patted my arm that was still in Sister's vise-like grip. My gaze went from the worn silver ring, imbedded in Mother Colette's fleshy finger, to the penetrating eyes. I was startled by their serenity. "Take Sister into the refectory and see that she gets a cup of tea."

"Yes, right away, Mother," I babbled, almost genuflecting on the spot.

"Who was that?" Sister Patrice asked hoarsely.

"That, Sister, is our Mother General," I whispered, wondering if it was still true.

It was nearly 4:30 when we arrived at the convent in the Mission District where several of us were staying while we took classes at U.S.F. As the bell began to toll, we filed into the chapel to recitation of the psalms of the Office. Sister Gloria sat at the organ and began a hymn. Abruptly, Sister Superior walked to front of the altar and held up her hand, interrupting the music.

"Sisters, I have an announcement. I've just received word that Mother Mary John has been elected our new Mother General. Let us sing this hymn in thanksgiving to the Holy Spirit for His Guidance." A cold fear crept through me and knots tightened in my shoulders. I clutched the crucifix on my large rosary and I began to shake. My leader had fallen in a bloodless coup! After this communal prayer, we would move to the refectory where the tables would be set with bread, fruit and milk. Sister Servers would pass steaming bowls from the kitchen. It would not seem different, but nothing would be the same again. How many ballots had it taken? I'd never know. Everything was secret.

My fate was now in the hands of someone who didn't know me, who had no sense of my strengths or desires. I was just a pawn that could be selected for any job at any convent. My most urgent question was: will Mother John Mary allow me to return to Seattle where I was almost happy? Mother Colette must be feeling rejected by her own Congregation that she tried so hard to guide. I seemed to hear her voice: *O ye of little faith, behold the lilies of the field, they neither sow nor do they reap; yet your heavenly Father takes care of them.* Would He take care of her? Would He take care of me?

The next day at lunch, the high school cafeteria was abuzz with rumors. Supposedly, it had been a close election with many ballots and finally decided by only one or two votes. Sister Sean plopped her lunch tray down next to me. "Theo, what happens to ex-Mothers General? What do they do?" I only shrugged as I was feeling a deep empathy for Mother Colette.

From across the cafeteria came a loud, 'Yippee, we won!' Sister Vincent was in the midst of a group of Mother John Mary's supporters, linking arms in a tight bouncing circle. Disgusted, I turned away from the scene and played with my mac and cheese. "Sean, as long as we've been here, Mother Colette has decided our fate. Now, someone I've never even met is going to decide my future. In September I want to return to Seattle. It was a such a good year."

"Does it rain all the time like they say?"

"Almost all the time, but we visited many places, Hood Canal and Victoria; the school was great. On weekends I got into painting watercolors."

"So this is scary, huh?"

"Very!"

For awhile nothing changed. We went to our classes at U.S.F., had lunch in our high school cafeteria. Then one afternoon, not long after the election, I had an unusual visitor. I hurried to answer the convent doorbell. I knew who was at the door--my best friend from high school, Marilyn, who had left after a year in the Novitiate. I hadn't seen her in years, but she'd called and I'd gotten permission for her to visit me. I was hoping it would be like old times. When I opened the door, I barely recognized her.

"Come in, Marilyn. You look . . . great."

In place of the tight curls, was a huge mane of black hair; her voluptuous body was squeezed into a tight, red dress. Gone were the thick, black-rimmed glasses. She followed me into our stuffy parlor, chattering away, her patent leather heels tapping an irreverent staccato on the polished corridor. I was glad to see her bubbly manner was the same. She struggled to pull her skirt to her knees, then, gave up and her skirt rose high on her thighs. I adjusted my habit over my oxfords.

"You look great, Sister, like a real nun."

"I am a real nun. Marilyn we have years to catch up on. I want to hear what are you up to these days?"

"Oh, I'm teaching fourth grade in a school in North Beach, but that is so boring. Let's talk about the real news-- Mother Colette voted out of Office! You remember how we feared her, but still loved her as our Novice Mistress. Why, Judy? You don't mind if I call you Judy do you? Sister Theophane is such a mouthful. Why is she out? She was so holy. Was the election close? She must be so hurt. Do you think the nuns are just tired of all that strictness? Is that it?" I resented her her prying. She left long ago. What does she know of our lives now?

"It surprised me too, but as you know, I can't really discuss the goings-on of the Order. The voting is secret. Tell me, Marilyn, are you wearing contacts?" She re-crossed her legs. How could she be comfortable with miles of exposed white thighs?

"Yes, yes, I'm happy with them but tell me, do you think they'll change your habits? I hope they don't tamper with them. You know those Orders that are changing to short skirts and tiny veils with their hair showing. Just awful! They don't look modern; they look like they shop at Goodwill."

"I do think the newly-elected Mother John Mary will want to make some changes. We have to adapt, keep up with Vatican II. They're throwing open the windows over there in Rome. Say, do those contacts hurt? "

"Only at first; then you get used to them."

"Marilyn, do you recall when you left the convent and we had that last secret conversation in the bathroom and I asked you, 'why you were leaving?' And you said, 'It's the boys.' You and I never had many dates in high school. We were always hanging around the nuns. Tell me how are the boys?"

She laughed, "Well, I'm not married, not even going with anyone. But now promise you won't tell anyone, especially Toots." She meant Sister Joseph. "After I left the novitiate I got involved with a seminarian, a Jesuit. He was teaching at a high school where I was working as the secretary."

"Wow! Did he like you? Did he leave to be with you?"

"Yes, he left but . . . .Oh, it's a long story, don't want to go into it, just can't talk about it now." Tears started and she reached into her purse for a tissue and dabbed at her eyes, trying not to disturb her heavy mascara. "You see, God punished me for leaving by letting me fall in love with a Jesuit, someone really not available! Anyway it's over. Not a word to Toots."

"Oh, no!" I smiled at the way she still called her high school idol, Sister Joseph, Toots, a way we had used to conceal who we were really jabbering about.

"You know, I'd love to try contacts".

"Would they let you get them?"

"This last year in Seattle an optometrist offered them to me for free. He said I'd see better. But Mother Colette said no, it would be a sin of vanity!"

"Oh, that was so mean of Mother Colette."

"I felt angry and it was horrible. When we were asked for suggestions about changes in our Rules and Customs that might get passed by this current Chapter, I submitted a change: *Sisters with serious eye prescriptions could choose to wear contact lenses.* I think that change will go through under Mother John Mary."

"Anyway, how do you like teaching high school? Big change from first grade, right?"

"Teaching biology is work. Sometimes I'm only one page ahead of the girls, but I like it."

She drew her chair closer to mine and asked, "What do you really think of the kids in high school?"

"Mostly, they're nice girls, Marilyn. They don't love to study and try to get me to listen to their music albums and stuff, but, of course, I can't."

"But Judy, really they're not like we were. They smoke, they go steady by thirteen and they make-out all the time."

"How do you know this? You teach fourth grade."

"I live next door to a teenager. She can't talk to her mother. She comes over everyday--tells me everything! Straight talk. You know, I bet you don't know half of what goes on."

"Where did you get your contacts, Marilyn?"

"Just here in town. Judy, do you know that some of your sweet Catholic girls are already screwing around. Of course, they wouldn't dare tell you. Listen to me, Judy, did you ever see the number 69 written on the kids binders or PeeChees?"

"No, I can't say that I have."

"Really, you've never heard of sixty-nine? You know its like a diagram- one number goes one way the other number is upside down, You don't know what that means?"

"I don't know what you're talking about."

"Sex, Judy sex! If you're teaching high school, you've got to know what's going on." She clapped her hand over her mouth as if afraid other sisters might hear her.

"Okay, tell me what is really going on. 69 means they're doing it? Having sex?"

"Judy, it means, eh...." She lowered her voice and looked around, checking to see we were really alone. "that the girl sucks the boy's thing, his dick, his penis and at the same time, he puts his tongue down there on her." She pointed between her legs. I was silent and blushing while she was checking her long red nails.

"Marilyn, I think you're making this up. You always exaggerate things! You remember that time in high school when you thought I had a real vision of the Virgin because of something I said about that holy card, that one I said looked like the real Mary."

"I'm not making this up, Judy!" she screamed, then cupped her hands over her mouth as if she expected another nun might enter the room at any moment.

"Marilyn, what has this got to do with the sacred act of procreation, that is what the Pope calls it? I'm sure what you're describing is a mortal sin and it probably only happens with public school kids." I pulled out my pocket watch and sighed, "Uh-oh, where did the time go?" I stood up, "Already time for Vespers." She continued to chatter as we left the parlor and moved to the front door.

"Listen, Judy, I can tell you've matured and now you'll be the nun that knows what's really going on and you can even look for '69. You can counsel the kids and they'll like you since you know the real score." She was still talking as I opened the huge door and a welcome breeze came in. I tried to give her a little hug, but then nearly pushed her out the door. She managed the stairs in her high heels, pulling on her short black jacket. Over her shoulder she counseled, "Now don't say a word about this to the other nuns."

I slammed the door and leaned against it, breathing hard. I wanted to shut out what she'd babbled about. Right! Don't tell the other nuns! Was she insane?

A door opened and Sister Sean stuck her head into corridor, "Come on, Theo, you're missing a great discussion in the Community room about the changes that might be coming for us."

"Oh, yes" I said relieved, "I'm coming. I'm coming right now."

As I entered the Community room, the Sisters were talking animatedly about changes they hoped would occur. I dropped into a chair next to Sean, happy to listen and grateful to be with them, safe and familiar.

That night in bed I thought about my afternoon conversation. Sixty-nine? Sucking each other? Sex? I've never even seen a penis. Why on earth did she tell me these things? Perhaps, when she first learned of these things, she was shocked as I was today and that's what made her go on so. In her own way, she was trying to educate me, prevent me from perpetuating the myths that kept us naïve for so long and to know what my students were really up against. My ignorance stretched out, an endless horizon of unknowing. I drifted off, worrying about where I'd be sent next year.

CHAPTER TWENTY

THE CHANGES

THE GENERAL CHAPTER had lasted only three weeks and the Sister delegates, sworn to secrecy, returned to our midst, wearing Cheshire Cat smiles. "You'll know everything soon," they said. Later in the week, after my class with Millikan, I entered our cafeteria and noticed knots of sisters talking in hushed tones. Earlier in the day, a list had come out naming the Superiors for each of our twenty-two convents for the coming school year, 1964-1965. Usually, that information was announced on the same day we received our Missions for the coming year.

As I finished my plate of stew, I spied Sister Sean standing by the cafeteria door talking with two other sisters. I suspected from her expression that she knew something. I weaved through the cafeteria and stood next to her. Sean's face flushed, but she didn't make any move to include me in the conversation. Then I knew: she did know something secret and part of it included me.

I whispered, "Sean, let's take a little stroll." Forcibly, I guided her out of the door. I squeezed her arm and looked up at those blue eyes, now avoiding my glare. "Jesus H. Christ, Sean, you tell me what you know, right now! Someone has given you secret information. What's going on?"

She tucked her chin down and spoke with no emotion, as if this would minimize the impact. "Theo, I don't know much. I heard from my Superior that I'm going back to L.A. as vice principal, same deal, but that you're not going to return to Seattle."

"Then, where am I going?" I squeezed her arm harder.

"I honestly don't know. I'd tell you if I did."

"O Lord, Sean, I want to go back to Seattle! Remember I told you we're just going to be pawns. Mother John Mary doesn't know us. Now she's over there throwing darts to see where we'll go." I stamped my foot and exhaled angrily.

She put her hand on my shoulder. "Theo, Theo, take it easy! I think tomorrow afternoon we'll get our Missions. You can wait one day."

I couldn't believe I was standing here in this cold locker room, getting information from Sean that was supposed to be God's Will for me? I began shaking. Tomorrow was light-years away. Never before had the Missions been leaked before the whole Community was given their envelopes from the hand of the Superior. Here was this new Mother General playing games with my life. What could I do? Suddenly, I dashed into one of the student bathrooms and threw up my stew.

In mid-afternoon, five of us piled into the car to return to our summer convent in the Mission district. I couldn't even speak to anyone. Once back in my cell, I threw myself on the bed. Exhausted from concealing my panic, I began to cry and then to sob violently. The tightly wound skein of my life was unraveling. Nearly every year I had been assigned a new Mission and had to start all over, but finally in Seattle, I was almost happy, far away from the rigid Motherhouse. I enjoyed the company of Sister Maureen's sister. I liked teaching in the coed high school with different Orders of nuns. I wanted to return. I thought this would be a good day to die; but the Lord had taken old Sister Malachy instead. At this moment her satin-lined casket was being wheeled into the Motherhouse chapel to rest in front of the altar. At five o'clock the community would convene for her rosary.

Suddenly, I sat up and stopped crying. I was going to find out my fate. I washed my swollen eyes, stuffed two linen hankies in my pocket, raced downstairs and joined the other sisters who were pulling on black gloves, straightening their veils. The Superior was surprised to see me. "I thought you didn't feel well enough to go in for the rosary, Sister Theophane."

"I changed my mind, Sister Superior. Is there room for me in the car?" She nodded. I squeezed into the back seat.

Once in the Motherhouse, I saw Sister Sean at the top of the stairs of the second floor. I raced up and dragged her outside to the balcony that overlooked the convent garden. We were forbidden to use this private porch as it bordered the cell and office of the Mother General, but today I was in no mood for the Rules.

"Sean, I can't stand this. Where do you think I am being sent? I want to return to Seattle." I burst into tears; then blurted out, "You know where I'm going, Sean? I'm going home, that's where I'm going!"

"Theo, Theo, stop this! You are not going home. You are going to find out what is your Mission. You go into that office right now and talk to Mother John Mary. I know her and she's not like Mother Colette. She'll listen. Go knock on that door right now!"

"O God, Sean, do you think I should? Just burst in? I've never even met her."

"Go, Theo, go right now." She grabbed my arm and walked me down the corridor. Frightened, but determined, I knocked on the large door.

When I heard the unfamiliar, booming voice, "Come right in," it struck me clearly that Mother Colette was really gone. In her place at the large uncluttered desk, sat a hefty nun with a round Irish face. Her blue eyes, behind clear-framed glasses, were squeezed into half moons by the breadth of her smile. It was a surprising contrast to Mother Colette's piercing eyes and stern gaze. As was customary when speaking to a seated Superior, I fell to my knees at the side of her chair. The western light fell softly in the room; outside the window I could see the gently waving fronds of the big canary palm. A large painting of the Our Lady of Good Council looked down on us from the wall facing the desk.

"Mother John Mary, I'm Sister Theophane"

"Ah, yes, you're the artist. What can I do for you?"

I burst out, "I want to go home!" I almost felt pity for her that she had deal with me in such a state after only few days in power.

"Sister, Sister dear, please sit down," she said gently. "What's happened to you?"

I stumbled to a chair in front of her huge desk. She questioned me but it took a while before I could formulate coherent answers. I was amazed how comfortable she was with power. She reminded me of Millikan, both because of her build and her sense of authority. When she learned what was upsetting me, she said, "Sister, in one minute, the bell will toll to call us to say the rosary for dear Sister Malachy, but would you please return afterwards? Then we can talk as long as you like."

The bell began to toll. We filed into the chapel, rubber heels squeaking softly on the polished floor. Sister Malachy's casket rested in the center aisle surrounded by six large lighted tapers. I genuflected and slowly passed by the casket. In Sister Malachy's hand was a rolled copy of her vows and a thin black wooden crucifix. On the crucifix, there was no Corpus, no Body of Christ. We each had one to remind us that we were to be the crucified ones. Sister Malachy's crucifixion was over. I almost envied her. In the back of the nearly-full chapel, I knelt and took out the rosary beads that I kept in the pouch Sister Maureen had made for me long ago.

In her clear voice, Mother John Mary began the Sorrowful mysteries of the Rosary. We responded, rote-like, to the oft-repeated Hail Mary's and Our Father's, but my mind traveled home to where Mom and my sister, Ellen, lived, not far away. Mom would've returned from Ulloa elementary school where she was principal and was supervising the summer session. Ellen, who'd left her alcoholic husband, would be there, too. She would've picked up her young son, Jimmy, from the babysitter on her way home from her job at the advertising agency. They'd be at the kitchen table talking over the day. Jimmy would be in his highchair, fussing, waiting for his dinner. Mom would be having bourbon on the rocks, Ellen, a diet coke and hoping Mom wouldn't have second bourbon.

If I phoned, one of them would answer and whisper to the other in surprise, "Its Judy." They would be even more astonished when I announced, "I want to come home. Will you come and pick me up right now?" It was comforting to know, however baffled, they would come pick me up in Mom's turquoise and white Chevy BelAir. While the rosary droned on I delved deeper into this scene. Where would I sleep? Would any of my sister's clothes fit me? What about my classes at U.S.F. and Millikan? Would Mom be happy to have me home or ashamed I 'd left? She was always proud of me. To go home now would be difficult. Mom was seriously alcoholic and she wouldn't change. Where would I find a job? What I really wanted was to return to Seattle.

I envisioned another scenario. I'd go back to Mother John Mary and demand to be sent back to Seattle. By the time the rosary was over, I hadn't settled on either course of action. Minutes later, I sat across the desk from Mother John Mary. If Mother Colette were still at this desk, I'd be on my knees, listening to her tell me God's Will for me was to stay and take the assignment I was given.

"May I ask, Mother, where did you plan to send me?' She sat with her hands clasped on the desk, blue eyes looking directly at me.

"To St. Martin's in San Jose to teach seventh grade," she replied.

"Oh no! I won't go there! I'd rather go home than go back and teach at an elementary school again," I stated firmly, startling even myself. It was two years ago since Mother Colette elevated me to the ranks of the high school teachers. To teach elementary school again would be a demotion, a humiliation. I would go home before I'd do that. I continued, "Mother, I'd really like to return to Seattle to teach biology again at Blanchett High School. I was quite happy there. They liked me. Even the principal said he hoped I'd return."

"I'm afraid that is not possible. Sister Esther needs to go to Seattle for medical reasons." I knew Sister Esther who'd been teaching biology here at Presentation High School and I doubted the truth of this medical excuse.

"I know it was Sister Angel who spoke to you about me, wasn't it? She said some bad things about me, didn't she?"

"Perhaps, she did mention you had some trouble with teaching and getting along with the other Orders of nuns at the high school."

"She's lying! Everything she said is a lie. I got on very well. She's describing herself. No one likes her! No one except Sister Superior! She's her pet." I said, furiously.

"Now, now Sister, let's not make judgments," said Mother with a nervous laugh, but without any accusation in her tone. "You really cannot go back to Seattle. She paused, smiled, "So where would you like to go?"

I savored the moment. "You mean, if I don't go home?"

"Yes, I truly hope you don't go home. You have so many talents to contribute." She paused. "Would you consider going back to Presentation High School, right here?" I was surprised at the way she phrased it and I didn't answer right away. I was relishing the moment of a choice.

I replied, "That would certainly be better than going to St. Martin's in San Jose. But there is another problem. Sister Andrew and I didn't get on well. She may not want me back."

"Well, I'll just have to ask her, but I'm pretty sure she will," she chuckled. This was a strong woman who spoke her mind; then moved to immediate action. I walked out of the office with admiration for her but also with a new respect for myself. I could handle the high school again. It would be difficult with Sister Andrew and Sister Vincent still there but I loved the students.

Late in the afternoon after our day at U.S.F. was over, a day when it was my turn to drive, I pulled the car to the curb outside the convent in the Mission where we lived for the summer. The Sisters piled out. I was still worrying about everything. I said, "Sister Sean, could you wait a minute? Do you have a few minutes to talk?"

She was already out, but poked her head back in. "I've got to get the dining room set before the Office, but I have a few minutes." She slid into the passenger seat beside me. She was uncomplicated and funny and a good friend.

"Sean, I'm really mixed up."

"Because Mother Colette is out? Because there's so much uncertainty?" She stared at me with her intense blue eyes, waiting for me to speak.

"That and other things. But you know what is my real problem?"

"Sister Maureen."

"You are brutal." I put my head in my hands. "It's always been her, but I think it's deeper than that. I have a need to love someone and be loved back and . . .well, its forbidden by our Rules."

She stretched out her hand and held mine. "Theo, things are changing."

"That'll never change. I want to ask you: do you think my attraction to Maureen is a misplaced sexual attraction? Like I really need . . . a man?" I started crying again. "Do you think I should just face that and. ."

"And leave? No, no, Theo! You're a good nun. I've known you for years and seen you struggle. You feel things more deeply than most of us because you're an artist and more sensitive; things get under your skin. You're too hard on yourself." She squeezed my hand.

"Thanks for choosing to talk to me. Your friendship is special." I envied her self-control, but I knew she didn't need the kind the strong emotional love I wanted. I was a misfit.

After I spoke with Mother John Mary about next year's assignment, I did not yet have peace. When I learned that as a summer school student, I could ask for a private counseling session with Dr. Millikan. I decided to approach him. I thought he might hear my heart pounding as I asked for an appointment, but he didn't even ask why, just pulled a calendar from his jacket pocket and said: "I'm free Thursday morning. You come down to the Counseling Center. You know, I'm Chief there, yes, siree. You come down to the old bungalows to my office, eight o'clock sharp."

I giggled with relief. It was against our Rule to be alone with any man, but I was desperate. This summer was earthquake season; everything was shifting.

On Thursday morning I asked the sisters if we could get to school a bit early as I needed to do some research at the library. When we arrived, I sprinted down to the old bungalows to Millikan's office. I couldn't begin with the Maureen problem. That was too complicated. I'd start with the most pressing problem--going back to that "hellhole," as Sister Vincent once characterized the Motherhouse, where I'd have to teach biology again under the difficult Sister Andrew. In his modest bungalow office at the edge of campus, he relaxed in a swivel chair while I perched like a terrified bird on the edge of my seat. I could smell his scent; I could hear his breathing; I could sense his strength. I felt as if I was in a room with a large animal. He put his hands behind his head and asked, "Sister, what's on your mind?"

In a shaky voice I began. "Dr. Millikan, I'm hoping, I mean, a what I want to say is, . . .uh, just can't find the words. Er, I don't know how to begin."

"Sister, just spit it out. It doesn't matter how it comes out in here," he said gently.

For years my important feelings were kept under the surface, bobbing around like great pools of kelp. Occasionally when a piece washed ashore, I inspected it with awe and tears, but most of the time my true feelings were unaccessible. What should I spit out now? "I hope you can help me with a difficult situation. I wanted to go back to teach in Seattle but I've been reassigned to the high school a few blocks from here. I taught there before, but I had a hard time, especially with the principal."

"Are you one of the counselors?"

"No, they don't trust me to do anything like that," I said with a derisive snort.

"I just teach biology." I almost added, but I wish I was teaching art.

"That figures. You strike me as an earthy, practical type. I bet you do a good job explaining to the girls how nature works."

"Yes, I do get on well with the students. They approach me with all kinds of personal problems, but the principal, . . " I began to cry, "Sister Andrew, she doesn't like me." I couldn't continue. He made no attempt to comfort me. He nodded slightly, looking grave, just waiting.

"I'm sorry."

"That's quite all right. I see you have some strong feelings about returning to that situation."

I continued, sobs punctuating each sentence. "I don't really want to go back. I want to return to Seattle where I was happy, but we have a new Mother General; she was going to send me to teach seventh grade and . . . , I stood up to her. Oh, it's all too complicated. . . Do you have any advice on how to handle this situation the second time around?"

"Hmm, they won't let you return to a situation where you were happy and successful?"

"No, it doesn't work that way," I said with a little laugh. Somehow I expected him to be nearly omnipotent, to divine the inner workings of the convent that had unfathomable rules of their own.

"Sister, you've had some painful experiences that you've been bottling up. Right now we're running out of time. Let's make another appointment and see if we can discover what those feelings are all about."

When I stepped outside, I felt extraordinarily calm. I trusted this man. I knew he would help me. We had several more sessions, talking over my situation.

On the last day of classes, I felt sad Millikan's class was ending. I hurried to speak to him outside the building to thank him for his help. He wished me the best in my September assignment. Then, in a sudden, intimate move, he jerked his head toward a secluded alcove in the building. I followed him. He ran his hand over his greying, crew cut, and looked at me for a long moment. His collar was open at the neck where he had loosened his tie. He slipped a Camel from the pack in his pocket. He lit the cigarette, cupping his hand in the same way my Mom did. I had an urge to throw my arms around him, to hold on tightly.

"You know, Sister, it seems the talks you and I have had are important. We could continue. I have an office downtown where I see people in the afternoons." His grey eyes looked at me intensely. "You could ask that new Mother General of yours if you might come on down. My fee is reasonable."

When he spoke, I felt a cloud descend over me. It was as if he'd said: I see you have cancer, but I might be able to help you. I thought of myself as confused, frightened, but did he see something in me that could be cured? I felt both fear and relief.

"You think there's really something wrong with me?"

"The way I see it, Sister, is that getting one's feelings out, the way we've been doing this summer is healthy. It enables you to be more effective with the other nuns, with your students, even with your Creator." He smiled, reached out, pumped my hand, and strode off into the brilliant sunshine, leaving me under a cloud.

I stumbled to a bench and closed my eyes. What could I do? Nuns were sent to priests for help, not therapists. Could I go to Mother John Mary again, admit I'd been alone with a man at USF, tell her that he thought I was . . .well, crazy? I stared out over the City where buildings and the distant Bay Bridge rose in silhouette. Where was his office? As I gathered up my books, I took one more look out over the City. Yes, I would find a way to see him at his office downtown.

CHAPTER TWENTY-ONE

———— ⚬⚬⚬ ————

VACATION,
SANTA CRUZ MOUNTAINS
AUGUST 1964

THE NIGHT BEFORE vacation at our property in the Santa Cruz Mountains, I dreamt about Sister Maureen. We were young again, laughing and hiding from Della. When I awoke, I even smelled her scent, the English lavender that always clung to her. Now that we were both Final Professed Sisters, we could speak freely to each other. I couldn't wait to see her and to tell her about this summer and, of course, later to dance with her

As soon as we arrived, I grabbed my suitcase from the car and ran to the small room in St. Martha's cabin where I was assigned, threw my suitcase on the bed and dashed over to the larger cabin, nestled in the shade of the oaks, where Maureen was assigned. I was in the grip of my usual anxiety--that fear that somehow I'd be deprived of her presence. Possibly her real-life sisters, three of them in our Order, would already be with her. On vacation, they gathered together and read Agatha Christie mysteries aloud to each other- a family tradition.

It was dim inside the large cabin, but in one of the bedrooms some-one was humming. Through an open door, I saw Maureen with her back to me, unpacking her bag. I tiptoed in and put my hands over her eyes. "Guess who?"

"Oh, Lord, Theo, you almost gave me heart failure! But please, don't crush my veil." She turned around and we hugged, but there was restraint on both sides that had crept in over the years. "So how did you survive teaching in Seattle with Sister Angel? And you're not going back? What happened?" she asked as she stood back, surveying me.

Was she checking to see if I gained weight or had crows feet 'round my eyes as she did? No, I knew what she was looking for—the old ado-ration in my eyes. But I looked away. I didn't want to talk about my teaching in Seattle, but about this summer-- the changes in our Order, about Millikan and the things that were discussed in his class. Maureen placed a stack of perfectly folded hankies and several pairs of stockings into the oaken dresser drawer. Next, she whisked in an old worn corset. Her waist was as trim as when I'd met her 13 years ago.

"Tell me how've you've been, really." I plopped on the edge of the bed.

"I took this marvelous molecular biology class at Loyola U and I got great ideas for student projects for the science fairs. I even had time to do a bit of knitting. Look at this." She took a black vest from her suitcase and held it up. "I made it myself."

I reached out, felt it. "Nice," but I was thinking, everything in my world is shifting and you're showing me a sweater vest you knit. "You always were clever with your hands. I want to talk about this class I had this summer." She came over and tried to hold up the vest against me. I grabbed her hands. "Listen, I had this great Adolescent Psychology class and the teacher. I never met anyone like him—tough as a ser-geant, but kind and wise." She pulled free and continued, "You know at Loyola, the Jesuits showed us some good movies this summer. One was "My Fair Lady" with Audrey Hepburn. You'd have loved it." She started to hum a tune, while she folded the sweater vest and put it in the drawer.

"You should've heard the topics that came up in this class---sexual stuff, not like anything I've heard before--masturbation, homosexuality. I even went to Doc's office at USF for counseling and he was good with me."

"You're not supposed to go to teachers for counseling. We go to priests," she admonished.

Frustrated, I got up and put my hands lightly around her waist. She shook free and turned, "Theo, this whole thing sounds quite strange to me. I just don't think..."

"Hey, remember long ago when you told me about dancing with those enlisted men at the CYO dances? Did you ever think what it would've been if..."

"Theo, that was eons ago. I never think about that," she snapped.

"So you never questioned your choice? I mean, about being here; you never thought about, . . .well, about leaving?"

Her eyes clouded and she moved to her suitcase with her back to me and said irritably, "It's never crossed my mind. You know, Theo, I'm really not interested in this kind of talk."

"Maureen, Maureen, why don't we get out of here and take a walk to the creek so we can talk without being interrupted before your sisters come?"

"Theo, we are alone. We are talking. What more do you want? My sisters will be looking for me and I want to see them."

Suddenly, deep inside something gave way, like an ancient redwood tree slowly toppling to the forest floor. I was nearly split in two by the weight of my feelings. I stood for long moment, breathing deeply. The obsession that held me captive for years was releasing its grip on me. Yes, I did want more, though I was uncertain what it was. Slowly, I turned, and staring straight ahead I walked out the door. If Maureen had uttered a word, even a peep, she would have shattered my fragile freedom but she was silent.

I bolted up the path, then started running wildly, breathing deeply, experiencing my new independence. High above a hawk circled. I walked past the Novitiate building and climbed the hill to the apple orchard. My spirit was soaring. Overripe fruit clung to the branches and the air was rich with a pungent cider smell. I sat under a tree and laughed aloud. A crow loudly mocked my laughter and I sang alleluias in return. When the bell rang for community dinner, I realized that instead of plotting how to sit next to Maureen, I could sit anywhere. Later at folk dancing, I smiled widely when I realized I could dance with anyone and I wouldn't care with whom she choose to dance. My independence was intoxicating, but never did I imagine that I wouldn't speak to her again, not for twenty years until the day she lay dying of cancer in a San Francisco hospital.

PART FIVE

CHAPTER TWENTY-TWO

MOTHERHOUSE
SEPTEMBER 1964

AT THE POINT during our Mass where the priest faced us and asked for special intentions, our new Mother General, Mother John Mary prayed aloud, "For the joyful renewal, in our Community, of love and compassion as Christ practiced it."

"For social justice, right here in San Francisco," prayed Sister Margo, who'd just been appointed to the Mayor's commission on social justice.

"That we may regard each Sister as a dear friend," prayed young Sister Nathan.

The priest continued, "Holy, holy, holy, Lord God, heaven and earth are filled with your glory. Hosanna in the Highest"

I had returned to the Motherhouse according to the arrangement made with Mother John Mary and was teaching biology and religion at our high school. Except for Sister Vincent, the other nuns that been new that September of '62, when I was first was assigned to teach at the high school, were no longer teaching here. The Old Guard had ground them up and they'd been reassigned to other schools. Now I wanted to cry aloud: Love, community, friendship—where is it in this Motherhouse?

With Mother John Mary as Mother General, it wasn't the same as my first year teaching here in '62. The atmosphere was far more relaxed with penances, corrections, confessing faults aloud on our knees no longer part of the routine. I was no longer being reprimanded; the older faculty wasn't reporting on me; I didn't have more tasks than I could possibly do. Mother John Mary's booming laugh could often be heard breaking the silence in the convent. In fact, she could often be found in the kitchen after dinner, washing the pots and pans

Yet for me, the newly relaxed spirit was a problem. New alliances had formed while I was away teaching in Seattle. Many Sisters now went about in pairs, smiling, busy. The volatile Sister Vincent was the constant companion of Sister Hubert. Even a chatty foursome had formed--Vincent, Sister Hubert, Sister John Mary's real sister, Sister Clara, and Mother John Mary, herself. They often gathered in Mother's office or even her cell for private get-togethers, perhaps watching TV together. We could overhear them when we passed by the office and cell on the second corridor. What would Mother Colette have thought of this?

Even Sister Andrew, the principal, now had a favorite, the barrel-shaped Sister Aquinas, who'd replaced my dear friend, Sister Loyola, at the high school. Sister Aquinas moved with irritating aloofness in her flat policeman's shoes and was said to be doing a brilliant job teaching math and directing the glee club.

Once Mass was over, my stomach tightened with dread of the day: six classes to teach: four of biology, one of religion, one of Christian Family Living, and then, lunch time supervision. Sadly, I had no art class as Sister Dorothea had a monopoly on all things artistic. This year I felt differently than my first year here. Now I was depressed and confused and wanted to hide in my cell with the curtains drawn and read Carl Rogers "On Becoming a Person" and figure out what was wrong with me. Often, I wanted to slip down to North Hall and talk to the cheerful Sister Brian, who was still trying to make order out of the twenty plus years of accumulations of the former Dean of Studies. She had come to the Motherhouse the same September 1962 as I did, but it was only during the vacation at Los Gatos, after I had broken with Sister Maureen, that we became friends. She confessed, she, too, found the Motherhouse cold and repressive. She missed being a Superior and Principal, but she knew it was God's will for her to serve as Dean of Studies and Supervisor of our Elementary Schools. Her wisdom and competency were obvious, but what came through in her Italian deep-set brown eyes, was warmth and caring.

For my first appointment with Doc Millikan at his downtown office, Sister Brian went with me. Mother John Mary told me Sister Brian would have to approve of him and report back to her before I could start sessions. I'd admitted to Mother John Mary that during summer school at U.S.F., I had talked with Doc Millikan, even been alone with him, which violated our Rule, but that didn't concern her. Nuns never went to therapy, especially with a lay person. Priests were our occasional counselors but she was progressive and anxious to see me become a less-troubled soul, a well-functioning nun. However, as I was leaving her office she said something disturbing. "Mind you, Sister, Sister Brian is of the Old School, an appointee of Mother Colette, not one of our most progressive Sisters. If you rely on her for counsel, she may not be the best for you." I was puzzled by this remark. I knew Mother John Mary was trying to modernize our Order, but in my experience Sister Brian was one of the kindest nuns I knew and was moving forward, perhaps not at the speed of Mother John Mary, herself, but now I only needed Mother's permission to continue my talks with Doc Millikan.

On a fall afternoon, I eased into a huge leather chair across from Doc Millikan in his office downtown on Sutter St. while Sistser Brian sat in the waiting room. As I settled into the chair, I wondered about the sofa. Was this where he saw that woman who thought she had a 'dick'? The one he'd told us about in summer school.

"Doctor Millikan," I began, "I brought Sister Brian along today. She has to approve of you."

"That's fine, no problem and just call me Doc or Millikan. See, we don't have to be formal in here. We're gonna get along fine. See, I'm an eclectic. I take a little of St. Aquinas and St. Augustine and Freud and Jung and Rogers--they're all in here." It was comforting to find Aquinas and Augustine. It seemed so intimate, just the two of us, me calling him, Doc, that it flashed though my mind that it was a bit like sitting at the foot of uncle Hube's big chair as he told his wonderful stories.

"Doc, I haven't been doing very well. I hope you can help me."

"Tell me what's going on with you."

"Doc, I feel like I'm worn out and I get anxiety attacks, then I start crying for no reason. I don't really care about teaching anymore. The only person I trust is Sister Brian. She's my friend. She wants to know what we younger nuns are thinking. She doesn't want to ossify like a dinosaur and end up on the wrong side of the chasm she sees developing in our community."

"I'm glad she's interested in you. Sounds like she treats you as if you're important to her." I nodded but I still felt my life was hanging by threads, barely held up by the rites and rituals of convent life. The old Sister Theo was collapsing but what would the new one be like. What would she do?

At the end of the first session, he put his hand on the doorknob, ready to throw open the door, but kindly, he waited, looking at me. When I nodded, he opened the door and greeted Sister Brian.

"How long will this take, Dr. Millikan?" asked Sister Brian, pulling on her leather gloves. I knew what she meant; how long would it take to make me an efficient cog in the machinery of our Congregation that had twenty-two convents and schools, delivering Catholic dogma and discipline to our many students?

"She's smart," he remarked. "In fact," Millikan continued, "I don't know if I'm as smart as she is, but we have a lot of good work we can do here. My fee is reasonable. It'll be ten dollars a session. "

They spoke about me as if were an errant child in the principal's office, but I didn't mind. I was exhausted being an adult. I really wanted to go back and figure it out all over again. Wouldn't it have been marvelous if he could've fixed me up like a surgeon removing the diseased part and putting in a shiny new plastic replacement that would have functioned perfectly? Then all that was to come, could have been avoided.

As we left his office and strode along the corridor smelling of dentist's anesthesia, Sister Brian quizzed me. "Is he Catholic? Married?" I answered in the affirmative to both questions and added, "He has two boys in school at St. Emydius parish."

"I liked the man, Theo, but do you think he understands us nuns, comprehends our values?"

"I think he has good values and it feels to me like he's promised to fix something, like a horrible, aching tooth where the pain is so bad, I can't function. I need him." I went on to describe how eclectic he was and that Aquinas and Augustine were in there."

She pushed the button of the elevator and straightened the pleats of her habit while she waited. Once outside Sister Brian lead the way up Sutter St. into the crowd of pedestrians in the five o'clock rush. She marched up the street without a glance at a blind man playing, "Lady of Spain" on his accordion. At his feet was a battered hat with a few crumpled bills and a scattering of coins. I wished I could've given him something.

Sister Brian was the first one off the curb when the signal changed. I hurried to keep up with her. In the car she efficiently pinned back her veil to see clearly when she drove while I slumped in the seat and stared out the side window at a crowded bus. It was dark now and the light was on inside the bus. Sister said she would recommend that I see Dr. Millikan once a week, but she wouldn't have time to be my partner. She would find a discreet partner for me. I now had the stigma of being the first nun to see a professional therapist instead of a priest counselor.

My eyes were still on the bus. I could see the crush of bodies that swayed in one motion as it lurched forward. I recalled from my high school days the smells of cheap perfumes and body odors in the crush of ordinary folks in a bus. I closed my eyes. What would it be like to ride home with these people, to have the choices in one's life still ahead?

That night in my cell, I listened to the two Sisters in the adjoining rectangles, snoring softly. Uneasiness gnawed at me and I began to shiver, than shake uncontrollably. Faint chimes striking midnight came from the first floor. Steathily, I rose, slipped on my black seersucker robe and tied my short white cotton night veil tightly over my close-cropped hair and crept down the polished corridor dimly lit with archaic fixtures. In every cranny a nun was sleeping. I stumbled into the short hall that led to three cubicles separated by thin plywood. The first one was Sister Brian's. At the doorway, I could smell Vick's Vapor Rub and recalled she was battling a cold. My light knock vibrated on the flimsy door and without waiting for an answer, I burst in and threw myself on my knees, shaking, at the side of her bed. She looked up bewildered, rubbing heavy lidded eyes. As she pushed herself to a sitting position, her light green rayon pajama top hung loosely. She tugged her white night veil forward over her close-cropped dark hair.

"What is it, Theo? What's wrong? What time is it?"

I burst into sobs. "Shh, Theo, shhh, you'll wake Sister Andrew and Sister Agnes Ann."

"I'm so frightened I can't sleep. I'm just shaking," I cried. Like one drugged by sleep, she reached for me, the dark hair on her arm stood out against her pale skin. She pulled me to her shoulder. For a long moment, she held me. As I felt the warmth of her body, the sticky grinding fear released its grip on me and I stopped trembling.

"Feeling better now? Think you can sleep?" Ashamed and embarrassed, I nodded and retreated to my cell.

The next day we faced each other across her desk in North Hall. "What happened last night, Theo?"

"Its hard to explain. Panic takes over. I know I'm kind of sick, but I don't really understand it. I feel anxious and depressed all the time. Please, forgive me." I said, but I wasn't really sorry. I needed her. Her brown eyes looked worried. I think I frightened her, but I also touched a nerve. She was a capable woman and before coming to the Motherhouse she had been an efficient principal, a warm superior, a care-taker when it was necessary, but now all she had was this huge office with hundred of records and files. No one needed her—except me.

"I think you woke Sister Andrew. I wonder if she . . ."

"I'm sorry, but I don't care about Sister Andrew anymore."

"You should. She's your principal. She doesn't know you are getting professional help. Maybe if you told her, she'd be more understanding."

"Too late for that. I don't want her to know."

"Theo, I don't really understand this psychology stuff. I'm from the old school--blind obedience, no dialogue, penances, discipline, but I realize things are changing rapidly. I can see you are not yourself anymore. I recall that day when you came to my school in San Jose and gave that fabulous art demonstration to the faculty, showing them how to do art lessons in their classrooms. I thought you were the most talented, confident, young nun . . ."

"Well, I'm not that person anymore," I snapped. It came out more sharply than I intended.

"Dear God," she looked at me for a long moment. "You have so much talent. I do want you to get well. I guess if you need a hug or a moment of holding, I can do that, but I want you to talk to the Doc about it. This is all new to me." She walked to the window and stood looking out at the garden. Her hands gripped the sill tightly and she said, "A hug is a measure of comfort, but if you ever try to put your lips to mine-…well, I can never tolerate anything like that." She turned and faced me with her deep-set eyes blinking. I admired her courage for speaking so honestly. She was rare. I wanted to assure her it was a bit of mothering I needed, but the ringing of her phone on her desk interrupted us.

When she picked it up I knew by her expression that it was Sister Anna calling from the next room. She sighed, covered the receiver, and said, "Sister Anna needs some questions answered about schedules she is typing for me. We'll finish this later." Reluctantly, I left North Hall.

When I complained of Sister Anna's frequent interruptions, she said, "When I'm with Sister Anna, I can give freely of myself because its painful to hear her drone on and on, but when I'm with you, I enjoy our discussions so much, I feel guilty. Can you understand that?" I knew what she meant, but I didn't care about guilt and all that other stuff anymore; My insides were crumbling and only the shell of a nun remained.

One evening Mother John Mary invited two Jesuits to the Motherhouse that had often come to the Novitiate when she was Mistress of Novices. In the Community room, they showed us a film, Fellini's "La Strada." After the viewing, we formed small discussion groups room. "Be open, share freely your ideas, Sisters," the two priests who'd studied with Carl Rogers, the well-known psychiatrist, encouraged us. I nearly froze when Mother John Mary with the swoop of her hand, assigned to me to the same discussion group as Sister Andrew who drew a chair to our circle. She stumbled and it looked as if she might fall. I moved a hand to assist her, but she caught herself. That small incident of her vulnerability gave me hope that something genuine might emerge in this group discussion. Young Sister Nathan, familiar with these discussions from her time in the novitiate, spoke first. "I'd be happy to act as the group recorder."

"I don't think there'll be anything to record, Sister," retorted Sister Andrew, her eyes puffy slits behind her glasses. With the students at school, she was often comic, but here she was serious, almost angry. Her face was chalk-white, her flared nostrils too pink, and I couldn't help noticing how homely she was. You could almost feel pity for a face like that except that her overbearing manner stifled any sympathy. She continued, "To me it was just a film, a movie. I saw characters on screen; I watched a story. Nothing more than that."

As the plaintive theme song from the film ran through my head and I recalled the poignant expression in Gelsimina's eyes, it reminded me too much of my own vulnerability. Meanwhile the other Sisters in the group, all senior to Sister Nathan and me, looked down at their hands or cleared their throats. Sister Nathan sat up straight and bravely directed a question to Sister Andrew. "Sister, didn't you think that The Fool, who attempted to rescue Gelsomina, and was killed by Zampano in the attempt, could be considered a Christ figure?" Her shiny optimism made me cringe.

"I didn't see any such meaning, Sister Nathan. In fact, I saw a lot of bad acting. Give me Perry Mason or something where I can relax and enjoy myself. Perhaps, it did mean something to you. As for me, I never read beyond the screen."

"Could someone explain to me what we are doing here?" asked the heavy set Sister Aquinas, her eyes as challenging as her tone. She'd settled into one of the new comfortable chairs that Mother John Mary had placed in the community room and spoke as if it was an effort to rouse herself. The others in our group shifted in their seats. Andrew and Aquinas—quite a duo.

I sat, afraid to open my mouth. I was like a photo negative among these crisp positives. This afternoon Sister Andrew had appointed Sister Nathan as chairman of the biology department. Even though I didn't want the job, it hurt that it was awarded to the younger biology teacher with more science training than me. Sister Nathan took a deep breath, trying to answer kindly, wisely, to Sister Andrew's cynical remarks. I glanced over at another group where Sister Brian sat, deep-set eyes earnest, nodding as she listened. She caught me looking at her and she winked. Ah, to be in her group. Elsewhere in the room, I could hear other groups of Sisters easily sharing ideas.

Mother John Mary stood at the front and with her habitual little laugh directed, "Now, Sisters, let's pool our insights in a general discussion here with Fathers McMurray and Jones." She stepped aside and let the two Jesuits move to the front. The tall one had smooth skin, amber hair with eyes that matched. His slender hands made gestures that were a ballet of their own. The dark one with a five o'clock shadow spoke with the bullet speech of Bogart. I liked them both.

With a confidence I would never have, Sister Nathan moved to the front and began a summary. "Fathers, we were not all in agreement," she said with a pleasant expression, extending her smile to Sister Andrew. I pulled my chair next to Sister Brian, who turned to me and whispered, "This is great. Our group brought out so many things I missed in the film. I'd like to see it again." Her enthusiasm made her seem more youthful than her forty plus years. The Fathers drew analogies of Christian principles that operated in the characters in the film. They spoke with concern, listening to each Sister who raised her hand, careful to learn the speaker's name. This was a refreshing change from the usual preaching of priests. I noticed that Sister Andrew had slipped away as soon as the general discussion began.

During the course of the year, Mother John Mary brought the two Fathers back several times to show other films—among them, Ingmar Bergman's *Winter Light* and *Wild Strawberries*. The discussions that followed were similar to this first one. I avoided being in a group with Sister Andrew, but then thankfully, she began to absent herself from these gatherings. I wondered if Mother John Mary's efforts at modernization would ever have an effect on Sister Andrew.

In Doc Millikan's downtown office, a copper fish in a simple wood frame gazed down on us from the wall behind his large chair. For the second time, I sat opposite him, my habit arranged covering my shoes, my feet barely touching the floor. Millikan leaned his huge frame back in his leather rocker, threw his feet up on his desk revealing white socks and a pack of Camels jutted from the pocket of his white shirt. I'd rambled through the litany of tasks that made up my week. I spoke of these things to fill the void because he'd just sit in silence and wait for me to speak. I was wondering about the plaque of the fish on the wall. Was it something he had round the house and perhaps his wife said, 'Here, Robert take this to the office. It doesn't fit in our house?' Or had he chosen it with care, a fish, an early symbol of Christ, as something special for his office? I would stare at that fish for some years to come.

After listening to my litany of tasks he said, "People ask a lot of you and you ask a lot of yourself. You seem to have trouble saying *no* or *setting limits*," he commented.

I taught six classes of teenagers a day, half of them dying to challenge me. I had to say no to them but whenever another sister asked a favor, I couldn't say no. Charity is our rule. The household tasks were assigned, done without question. I had a vow of obedience.

Could it possibly be that he meant saying no, as in: no, I won't get on my knees and polish the school corridors on Christmas Eve? Or no, I won't teach biology because I want to teach art? Or no, I won't be the sister who serves the priest his breakfast after Mass in our chapel and who has to gulp down her own breakfast? Even no, I won't ever go back and teach sixty first graders in East L.A.?

"See, it wouldn't hurt to say 'no,' when you are feeling overwhelmed."

"Good nuns don't say, 'no'."

"This is not about being a good nun."

"Not about being a good nun?" My, God, then what? I put my hand over my mouth. Tears threatened.

He swung his legs off the desk and leaned toward me. "It's about being yourself."

My God, who was that? If habits, rules and rituals fell away, what would be left? I felt naked and sick to my stomach. Would my legs hold me up when I left his office?

The Vatican Council II in Rome had instructed all Orders and Congregations to adapt a modern habit. In November Mother John Mary made her first move to update our habit. Sisters came to the motherhouse from all our Bay Area convents and a few came up from L.A. With an air of anticipation, we filled the rows of folding chairs in our high school gym. My friend Sister Sean accompanied her Superior from Los Angeles. As I came in, she waved and motioned me to sit beside her. Mother John Mary, herself, stood at the podium at the side of the stage and began to introduce each model. Wisely, she'd chosen four middle-aged nuns to show four versions a modernized habit. The models walked out the stage with confidence, but under our scrutiny, they blushed and even giggled. As they crossed back-and-forth, Mother introduced each outfit, pointing out the new features and up-dated fabric. Sean sat straight up, straining to see each one, while making little asides to me.

"Oh no, not that short skirt, especially with my legs and shoes." I smiled. Sean had fallen arches and wore flat, size 11 shoes. Look, even dowdy Sister Constance looks good in that one. The changes were not dramatic. All, but one of the four outfits, had a floor length skirt and a shortened veil that completely covered the hair. Only one resembled a modern suit with a skirt just below the knee. The main changes were the absence of the stiff, bib-like guimpe, the leather cincture and the choking linen and serge around the chin and neck. Drip-dry polyesters and cotton blends replaced the serge. The models paused so that those near the stage could finger the new materials. A hubbub of comments accompanied the modeling. Sean and I agreed that our favorite was the floor length skirt and a bolero jacket over a long-sleeved black blouse with the white dickey and a shortened veil, held up with a soft white bandeau that covered the hair. Finally, Mother called for quiet. I sat back, expecting that after a few questions, we would make a choice by a show of hands.

Mother recognized the former Dean of Studies, who sat in the first row with raised hand. She turned sideways so we could all hear her. With gray eyes, magnified behind thick lenses, she looked over the assembly. She began by grasping the hem of her long serge habit and dramatically pressing it to her lips. Then she said, "Mother, I believe I speak for the majority when I say we are not interested in any change whatsoever." A hush fell over the gym. Heads snapped up. The dean was well respected. She continued, "My holy habit in which I serve God and I've worn as I traveled around this country doing God's work, is more precious to me than any comfort or ease that change would bring."

Sean and I stared wide-eyed at each other. Several heads were nodding in agreement including Sister Andrew and Sister Aquinas seated a few rows ahead. The former Dean showed no signs of concluding. "Everywhere, I am recognized as a sister of our Community, as a Spouse of Christ, even united with our Sisters in Ireland . . ." At the podium. Hands began signaling for recognition. Mother tried to give others a chance to speak. "Sister, Sister dear, I appreciate your view, would you give others ..." The former Dean kept on speaking. She litanied the names of our oldest sisters, then flung her hand at the short-skirted model near her on the stage and asked: "Will we impose 'this cruel fate' on our dear elders in their remaining years." Some in the assembly applauded. Mother John Mary's face turned as red as a Heinz tomato.

Sean and I elbowed each other. No one ever treated a Mother General in this manner. I glanced around to see if Mother Colette was in the gathering but I didn't see her. Another older, respected nun stood up and former dean relinquished the floor only when she knew that the next speaker would agree with her. This nun, a principal of one of our schools here in the City, spoke in a melodious tone, but she too, opposed change. I was astonished at her view. Long before any talk of change, she'd worn the sheerest of stockings, the highest of heels and seemed knowledgeable on current topics. Now she was fiercely opposed to any changes?

Another sister stood up and argued for some small changes, but she lacked eloquence and status in the group. Another sister stood and agreed with the last speaker, but she was drowned out by sisters shushing her. Sisters were now speaking at once, some were even shouting at Mother, who volleyed remarks right back. The models were blushing, looking as if they wanted to disappear. The former Dean never took her seat, but rambled on, speaking over others. I looked at Sean in astonishment. I couldn't believe these mature women who administered schools, dealt with pastors, wrote books, argued with bishops, and raised funds, were responding like this. At a certain point Mother John Mary took a few steps back from the microphone and become an observer of the chaos. I sat spellbound. So much for holy obedience.

Finally, Mother shouted for order and motioned the models to exit the stage. "Sisters, thank you all for coming today. I realize there is no definitive answer. We shall continue to study the matter as this is a direct mandate from Vatican II."

For days everyone bristled about the habit. Factions formed and reformed. It was whispered, with horror, that Mother John Mary removed her veil while visiting local convents. I could see her pyramid body, her round face, but I couldn't envision how her hair, likely strawberry-blond with a few streaks of grey, was styled.

A few days after the fashion show I received a phone call from Sister Sean. She was worried about me. She thought I looked pale and seemed tense. Was anything wrong?

I replied, "Its just that I'm tired all the time. I went for a checkup and the doctor said I was slightly anemic. I'm receiving injections of a vitamin B complex and I'm taking iron pills. I'll be all right. How are things in your convent?"

"Our whole convent is in an uproar. I can't believe they are so wild against small changes. Don't you think its crazy?"

"Yes, I do," but I almost said "I feel like I'm going crazy myself." I didn't elaborate nor did I mention that I was seeing Doc Millikan regularly.

At one of our sessions, Doc Millikan had suggested that I speak up and ask for what I needed instead of keeping everything bottled inside. What I wanted was more time with Sister Brian. I was ready to lie at her feet like a tired dog and wait for a pat on the head, but she already had the moping Sister Anna who'd come with Sister Brian to the motherhouse. She was a frail soul, a few years older than my twenty-seven years, who'd had a serious breakdown at the San Jose convent where Sister Brian was Superior. Sister Brian nursed her back to some degree of functioning though teaching in a classroom was now beyond her capability. When Brian was appointed Dean of Studies, she arranged for Sister Anna to come along to the motherhouse as her secretary.

When I walked into North Hall, Sister Anna was typing. I sat down across the desk from her.

"Sister, could I talk with you for a minute?" She turned, nodded, and grinned, a wide, inappropriate grin.

"I'm going through some personal problems right now." Then my voice cracked, my façade of self-control as the capable biology teacher was disappearing. "Sister Brian is one of the few sisters I can talk to in this place. I hope you'd be willing to share her." Still grinning Sister Anna rose from her chair and came round and put her painfully, thin arm around my shoulder.

"Of course, of course, I want you to have help. You can count on me. Sister Brian is a wonderful woman. I can attest to that. When I was in that convent in San Jose, I was a real mess." She went on grinning and relating her past and praising Sister Brian. When I left, I thought how easy that was. All I needed to do was ask.

However, the next morning Sister Anna did not arrive at the chapel for meditation and Mass. In fact, she stayed in bed for several days though she had no physical symptoms of illness. When Brian discovered my conversation with Sister Anna, she called me to her office after my day of teaching. I wasn't prepared for what was coming.

"I don't know if I can go on with the two of you! One sickie for three years is enough," she yelled at me. "I'd just gotten her on her feet, feeling independent, getting up for Mass. Then you come along and knock everything out from under her in one day. Its more than I can take!" Her voice choked up. A sob escaped her throat just before she slammed her fist on the desk in frustration and left the room.

In shock, I went to the chapel and tried to pray, but Jesus seemed distant. I sat still until the Sisters gathered for Office. After dinner I saw Sister Brian coming out of Mother John Mary's office and thought, this must be serious. Sister Brian beckoned me to follow her down to her office where we sat across the desk from one another.

"I want you to get some things straight. It's amazing you have an ally in Sister John Mary. She is going to let you stay here. I thought it might be better if you moved to another convent nearby and just come in to teach. Then you and Anna wouldn't get into clashes and..."

"You wanted to send me away because of Sister Anna? Because I asked for what I needed as Millikan suggested?" She went on talking but I wasn't listening. I slid down a long, dark tunnel to a place where I'd been before, where I was ugly and worthless. I stood up and left her without a word and went to the chapel. It was dark and empty, lit only by the red flickering sanctuary lamp, which cast a shimmering reflection on the highly polished floor. A passage I'd read earlier came to mind: A Christian is one who accepts a God of love, who is daring enough to believe that he is loved by God, who will not be put off by the suggestion that it is too good to be true.

For years such passages had sustained me. Tonight nothing made sense. I prayed: Jesus, let me feel Your Presence. But there was only profound silence and the long terrifying night ahead.

After I left the chapel, I crept down to the first corridor and slipped into the phone booth. I was going to use the phone without permission. With shaking hands, I dialed Doc Millikan's home number which he had given me for an emergency.

"Hello," a gruff voice challenged the caller.

" Hello, Doc. It's me."

" Yeah, How are ya?"

"Not good."

"What is it?"

I began to cry.

"You're feelin' sad?"

"Yes, I tried to ask for what I needed, like you told me. But it didn't work out. Sister Brian wanted to send me away to another convent."

"Is that going to happen?"

"Not now."

"You feel rejected and sad, huh?"

"Yes, and I needed to hear your voice."

"Well, I'm here and I'm glad you called. I really am."

"Thank you for being there. I'll be all right now. I'll see you Wednesday, right?"

"Right! I'll be waiting for you."

The men in my life didn't just leave, they died! First, my wonderful, caring father---gone from stomach cancer when I was three; then my adored uncle Hube, who stepped up to help my mom after dad died. Then he got multiple sclerosis. By the time I was fourteen, he was gone of a heart attack. Even Jesus, hanging on the Cross didn't seem to be around these days. I felt like a thin, beaten animal, limping along, going God knows where, but on Wednesdays, I'd sit in the big leather chair and Doc would be there for me. In his office he'd told me, "You can break your head against my no. My no's last forever and when I say: I won't leave you or let you down, you can count on it."

But of course, I knew it wasn't true. Men always let you down.

Why would he be any different? I'd have to test him.

When I went to see Doc, he threw open the door and welcomed me, "How ya' doin' today. Glad to see you."

I began by thanking him for taking my call the other night. Then I said, "Doc I've not been doing very well. I was frightened when Sister Brian said she wanted to send me to another convent and just come in to teach. She's protecting that wimpy Sister Anna. I was scared it might really happen, but the Mother General, Mother John Mary, stood up for me. I'm getting these anxiety attacks where I'll start crying for no reason and still the only person I want to be around is Sister Brian"

"Uh, huh. What is it about her?" He leaned back and swung his feet up on the uncluttered desk and put his hands behind his head. He wore the same white socks, black shoes and baggy pants that he'd worn in the summer school class.

"She listens to me. She misses being a superior and principal, being with people. She likes my company and says she wants to stay in touch with younger sisters and hear what they are thinking. She's bogged down in lots of paperwork and even though she's twenty years my senior, I feel like we are friends."

"Sounds like she treats you as if you're important to her."

"Yes, but I'm afraid I'm beginning to care for Sister Brian too much. That's been my problem: I always need someone special. Our Rule forbids particular friendships." My long love affair came to mind. It was only this summer when I'd miraculously broken the emotional stranglehold Sister Maureen had on me. Was I repeating my pattern?

"It sounds like dependency needs to me. Yep, plain old dependency. Nothing wrong with that."

I perked up, hopeful for a diagnosis. I reached into my pocket and took out a little pad and wrote down his words. "I'd like to be rid of these dependency needs," I said.

A low chuckle rumbled in his throat. "It's a good thing you're bringing it up here. Do you ever want her to hold you?"

The question took me off-guard. My feet jerked and I stared at the copper fish. "Sometimes I do," I murmured softly, "but our Rule doesn't allow it. I'd be in trouble with that." I laughed nervously.

"He smiled and said, you know, Sister, it looks like our time is up. I'll see you right back here, same time next week."

In the waiting room was my nun partner, Mother Colette's former secretary, now inherited by Mother John Mary. She was an older dear nun who had been a secretary before she entered the convent. She was never destined to teach, but was a loyal, efficient nun who served the Mother General well as her secretary. She would read until I emerged, then ask the same question, "Are you feeling better now, dearie?"

I gave a similar answer each week. "Yes, Sister, so much better. Thank you for coming with me." I was grateful for her patience, but I knew she had no idea what this therapy business was about.

Some evenings Sister Brian and I would slip out to the ball court and walk up and down in the chilly evenings and I'd tell her of the insights I was gaining. She listened eagerly, nodding her head, punctuating my account with affirming remarks, "I see what he means. Yes, that is enlightening. Indeed, this is an education for me, too."

Many nights before I could retire peacefully to my cell, I'd need a hug, like a child needing a goodnight kiss. I had to find moments when Sister Anna was not around. I'd kneel at the side of Brian's desk where she was attacking the endless paper work. She'd pat my cheek or let me rest my head in her lap.

One night she said, "Theo, I have some good news. As I was going through all the records, I noticed you haven't actually graduated from U.S.F. though you have more than enough credits. I'm putting in the proper request and you will graduate this June."

"Wow, that's great news. It's only taken me nine years."

And what's more you are going to graduate cum laude."

"Whoa, what does that mean?"

"It means you did a good job in your classes. The translation is: with honor. Congratulations!"

Nice job, Theo, I thought to myself but it didn't change anything.

CHAPTER TWENTY-THREE

DECEMBER 1964

ONE BITTERLY COLD day in December, I hurried across the garden after school hoping for a hot cup of coffee, but knowing it would be luke-warm. Sister Brian was away visiting our schools in Los Angeles in her capacity as our Education Supervisor and I was lonely and hanging on by my fingertips while I awaited her return. When I went into the refectory, Sister Aquinas, a stocky nun who'd come to the mother-house while I was teaching in Seattle, was also approaching the coffee pots. Until now Sister Aquinas and I had never spoken more than two words, though since September, she slept in the cubicle next to mine, separated only by an opaque yellow curtain. Behind her glasses, her close-together eyes looked wise.

"Hi, there, I'm going to have hot chocolate. Would you like some?"

"Sounds great but how?" Even this simple conversation was welcome.

"Leave it to me." She winked and disappeared into the kitchen.. Moments later, she returned carrying steaming cups of hot chocolate with marshmallows bobbing.

"Wow, how did you do it?"

"My secret." We sat down together, sipping in silence. "You're awfully quiet. Are you depressed?" she asked.

"I have my ups and downs."

"Is it something at school?"

"Possibly."

"Sister Andrew?"

"Sometimes."

"You know she appears unfeeling, but she's a good soul. The trouble is she doesn't know how to listen. She talks at people, instead of to them, and she hides behind a wall of words."

"That's quite an apt description but I thought it was only me that she treated that way." As I sipped my drink, I marveled that I was having a serious conversation with this nun who had never spoken to me before.

"Oh no, you shouldn't take it personally. To deal with Sister Andrew, you've got to know how to handle her."

"And you do?"

"Yes," she laughed, "I do and I absolutely love it here." She began to elaborate. "I've a passion for music and I never had the chance to teach it until Andrew gave me the glee club and the class in music appreciation. We're studying Aaron Copland now. Do you know his work?" I shook my head. "Then there's my trig class, a positive joy. Math is my second love."

"Glad it's working for you," I got up to leave. I couldn't bear to hear more.

"You know, Sister Theophane," she called after me, "I'd like you to hear the glee club. We're rehearsing in the Little Theater after school for a concert. Why don't you stop in sometime?"

"Thanks, I might." I left the refectory and headed to the chapel. Mother John Mary was coming the opposite direction. She stopped me in the corridor and from long experience, I worried, what had I done?

"I've been meaning to ask you, Sister Theophane, would you like to get contacts? There's an optometrist that provides the novices their glasses without charge and he'd order the contacts for you."

"Y, y, yes," I stammered, "I would like that." I was ready to kiss her hand in gratitude, but she was gone before I could even say thank you.

The week before Christmas I sat in the optometrist's office in San Jose where the technician in a crisp white coat demonstrated how to put the hard plastic dot in my eye.

"You insert it like this." He pulled his lids apart. "Now you try."

I set my thick, rimless glasses on the table. My fingers trembled. These thin plastics would replace my coke-bottle bottoms? I leaned forward but to see without my glasses, I had to get so close to the mirror that my breath clouded it. No matter that he placed the mirror at different angles and showed me numerous times how to insert the lens, I couldn't force the tiny plastic past my nervous, fluttering eyelid. With an impatient sigh, he slumped back. Desperate to please, I jabbed at my eye and the lens went in but it missed the cornea and disappeared under the lid. Neither of us could get it out. I was close to tears as I was condemned to wear my thick lenses forever.

The technician sat back, smoothed his hair and murmured to the air, "I've never had anybody like this."

"I'm sorry but I do have a bit of resistance to putting something in my eye."

"If you knew you were like this, why didn't you take a tranquilizer?"

Did he think me a skittish animal to be anesthetized? Didn't he realize that we nuns offered our tribulations to Jesus with joy? Yet his words were a revelation: ordinary people took tranquilizers to deal with stress? An hour later with eyes stinging and swollen, but with the hard lenses fairly glued to my corneas, I drove home triumphant.

When my partner and I reached the convent, Mother John Mary, herself, opened the door.

"Ah, Sister Theophane, you look different. What is it?"

"It's the contacts, Mother. I got them an hour ago."

"Oh, that's it. You look a little red-eyed," she laughed, "but that will pass."

Over the Christmas vacation, I got used to wearing contacts, first for just a few hours. Then I worked up to a full day, though it was agony getting them in at 5:30 each morning and I was nearly late to the chapel every morning. On the first day after Christmas vacation, I wore my new contacts to school. The students followed me like a pied piper--staring, asking questions and giving me tips on how to find them if I dropped them. One biology class burst into applause when I entered the room. A senior, a former biology student of mine, caught up with me in the hall. "The word is out, Sister. You got contacts! Stand still and let me look at you." In the jam of students surrounding us, she pronounced judgment: "You have terrific blue eyes, Sister. Before, behind those glasses, you had little mosquito eyes." Although they itched so badly that I had to restrain myself from tearing them out, they made me feel young and new, as if I'd come out from behind a mask.

One day after school, I decided to take up Sister Aquinas on her invitation to see the glee club in action. I tiptoed into the darkened theater where the girls stood on stage in tiered rows, bathed in yellow light. Every eye was focused on Sister Aquinas' upheld hand. With a commanding drop of her arm, they began to sing, but she stopped and started them over and over, until they began as a single pure voice that she directed as if it were attached to her hand by an invisible thread. When they finished, I clapped.

"Who's out there without my permission?" she shot.

"I took you up on your invitation, Sister. Marvelous performance." I said.

"Ah, Sister Theophane, I'm so glad you liked it. Girls, take a

five-minute break. Sister, come on up here. Listen to this new piece."
She waved away the student pianist and seated herself at the baby grand
and played something unfamiliar to me.

"Do you hear it?"

"Hear what?"

"Listen again. Do you hear the dissonance and the way it changes
key, yet it works," she beamed. "The girls are having a little trouble
with it, but soon, they'll get it."

I couldn't hear the finer points but her talent and confidence awed
me. Although we had never conversed until a few days ago, she was
treating me as if we were good friends. Would this last?

The next morning when she saw the curtains of my cubicle still
closed before the school, she whispered, "Theo, are you sick?"

Through tears I answered, "I've got one contact lens stuck under
my lid and can't get it out. I'll never get to school." She laughed and
parted the curtain. While I pulled on my lid, she moved the lens into
place. Her touch was amazingly gentle for a large woman. Together we
hurried across the garden to school, hoisting our habits and breaking
into a run when we heard the final bell ringing. Sister Andrew stood
with scowling face and folded arms at the school door.

"Sister was having trouble with her new contacts," said Sister
Aquinas, smiling broadly. "I had to give her a hand." I heard her add
with a chuckle, "Well, it was a finger, really!"

One afternoon Aquinas came into the room of cells. I was sitting
in mine and she said, "Hey, Theo, are you in there?"

"Yes, yes," I answered, sobbing. She peaked through the curtains.

"What's wrong?" I only shook my head. Boldly, she walked in and
put a cool hand on my forehead. "You feel a bit warm. Maybe a little
fever?"

"No, no, I'm not physically ill."

"Then let's take a walk in the ball court. You can tell me what's troubling you and I'll share with you the details of the musical that I've picked out for the spring performance."

As we paced outside in the overcast afternoon, I confided that I was prone to anxiety attacks. "I cry for no reason at all. Now I'm confiding this to you but you mustn't tell anyone. I'm also seeing a therapist downtown but I don't see that I'm improving. In fact, I think I'm getting worse."

"I'm sure these things take time, Theo. You've got to be patient with yourself. Whatever is causing this, it didn't start overnight. Now," she bubbled, "let me tell you my news. As this year's musical, I'm going to produce "The Wizard of Oz!" She hummed bits of melodies. I listened and was grateful that after my confession she didn't treat me as if I were diseased.

Now, Theo, I'd like you to take over the costuming." She stopped right there in the ball-court and faced me, taking my hands, her eyes glittering like a child's. "You can decide what the characters will wear, choose patterns, the materials and so on. The kids or their mothers or aunts will make them."

"Oh, goodness, Aquinas, I couldn't. I've never done anything like that. This is an ambitious project."

"But Theo, you're an artist. You have a visual sense. You'll do it much better than me. Please?"

"Ask Sister Dorothea. She's the art teacher."

"Oh, she's too busy. Besides, I want you."

"What about Sister Andrew?"

"Leave her to me. You'll do it then?"

With a deep breath I replied, "I'll do the best I can."

She clapped her hands and as we turned back toward the convent and punched my arm lightly and said, gleefully, "Together we'll do a great show, partner!"

I felt a strange lightness coming over me, an unfamiliar joy, a feeling of being wanted.

After school Sister Aquinas and I worked together on the musical. When Sister Brian, who was supervisor of our schools, returned home from visiting our schools said she was pleased that I wasn't moping around and depressed. At my next therapy session, excitedly, I told Millikan, "I have a new friend and she's involved me in the school musical. We're doing *The Wizard of Oz*. For the first time I feel I'm part of something at school. It's as if suddenly, I belong."

"Good. I'm glad to hear it," he responded with one of his rare grins. When he swung his legs from the desk, signaling our time was up, he said, "Let's cut our sessions back to twice a month now and see how it goes." I smiled. I felt I was getting well. Sister Brian would be delighted.

When I got back to the convent, I went immediately to North Hall and kicked off my shoes and danced around her office relating my good news to Sister Brian. She seemed pleased but I detected a slight reserve in her response.

One day after school Sister Aquinas and I were sitting in her classroom with heads bent over sketches of The Cowardly Lion and The Tin Man when the door opened. Sister Andrew's grin vanished when she saw me and she shut the door with a flustered, "Excuse me."

I'd never seen her act like that. "Aquinas, she came to see you. You'd better go after her right now," I warned.

"No, no, I'll take care of her later." She waved her hand and went on discussing the costumes. When she was satisfied, she put her hand over mine and looked at me. "Theo, you're such a help to me. The performance will be better because of you." Her skin was alabaster and the texture smoother than mine, an unexpected contrast to her amazing strength. Our eyes held and a rush of warmth passed between us. When she stood she leaned over and gave me a kiss on the forehead.

"You're a good kid, Theo." I sat very still. "Let's go," she said. I felt I should have warned her again that I was under a doctor's care, possibly infectious, but I didn't.

At a rehearsal in the Little Theater we stood in the wings of the stage amid the ropes, cables and colored gelatins. My presence back stage was unnecessary, but Aquinas wanted me to be with her. To my right was an intimidating panel of large switches with red and green lights that controlled all kinds of things throughout the theater. I wasn't comfortable back stage and worried I would trip or pull a wrong switch or do some type of damage. The girls were on stage rehearsing a scene for the umpteenth time. Sister Aquinas was behind me, leaning back against the panel with closed eyes, listening intently. She had rested her arm on my shoulder. Very gradually, she pulled me back against her. My body melted into her cave of warmth. I knew this was daring and dangerous but I didn't resist. As the number concluded, she squeezed my shoulders and her cheek grazed mine. Then, she was center stage barking commands.

The mother of one of my sophomores died suddenly and many of us wanted to attend the wake and Rosary. In the community room, I scanned the list Sister Andrew had posted that assigned sisters to cars to attend the wake. My name was omitted, yet as one of the girl's teachers, it should've been on the list. I knew Julia well and I wanted to attend the rosary. I realized Sister Andrew was behind this. Nearby Aquinas was checking for mail in her box. She pulled out an envelope. "It's Andrew's handwriting," she murmured.

"It's ridiculous that neither of us are on this list," I complained. She was slitting the envelope with a letter opener. "This isn't going to stop me, Aquinas. I'm going anyway," I said defiantly. But she was already leaving the room while reading the contents of the envelope.

"Aquinas?"

"Later, later, Theo." She fanned the air behind her.

After dinner I rustled the curtain of her cubicle next to mine. There was no response yet I had heard her enter. I parted the curtain and saw her sitting at her desk, looking solemn with pen in hand and paper in front of her.

"Aquinas what's wrong? Can we talk?" She took off her glasses, cleaned them with her handkerchief and shook her head. "Is it the letter from Andrew?"

"Your friendship is too costly," she said, rubbing her nose where her glasses left a red mark.

"What did she say?"

She pushed back her chair and strode out of the cell. I followed her, but she fairly flew down the stairs. "Where are you going?" I called. She shrugged and rushed down the next flight. I didn't follow. In my cell, I put my head on my desk and closed my eyes.

The next day she reverted to the old Aquinas, gruff and business-like, clearly wanting to be left alone. I was startled at the sharpness of pain I experienced. However, three days later, she asked brusquely if I would be her partner as she had permission to buy new shoes. She was going to take the bus downtown. After school we boarded the bus crowded with our students. They hovered over us, giggling and joking. I pretended to read Vespers from my Office book, but it was impossible to pray.

After the girls got off the bus, Aquinas took a deep breath and tried to explain to me what was going on within her. Though I was disappointed that she wouldn't reveal a word of what Sister Andrew had written, I felt a revengeful pleasure in the knowledge that my association with Aquinas irked Sister Andrew who had caused me so much pain during my years at our high school.

"Andrew cares about me and I hurt her by being with you so much. You see she is all head, afraid of emotions, the way I was before I met you. I've got to keep talking to her, letting her see that I do still care for her." She talked about the changes happening in the Church, of how emphasis on self-denial was gone and how we should accept our human needs. "Even the Church is acknowledging our humanity, admitting to our need for friendships. You and I, we're avant-garde, right at the tip. It's you, Theo, who opened me up to the first real emotions I've felt in years." She squeezed my hand. "It's my mission to bring Andrew along, too." I wondered if even she could do that, but I merely listened, content that we were close again.

In the department store, we acted like adolescents, picking up fancy heels and giggling. "Theo, you've made a loose woman of me, she said as she grinned at the salesman who was slipping a soft, low-heeled pump on her foot. "Look, Theo, these are dancing shoes." I laughed as I watched her do a clumsy pirouette in front of the mirror. Since she and I began to work together, she had been dieting. She had lost nearly thirty pounds and that had shifted her figure from barrel-shaped to hourglass.

"I'll take them. In fact, I'll wear them,'" she said to the salesman, who was smiling, too, as if he was a co-conspirator. He plunked her worn, flat clodhoppers in the box. We walked out grinning, arm-in-arm to catch the bus.

That night it was Sister Aquinas' turn to serve in the refectory. As she passed the steaming platters, she couldn't suppress a knowing grin. With her new waist cinched in by the ties of the long apron and her new heels clicking on the vinyl, she was aware of the swivel of heads. Given the slightest encouragement, I was sure she would have tap danced between tables. When she passed a bowl of green beans to Andrew, she elicited a reluctant grin from her.

On the afternoon of the dress rehearsal for the Wizard of Oz, Aquinas was a wild woman; she bellowed directions, demanded numbers be repeated and sent the Cowardly Lion off in tears. I spent the afternoon spraying silver on new parts for the Tin Man's costume that had gotten wet. However at the end of the long afternoon, everything fell into place, girls, music, lights, and costumes. Aquinas knew it was working and she beamed. For each of the four nights the school theater was filled to capacity. The cast took two and three curtain calls. On the last night, Sister Aquinas was called onstage and the applause escalated to whistling and shouts of bravo. She smiled triumphantly and took a modest bow as a student pressed a bouquet of red roses into her arms. Standing in the balcony, clapping, I felt in love with her and grateful that she was giving me new life.

That night the sisters who had ushered for the evening performance, gathered in the convent kitchen for hot chocolate. When Aquinas came in, they burst into applause. Even Sister Andrew had a big grin and made a toast, raising a cup of hot chocolate: "To Sister Aquinas who has given us the best performance ever at our high school."

Aquinas blushed and grinned. I could see that this tribute moved her more than the accolades in the theater.

When at last we climbed the stairs, we both felt heady with success, but also afire with unspoken passion. It was fortunate, I thought, as we entered the room and our hands brushed and eyes connected, that Sister Stephanie was asleep in the cubicle by the window. When the lights were out, Aquinas inched the curtain back between her bed and mine. She tiptoed to my bedside. Breathing heavily, she leaned over me and stroked my lips. I put my cheek to hers. We held each other for long moments. Then, she drew the curtain and slipped back to her bed and left me to dream.

The next weekend we received permission to go to the de Young Museum in Golden Gate Park where the Society of Western Artists was exhibiting. The day was warm, after a spell of grey, the kind of day that dries up the winter mold that has grown on the soul. The gnarled cherry limbs delivered up a frothy pink confection. As we walked from the bus stop, Aquinas reached for my fingers and hand-in-hand, we sauntered toward the museum, two aging adolescents.

Inside the paintings cast a spell over me; I moved from room to room in a near trance, while Aquinas trailed behind. I returned a third time to my favorite, Robert Elsocht's Ironsprings, a tree, nearly abstract, spreading its tangerine foliage over an ochre spring. As I absorbed the freedom of that painting, I knew in the core of my being that I had to paint soon. When I spoke of my desire to Aquinas, she said, "Then, Theo, you've got to do it. You just march into Sister Brian's office and tell her: Sign me up for painting this summer. You've finished your B.A. degree, right?" I nodded, sucked in my breath and gritted my teeth. I knew that after this experience, I'd get ill, if I didn't paint soon.

The next week an unforeseen event occurred. Sister Stephanie was sent to the hospital for tests. She would be away for two nights. Meanwhile, Sister Brian was also gone for a few days. The anticipation of our being alone in our cells that night rose between me and Aquinas like a fever. By some intuitive ritual, we avoiding speaking to each other during the day, but even before dark, we retired early to our cells.

In solitude we undressed, put on flannel nightgowns and short white cotton night veils, each aware of the rustling of the other. I slid between the sheets and waited. Like the first movement in a wordless tango, she snapped open the curtain and advanced to my bed. I was breathing heavily. In a teasing foreplay, she sat on the bed and traced the line of my brows.

"Did you know I love your eyebrows? They're like a child's." Then she ran her fingers lightly over my lips. I bit her finger. Slowly, she led me to her bed where I lay next to her, rubbing my fingers over her closely cropped hair. It was soft, like down, not bristled, the way it looked. I bit her shoulder, playfully, felt the warmth of her large breasts, swinging free beneath her nightgown. As she rubbed her porcelain cheek against mine, she confided she hated her breasts until she met me, but I had brought out a nurturing that she never knew she had. We clung to each other hungrily.

"I never want to hurt you, Theo," she said and we moved delicately into a forbidden paradise. I felt her glowing, hot, drawing me close.

She was going to sizzle my flesh. I let out a silent scream of pleasure and lay panting. Even when I felt tied to a rack of guilt, I could not leave her. The chimes of the clock on the first corridor marked three and I left her warmth and slipped through the yellow curtain and returned to my own bed, knowing we had to face the day at five-thirty.

In the morning, I couldn't face Jesus in a meditation before Mass. Instead I sat shivering in the cold outside on a bench on third floor balcony, feeling numb and sick, at one with the fog. How would I even get through a whole day of teaching? When I truly awoke, I was teaching third period biology. When the girls asked what was wrong because I was so distracted, I proceeded in silence to pin the chloroformed frog's foot under the microscope. We all watched in awe the ballet of blood corpuscles as they hurled through the capillaries, one by one and under the lens, I discovered again the beauty of the Creator, and I recalled, sadly, that once I was in love with Him.

Aquinas and I had another night of magic.

When Sister Brian returned, I couldn't hold her gaze and though my greeting was bright, I chattered too loudly and she was immediately suspicious. Later in the day I saw her go into Mother John Mary's office. Soon afterward, she called me to her office in North Hall.

"Okay, Theo, what's going on in that cell? Mother told me Sister Stephanie's reported odd noises between you and Sister Aquinas during the past few weeks. Mother believes you're 'infecting others,' her exact words. What is really happening?"

I turned deep crimson and wished I could explain, but I merely shrugged. It was too much to ask her to understand. I didn't fully comprehend it myself. What I did admit was that occasionally, when I was upset, Aquinas put an arm around me. She began to pace furiously. I thought she was holding back tears, but I was wrong. She pounded her fist on her desk, "Damn it to hell, I've had it, Theo! I'm calling the

Doc." I overheard her speaking to Doc Millikan. "Yes, Doc, that's it exactly. I've reached the end of my rope and so has Mother John Mary. You bet, I'll send her to you tomorrow." I dreaded tomorrow.

When I arrived at his office, he didn't throw open the door and greet me with his usual cheerful, "Hi ya." He sat with his feet up and his face chiseled in a scowl. "Sounds like a lot of acting out going on out there. You've pushed the big brass to their limits," he said, looking at me for only a second, and then tossing a book of matches in his hands. "You're on a destructive path. You've ticked off the authorities and now you've got to quit acting out." I'd never seen him like this. He was siding with them, against me.

"You don't even know what's going on," I challenged.

"I don't have to know the details. When I get calls from the big brass, hollering, 'Uncle,' I know you're acting out. You're gonna get pummeled. You gotta cut out whatever you're doing and bring all the feelings in here."

"You mean not be friends with Aquinas?"

"If that what it takes. You're pulling out that woman's pathologies. They're not equipped to handle everything in there. See, they're trying to learn, but you're pushing them too far. You're not getting any insights. In fact, you're blocking them."

"I don't care about their damn rules anymore. I won't give up Aquinas. I don't care what they want. I won't promise anything to them or to you. It's you that taught me not to set myself up, not to make promises I can't keep."

We were locked in a battle of wills. He wasn't going to soften or get into any discussion. One could break one's head against his 'no.' I was cornered. Millikan lit a Camel, inhaled deeply and blew the smoke out slowly. After a minute, he crushed it, grinding it in the amber ashtray.

"Yep, what I see going on is egocentric, masochistic, sadistic, homosexual love." He gave a final grind to the butt. He faced me, waiting. What he said, terrified me. Ordinarily, we would've examined the pieces, one by one, with me straining for insight and understanding, but today I was too angry.

"Millikan, I'm telling you, I can't stop loving her. I can't promise I won't touch her. I can't promise anything!" I said, shouting.

"You've pushed those authority figures to their limits and you've got to halt."

"I can't."

"You mean, you won't."

"I can't and I won't. You don't know what it's like living there. Aquinas is the only person in that whole school that's ever been kind to me."

"But the way you're acting out is, not a solution." He looked at me, his hooded eyes wary, his face granite

At that moment I hated him. I made as if to rise. "I don't need to come here anymore."

"Come back when you're ready to talk things out, instead of acting out."

"I won't ever come back!" I stood up and moved toward the door, wishing at every step, he'd call me back.

When I returned to the convent, I went straight to North Hall. With forced confidence, I told Sister Brian I was finished with the Doc. In truth, I felt like some half metamorphasized form, plucked from the cocoon in mid-development.

"You quit the Doc?" Her sallow skin blanched.

"We can handle it right here," I told her. "He doesn't understand us. We can control ourselves. Sister Aquinas doesn't want to hurt me. She loves me. We'll do whatever you say, Brian." She said solemnly that she'd meet with Sister Aquinas in the evening and I was to leave them alone.

After dinner Sister Brian and Aquinas met in the seldom-used dining parlor with the fake daisies in the center of the table and the Archbishop, in violet-trimmed robes, eavesdropping from a gilt frame on the wall.

"Go up to your cell, Theo. Let me handle things," she had said after dinner. I knew she was furious with Sister Aquinas because she thought she was undoing the work that she and Doc were doing to make me well. I went to bed but I couldn't sleep. When the clock in the corridor chimed ten, I wrapped my robe around myself and padded downstairs. The light shone through the opaque glass in the parlor door. I could hear muffled voices. I stole into the other large parlor, the one where I had gotten dressed in my wedding dress as a bride of Christ about a hundred years ago.

Sitting in the dark on the brocade sofa, I listened to the muffled voices in the other parlor. I recalled that summer a few years ago when it was discovered that two of my peers spent the night together during our ten-day vacation in the mountains. Mother Colette was summoned and she confined them both to separate cabins for the rest of the vacation. The young one was dismissed from the convent immediately. Later, the older one was also asked to leave the convent. I remembered the suppressed twinge of envy I'd felt when I heard they'd left. What would be my fate?

Breaking my reverie, I heard chairs scraping and I saw a form silhouetted against the glass, a hand was turning the doorknob. They were coming out. I scurried away, frantic for a hiding place. In nearby North Hall I stopped at the broom closet. When I opened the door, I nearly screamed. A white-faced Sister Anna, plastered against the jumble of mops, stared out at me. I fled to the next closet. After their footsteps faded, I began to laugh hysterically. The line between sanity and madness was stretching dangerously thin.

The next day Sister Brian laid down new rules. Aquinas would continue to be a good friend, but she was the one I would go when anything upset me. There was to be no communication in the cells and absolutely no physical contact, not so much as a hand held. Both Brian and Aquinas knew that they would not let me manipulate the situation any longer, playing one against the other. I sat there nodding, wondering what was ahead.

Though Aquinas and I tried to live up to the new rules, but it was too late. Often we held hands or stole an embrace. It was a closed system with no escape valves. Aquinas, Andrew, Anna, Brian, and I kept bumping into each others needs, limits and passions. Love, jealousy and fear oozed all over the place. We hadn't enough fingers to plug up the leaks.

Late one night, racked by anxiety and confusion, I called Millikan. When his wife answered, she sounded ordinary and calm and I envied her as I heard her calling the Doc.

"Doc, could I come back?"

"You betcha, we haven't finished our work."

Shortly after my admonishment, Aquinas did me a huge favor. Though Sister Andrew wanted me to take more biology classes, Aquinas advocated for me to take a summer. painting class. She told Sister Brian that it would be a good for my mental health. To my amazement, Aquinas prevailed against Andrew. Together Aquinas and I explored summer school art options, but as none of the nearby Catholic institutions offered art in a summer, she insisted that we look at other offerings, even those of the well-known Art Institute on Chestnut St and indeed, they had beginning painting class that met every afternoon in July.

Near the end of the school year, Aquinas and I took a bus to famous Art Institute in North Beach so I could register. We pushed open the rusting gates and entered the unkempt courtyard where the central fountain hadn't been operational for ages. Art hung everywhere, but it wasn't what I called art. Toilet seats tacked to canvases and wild-colored nudes lounged on canvases, pieces of wood formed abstract creations. Fortunately, Aquinas began to laugh at the scene and that eased my anxiety. Down a dark hall we found the registrar's office. As I completed the paper work, I timidly asked if any other Catholic nun was attending. The registrar smiled and assured me there was one other nun. She was from Lone Mountain College and was taking printmaking. I wondered if I'd run into her in summer. At least the students and teachers would have seen another woman in a habit

The school year ended in mid-June and we bore the scars of the year's battles. Before Aquinas went to her summer assignment, we walked together in the ball court. We both knew the year had been unlike any other and we didn't know what the future held. We cared for one another and were trying to keep our friendship viable without 'acting out', as Millikan called it. She hugged me and told me to become a great painter. I squeezed her tightly and let my head rest on her shoulder. She put her smooth hand on my cheek and I kissed her fingers. Then she turned and bolted to the car waiting at the curb that would take her to her summer convent in Berkeley.

Before I left for St. Elizabeth's convent in the Mission district where I'd been assigned for summer, Sister Brian asked me to come to her office.

"Theo, are you ready for your painting class?" she asked too brightly.

"Okay, Brian, what's wrong?"

"Damn-it-to-hell, Theo, you have a sixth sense! I can never fool you."

"I know you! You can't deceive me."

"All right, sit down. Mother John Mary and I have talked to the Doc about you. Your progress seems to be at a standstill and she has decided there will be no contact with Sister Aquinas or me this summer. The Doc says you're acting out, not bringing your real feelings to him."

"This is Gestapo tactics! Once Aquinas is out of the house, you and

Mother gang up on me. I've been getting better. I've returned to the Doc on my own. Why cut off my support system?" I paced the floor, picking up things, banging them down.

"Theo, calm down. The Doc will see you every day in the morning at his university office. He'll take care of you. I'll be around. I'll want to hear how well you're doing."

"You mean I can still talk to you?"

"Well, not everyday but from time to time."

I knelt next to her and put my face in her lap and broke down. "Brian, I hate this whole thing. I hate myself, I'm ugly and awful, a terrible manipulator, but I need you. Don't push me away. I'll get much worse." She stroked my face. Her face was lined and she had dark circles under her eyes. This was hard for her, too.

"Theo, I have something for you." She took a package wrapped in white tissue from her bottom drawer. I tore it opened and held up a bright, flowered apron, floor length and with a square bib and a big pocket.

"Brian, how can I paint in this? It's too gorgeous! You can't sew. Where did you get this?"

"I bought the material with as many colors as possible so the paint won't show. I had my sister, Flo, sew it up."

I was so touched by Brian's caring that I wanted more than anything to get better, to be a good nun, to make her proud of me.

Sister Theophane in the Biology Lab

Sister Brian

Dr. Millikan

CHAPTER TWENTY-FOUR

SUMMER 1965

JUST BEFORE WE left for summer assignments, Mother John Mary decreed that we all would change to a modified habit on August 1st. Happily, the model chosen was the one that Sister Sean and I liked. In the motherhouse bitterness ran rampant, some swearing they'd die before they'd change. Everyone was to begin sewing to make a floor length skirt from an old habit and two new black blouses. Some of us needed help. Fortunately at my summer convent, the Superior had engaged a generous parishioner to make blouses for the sisters. When I went to her home to be measured, I got on well with her and her husband. I had started my art class then and promised them a painting. Through the course of the summer, her handy husband framed several of my paintings. It was such a relief to be away from the tension at the motherhouse and have moments with ordinary folks. I also arranged for one of my favorite students to drive me to and from the Art Institute everyday. The summer was going to work out well after all.

Each morning I rode to U.S.F with a group of sisters who were still taking classes there but I would run up the jillion steps of Lone Mountain where I was taking a design class. At 11:30, I would race over to Millikan's office at U.S.F. for our half hour session. Then walk to our high school cafeteria for lunch. After lunch my dear student, Kathy, who lived in North Beach and had recently gotten her driver's license, would pick me up and drop me at the Art Institute for the afternoon class. Kathy was an attractive dark-haired young woman who loved to chatter about her boyfriends. I was a good listener and was grateful for the transportation. At the end of the day, she would pick me up and drop me at our convent in the Mission district.

On a foggy Monday morning, I pushed open the creaking gate of the famous San Francisco Art Institute. In the courtyard shaggy-haired students lounged around a defunct fountain, most of them sketching. A formidable rusty sculpture loomed above them. No one stirred as I crossed the courtyard, but I knew eyes followed me in my long black habit and veil. On my first visit here Sister Aquinas was with me and it felt like an adventure. Without her, it was unsettling. I hurried down the walkway hung with the same huge canvases we'd seen before-a garish nude, a filthy toilet and basin, a collage of wood scraps. We had laughed then and asked: Was this art? I was tempted to race back to the familiar University of San Francisco, but this was a real art school with a national reputation and many famous artists had passed through this courtyard and I ached to be a genuine artist. I didn't know it then, but this is where Joan Beatty Brown, from my senior high school art class, had risen to local fame.

Beginning Oil Painting was held in Studio 2. When I opened the door, I was confronted with a forest of easels where students had already begun painting. As I searched for the instructor, the smell of linseed oil and turpentine brought a flash of fond memories of my high school art class. Then in the center of the studio, I saw her---a huge, naked woman, mounds of flesh, reclining on a dirty platform. I staggered. Oh Lord, where is the still life-the bowl of fruit, the vase flowers? I never imagined they would have a nude model on the first day of a beginner's class. I had never seen a naked woman before. As I started to back out the door, a man in denim shirt and jeans planted himself between the me and the model.

"Can I help you?" He asked twisting his handlebar mustache.

"Mr. Oddo? I'm Sister Theophane. I'm registered for this class."

"I see. Umm, do you have your supplies-paints, brushes, canvas?"

"I do have paints-watercolors and oils, but no canvas."

"Here's the supply list." He grabbed a paper from a stack on a chair. "The supply store is just down the hall." He took my elbow, escorted me to the door, stepped out in the hall and pointed the way for me. Reading the list, I trudged down to the bookstore. It specified a four by three foot canvas and three-inch brush. I sighed as I looked at my tote bag with a few watercolor brushes. I couldn't paint a four-foot canvas of that nude. I'd have to drop the class. But then I remembered how Sister Aquinas had stood up to Sister Andrew and fought for me to take art, not more biology. I could do this.

In the damp cellar bookstore, I bought a giant canvas and huge brush. Luckily, Sister Brian had given me money for supplies. On the way back to the class, I stopped at a row of empty lockers and undid my stiff white guimpe. My hand clutched at the cool space between my collarbones now exposed to the air. Over my habit, I pulled on a brown oversized man's shirt that my friend, Marilyn, brought me when she drove me to my summer convent. With a deep breath, I opened the classroom door and sailed across the studio, holding the canvas high between my line of vision and the naked model. I landed next to Mr. Oddo at the far side of the room. I was sure I appeared like a freak from another era to the other students.

"It's a little late in the day to start the model. Why don't you just make some sketches today?" he said, twirling his mustache.

With relief, I replied, "Oh, yes, good idea." But I could not look at that huge, naked woman, let alone make any sketches. Behind me a small door was ajar. It led out to a balcony overlooking Chestnut St. I glanced at Mr. Oddo with a questioning look. He nodded. I stepped out into the bright sunlight. I looked up and saw Coit Tower, a sentinel against the cobalt sky. I took out my watercolors and brushes and began an easy rendition of the famous monument. That night I hardly slept, worrying about the naked woman.

The next afternoon my hand was tense on the studio door handle. With a thumping heart, I steeled myself for the worst but to my astonishment Mr. Oddo was positioning a new model on the platform. She wore a gauzy white blouse, a full blue skirt and black high boots. An orange nasturtium, like a protruding tongue poking out of a knot of black hair. Mr. Oddo's eyes darted to me and he motioned me to an empty easel. Was it because of me that he'd changed models? I felt relief, but worried that the other students would resent my presence. I set up my huge canvas and began to paint. At the break, I wandered among the other easels. Most of the students were adults and it seemed that they might have taken this painting class before. Many were still working on yesterday's figure. They had painted her in bright colors-vermilion, magenta, cobalt blue, greens. As I wandered around during the break, no one spoke to me, not that day, nor any day of the entire summer.

Mr. Oddo kept the same model for the week. Soon I was absorbed in my own painting and didn't mind that no one spoke to me. Mr. Oddo would come round and make suggestions. "I'd keep that background simpler. See like this." He'd take my huge brush and simplify the background so that the figure was more prominent. The hours of painting calmed me. I didn't consider myself one of the best painters in the class, but I saw that I was easily as good as many of the students. When I would bring home a huge painting to the convent at the end of the week, the sisters would gather round and admire it. But then, they'd ask, "What will you do with this?" We'd been taught to think practically. Everything, even paintings, should be put to good use. The watercolor landscapes that I had done made fine gifts for benefactors. They fit nicely in a doctor or dentist's office. What good were these enormous oil paintings of outlandish women? It didn't matter to me. I was learning to paint at a real art school.

At Millikan's first session of the summer, he announced, "We're going to use this time in concentrated doses; see if we can make some real progress." Then he rocked back in his swivel chair, settling his tree trunk legs on his desk. "You know, you really stirred them up this year. They can't handle that acting out. They're limited. See, I can handle anything here."

During the first week, I kept to the safety of topics that we've gone over before, but then one day the Doc pierced my armor. He recalled that I had used the word 'ugly' about myself. "I wonder where does that come from? Ugly is a powerful word," he said.

I closed my eyes. As long as I could remember I felt unattractive. Much of it had to do with the thick lenses of my glasses that only last year, I was able to exchange for contact lenses. Boys had teased me at a vulnerable age, called me 'four eyes 'and even worse, 'a four-eyed pile of shit.' I still recalled those hurtful incidents, but the damage may have been earlier. Being abandoned at an early age by the death of my loving Dad when I was three and then by my adored Uncle Hube when I was fourteen, may have impacted how I felt about my-self. Then, too, my Mom was tall, and attractive, never wore glasses. Men loved her. I couldn't compete. I brought up these memories up with Millikan.

"Sounds like pretty important feelings coming out now." He was nodding and looking at me intently. But our summer appointments were short and as I prepared to leave, I said, "I almost forgot to tell you the news. Sister Brian is going to be the new superior of the mother-house in September."

"Huh," he drawled, scratching his head. "So she's going to be the big cheese, the mother to all of them. Wonder how that's going to workout?"

When I heard the news, I had acted as if I were delighted for her. Yet it was unsettling because now she would belong to all the sisters. I had a sudden urge to cling to his comforting bulk.

That night in bed I begin to feel ill, like I was coming apart, dissolving. I wasn't sure who I was anymore. The feelings were far worse than depression. 'Theophane' as I knew her was disappearing. The next day while trying to explain these feelings to Millikan, I burst into tears, not just weeping, but great sobs as a tidal wave of buried emotions rose, repressed demons, dark and ancient, rose up. Millikan sat quietly, turning a pack of matches in his hands, just letting me cry and cry.

"Some real feelings are coming out today," he said at last. "Any ideas about them?"

"I feel so weak," I gasped. "Sick, in fact. I feel like I did when I first went to a camp at age seven, a camp run by nuns. I got so homesick that I cried constantly and even vomited. The nuns called my Mom. She came and picked me up.

"Sounds like you felt abandoned."

Now I was crying so hard I could scarcely breathe. Scraps of the scenes from my childhood rushed through my head: Tantrums, where I'd screamed at Mom and blamed her for my dad's death; Times of being punished; put in the closet-by our live-in housekeeper who favored my baby sister, Ellen.

"Millikan, I don't feel well," I whispered. "In fact, I can't make it to lunch or my afternoon class. Could you call Sister Brian?" He dialed the number I gave him. Then we waited in silence, though we'd gone well over my half-hour.

"I'm sorry I'm out of control today, Doc," I murmured.

"Control will never be your problem. You have control down pat. Some real important feelings coming out today. See this is good stuff, real good stuff."

Within minutes Sister Brian was at the office. She didn't ask questions, just took my arm, said thanks to Doc, and got me to the car. Once in the car, I put my head in her lap and sobbed. She patted my cheek and let me cry. When at last I sat up, she started the car. I sat back with closed my eyes. I'd lost all control. When the car stopped, I saw that we were at a fast food place on Geary Street.

"Chocolate or vanilla?" she asked, as she opened the door.

"What?"

"What kind of shake?"

"Uh, chocolate."

When she returned, the smell of burgers and fries filled the car. When we came to a stop, I saw that we were at China Beach, a place I'd come often as a teenager to think about things. The day was sunny, but cool. Only a few sunbathers dotted the crescent of sand. In the trunk she found an old towel that she spread out in a sheltered sandy spot. We sat munching hamburgers. I untied my oxfords; my toes ached to wiggle freely in the sand. With the warmth of the food and sun, I felt my physical strength returning, but mentally, I was drained. It seemed the old Theo was dying and a different person, less competent, but more honest, was emerging. I looked at Brian as she sat with her arms around her knees, enjoying the ocean. I was overwhelmed by a feeling of gratitude because between Brian and the Doc, I was being taken care of in a way I'd never experienced.

"Don't you love the sound of the waves, Theo?" She imitated the sound of a wave crashing and gave a swoop with her hand.

"Yes, the water has healing powers. Thank you for bringing me here." I sifted sand through my fingers.

After a long pause Brian began to speak slowly, choosing her words carefully. "Theo, have you given any thought to the possibility that our life may not be for you? Have you given it serious consideration, ever?

"No, I'm sure I belong here. Mother Colette often said that she never doubted my vocation, I protested. " in fact.. . . " I paused.

"In fact, what?"

"I'd like to be just like you."

"Is that so?" she frowned, mocking me.

The next day I resumed my routine, but deep down something had shifted.

By summer's end, I had painted four large canvases of unique women, none naked. Lonely as it was, I had enjoyed every day of the class. I gave two of the paintings to the generous couple where the wife had patiently made new, black blouses for the sisters in the parish. The other paintings I brought to the motherhouse and kept them down in the trunk room for the future. During the summer, Sister Aquinas called three times to check on me. Our conversations were brief, but I told her I was so grateful that she had helped me get into the Art Institute. I made her laugh with the description of my first day. She just wanted to check in, to see that I was all right. Everything was fine with her, she said. I had a premonition, however, it wouldn't be that easy once we returned to the motherhouse. Things had shifted for me during the summer and I wasn't the same person I had been last June.

PART SIX

CHAPTER TWENTY-FIVE

MOTHERHOUSE 1965

WHEN I RETURNED to the motherhouse in fall of 1965, it was time to change into the new habit. All summer in every convent the sewing machines were in constant use--everyone stitching up new skirts and blouses. We were given new headgear designed by one of our own Sisters, a radical change from the linen and surge that trapped us for years. The veil was shoulder length held up by a light bandeaux--a softer white band across the forehead and a white dickey of the same material. The Superiors designated a large table, sort of a dumping ground, where everyone was to put their old serge and linen gear--habits, veils, guimpes and leather cinctures. The next day we appeared at Mass in the new look. As I peered around the refectory after Mass, it appeared as if everyone had lost fifteen or twenty pounds. Compared to the former habit the new outfit was sleek, light and comfortable. A few hold outs refused to change, older sisters who were no longer teaching. All the sisters who taught at the high school donned the new habits and even Sister Andrew, grudgingly, put on the new look.

Because of my sessions with Doc Millikan, I was now a changed person and, though I was happy to see Sister Aquinas and it was clear that we were still attracted to each other, I was resolved that I wouldn't lose the personal growth I had made over the summer. Fortunately, she was assigned to a different cell/bedroom and I hoped that we could be just good friends. I think she knew, as I did, that it was best, though she didn't seem happy and it was hard for both of us to realize we should have no physical contact. Yet on several occasions we discovered moments for long sensuous hugs.

Afterwards, the Doc's warning would race through my head: *Acting out won't solve anything; in fact, it may block insights.* One day Aquinas wanted to check out some fabric for the gleeclub outfits. Naturally, I was happy to drive her, but when we returned home and I pulled into the tiny wooden garage, we bumped into each other in the small dark space. She kissed my cheek and declared, "I love you, Theo." Suddenly, we were again in each other's arms. Clearly, I was still attracted to her, but worried that we'd slide back into our old forbidden intimacy. I thought if Aquinas and I spent less time together and were just friends, all would be fine. I was deluding myself.

Sister Brian, in addition to her duties as Dean of Education, had been appointed Superior of the motherhouse. Gone was the privacy of North Hall as her new office was right outside the refectory. Late one afternoon, I was trying to get in to talk with her, but desk Sister Lorena sat with her back to me. I knew it was she from her shapely ankles encased in sheer stockings but she would be in there forever, droning on about her headaches and doctor's appointments. I could see Sister Brian facing her, eyes sympathetic, face intent as if she were hanging on every word. She had a gift with people.

I went into the refectory and as I sipped my coffee, my anxiety rose. Doc called it, separation anxiety. Since Brian became Superior, someone was always with her, but when I was with her, inevitably, the phone or her call bell would ring or someone would knock. Initially, I imagined it would be an advantage to be close to the Superior, but she was pulled in a million directions and if I was with her too frequently, it appeared I was being favored and others got jealous.

When I finished my coffee, I headed back to her office, but now old Sister Patrice was shuffling in. Even before she got to the desk, she began mumbling in her barely intelligible brogue, "Sister Superior, I spilled holy water in my cell. I spilled it. I know it's a sin. Give me a penance please, Sister Superior." It was rumored she drank holy water-- for her bowels or for her sins. Her large figure butted up against Brian's chair like a St. Bernard. It was sad to see her now because in her day, she was a fine Latin teacher.

"Sister, stop worrying; it's not a sin. I told you that before. Now go upstairs to the chapel and say your rosary."

I caught Brian's eye and made gestures toward myself. She rolled her eyes, then she took the sister by the arm and walked her into the hallway. As they passed, Brian winked at me and pointed toward the parlor. To get a moment of peace, we had to hide.

I sat on the edge of the padded parlor chair and waited. It was the same chair where I often sat as a high school girl waiting for Sister Maureen. I was pathetic. Would I ever be independent?

With teeth clenched, Brian entered and slammed her fist on the table. "God, give me patience! Sister Patrice has been in at least fifteen times today, always repeating the same thing. If I get like that, Theo, will you shoot me? Promise?"

"You won't get like that," but there was an edge to my voice. I was being sulky. She began shrugging her shoulders and putting her hands to her neck to ease her tension. She plopped into one of the brocade chairs. I paced in front of her. "It's been a difficult day for me, too. Something crazy happened on Haight St. when I took the watches to be repaired. I've been waiting to share it with you."

She sighed and forced a little smile. "Well, we are here now. Tell me what happened."

"Remember, yesterday you told me to take the Sisters' pocket watches to Holcombe's Jewelers for repair?" She nodded. "Well, I drove over to Haight St. I parked the car and started walking toward the corner of Ashbury when all of a sudden a huge black man lunged at me from a doorway. I dodged him but he followed me down the block, trying to embrace me, yelling: 'You stand for love and I loves you.' His eyes were bloodshot; his speech slurred. Some young people were sitting on the sidewalk laughing. He wouldn't let up. I had to run to escape but I kept calling over my shoulder, 'I love you, too,' just to show a Christian spirit. He chased me all the way to the jewelers. It was terrible."

"O Lord, Theo, I'm so sorry. What an experience. Do you think he was drunk?"

"I don't know but he was on something."

"Yes, I've noticed the neighborhood is changing. Our Sisters at St. Agnes Convent on Ashbury St. have been complaining the neighborhood is "going downhill." They're even nervous about shopping there. I should've warned you."

I continued, "I was out of breath when I got to Holcombe's jewelry. I dashed in saying a prayer of thanks. As the little bell jangled, Mr. Holcomb came from the back and hollered, 'Lock the door, Sister-just turn the top knob.' He was shaking his head and peering at me over his spectacles. Said he hadn't seen the likes of what's going on out there in all his years. Told me lots of the merchants are selling out, closing up, but he's going to stay and I noticed he has bars on his windows now. I feel afraid for him. I mean, a robbery could happen anytime."

Suddenly the parlor door flew open and in strode Sister Aquinas yelling, "So there you are, Theo with Sister Brian as usual! Well, I want to talk to you, right now! Would you mind coming with me?" She stood glowering at me, possessively. When I saw how angry she was, I felt badly and wanted to leave the room with her to calm her.

"Please sit down, Sister Aquinas," said Brian kindly. "What has you so upset?" For a moment Aquinas continued to glare. Then she sat at the table and started to speak but suddenly she burst into tears, threw her head on her arms and wailed. I had never seen her cry. I reached out and touched her arm and she clutched my fingers. Millikan's warning flashed in my head: *you are pulling out that Sister's pathologies.*

Aquinas wailed, "My world is falling apart. I need you, Theo. It's crazy, but when I see you with Brian, I feel cut-off, unloved." She blew her nose loudly.

Brian said, "Sister dear, last year Theo was dependent on you. Now with the Doc's help over the summer, she's become stronger. Though it may seem she doesn't care for you that's not the case. I'm sorry that you're feeling so badly." Brian was trying to be impartial, but I knew she feared Aquinas would undo the progress I had made over the summer.

"It's strange," she said, "how I've come to need Theo. I've always been in complete control of myself. Now I can't will myself to be the old controlled Aquinas anymore." She wiped her runny nose with the hanky Brian handed her. At that moment she looked so vulnerable that I wanted to hug her, to say: 'Everything will be all right.'

"You know, I'm furious with you, Theo. I just want to wring your neck, but on the other hand, I just want to be with you," she said. She squeezed my hand hard.

"Aquinas, we are still friends."

Brian bit her lip.

That evening Sister Brian asked Mother John Mary if she could send Aquinas to the Doc, too. She knew that she could not handle both of us. Mother gave her permission. After breakfast Brian called Aquinas aside to ask her how she was feeling. Then she offered Doc's help. Would she like to have an appointment with him?" Aquinas knew the Doc. She'd often been my partner last year.

She said sharply, "I'll think about it."

After school the next day, I foolishly raced to Brian's office to see if Aquinas would go to see the Doc. We were whispering together when Aquinas marched into the office with clenched fists. "What kind of conspiracy are you two cooking up now? Talking about sending me to the Doc? Let's get her out of here, so she won't bother us. We've used her up. She's a throwaway!" she shouted, "Well, I'm not going to your precious Doctor. I'm going to stay right here and hang around and watch you!" She pounded her fist on the desk. Her words struck like blows. Brian swayed slightly, looking frail next to the robust Aquinas.

"Sister, no one has any intention of throwing you away. We both care about you. My offer this morning was made with honesty as I thought it might help you to talk with a professional. You certainly do not have to go. Theo and I want to be your friends." She met Aquinas's scowl without flinching.

"Yes, I'm sure you do. I'm sure as hell you do!" she interrupted, her face contorted. She stepped closer to Brian, her face inches away. "Just try to get rid of me," she snorted, raising her fist. "Just try!" After what seemed like an eternity, she stalked out.

"Boy, she hits hard," exhaled Brian. "Maybe you can talk to her when she calms down. She'll listen to you." It was as if an angry bull had rampaged through her office and raw anger unleashed in a place where everything was negotiated with soft voices and restrained self-control. My God, what now?

After dinner, I found Aquinas on a bench in the garden. I sat with her and tried to comfort her. "I want you back, Theo," she moaned. I held her hand and protested, "But we are still friends." Yet in truth at that moment, I didn't want to be with her. I hated the way she treated Brian and I feared that she would bury me under an avalanche of need and fury.

When I went for my next session with Doc, I told him that Aquinas was coming apart and spewing anger everywhere. He didn't say, 'I tried to warn you.' In fact, he grinned, like he was expecting it.

"She might as well come in here. I can handle this stuff. She doesn't scare me. Back there in the convent they have goodwill, but they don't have the skills. This stuff pushes them to their limits."

"You know, Doc, it's odd. When I see her crying, somehow I feel stronger. It's as if we've reversed roles." I was happy that I was becoming better and imagined I might soon become my ideal: a nun who could control her feelings and operate without being dependent on another nun, like Aquinas or Brian or Maureen.

Aquinas wore her anger like armor, swaggering through the convent with clenched fists, slamming doors, scowling. She returned to wearing her old policeman's shoes and was gaining back the weight she had lost. After breakfast she would sit in the community room reading the paper while the rest of us ran around in our blue check aprons, dusting, mopping, and cleaning our assigned section of the convent. Her charge, the stairway from the first floor to the third, became thick with dust collies. She never cleaned it.

I overheard another Sister quip to Andrew, "What's with Aquinas? She's like Attila, the Hun."

Sister Andrew muttered something under her breath; then faced the sister and said, "I really don't know. You'll have to ask her yourself."

"No, thanks," retorted the sister, "I don't want my head decapitated."

She even threatened Sister Andrew and said she would abandon the glee club unless she could have everything exactly as she wanted. Frequently she followed me around the convent, taunting: "Can't find your dear Brian now? Feeling upset? Can't stand the sight of me anymore? Well I'm going to hound you, to chase you until you have nightmares!"

I crept around the convent and school, praying she'd go to the Doc. Only he could help.

Then suddenly, Aquinas decided to go see the Doc. She went alone, taking the bus to his office. Sadly, her behavior didn't change. I didn't know if she would keep up the visits. If he couldn't help her, we were doomed. But she only went a few times.

After school one slate gray day, I brought Brian's clean laundry up to her cell. Possessively, I still vied with Sister Anna to do some personal things for Brian who was always busy. As I was leaving Brian's third floor cell, I ran into Aquinas. She may have assumed that Brian was in the cell and that I'd been with her, but I had no idea where she was. Aquinas lowered her head like a bull and stalked me as I scurried away along the third corridor. When I got to the other end, she accosted me.

"Would you mind stepping out on the third balcony with me?" I hesitated but when she held open the door, I walked out on the balcony which ran the full length of the convent and overlooked the garden.

"Theo, I feeling you're avoiding me and I'm really tired of it." She didn't shout, but spoke softly, perhaps in her way trying to offer a truce.

I replied, "What do you expect with the way you've been acting? Its not the same between us anymore."

"Well, I'm sick of seeing you with your precious Brian."

"Now that's your problem," I snapped unsympathetically. She moved closer, nostrils flaring, breathing heavily.

"Well, I'm just going to keep you out here 'til I am good and ready to let you go."

Instead of standing up to her, I backed away to the farthest corner of the balcony as she glared at me. When I made a move to go, she blocked my path with her body. Then, she grabbed my wrist.

"Let me go," I yelled. I jerked my wrist free and ran the length of the balcony.

"You can't escape me," she threatened. With slow, deliberate steps, she followed me. I ran into the corridor. My heart pounding, I dashed into my cell. I yanked the yellow curtains around my bed but I knew in a minute she'd open the door and then what? Could I hide under the bed? No, she'd find me.

I could hear her coming after me with slow deliberate steps. I was hiding , but she would find me. She always found me. How could I escape? I looked at the window of the bedroom cell. I hesitated a moment. Then, I hoisted it wide open, wider than it had ever been opened. I tucked up my habit and pulled myself to the sill. I swung my black stockinged legs outside and eased my headgear out the window frame, hoping my veil wouldn't catch and pull me back. Slowly I stood up on the ledge three stories above the manicured lawn of the front of the motherhouse. I pressed my back against the outside of the convent and though my palms were sweaty against the wood, it felt warm against my back. I squinted as the sun was startlingly bright after the dim bedroom.

To calm myself, I recalled that I'd never been afraid of heights. Then my body sagged. I was weary of the struggle to be a good nun. And lonely. Now I could just fall forward into space and I'd be free. The whole struggle to be a good nun would be over . . peace, yes, peace. It was so tempting. I stood there a long time away from everything. Then my thoughts went to consequences. Suicide was punishable by everlasting hell fire. Hell? No, no, I didn't want hell fire. Slowly, I edged back to the open window. When I slid inside, it was dim and quiet and cool. I collapsed on my bed. I had a sense of having been away a very long time.

One Saturday Brian annouced with a smile that she had a surprise for me. I followed her into the garden and she led the way to the laundry then up the rickety outside stairs to a weathered door. She struggled with the key for a minute, then swung open the door to the unused bathroom above the laundry. It was a modest room with a full tub and toilet.

"Poor Frank used this when he was our gardener but he drank too much so we had to let him go." She wrinkled her nose at the smell, swiped dust off the toilet seat. "I was wondering, Theo, if we cleaned it up and brought in a table, would it serve you as a painting studio?"

The gift she was offering was priceless—a place of my own to spread out my paints, not have to pack them away before I finished the piece in my cell.

"Sister Dorothea has the art room and you can't set up your easel in the biology lab, so I thought you should have a place of your own to work. You've taken several art classes now and I know this is your God-given talent. I'd feel much better if I knew you had a place to work, undisturbed."

The way she emphasized 'undisturbed' I knew she meant away from Aquinas. I stood speechless as I looked around the bathroom. In spite of its run-down appearance, this was an amazing gift. With tears in my eyes, I gave Brian a hug. The next weekend, I went about transforming that bathroom to a studio. I put a big piece of plywood over the bathtub and found a wonderful table that fit perfectly. I had a view of the garden from the window and I put up little curtains and tied them back with red ribbons. It was my own space, a healing place. When I was alone inside, I could breathe, even sigh or sing aloud. I could be myself.

With permission from Brian, I had enrolled in an evening painting class at the nearby Jewish Community Center. The Jewish woman who taught the class was surprised and delighted that a Catholic nun would take instruction from her. Most of the other students were adults, some older men who said that painting relaxed them after work. Everyone was respectful of me, but she treated me as special. Sometimes I would almost tear-up at the kindness. She was interested in my progress. She told me of other galleries to visit on Union Street. I was grateful for everything she did for me.

The first assignment was a self-portrait. In the mirror of the old medicine cabinet in my new studio, I peered at my image. Using only blue acrylic on a large canvas pad, I began the portrait, painting boldly, without pre-sketching. When finished, I tacked it up on the wall and settled back to examine it. I was shocked. The face in the habit was that of a frightened child. In the background, I had painted an imaginary French window that now gave the appearance of bars. It was far too disturbing to bring to class. Quickly, I painted another in sepia tones, a portrait of an artist at work, an acceptable image, but the insight that art was a process of self-revelation, startled me.

Painting alone in my new space after school and on weekends, I realized I was running away, not just from Aquinas, but also from everyone, except Brian. Once or twice, after Aquinas discovered my hideaway, she'd come up the stairs, but I always locked the door. When I refused to answer her pounding, she went away. Finally, she left me alone. Only then, could I begin to feel sympathy for her. The painting hideaway gave me a joy I had not felt before. Soon my watercolor paintings, mostly landscapes, sold to relatives of the sisters and happily, I could now buy my own supplies.

Aquinas and I rarely spoke now, however, still she carried her anger everywhere like a burning torch. Mother John Mary talked to her several times, but nothing, not Mother, nor Sister Andrew, nor even Doc seemed able to subdue her fury. I felt sorry for her, but I could not engage with her. I wasn't strong enough.

One warm evening in May, as the school year was winding down, Sister Brian and I went on a special outing to Grace Cathedral to hear Abraham Maslow speak. I 'd recently read his book *Toward a Psychology of Being* and was excited to hear him in person. I was deeply interested in psychology. When we entered the Anglican cathedral, formerly forbidden to all Catholics, I stared at everything as it was the first time I entered a non-Catholic Church. To my amazement, this majestic structure was not unlike our Catholic churches with stained glass windows, pews, pulpit, altar--everything. We sat near the front of the half-full church.

Maslow began with a personal anecdote. He told of a family meal where they were serving rare winter strawberries for dessert. After his children had gobbled down their own portions, he gave his share to his children. "I enjoyed the taste more in their mouths," he said.

Brian squeezed my hand and whispered, "Isn't that beautiful? I'm so glad we came." It was rare that she took time out for anything for herself. I was happy that she had agreed to come with me that night as I couldn't have come alone.

He related the story to basic needs—for belonging, for love, for safety--needs that must be met in childhood in order to produce a neurosis-free adult. "However," he remarked, "a perfect childhood is rare, but the deficits can be modified by therapy. What a man can be, he must try to be. We call this self-actualization." I was interested to hear more of that topic, but he moved on to the main subject of the evening--the peak experience. He couldn't expand on the remedies for those deficient in basic needs he said, because of the evenings time constraints.

While he spoke, it dawned on me that I was getting well because of the healing love of Brian. It was her acceptance of me, even of my immaturity, that I begin to value myself. She was the 'good mother.' This heightened awareness of the power of her love, undeserved, but freely given, transformed the evening to a near mystical experience.

When the lecture was over, we moved slowly toward an exit while I admired the beauty of this cathedral. A woman approached us.

"May I ask, are you Catholic nuns?" When we answered in the affirmative, she continued." I went to a Catholic school, but in all my days I couldn't imagine that I would see Catholic nuns here in an Episcopal cathedral willing to listen to such a scholar as Abraham Maslow. This is remarkable."

We smiled and Brian grasped her hand. "Yes, there is progress in the Catholic Church." We drove home in a state of euphoria, feeling we were in the avant-gard of the changing Church.

What would summer bring for me? When Sister Brian called me into her office in North Hall and said, "I think, Theo, that getting out of town for the summer could be a test of your strength. See if you can function independently," I gritted my teeth and asked, "What do you have in mind?"

She pulled out a brochure from Mount Saint Mary's Catholic College in Los Angeles. "Look, these look like good art classes: figure drawing, painting in oils."

I took the brochure, but I had doubts that emotionally I could go it alone. She told me she'd found some good language courses also offered at the college so another Sister, who was majoring in languages, could also attend. I didn't know her well, but I took a deep breath and said, "Okay, I'm up for it."

She smiled and patted my arm. "It'll be fine, Theo!" I knew she was glad I would be out of town for the summer. She would have peace and know that I would be safe. Even the Doc thought it was a good idea that I was going to L.A. for a new adventure. I didn't ask where Aquinas would go for the summer. I knew we would have true space between us now.

CHAPTER TWENTY-SIX

VACATION IN THE SANTA CRUZ MOUNTAINS

IN A RARE moment of relaxation, I sat with Sister Sean and Sister Gloria on the cabin floor at our vacation property in Los Gatos at the end of the summer. I proudly arranged my new art pieces around the living room of the cabin where several of us had been assigned for the retreat. I had made it through my classes in L.A. without help from Millikan or Sister Brian, but even more amazing, I had found absolute joy in the art classes at Mount St. Mary's College.

Mr. Dibbs, who taught the figure drawing class in summer school, had been very encouraging to me. The model should have been nude, but much to the annoyance of Mr. Dibbs, the Sisters who ran the college insisted she wear a bathing suit. However, we painted her as if she was nude and Mr. Dibbs would go round the classroom and comment on our work, calling aloud our strong suits. "Sister Theophane, the brush!! Yes, the brush, that is your strength."

I think he liked the looseness of my technique and I thrived under his encouragement. Since we had no nude model, I had gone into my private bathroom and drew a charcoal nude rendition of myself from my reflection in the mirror. What a freeing experience that was but it was one piece I didn't pull out for the sisters' viewing. At this moment, sitting on the floor with my peers, I was happier than I had been in years.

"To be honest, I don't understand half of these paintings," exclaimed Sister Sean. "I love the sailboat, but I'm puzzled by the unfinished faces with squiggly pencil lines or this one with only a few brushstrokes. Is this one a naked lady? This will really shake them up when you frame these for Mother John Mary's feast day!"

The best compliment came from Sister Gloria. "These are as good as Sister Dorothea's work, Theo, and maybe more interesting."

Yet in spite of their praise, I knew I still would not be allowed to teach art at the high school as Sister Dorothea had a monopoly on everything in the arts. The tolling bell cut off conversation and summoned us to night prayers and the beginning of our annual eight-day retreat. Sean and I whispered a few last words before the silence as we hurried down the path toward the chapel. Outside, we crowded around the posted list of Employments for the retreat.

"I've got the sacristy," whispered Gloria. "Nice, I love the new chapel."

"Look, Theo, you are serving the priest's meals.

"Ugh, no," I moaned.

"I've got the vegetables," laughed Sean.

"I'll trade you the priest for the vegetables, Sean," I begged.

"No way! I love the vegetables."

"But I do, too. I'm a maniac with a peeler," I said.

"Offer it up, Theo. No trade!"

Now our lips were sealed for eight days and we joined others streaming into the modern recently-built chapel, adjacent to the pink stucco novitiate building. I would hate serving the priest--all that running back and forth from the building that housed the kitchen to the cabin assigned to the priest, and worse, having to make small talk while

I served him. What would I say to the renowned Father Phil Berrigan who our progressive Mother John Mary had arranged to give our eight day retreat?"

At nine the next morning we sat in the light, airy new chapel. Nine-ten, nine-twenty and still the chair behind the table in the sanctuary remained empty. Outside nothing stirred. We were awaiting the arrival of Father Phil Berrigan, a Josephite father who with his better-known brother, Daniel, were taking increasingly radical steps to bring attention to the anti-war movement, leading draft board raids that galvanized opposition to the Vietnam war. This activism met with deep disapproval from the leadership of the Catholic Church. However, we considered ourselves a progressive Order and we were excited to hear from Father Berrigan. By nine-fifteen, sisters fidgeted, sighed, a few took out their beads and began a rosary. Sister Cloris moved to the front of the chapel. Genuflecting with difficulty, she pushed herself up with one hand, sighing from arthritic pain.

"Sisters, we have an emergency. Our retreat master took ill yesterday, but the Good Lord always provides. We've found a replacement and he's on his way from the airport now. I ask your indulgence a little longer."

Fifteen minutes later a stocky priest in a plain black cassock, came rushing out, made a hasty genuflection that any nun would be ashamed of, noisily dragged the chair from behind the table, and plopped his bulky figure down in front of us. His face was broad and pale, crowned with a halo of fine blonde hair. Beads of sweat glistened on his forehead. He adjusted his black-rimmed glasses. "Good morning, my dear Sisters. Good to be here. Yesterday when cousin Clo," he nodded toward Sister Cloris, "called and asked me to come out here, I dropped everything and jumped on a plane. A chance to visit with her and see your beautiful state, well, I couldn't pass that up."

With his hair slightly mussed and his wide grin, he struck me as only a teenager, impersonating a priest. When he spoke, he sounded as if he had a speech disorder, but as he drawled out each reluctant syllable, I realized it was his unfamiliar Midwestern twang. We had been sitting as restless as Roxanne, waiting to be dazzled by Christian's lyrics, delivered by Cyrano, but there was no Cyrano today. McGowan's jokes fell flat and his platitudes were simplistic. He referenced Ma Bell several times. I wondered: who was she? Sister Andrew yawned. I saw others exchanging glances that said: Can we stand this for eight days, especially as we were looking forward to the renowned activist?

That evening I carried Father's dinner from the kitchen to his cabin, murmuring rules to myself: serve from that right, remove from the left or was it the other way around? The cabin reserved for the priest was elegant compared to our Spartan quarters and Father was sitting with his back to me at a damask covered table, set with crystal and silver. I padded across the thick Oriental carpet and set his salad and another plate with roast beef, potatoes and steamed carrots on the table. I was about to hurry away when he looked up at me with blue eyes, magnified behind thick lenses, and asked, " Sister, what did you think of my talks today?"

Slowly, I refilled his water glass, racking my brain for something positive to say. "Ah, I liked the point you made about our having to be real, so that God can live in us, not 'being 'dead to ourselves' as we've often been taught." He nodded vigorously as he chewed a piece of meat.

"Sister, sit down a minute. It's no fun to eat alone." With his fork, he pointed to a chair. I froze.

"Really, Father, I should get your dessert and coffee."

"They can wait; please, sit down." He spoke as he ate, sometimes with his mouth full, talking of his parish back home in the Midwest, about his job before he became a priest. "Worked for Ma Bell," he said, twanging the vowels unmercifully. I had no idea who Ma Bell was though he referred to her several times. Then he paused and said," Tell me about yourself, Sister."

"I teach biology at our high school in San Francisco." Then, I added softly, "and I also paint."

"Really, you're an artist?"

"Yes, I've been taking some art classes and I had a wonderful summer of painting at a college in Los Angeles."

"Say, I'd like to see your work. Do you have some of your paintings here?"

He seemed genuinely interested and I surprised myself by replying," I'd be happy to show you my work."

The next day after lunch when the others had retired to their cabins to nap, read or sew, away from the mid-day heat, I hurried to his cabin with my portfolio. He left off his scribbling at the desk and helped me prop up my figure studies and watercolor landscapes around the room. He was genuinely enthusiastic about the pieces and I realized I liked an audience. I started babbling about the figure drawing class where the model had to wear a bathing suit at the nun's insistence and how it made the teacher angry. He laughed so heartily that I blushed and hoped Sister Cloris wouldn't stop in and find me showing off to the retreat master.

"Sister, these are fantastic ! Would you consider doing one for me? I could use something beautiful to hang in my office back home. I could pay you."

"Oh no, no money, Father. It would be a privilege to do one for you. What would you like? A landscape?"

"Ah, Sister, you're the artist. Surprise me."

When I brought his dinner that evening, Sister Cloris was with him. As I was leaving, I overheard Sister say," You know, Bud, the group here is pretty intellectual. I'd say a little more theology might be in order. They're more sophisticated, theologically speaking, than your parishioners. In fact, they may appear even stodgy at times." She laughed, trying to soften her message. I'd noticed that some Sisters, rudely, were reading during his lectures.

The next day Father omitted any jokes but spoke of obedience and the work of the apostolate. "Every since Papa John, as he called Pope John XXIII, opened the windows, it's no longer enough to say: Yes,

Sister Superior, I'll do whatever you command or to do as the monk was commanded: water a barren stick in blind obedience. Today obedience must be reasonable and the Order now has obligations to consider the personal talents, even preferences of the sisters."

Some of our sisters would think this heresy, but I was nodding in agreement. He continued, "And your Order is blessed to have so many fine women with intellectual gifts. You are fortunate too, to have such a grand artist such as Sister Theophane."

I wanted to die. No priest ever singled out an individual nun for praise. Ever! Yet in front of that whole staid high school staff--Andrew, Dorothea, Agnes Ann, and the rest -- their biology teacher was recognized as a fine artist.

A few days later on a hot afternoon, I knocked at Father's cabin. My palms were sweaty. I was tempted to simply leave the new painting at the door and sprint away but he opened the door quickly and motioned me in. With a nervous smile, I propped the new watercolor up against a chair. He stared, looking from the painting to me. In truth, it wasn't an ordinary painting. When I begun to paint, I had tried to let my subconscious direct the work as I discovered this was an honest way of painting. I, myself, was astonished by what appeared.

In the foreground was a face, painted wet-into-wet, without fussy details, bearing a resemblance to a clown. In the background, a young woman was dancing or running, looking back seductively over her shoulder at the clown-figure. The colors bled and ran into one another, giving the painting a dreamlike quality. As we viewed it together our shoulders brushed with unmistakable excitement. Thankfully he did not ask for an explanation as we both realized it was us. He broke the long silence by telling me where he would hang it and that it would always remind him of me.

The day before the retreat was over, I began to look for excuses to go to Father's cabin in addition to serving his meals, The evening before I had noticed his wrinkled cassock hanging on the bedroom door. Now that seemed a good reason and I hurried over, knocked, and getting no reply, I slowly opened the door. Sounds came from the bedroom. "Gigi, oh Gigi, da ,da, da, da, Gigi." I tiptoed to the doorway. Father's suitcase was open on the bed and he was folding a pair of striped pajamas. His Roman collar was on the bed and his black shirt was open revealing a few golden hairs gleaming on his chest.

"Ah, Theophane, have you ever seen the film, *Gigi*? I thought back to the films the Jesuits had shown over the summers. *Gigi* was not among them. I shook my head.

"It's a marvelous film. You've got to see it. "He went on singing snatches of the tunes, holding up his pajamas as a partner and waltzing a few steps. I could tell he was glad the pressure of retreat was over.

"Father, I was wondering if you'd like me to press your cassock before you leave?" I giggled nervously.

"You know, the sister who cleans the cabin has taken care of my laundry, but I'd be mighty pleased if you'd press this old cassock." Handing it to me, we seemed to move in slow motion, our hands brushing, the steady gaze of his blue eyes riveted me to the floor. When I walked the dusty path to the laundry in the broiling sun, I noticed the underarms of the cassock smelled musky with perspiration. I didn't find this offensive, but in fact, enjoyed the smell. Once alone in the large cool laundry, I stuck my arms through the garment. It could have wrapped around me twice. I held it up and waltzed around, using the cassock as a partner. Finally, I pressed it.

Usually at the conclusion of the retreat, I felt renewed, joyful and ready to end the silence, but today I felt sad. The night before I'd rolled around in the stifling bed, unable to sleep. Finally, at midnight, I got out of bed, threw my habit over my nightgown, slipped on my veil and tiptoed out, through the cacophony of snores and wheezes that came from other rooms.

Outside a cricket concert sawed at the stillness and a full moon hung like an egg yolk over the mountains. As if with a will of their own, my feet took me in the direction of Father's cabin. I was surprised to see soft squares of light shining through his drawn shades and hoped I might glimpse his shadow but there was no movement or sound, other than fluttering moths making overtures to the glowing porch light. I stared at the door. Could I will him to open it? Powerful feelings stirred inside me. *Father Bud, I am here.* The female in the painting I had done for him seemed to sprint before me, dancing toward the door.

After a time, I wrested my feet from the path to his door and walked to the nearby lake. What was this yearning so intense I could taste it? Could it be possible that I wanted to make love with Father Bud? Yes, I admitted that was what I want. I smiled, then laughed aloud. I twirled under the stars. My God, I am redeemed! I am no longer alone but part of the great communion of women who want to make love to a man. Salty tears streamed down my face. In time, I returned to my solitary bed a changed woman.

The next morning after Mass and breakfast, I went to his cabin. I knew he was gone, but I wanted anything he left behind. I pushed open the door and looked around. Without him, it was desolate and bare. I sighed and turned to leave, then I saw an envelope propped against the salt shaker addressed to me in bold, black script. I tore it open.

Sister Theophane,

You must keep up your art because you are at the tip of your brush. More of you can come out there, then in the chapel, the classroom or even in a sweet prayer.

You pepped up a young priest who knows his own reality, but was afraid of religious sophistication. It was a moment of meeting that I hope will bring years of mutual prayer and exchange. You are you, don't change, just stay what you are: smashing, excitable, imaginative, and above all, real. Keep on becoming the artist that you are.

An admirer,
Father Bud

Me? Smashing, excitable? Yet when he reached for my creativity, he unleashed a part of me that I was just beginning to understand. God bless Father Bud!

CHAPTER TWENTY-SEVEN

MOTHERHOUSE
SAN FRANCISCO FALL 1966

THE OCTOBER SKY was brilliant blue on this special Saturday, a day full of possibilities. Miss Collins, one of the lay teachers at our high school, invited me to visit her friend who was a real artist and was studying at the Art Institute. I often found it more enjoyable to sit with Miss Collins in the school lunchroom than any of the sisters. Through our conversations she realized that, though I taught biology, I ached to teach art. Yet Sister Dorothea had a monopoly on all the art. This morning I had raced through my housekeeping chores, sped through the rosary and the fifteen minutes required spiritual reading. After lunch in the refectory in customary silence, I went to my third floor cell, changed into my best floor-length habit, looked into the tiny mirror to straighten the white bandeau across my forehead and made sure there were no unsightly hairs showing. I grinned conspiratorially at the blue-eyed nun reflected in the mirror. I'd be twenty-eight in a few days and today I was about to meet a real artist. I sighed wondering if I'd have to teach biology forever.

As I backed the car out of the small wooden garage, I was feeling independent, even worldly. I thought of Father McGowan as I had a letter from him the day before. He wrote:

I'm praying you'll pour your energy into the canvas. I'll be standing by to hear your success stories. But I know you'll go through many a cross before you'll be yourself and accept yourself as you are.

He signed it, a hug and a kiss to you. It was a wonderful letter, but his intensity scared me. He expected too much of me, his projections were too grandiose, but he was back in the Midwest and I probably wouldn't see him again. I wrote him that I had a painting accepted for the San Francisco Art Festival where it would be on display in front of the City Hall during the Art Festival. I also told him, a framer, a generous man, was teaching me to frame my own work on Saturday mornings before he opened his shop. We became friends when I had taken several of my paintings to be framed. On Saturdays Sister Brian would drop me at his Clement St. shop where he taught me how to use the framing equipment. Just before ten, when he was to open his shop, he rushed me back to the motherhouse in his TR convertible, my veil flying in the wind. What I didn't tell Father Bud was that the Motherhouse was closing in upon me again. I was seeing the Doc, entrenched in my dependency on Sister Brian, but grateful that Sister Aquinas now left me alone, though she still went 'round with her constant aura of anger.

I turned the Ford down Masonic toward Haight St. As I drove through the Panhandle of the Golden Gate Park, I jammed on the brakes; the traffic was at a near halt. Was it an accident? I rolled down the window. I saw a huge crowd of young people, a kaleidoscope of blue jeans, long, bright dresses, beards, long hair, streamers and balloons. Then a guitar twang split the air. My students had told me a group often played here--something about an airplane with a Slick singer. I spied a band under the trees. Could that be the group? On

Monday, I'd love to brag to my students that I saw that music group. They'd never believe me. After biology class when they had jabbered to me about the group saying something about an airplane. I'd asked, 'Is that something like the Freedom Train?' They'd howled. They'd never heard of the Freedom Train, which was a real train.

'It's a music group,' they'd screamed, "The Jefferson Airplane." The last worldly music I recalled was Nat King Cole crooning *Mona Lisa* and Johnny Ray belting out *Cry* when I was a high school senior.

I moved slowly across Haight St., crowded with young people, colorful posters on every post. An old car with writing on the rear, pulled in front of me. As I got closer, I read: James Bond is a Virgin. I am, too, but who is James Bond? When the car pulled over, I couldn't tell if the driver was male or female. On the side window, painted black with white letters, I read: *Don't laugh, your girlfriend may be inside and God uses LSD.*

I had an urge to return to the convent but then I spied the apartment address, 1301 on a Victorian. The '0' had fallen off, revealing the bright blue of the building's original color. I pulled into a parking spot. On the sidewalk a young man, two women and a child were passing. They were laughing and handing around a cigarette. They looked unkempt. The child, whom I couldn't identify as a boy or girl, dragged a legless teddy bear. The young man wore only one sandal; the other foot was bare. I sat in the Ford a few minutes fingering my rosary beads before I walked to the old Victorian and noticed the once-proud windows were hung with sheets of various colors; stains from the rusty hand railings made Rorschach patterns on the stairs. Green mold grew under each step. I rang the bell for apartment 3, wishing I hadn't come. I jumped as the buzzer sounded loudly and pushed open the heavy door; inside was a stale musty odor. I climbed a flight of the worn carpeted stairs, encouraged by the sweet call of Miss Collins, "Up here, Sister." She was leaning over the railing, smiling. Instead of her conservative school dress, she was wearing a crocheted top and a tiny mini skirt revealing miles of white freckled legs. Her auburn hair was now free, frizzy and vibrating like an auburn halo.

"Hi," I called, suddenly self-conscious in my layers of fabric.

As I entered the apartment, I was startled to walk directly into the outstretched hand of a tall, thin, black man with a droopy mustache and piercing eyes.

"How do you do, Sister, my pleasure? Ben Taylor, here. Come in." His hand felt cool against my sweaty palm. He wore a silky yellow shirt, black vest and jeans that flared at the bottom. Miss Collins was standing in front of a worn velvet couch and the window behind it was hung with a dyed sheet that cast a greenish glow over her. Ben gestured to a straight-back chair. I nearly tripped over a rusty bike, minus its front wheel. On the seat of the bicycle which served as a coffee table, sat a plate of shiny red grapes; on the handle bars, was tied a bouquet of fresh daisies. I thought of my mother's home nearby with her faux marble coffee table and its tidy cork coasters for the bourbon drinks she served.

I stammered, "What a unique coffee table." The room smelled sickly sweet; I noticed thin sticks smoking in one corner. Ben sat on the couch close to Miss Collins and tugged at his mustache as he examined me. Then he stood and went to the hallway calling, "Sister, come and see my latest."

I stood to examine his large canvas. It was the head and shoulders of a very thin black figure. The face was featureless, except for the tiny pinpoint white eyes. It was a frightening painting. Racking my brain for something complimentary, I said

"Interesting treatment of the figure."

"Sister, isn't his work extraordinary? Say, would you like a cup of tea?" asked Miss Collins.

Tea, yes, hot, calming tea. "Yes, please."

"Lipton's or Jasmine?"

I'd never heard of Jasmine. "I'll try Jasmine. "

"And you, Ben," she said to Ben.

"Jasmine for me too, darling." Miss Collins disappeared into the kitchen where I could hear a kettle whistling. Why doesn't he get up and make the tea? This is his apartment. Do women always wait on men? Miss Collins handed me a battered tin cup. I held it gingerly, trying not to burn myself.

As Miss Collins handed Ben his tea, I saw the look that passed between them. "Thanks, girl," he said, taking her hand and pressing it to his cheek.

My God, she is his girl! Our precious theology teacher is with this man. Sipping the hot tea, I was beginning to plan my escape.

"Sister, I'd like you to see one of my favorites." He beckoned me to the bedroom. I hesitated. I'd never been in a man's bedroom. "Come on over here, Sister" he called. Clutching my tea, I tiptoed in. An emaciated black woman stared out from a canvas with those same pinpoint eyes. The only furniture in the room was a double mattress with an Indian print spread and two plump pillows. Could Miss Collins? Oh, no! This is their bed! I was perspiring now.

"Oh, yes, that is special, Ben."

As we moved back out to the living room, I passed other paintings on canvas in the hallway, almost all identical with black face and pinpoint white eyes. "Ben, this has been a real treat but I'm going to have to get home soon for Vespers." I moved toward the front door.

"Sister, I'd like to see some of your paintings," Ben said as he followed me. I thought of my watercolors--seascapes, old barns, crisp snow scenes, even the figures I'd done at the Art Institute which actually resembled the live models. I realized the disparity between our aesthetic and knew I wouldn't be inviting him to my studio.

As I bolted down the stairs, they stood with arms around each other's waists. I got into the car, locked the doors and breathed deeply. Then I headed up Masonic. In the Panhandle the crowds were larger, the music louder, but I looked straight ahead. After parking the car in the convent garage, I sat in the garden with an unsettling feeling. Pale fingers of fog snaked through the pine trees. Why am I upset, I asked myself? Was it the awful paintings? Was it the intimacy between Ben and Miss Collins? I supported racial equality. Last year I'd done some parish work with the families in the Fillmore with Sister Margo. What was different today?

Inside the convent the sweet aroma of cinnamon rolls wafted from the kitchen. Elva Lee, the hired African-American woman in the kitchen, smiled and waved. I went straight to Sister Brian's office. Her desk was clear except for a book she never had time to read, *Nun in the Modern World*. I rang her other office in North Hall. No answer. I wondered if she had gone out with that simpering Sister Anna. The tolling of forty bells called me to the chapel, but I wanted to see Brian first. I confronted myself: Would I be a permanent appendage to Brian, having to be transferred from convent to convent with her as Sister Anna was and never be able to stand on my own? I forced myself to climb the stairs to the chapel, entering on the 39th toll, genuflecting deeply in the center. The stained-glass windows created a soft rainbow that spilled on the polished floor. The crucified figure of Christ hung above the white silk draped tabernacle--all calming and familiar, but during the recitation of the psalms, the churning began.

"Unto you will I cry, O Lord, my Rock. *James Bond is a virgin*- Be not silent to me. For if you are silent to me, I will become like those who go down to the pit." *I'm an alchemist of the unconscious.* "Draw me not away with the wicked and with the workers of iniquity which speak peace their neighbors, but have mischief in their hearts." *A black hand pats a white knee.* "Hear the voice of my supplications when I cry to You for help!" *God uses LSD!*

That night I heard the chimes on the first floor clock strike midnight. I rose, tied the ties of my white night veil, tugged on my black seersucker robe. Dim lights burned in archaic fixtures. I stole outside to the balcony overlooking the garden where I was assaulted by night sounds: the deep moan of the foghorns, a car backfiring, a siren screaming in the distance. What would it be like to be out in San Francisco on a Saturday night? Returning to my bed, sleep came and the dream began.

My head was underwater. I felt my body float away. My head watched my naked body drift through the water. Now caught up in a current, it moved toward a Black man who was standing in the water, laughing, extending his arms toward the body. The pubic hair on the body was auburn and frizzy, waving like kelp underwater. The man's arms grew longer and longer as he reached for my body; his laugh became deafening. The detached head tried to scream, but was mute.

"Let us bless the Lord, "called out the Sister ringing the bell at each cell door.

"Thanks be to God!" I swung my feet out and got up, splashed cold water on my face. I did not kneel and kiss the floor in the act of humility as I'd been taught. I dressed quickly and walked to the chapel.

Early in January Sister Brian began her tour of our southern California schools in her additional role as Supervisor of our Elementary Schools. One cold Sunday soon after she'd gone, I walked across the garden to the school biology lab to do some weekend chores. I passed Sister Vincent and Sister Clara walking together, laughing. They didn't even notice me on my way to the third floor. My biology classroom was a lifeless classroom without the chattering students, just scuffed black-topped tables, cases of musty stuffed birds, drawers of insects pinned forever in mid-flight, frogs soaking in formaldehyde. Absentmindedly, I watered the plants, sprinkled food in the goldfish bowl. When I lifted the glass lid, the King snake slithered away and buried itself in the sand. I tossed in a few live mealworms, in fact a few extra, to guard against another untimely escape.

I snapped the shade of a window and peered out at the fog. Grey, nothing but grey, wet fog, as grey as my mood. I'm pinned to this life as surely as the frogs that the students will pin onto dissecting trays next week. I'd always teach biology and wish I was teaching art. I'd always feel on the fringe and lead a lonely life that would end like poor Sister Patrice's.

Yet, something was trying to break through my fog—it hit like a jarring bolt of insight: *I am my own jailer! It's me that's keeping a lid on my life as tightly as the lid on the King snake! I am keeping me here!* I held on to a table. *It's me imposing my own life sentence. What have I done to deserve this? I don't know, but whatever it was, I've paid my dues. I can't go on punishing myself.*

I was shaking. *Could I turn my back on Jesus, forgo my vows, go alone into the world? No, that is madness! But it couldn't be worse than staying here.* I felt weak and steadied myself against the table. Out there I'd have a slim chance for happiness. My former girlfriends were now all married, had families. I'd be alone. Yet I had to free myself. I pulled out the connecting sockets and my mind went blank.

I raced around straightening things, opening cabinets putting away petri dishes. I knocked a beaker to the floor; it smashed. Theo, stop! For a moment, now only pretend that you're going to leave. Think: where would you go, what would you do, where would you live? I couldn't go home because of Mom's drinking. I couldn't teach rowdy kids in a public school. I wouldn't be able to support myself. I'd go mad with loneliness. No, no, I couldn't do it!

Frantically, I swept up the broken glass, and mindlessly dusted the window ledges, to rid my mind of these thoughts. To escape the terror of a decision, I fled to the convent and ran, not to the chapel, but to the cold pantry where I feverishly started to unpack the boxes of canned goods. This had been my job last year, but surely the sister in charge would be grateful for my help. As I ripped open a carton, my finger caught on a staple. Blood spurted. I sucked the finger, kept on working. Now, blood on the large cans of tomatoes, blood on the cans of asparagus, blood on the cans of peaches. Bloody prints everywhere. I scarcely noticed. The new insights were in hot pursuit. *You must leave. You can't stay. Don't you see it now?*

No, no, no, I can't leave! I can't do it!

You're an artist you need to be true to that part of yourself. You've done your penance. Now its time to go.

The lined face of the old Sister Cook appeared at the door.

"Sister," she said. I nearly jumped ten feet. "Ah, Sister, so nice of you to do that. Should I help you?"

"No, I nearly shouted. "I can do this alone." Startled, she tripped backwards and scurried away. Fiercely, I went on unpacking the cartons. What about Brian? She would be hurt, but she doesn't need another parasite. You can't hang on her forever.

Stop! Just pretend you are going to leave. I plunged into the unknown world. I felt I was on a terrifying roller coaster. A sharp pain took hold of me. Then I heard the bell tolling for Vespers.

I went to the chapel, slowly genuflected and it dawned on me how privileged I was to be one of God's chosen ones. Where else could I experience such a community of dedicated souls? Yet at dinner, I could scarcely eat and heard little of the sister's prattling next to me. In bed I could no longer escape my inner voices. The truth assaulted me without mercy. The clock on the first floor chimed, marking endless hours. I slid down shafts of time, reviewing the years. I saw that earlier I had wanted to leave, but had lacked the courage. This time I would really go! I would be an artist, freed from the demands of religious life, freed from the yoke of obedience that told me what I could teach, where I would live, what I could do. My creativity was my key. In the parched desert of that night, I tasted the first intoxicating drops of freedom.

When the 5:30 a.m call bell pierced my restless slumber, my decision was immediately on the surface. Yes, I had to leave. I thought I would feel teary and vacillating, but I felt a reassuring certainty. I needed to talk with Jesus. I settled into my stall and in the silence of meditation, I spoke to Him:

Jesus, I've got to talk to You. You know how hard I've tried, Lord, but our marriage is not working. I know I made vows forever but I'm sorry, I need a divorce. I don't blame You, Lord. You've been there, forgiving and loving. It's me. I'm not right for this life. I realize I'm an artist. In truth, that is a gift from You. Yet it is not appreciated here. This need to create is devouring me. I still love You. I'm just going to do it somewhere else. I know you'll take care of me each step of the way.

I listened for His response. It came in the form of an exquisite peace, like a warm sun that filled my soul.

As I went about my duties on Monday, I was aware I was no longer a true nun. I was a quitter, a deserter and I was terrified someone might discover it. Sister Brian hadn't yet returned from her visitation of our schools. I called Millikan for an appointment. He could see me on Tuesday at 11 a.m. at his university office.

During my forty-minute free period, I slipped away from school and hurried the few blocks to the university. I sat in his waiting area. My decision was to be spoken aloud, given a shape and color in reality. Five long minutes passed; then a few more minutes. He never kept me waiting! The minutes dragged on. I had to return to school as I had to teach three more classes of biology. I was nearly ready to burst into the office and drag the person from the chair. Finally, a girl, too young to have problems, calmly emerged from the office. I glared at her. If she'd seemed upset, I could've forgiven her.

"Come right in," Millikan motioned with a dramatic swoop of his arm.

"Why have you kept me waiting so long? I have something very important to tell you."

He looked at me, shook his head, rocked back in his chair, and said, "Other people have problems, too."

"Millikan, I ... I have something important to tell you." I paused, sat up in the chair and looked directly at him. "I have to leave the convent." I waited but there was no change in his expression. He continued to stare at his hands. I wanted to shake him, to scream: *Aren't you surprised? We've never discussed this! If you knew I was going to do this, why didn't you tell me, instead of letting me stumble through years of pain?*

"I see that I'm punishing myself by staying here. I don't deserve to be punished anymore. This insight came out of the blue while Sister Brian was away. I'm the only one who can change it. I'll have to go."

"I guess you'll have to," he said with conviction, still not looking at me.

"You think this is the right thing to do?" I was dying for some reassurance from him.

"I think it's a good thing to do," he said at last.

"I'm not sure when I'll leave. I need time to plan. It feels scary. I still have to tell Sister Brian." I sniffled and a melodramatic sob escaped. I wanted his empathy for the terrifying process ahead. I strained to experience any doubts but none surfaced.

"I know it's hard. I'll be here for you. I'm not going anywhere. I think Sister Brian will understand."

"Okay, but I'm going to call you if I need you"

"Not to worry. I'll be here."

"I've got to go."

My time was up. I had to be back at school before I was missed. Yet I didn't rise. He and I now shared a special secret. I'd changed sides. Only he knew I was almost a secular like him. I wished he would've acknowledged something, a new closeness. "So long for now," I said with a slight flirtatiousness. Inside, a giddy girl was stirring.

After my decision, I could scarcely eat or sleep. It wasn't doubt that assailed me, but euphoria coupled with anxiety. How would Sister Brian and Mother John Mary receive my news? Would they be angry, try to talk me out of my decision? Or worse, ask that I leave immediately? Mother John Mary made decisions rapidly, forcefully. I needed time to plan. Would Brian reject me after all the work she had done and in spite of my protestations that I wanted to be just like her?

Late Wednesday night Brian returned, tired but elated from a Superior's workshop. I met her at the front door. "Oh Theo," she exclaimed with a smile, "I see so much change ahead and it will be so good for our Congregation. Our future looks bright."

I carried her suitcase to the third floor where as Superior she'd been given the comfort of a solitary cell that afforded more privacy. I turned to her. "Brian, I have something to tell you."

"Theo, if it's a problem, I hope it can wait until morning. I'm bushed!"

"I don't think I can wait and it's not a problem." She plopped down on the bed. I stood, facing her. "I'm sorry I'm not going to be here to see the progress ahead. While you were away I came to a decision. I have to leave. The only thing keeping me here is you."

She gasped, stood and put her head on my shoulder. Then, she went to the window and stared out at the black night. I could see her knuckles whiten as she grasped the sill. Her shoulders slumped but then she straightened up and turning said, "You know, as much as I hate to see you go, I believe it's right for you. I confess it's almost a relief. I want you to be independent but it seems hopeless here. If I was honest with myself, I'd have seen earlier that our life is not right for you." She gave me a gentle embrace. "I still care for you, Theo, no matter what decision you make, but I can see the artist in you is straining to be free."

The next day I sat across the desk from Mother John Mary. She looked much the same as the day I burst in two and a half years ago, threatening to leave, but now her expression was tempered with weariness in the eyes and tightness around her mouth that spoke of the toll of the office and the resistance to her efforts to implement change. She leaned forward expectantly, an efficient administrator, waiting for me to state my business. Usually I was on my knees, often crying. This conversation would be different than any I had in this office. I was no longer a subject asking permission; I was taking charge of my own life. Without any emotional display, I told her of my decision. She slumped back in her chair, pudgy fingers clasped in her lap. "You know, Sister, when I let you go to see Dr. Millikan I thought this might happen but that's a chance I took," she said, ruefully. She was obviously disappointed but there was no hint of condemnation.

"But Mother, it wasn't he who suggested I leave," I protested, anxious to protect Millikan's integrity. It was my own insights. I feel as if I'm punishing myself by staying here."

However, she wasn't interested in debating the origin of my decision. "Sister, the formality is that you must request a dispensation from your vows from Pope Paul VI. In actual fact the Sacred Congregation of Religious in Rome will handle it. I don't think there'll be a problem. Just state your reasons and I'll send off your request immediately. It may take a couple of months before you get an answer. Can you wait that long?"

"Oh, yes, in fact, I don't want to leave before Easter. I need to make plans. I can't go home because my mother is an alcoholic. I don't know what I'll do." She nodded sympathetically.

"Sister, could you possibly stay and finish the school semester? I'd be grateful if you could. It would be difficult to find your replacement in the high school right now."

I asked myself: Can I keep up the façade of good nun until June? Yet the idea of stepping into a hostile world in the warmth of summer, my favorite time of year, was inviting. It would give me time to make plans.

"Yes, Mother, I can wait until June."

For several weeks I basked in the peace of the decision, absorbing it, marveling at the rightness of it. Now I could teach at Sister Andrew's school with detachment. I no longer cared what she thought. It didn't bother me that I was not part of the in-group. I could even listen with tolerance to Sister Anna's ramblings. I moved unscathed through arguments about change, new apostolates, while wrapping myself in my secret like an invisible armor. However, now I had to write for my dispensation and make plans of my own.

After dinner, I sat in my cell trying to compose my request. I had received the proper form for addressing the Pope. Pope John XXIII had died not long after he opened the Second Vatican Council. Now a new Pope was left to carry out his reforms.

Your Holiness, most Holy Father, Pope Paul VI,

Humbly prostrate at your feet, I, Judith Lyons, called in religion, Sister Mary Theophane, having taken Simple Vows on January 18, 1958, do now request a dispensation from my vows.

Now the difficult part: the reasons. I couldn't write that it has now come to me that I am punishing myself by staying in this life; nor did I dare say: I entered because I was completely infatuated with Sister Maureen or that it was likely I entered to get away from my mother who was becoming dependent on alcohol or that I was escaping the world because boys thought I was ugly. What would I say? Few sisters ever left our Congregation and rarely any nun who had taken Final Vows. Over the years, two or three had just disappeared. They were mourned as if they'd died; their names never mentioned again. There was no one to ask for help.

Then slowly I began to write:

Recently, I have become aware of unconscious motives that drew me to the convent. However, these motives, my inability to face the responsibilities of adulthood, my desire for security, are not valid ones for me to continue under my vows. I realize that commitment and maturity are necessary for living the religious life. Therefore, I humbly request a dispensation from my vows of poverty, chastity and obedience.

I signed all the forms in the proper places, put them in the manila envelope and raced down to Mother John William's secretary and asked her to be sure the envelope was given to the Mother General.

Then I ran out to the garden and up the steps to my little studio and looked at my newest painting of a thin woman racing up stairs, nearly leaping out into space. I suddenly understood it was me! Yet I had to be practical and think about a job. I didn't want to teach in a public school where it was likely the students would know far more about the world than I did. In fact, right now I didn't feel I had anything to teach anyone, but only a lot to learn.

Furtively, I slid the Classified Ad section out of the Chronicle and in my cell poured over the Help Wanted and Job Opportunities. Some jobs I didn't even understand. What was a keypunch operator? Lots of ads for that skill. I did find a job that I might be able to handle. A Montessori school was advertising for a teacher. I knew the philosophy behind those schools from one of my education courses. I saw another one: a teacher in Project Head Start. It didn't require a teaching credential. It was unbelievable, but after all the classes at U.S.F. and now in my ninth year of teaching, I didn't have a California Teaching Credential. We taught in our own schools and in parishes where the pastors never asked for teaching credentials.

I had to start somewhere. The next day I used the phone in Sister Brian's North Hall office. The first call: Project Head Start. The job was already filled. I felt relieved. Next I dialed the number for the Montessori job. It required Montessori training. I explained to the gentleman who answered the phone that I had several years experience teaching first grade and was familiar with the Montessori philosophy. I also mentioned I had no teaching credential. Then in a whisper, I told the kind voice, "I'm a nun now and I'm planning to leave in June and I need a job."

After a long pause, the kind voice responded, "You know, I think you'd be fine. Why don't you come in for an interview?"

I wanted to hug the voice. You would take me? But I was not quite ready. "Thank you so much but let me give it a little more thought."

I made more calls about selling kitchenware door-to-door, telephone soliciting. These seemed safer, easier jobs. Compelling voices tempted me: Yes, come in for an interview. You sound right for this. I wasn't ready.

One day after school, I arrived at Sister Brian's office to find her in the midst of her usual futile conversation with Sister Patrice about sin and Holy water. Now it seemed comical. Many things that used to upset me now seemed humorous or pathetic. It surprised me how easily I omitted the daily prescribed readings and prayers, sloughing them off like a worn skin. Of course, I still joined the community for Vespers and prayers we recited together. I mouthed to Brian, "In two minutes, I'm pouring you a cup of coffee."

"In two minutes, I'll be there," she responded. I poured our coffee in the refectory but we went through the kitchen out to the back pantry, one of the few places we could talk without being interrupted. We sat on the large unopened cartons of canned goods

"You look good today, Theo," Brian remarked. "You've become a different person. Six months ago you would've gone crazy with Sister Patrice in my office; you trying to reach me, upset because I wasn't instantly available. Now, look at you-- calm, mature and getting coffee for me."

I nodded, chagrined at the truth and delighted with the changes. "Brian, if I'm going to get a job . . ."

"Yes, how did that Montessori spot work out?"

"It's still open. I said I'd call back. He wanted to interview me, but Brian I think I need to buy some clothes."

"I'm ahead of you. I already spoke to Mother John Mary. She said I could go ahead and give you some money from my household fund. Isn't that great? Why don't you go downtown this week after school and look around." She said it with the pleasure of the mother who discovered she could afford a prom dress for her daughter after all.

My forays into stores were painful. Still mindful of the vow of poverty, I shopped mostly at bargain basement and clearance racks. When I first tried on dresses, it seemed something was wrong with my body. Nothing fit or looked right. The thought of wearing unfeminine slacks or God forbid, jeans, was intolerable. It appeared my body was only suited for styles of the fifties. I was tempted to call Mom and ask if she had still had my long skirts and cashmere sweaters or even my saddle shoes.

Finally, I acquired a a conservative navy blue dress. Still, if I had to take a teaching job I should have one suit. That's what mom always wore when she taught, a suit. At a sale at Joseph Magnin's a cheerful, discreet saleswoman read my frustration. She noticed I was wearing a nun's habit yet preparing to try on suits. She took a hold of the drab suits I'd brought into the dressing room and with a smile said, "Let me help you. Wait here." She brought me two, a red one that seemed to be made of burlap and another, powder blue with a matching check jacket. The red was too worldly, but the blue was youthful and cheerful--the way I wanted to feel. When the saleswoman returned, I had on the blue suit. She commented, "With your figure, you ought to model; everything looks terrific on you."

"Oh, that's nice of you to say." Her startling words made me blush and I mumbled, "Uh, you see, soon I'm going to . . ." I gagged on the words. I thought it would be simple to say: I'm going to leave the convent, no longer be a nun. But in fact it was difficult, if not impossible, to say it aloud. I thanked her and purchased the blue outfit and happily Sister Brian approved.

On Holy Saturday, the eve of Easter, I received extraordinary news from Mother Mary John. She told Sister Brian to give me the news that our Congregation would send me $400 a month for my first six months. Mother John Mary felt that since I was going to be living on my own and had given long service to the community, it was only Christian to provide me with some support. This generous move provided me with options. I could work part-time and fulfill my dream: going to school part-time to get a degree in Fine Arts. Now I would enjoy the Easter liturgy--the celebration of the mystery of the Resurrection, from death on the Cross to the resurrected Christ, death to life, a fitting celebration appropriate for my final days in the convent.

Two schools offered the Master of Fine Arts degree that I coveted: the San Francisco Art Institute and the California College of Arts and Crafts. I favored the latter as I wanted to leave San Francisco so I wouldn't run into my former students. This embarrassing event happened once when I was shopping for a dress and I made some crazy excuse for being in the women's dress department. I was a lobster molting; soon I'd be without my shell, tender and vulnerable.

Meanwhile with Sister Brian's encouragement, I had enrolled in a Figure Painting class at the California College of Arts and Crafts in North Oakland. Each Saturday morning I escaped to this rural setting where Eucalyptus towered over turn-of the-century buildings, city sounds were absent; activities seemed to move in slow motion. When I signed up for this class, I had no idea how fortuitous it would be for the next phase of my life. This time, unlike the summer class at Mount St. Mary's where the model had to wear a bathing suit, I would have to deal with a nude figure. The class was taught by a woman, Mary Snowden, who didn't seem put-off by having a nun in full habit in her class. The model was a Black woman, Florence, but she preferred Flo. She strutted into the studio, tossed off her robe and planted herself on the chair on the platform, holding her chin high. Her body was partially draped with fabric—watermelon pink, lime green, and magenta. With pouty lips and long fingernails as fuchsia as the ribbon binding up her thick hair, she appeared so regal that I could imagine spear-carriers kneeling at her feet as we, her humble subjects, looked on, painting her with admiring eyes. At the class break, she moved among us making sassy comments about our work in her rich mahogany voice. " Sweet," she remarked to me.

After Easter I began the process of admission to enroll in an art degree program. I was hoping to get into the Master's of Art painting program. One Saturday I brought a portfolio of my work to be evaluated by the head of the painting department, Jason Schoener. For support, I asked Sister Brian to come with me. I packed my best watercolors in a portfolio and brought along one canvas. Schoener was teaching a painting class and at the break, he called me to one side of the studio. He looked at my work seriously, puffing on his pipe. I felt the students' eyes were all on Sister Brian and me. Nuns were not common on this campus.

"Looks to me as if you'll need more work on the basics," Schoener replied. If you continue like this you'll be eligible for the Society of Western Artists, but you won't get into our Master's program. He was very matter-of-fact and didn't show the least bit of warmth that we nuns were used to when speaking to lay people. I resented his remark about the Society of Western Artists as I admired the members' work. However, to get Financial Aid I had to enroll in a degree program. Though I already had a Bachelor of Arts from the University of San Francisco, I would not be deterred. That left me no choice but to apply for the undergraduate Bachelor of Fine Arts program that did not have any portfolio requirements.

One Saturday at the break in the painting class, I went over to the administration building to get the necessary papers. As I navigated the twists and turns of the old building, my eyes were drawn to the work on display: breasts and genitals leaped out at me. It took my breath away to imagine myself spending my days here in a place was so wild and sensual. The registrar was a short woman with large lips and eyes magnified by thick glasses. When I told her what I was trying to do she said sourly, "You'll have to have transcripts sent from every school you've attended and we'll evaluate these transfer credits. We have strict standards." I nodded and took the forms.

In the warm courtyard, I discovered the bulletin board with a jumble of handwritten notes offering to sell all kinds of things from tattoos to photo equipment. Then I found what I wanted: the notices of local rentals and sublets. I copied down several. I even got a coffee from a vending machine and sat on a bench in the sun. I mused; it might not be so bad to be a freshman. Though I was twenty- nine, in many ways I might as well have been eighteen.

One bedroom apt. Near College $65. a month.

Sounded perfect. The voice on the phone said students were still occupying but they'd be gone by summer. They would leave the door unlocked between noon and one next Saturday. That day I packed a shopping bag with a cotton print dress, nylons and sandals that Sister Brian had allowed me to purchase.

After the painting class I darted into the Ladies room of the Standard Oil station across the street. I bolted the door and tore off my habit and veil. My feet recoiled from the clammy floor; the nylons got a run. I slipped on the print dress, a pair of sandals and pinched my cheeks, fluffed up my hair that was growing out far too curly. I stuffed my habit in the bag and emerged from the Ladies restroom as Judy Lyons.

Luckily, the building was close to the school, but as I approached I saw the exterior paint was peeling. The carpet in the hall was worn and after knocking loudly at the appropriate door and waiting, I cautiously opened the door. Jeans, shirts, socks and dirty underwear, both male and female, made a path across the floor. From the kitchen came the rank smell of garbage. Dirty dishes covered the sink and drain-board. Half-filled coffee cups and beer cans were strewn about the room. How could anyone live like this, let alone show it as a rental? But it was the wrinkled stained sheets on the bed that made my skin prickle and my hands clammy. The bed was a tale of rigorous sexual activity. O God, this place is not for me. Was this typical of the students at Arts and Crafts?

A few days later, tense and depressed, I went to Millikan at his downtown office. Should I tell him about the apartment first or the horrible dream I had where a Black man held me by the leg?

"There is something bothering me," I said for the second time. "I don't know where to start."

"Just start. You don't have to be logical for Christ's sake. Start in the middle, start at the end, start anywhere."

This remark hurt because he had never talked to me this way. Now everything would be coarse and dirty and hard. Even Doc would treat me differently. "Millikan, please don't talk to me like that. Don't use Christ's name. Just because I'm leaving, doesn't mean you can treat me differently. Why aren't you helping me? Don't you see I'm scared?" I burst into tears.

"I'm glad you told me how you really feel." He took his feet off his desk and leaned forward. He looked sheepish. "What is it that has you so upset? Let's get right to it."

"I'm upset about sex, about men. Everyone knows more about sex than me. It'll be like I'm from Mars. I'm frightened."

"It sounds like you feel powerless; I know you like knowledge. That gives you power. Now your imagination is going wild, making things scary, maybe worse than reality but you're not sure."

"Yes, Doc, you got it. Suddenly, I feel like staying in the convent."

"I can see from where you are it does feel scary. But let's look at some of the realities."

"Like what?" I sniffled.

"Take what's happened between us. You 've made progress in heterosexual relations right here in this room." He leaned forward on his thighs, looking right at me. "You and I have had some pretty sensitive exchanges and you haven't run away." I nodded, enjoying the way he described our intimacy. "Evidently when your dad died, you felt deserted. Somewhere deep down you decided men were unreliable, never to be trusted, but you've tested me like hell and I haven't run away. I haven't let you down. Here you've learned to trust me and I'm not going anywhere. I'm going to be right here for you. We can deal with whatever comes up now and when you step outside."

Never were his words more welcome and comforting. I did trust him. I said to myself: O ye of little faith. Your savior is here.

The next week I called another number from the bulletin board that advertised a sublet, June through August. On the phone Cindy said, she 'just wanted to keep her good deal going.' She had a three-room apartment, a block from school that rented for $75 a month. I made an appointment to see it. The next Saturday after class I again appeared as Judy Lyons. The building was a three story brown shingle. Cindy had the top apartment. She showed me around and it was light and airy, sparsely furnished with a redwood picnic table in the tiny kitchen.

"I think I could trust you with my things though the building ain't much. You seem like the careful type."

"Yes, I'll take good care of everything." We were standing in the light kitchen. A door led out to a sunny fire escape where I could imagine growing potted geraniums or even stepping out to sunbath.

"Good, Judy. I'm happy this will work out for both of us." I was startled when she called me Judy. Time to leave before I broke down and told her my real story as she might reconsider. Back in the car, I put on my habit and drove home to tell Brian I had a place to live.

Everything was falling in place but I hadn't told Mom my plans. Recently, my sister, Ellen, had gotten pregnant with her boyfriend, Jim. He hadn't wanted to marry her but Mom insisted. She would not have the shame of an unwed mother in our family. She paid for a small wedding and reception in Carmel. However, Jim always drank too much and he and my sister only lived together a short time. Now Ellen and baby Jim lived with Mom in her home near Stonetown.

One afternoon at Sister Brian's urging, I made a difficult excursion. I went to buy some make-up. Not far from the convent was a store that sold Merle Norman cosmetics, the same brand that Mom used when I was at home. I begged Brian to come with me. The woman at the cosmetic store was blond and highly made up. When I confided my plans, she insisted on giving me a full makeover when I only wanted a lipstick. To me the make-up was completely overdone, but Sister Brian was laughing and enjoying the scene.

"This seems much too worldly, " I said to Sister Brian as she drove back toward the convent. Then I said, "Brian, do you think we could stop and see my mother?"

"With you dressed like this? You'll give her a heart attack. Oh, why not? I guess she has to see you in 'civies' sometime. Look there's a phone booth. You can call her." She pulled over. "Do you have a dime?"

"I do. In fact, I have two. I took them out of your petty cash box before we left."

The booth was dirty and smelled of urine. I tried to put in a dime but dropped it. I put in the next one and dialed.

"Hi Mom, It's Judy. How's everything? Oh, you're resting. Yeah, you sound a little groggy. Say Mom, Sister Brian and I were wondering if we could stop in for a few minutes. Yes, I know I'll see you on visiting Sunday but we won't stay long."

As the rules changed recently and I'd been allowed to come home several times on a Sunday. Mom continued to protest this wasn't a good time. I was becoming annoyed that she was so resistant. Perhaps she was afraid I'd nag her about her drinking. I continued to plead, "Mom, I have something important to tell you. What is it? I'd rather tell you in person. What? Am I leaving?" A false little laugh escaped. "You mean the convent?" I was trying to share the most important decision of my life and she wrested it from me in a filthy phone booth. When I told her indeed that was my news, she said, "All right, come on over, but you're not thinking of coming here to live are you?"

"No, Mom, I'll come over and tell you my plans"

Sister Brian drove over 19th Avenue to St. Stephen's parish near Stonestown. The day had been hot and now the evening blossomed into a rare tropical night. Mom had left the front door wide open. I could see her in the kitchen, removing her apron. I called out to her. She turned and stared without any recognition.

"Mom, its me, Judy."

She ran to the front door. "Oh Judy! I didn't recognize you. You are beautiful!" Then we were both in each other's arms, sobbing.

"Oh, Sister Brian, please excuse me for crying," Mom wailed over my shoulder. "I just never expected her to look like this."

"Mom, what made you think I was leaving?"

"Ellen and I were just talking the other day and I said, "Judy seems restless. It wouldn't surprise me if she has something on her mind-maybe even thinking about leaving. By the way Ellen's rented a flat for herself and Baby Jimmy. It's good they have their own place."

"I know you've been so proud to have a daughter who is a nun. I hope you're not disappointed or ashamed of me now."

"Oh, no, Judy. I'm happy to have you back."

She poured us 7Up and she put a shot of bourbon in hers. We sat in the living room jabbering, interrupting each other while munching chips and dip. I told her my future plans for art school but the details didn't interest her. Just having her daughter accessible again seemed all she could manage today.

I knew that to start a new life alone I'd need a car. Mom wasn't able to handle that expense but my favorite uncle, Phil, a successful businessman, might help me. With permission from Sister Brian, I set up a visit with Uncle Phil. Sister Brian said she would come with me. I decided to wear my new suit. We drove the convent Ford to his home in the Sunset and rang the bell. He, too, like my mom, barely recognized me. He hid his confusion by calling his wife, Henrietta, to come and meet the 'new Judy' and to open the champagne immediately. We sat sipping champagne in his well-furnished living room with the large floor to ceiling mirror framed with gold-gilt that had belonged to my great grandmother. Just as she did when we were kids, Henrietta ran for her camera and snapped several photos. Uncle Phil was happy to 'have me back' as he phrased it. He was never in favor of my decision in the first place and he would be able to fund a used car for me.

The pieces were coming together. Back to the classified papers I went and found an ad for a VW bug. I contacted the owner. Uncle Phil insisted I have it checked out before he plunked down the $400 cash price. At a garage on Geary St., the owner, a young man, met me and when it checked out, I happily handed him a check for $400 for my first car. It had a sunroof and low mileage and was a stick shift but I knew how to drive it. Years ago I had learned on a stick shift with lessons from annoying Ray, mom's boyfriend. I parked it on Masonic Avenue and moved it every other day so I wouldn't get a ticket.

Suddenly it was Thursday, last day of school. I was surprisingly nostalgic, especially with the girls calling out to me, 'See you in September, Sister.' Yet there was only one student I wanted to know that I wouldn't return in September. She was special--Marla Yturralde. Her parents had come from the Philippines and were quite strict with Marla and her older sister, who was also in our school. Marla was funny, smart and artistic. We often had little private jokes between us and I felt as if she could have been my own daughter. On the last day of school, I took her aside and told her my plans. She was cool and sad and said, "I have to go home and eat lots of peanut butter," which is what she did when she was upset. I said, "Yes, absolutely we'll be in touch in the summer."

Two days before I was to leave, Mother John Mary called me to her office. I sat across the desk from her and her Sister secretary came in and placed the papers in front of me that had come from Rome. My Indult of Secularization was to be signed with her secretary as witness. I was so nervous I signed without even reading it. While the secretary put her signature to the paper, I slid off my silver ring with the small raised crucifix and passed it to Mother. She closed her hand over it protectively and in that small movement indicated this moment was painful for her.

"Sister, I'm very sorry to see you go but I won't forget you. I'm surrounded by your lovely watercolors." Behind her head hung my cityscape, on another wall, a sailboat. It would've been easier if she hadn't been kind. "So you're all set? When are you leaving?"

"Friday at three."

"Is that all, Mother," asked the secretary. Mother nodded. I was glad to be alone with Mother as I wanted to ask a delicate question.

"Mother, would it be all right if I went around and said good-by to each sister." The few defectors customarily were whisked away, going from convent parlor to a waiting car at night. I'd hated the way a Sister would just disappear, leaving a gaping hole in our ranks with never a chance to say good-by. Mother's amazement was written on her face. "Sister, do you really think you're up to that?"

I realized she hadn't noticed what confidence I had gained in the last few months. For me, it didn't seem formidable but a natural thing to do, considering that the convent had been my home since I was seventeen. Now I was approaching thirty and moving on to become an artist, something that hadn't been possible here. I held no ill will toward anyone.

Recently I learned what happened when my friend, Sister Paula, who was in my group, had left. I was teaching in East L.A. then and wondered had she asked to leave or had she committed some scandalous act? I recalled sitting in the dark chapel with the tears streaming down and aching for more details. Later I heard they didn't want her to leave and had brought her to the motherhouse where old Mother Grace spoke to her kindly, persuasively, waving her long thin fingers in the air in same way she directed us singing the Gregorian Chant. Then Mother Colette got hold of her and put her through an hour on her knees, lecturing her on turning her back on Jesus but she wasn't about to be swayed. She had courage I envied. The evening she was to leave, they made her hide in the first floor closet in some old ill-fitting clothes and, when her father drove up to the curb, Mother Colette escorted her at a gallop from closet to car and they sped away. Her own mother was so ashamed that she made her keep to the house for six months so her friends wouldn't know she was home.

After praying for courage at Mass, I started my round of good-byes, taking the easy ones first. I found the Sister Infirmarian, who had sympathetically given me vitamin B shots as the Dr. ordered for my exhaustion. When I told her of my plans to leave, to go to art school, she gave me a wise smile and replied, "Stay healthy." In the kitchen when I told the Sister Cook, her brown eyes widened like saucers and she feigned surprise with a little scream, "Oh, Theophane, you bad girl," but then she hugged me as if she were now part of my conspiracy. I continued around, pulling one sister to the apron room or library or parlor. Some hugged me stiffly, obviously ill as ease. Others wanted to know every detail of my plans and seemed happy for me, some even a bit envious.

I didn't try to contact Sister Maureen. I hadn't spoken to her since that summer day when I walked out of her room in the cabin. The bond between us had snapped and could not be repaired, nor did I try to contact Mother Colette, afraid she'd disapprove of my action or try to change my mind.

Then Friday dawned, my last day. After breakfast I saw Sister Agnes Ann's triangular shape moving toward her third floor cell. Since high school she had terrified me. Now over seventy, she still was guardian of the gate. I knocked on her cell door. At her sing-song, "Yeess?" I crept in. In the dim light I saw her, back to me, standing at her dresser. I gritted my teeth and called, "Sister Agnes Ann." She turned with arrogance in her stance and tone, "Yes?" In one breath I rushed the words together, "I came to say good-by. I 'm leaving the Order this afternoon and I'm going to art school."

She cocked her head to one side. I saw the crows feet deeply etched in her full red face but her eyes held me motionless. "Well, well, Sister Theophane, you're leaving, are you?" She exhaled a long sigh, then moved her arms to shoo me out of her cell while muttering, "You know if I were your age, . . ." her words trailed off as she spoke softly, " I might consider doing the same thing." She brushed past me and sailed down the hall, leaving me with mouth agape. With the passing of what had seemed a changeless Church, even she was re-examining her life. Slowly I ferreted out each of the Old Guard who received the news stoically and nodded a brief good-by.

At noon Sister Aquinas was leaving for her summer mission. Sadly, she was still an angry woman and from remarks I overheard from Brian, Mother John Mary was losing patience with her anger. At this moment, she was near the front door waiting for her ride.

"Could I speak to you a moment, Sister," I asked. She hesitated, but then followed me to the parlor that was adjacent to the convent switchboard that was now operated by a student. The moment was deprived of privacy and that seemed best.

"I'm leaving the Order tomorrow. I'm going to art school." I hoped she might be pleased as she was the first to encourage my artistic pursuits.

"Well, well, well," she shrugged, barely making eye contact and turning her head, toward the window. "Oh, I think my ride is here." She picked up her suitcase and with slow deliberate steps in her flat policeman's shoes went out the door to the waiting car. In time they would no longer let her teach in the classroom as her anger continued to spew out everywhere. Much later, I heard she was asked to leave the convent, but had found a job in the public schools where her talents were quite appreciated.

In my cell, I stared at the two low cupboards and the slim closet where I kept my extra habit. I decided not to take anything. With the generosity of Mother John Mary and Sister Brian, I had clothes for my new life. But I did pick up the large rosary with the brass crucifix, the one I wore so long dangling from my leather cincture. I would take the crucifix as it helped me though many hard times. Who knew what lay ahead?

At 2:30 I poked my head into Sister Brian's office. "It's time for me to go. I'm going to my studio to get changed. I've been able to say farewell to everyone except Sister Andrew. I think she's avoiding me. What should I do?"

"She's uncomfortable with emotion and won't know what to say. I'll tell her later."

As I left her office I saw Sister Andrew's back as she hurried down the hall. When she saw me, she ducked into a parlor. Determined and still wishing for her approval, I stuck my head in. "I just want to say good-by, Sister. I'm leaving the convent today, moving to Oakland, going to art school."

"Well, Sister Theophane, we all have to follow our own conscience." Her mouth moved as if she was going to say more, but she coughed and disappeared out the other door. Even at this last moment, I'd naively hoped for her approval.

For the last time I went to my little art studio. In the mirror I took one more look at Sister Theophane; then I pulled off the headgear, slipped out of my habit and heavy cotton underwear. I put on nylon pants, a lacy slip, my pale blue suit with the check jacket, those new wonders--panty hose and stepped into patent leather heels. I brushed out my hair, which was full and terribly curly. Then I opened my new purse. Already inside were the keys to my new apartment as well as the keys to the blue VW bug, now parked at the curb. I added my linen handkerchief with my laundry number, #230, still sewn in the corner, my silver pocket watch and the rosary in the leather case that Sister Maureen had made for me when I entered.

Sister Brian appeared at the door bringing in two cups of coffee. We sat, she on the chair, me on the closed toilet, just enjoying our last few moments in privacy. Stripped of my art materials and paintings, the room had reverted to a dingy bathroom.

"Theo, oh, Judy, I'll be thinking of you and praying for you tonight. Next week we can have dinner together and you can fill me in on everything. Now we have to hurry down to the parlor. Mother John Mary is waiting to say good-by."

I'd expected to slip unnoticed out the side door. Now here standing in a reception line in the large parlor was Mother John Mary, her Councilors, and her secretary. The Big Brass Millikan would've dubbed them. I was overwhelmed and gave each a hug. I stood facing them, making a bit of small talk. Then Sister Brian said, "She has to be off. Don't want her stuck in a lot of traffic." Sister Brian picked up my suitcase and took my elbow and started toward the door.

"What time is it?" asked Mother. I reached in my purse for my pocket watch. "Nearly 4:15," I replied.

"Oh, Sister, I mean, Judy, wait, I have something," said Mother.

She whispered to one of her Councilors who left the room in a hurry. Oh no, I was the youngest and I should run the errand whatever it was. I felt uneasy, shifting from foot to foot, uncomfortable with my newly exposed legs. Moments later the sister returned with a slim box. Without ceremony, Mother opened it and removed a silver wristwatch and said, "Here, Judy, take this. Let me have that old pocket watch."

As I slipped it on, I felt a surge of bittersweet love, not only for her, but also for the whole Community that was no longer my family. I went down the front stairs, followed by Sister Brian who carried my suitcase with my new clothes. We hugged, long and hard. I slipped behind the wheel of the blue VW and with one last wave, I was soon devoured in traffic heading for the Bay Bridge. It was exciting to begin my new life, but I also felt an emotion that was hard to identify. It wasn't regret--I'd never experience that--but it was a certain melancholy for that innocence, that camaraderie with moral people who were sincere and trying to do good in the world. I knew I'd never be a part of that community again. I changed into the fast lane and sped off to Berkeley to start my new life.

CPSIA information can be obtained
at www.ICGtesting.com
Printed in the USA
LVHW041523120623
749513LV00006B/469